Russian Foreign Policy

*From Empire to
Nation-State*

Russian Foreign Policy

From Empire to Nation-State

Nicolai N. Petro
University of Rhode Island

Alvin Z. Rubinstein
University of Pennsylvania

LONGMAN

An imprint of Addison Wesley Longman, Inc.

New York • Reading, Massachusetts • Menlo Park, California • Harlow, England
Don Mills, Ontario • Sydney • Mexico City • Madrid • Amsterdam

Russian Foreign Policy: From Empire to Nation-State

Acquisitions Editor: Leo A.W. Wiegman
Project Coordination and Text Design: York Production Services
Supervising Production Editor: Lois Lombardo
Cover Design: Scott Russo
Manufacturing Manager: Hilda Koparanian
Electronic Page Makeup: ComCom
Printer and Binder: R. R. Donnelley and Sons Company
Cover Printer: Phoenix Color Corp.

Library of Congress Cataloging-in-Publication Data
Petro, Nicolai N.
    Russian foreign policy : from empire to nation-state / Nicolai N.
Petro, Alvin Z. Rubinstein.
        p.   cm.
    Includes bibliographical references and index.
    ISBN 0-673-99636-0
    1. Soviet Union—Foreign relations. 2. Russia (Federation)—
-Foreign relations. I. Rubinstein, Alvin Z. II. Title.
DK266.45.P48 1996
327.47—dc20   96-16348
                                                                                      CIP

ISBN 0-673-99636-0

12345678910—DOC—99989796

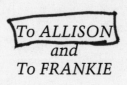

To ALLISON
and
To FRANKIE

Contents

Preface

The collapse of the Soviet Union in December 1991 from an implosion of economic stagnation, ethnic nationalism, and political ineptness, is, arguably, the most dramatic foreign policy development of the late twentieth century. Nearly five centuries of Russian territorial expansion ended; fourteen countries from the non-Russian areas of the USSR have emerged to independence; and Russia has moved to reinvent itself politically, economically, and internationally. Notwithstanding the loss of a vast imperial system, the Russian Federation, the largest of the fifteen republics resulting from the demise of the Soviet Union, remains a great power by virtue of its possession of the preponderance of the old regime's nuclear and conventional forces and of a wealth of natural resources. One of the big unknowns is how it will relate to the international system.

Under President Boris Yeltsin, the thrust of Russia's foreign policy has been to return Russia to easy and extensive interaction with the West—opening the domestic economy to foreign investment and market forces. Despite some successes, the ultimate fate of Russia's transformation is still in doubt. One reason is the ambivalence toward the West that has always existed among Russia's ruling elite. In the mid-nineteenth century, two competing conceptions crystallized: Slavophiles and Westernizers. The Slavophiles believed in the superiority of Russia's Eastern Orthodox and autocratic traditions as compared to the West. In the modern Eurasian form, Slavophiles have exalted nationalism, Slavic unity, the consolidation of the Eurasian land mass, and economic autarky. By contrast, the Westernizers argued that Russia was merely a less economically and politically developed part of Europe. Their modern interpreters have exalted the radical deconstruction of past Russian traditions, a greater focus on individualism and the rule of law, and speedy economic integration into the international economy. These currents are still very much alive in Russia today and their competition will affect the kind of foreign policy that Russia follows in the decades ahead.

The purpose of this book is to provide an introduction to the major developments that have characterized the foreign policy of Russia during the tsarist, Soviet, and post-Soviet periods. Keenly aware of the dramatic changes that have occurred since 1991, this book highlights the consequences of the collapse of the Soviet empire and the constraints that an emerging market economy and pluralistic government now place on the formulation and execution of Russian foreign policy. It focuses attention on the long-term historical continuities in Russian foreign policy, both as they undermined the status quo at the end of the Soviet era, and as they now condition Russia's search for a new definition of the national interest.

Drawing on Alvin Z. Rubinstein's *Soviet Foreign Policy Since World War II*, we seek to offer a concise, comprehensive analysis of the evolution, aims, and impact of Moscow's foreign policy; to discuss the range of new issues and the dilemmas and challenges that they pose for Russian leaders in the post-Soviet era; and to establish a foundation for in-depth exploration of the rich specialized literature that has been published in recent years. For those who wish to understand the foreign policy of Russia, knowledge of the past is essential, for the past is part of the present and informs our speculation about the future. In William Faulkner's words, "The past is never dead. In fact, it is not even past."

Skepticism abounds regarding Russia's prospects as a democratic state and its foreign policy ambitions. The unbridled enthusiasm that attended the demise of the Soviet Union has already given way to growing pessimism. Neither extreme is warranted, and can best be tempered by a useful observation made by Winston Churchill more than half a century ago: "I cannot forecast to you the action of Russia. It is a riddle wrapped in a mystery inside an enigma; but perhaps there is a key. That key is Russian national interest."

The authors gratefully acknowledge the helpful suggestions of Professor Richard M. Mills of Fordham University and Professor Mark N. Katz of George Mason University.

Finally, our thanks to Leo Wiegman of Longman, Lois Lombardo, and Angela Finnen of York Production Services for preparing the manuscript in such a timely fashion.

Nicolai N. Petro

Alvin Z. Rubinstein

Russian Foreign Policy

From Empire to Nation-State

Chapter
1

Sources of Russian Diplomacy

The foreign policy of Russia, like that of any great power, is a combination of discrete determinants. These include geopolitical considerations, historical memory, external threats, bureaucratic intriguing, exigencies of political power, economic capabilities, ideology, skill of the ruling elite, and so forth. At any given time, policy develops as the product of a complex process in which these determinants, although always changing, are in some fashion always present. Throughout Russian history its physical attributes—geography, climate, population, and resources—have played important roles. They have influenced the unique characteristics of the country's political, social, military, and economic developments; its belief system and culture; its reaction to external challenges; and key figures in its history.

THE HISTORICAL LEGACY OF TSARISM

The history of Russia is dramatic and complex. Sometime between the sixth and ninth centuries, various tribes or groups of East Slavs settled the vast East European plain. Over time, they developed into the Russian, Ukrainian, and Belorussian branches of Slavic culture we know today. The rich natural resources (timber, furs, ores) and numerous rivers provided opportunities for trade. Especially important was the contact between Kiev, which is situated on the Dnieper River, and the Byzantine Empire, which dominated the southern and western littorals of the Black Sea. It was from Byzantium, whose center was Constantinople, that the Eastern Orthodox branch of Christianity was introduced into Rus' (as the people called their land) through Kiev in the ninth century. At the time, Kiev was the leading Russian city, though there were also important principalities in Novgorod, Pskov, Suzdal, Chernigov, and Smolensk, among others. In the mid-thirteenth century, the expanding Mongols subjugated all of Russia. From 1240 to 1380 they were its unquestioned masters, exacting tribute, yet permitting cultural and religious autonomy to the many vassal princes. A shared language, religion, and ethos,

1

however, enabled the Russians to survive and eventually to surmount nearly a century and a half of Mongol domination.

In 1380, the prince of Moscow defeated a Mongol army at Kulikovo Field on the Don River. This victory greatly enhanced the prestige of the principality of Moscow, which had emerged as a separate entity in the middle of the twelfth century, and which had by then become the seat of the Russian Orthodox Church. In 1480, Moscow's Prince Ivan III (1462–1505) cast off the Mongol yoke once and for all and absorbed rival Russian principalities such as Yaroslavl, Rostov, Novgorod, and Tver, more than doubling the size of the Muscovite domain. At roughly the same time, St. Sergius of Radonezh founded a monastic movement that, over the course of two centuries, expanded Russian settlements hundreds of miles northward to the White Sea and eastward beyond the Ural mountains. Monks cleared away the forests, built churches and libraries, converted the land to cultivation and created islands of stability and prosperity in the wilderness that attracted peasants to settle there. Later, richer, established monasteries such as Solovetsk on the White Sea, the St. Sergius Trinity Monastery near Moscow, and the Kirillov Monastery in Belozersk, would aid in the national defense, even lending funds to the princes of Moscow to cover the costs of raising an army. In the most direct sense, therefore, the Church worked together with the princes of Moscow to preserve a unified Russian state.

The Mongol period was one of traumatic isolation from the West, arresting Russia's economic and social development, nearly severing close ties to Byzantium, and greatly bolstering the authority of Russian princes who, as military leaders responsible for the safety of the population, gradually absorbed more and more power from the Church and the citizen's assemblies (know as *veche*).

The end of Mongol overlordship and the ascendancy of Moscow also ushered in several centuries of conflict between Russia and its powerful western neighbors—Lithuania, Poland, and Sweden. These wars were fought as much for religious reasons as for real estate and stable frontiers. The sack of Constantinople in 1204 by Frankish and Venetian crusaders intensified fear of Catholic expansionism among the Orthodox Eastern Slavs, whose attachment to their church had deepened during the harsh period of Mongol rule. A national church also suited the political aims of the Muscovite princes, who relied on the Church's popularity to expand their authority. In 1472, Ivan III assumed the title of tsar (from the Latin word "caesar") and acquired an aura of Byzantine legitimacy by marrying a niece of the last Byzantine emperor who ruled in Constantinople before it was overrun by the Ottoman Turks in 1453. From the time of his reign on, tsars nurtured the view of Moscow as the "Third Rome" (after Rome and Constantinople), after which there would be no fourth. This doctrine, often erroneously interpreted as a political manifesto, was in reality a theological speculation about the fate of the Orthodox faith. It contained no specific political or diplomatic agenda, but sought to reaffirm the close relationship between church and state that Russia had inherited from Byzantium and that was already fraying in the West.[1]

In coming centuries, the struggle to determine the western borders of Russia in the vast area from the Baltic Sea to the Black Sea was invested with a religious as well as a strategic-political dimension: religious in that the Russian Orthodox tsars of Moscow were pitted against the Roman Catholic rulers of the powerful kingdoms of Lithuania and Lithuania-Poland; strategic-political in that each sought to expand and consolidate control over peoples and societies in transition and across lands with no natural defensible frontiers. The indeterminacy of societies and borders promoted conflict.

There was no accommodation; none was desired. Tsar Ivan IV ("the Terrible") (1530–1584) invaded Livonia (essentially, today's Estonia and Latvia) in 1558, but his invasion failed dismally, and in the process of a 25-year war with Lithuania, Poland, and Sweden, he lost the fortified Russian port of Ivangorod on the Gulf of Finland, which had been acquired by Ivan III. However, defeated in the West, Ivan succeeded in conquering the Muslim khanates Kazan (in 1552) and Astrakhan (in 1556), extending Russian control over the entire length of the Volga River, and turning it into a multinational empire. Eastward expansion continued throughout the otherwise trying seventeenth century, when Russia experienced serious internal problems and repeated wars in the West. The conquest of Siberia advanced Russia's border to the Pacific, and in 1689 Moscow imposed on a weak China the Treaty of Nerchinsk, which moved the border to the Argun River and the Stanovoi Mountain range. There the border remained until 1858, when the seizure of additional Chinese territory up to the Amur and Ussuri rivers established the current boundary between Russia and China.

Despite some early intermarriages with royal houses in the West, Russia grew increasingly distant from the West after the Mongol invasion. Typical of the growing ambivalence that Russian rulers felt about the West is the invitation extended by Ivan III to Western traders. While the court was curious to learn about foreign customs and technologies, their numbers were kept relatively small, and they were restricted to one area of Moscow. In Poland, Austria, and Sweden, Russia's interest in new technology coupled with its expansionist policy gave rise, according to Russian historian Sergei Platonov, to the perception in the West of a "'Russian peril' and the necessity of conducting a policy of isolation and repression vis-à-vis Moscow."[2]

Russia's emergence as a European power began in earnest during the reign of Peter the Great (1682–1725). Peter borrowed ideas, technology, and personnel from the West on a scale unmatched in Russian history, and he introduced far-reaching military, administrative, and economic reforms. Epitomizing his determination to modernize Russia, he moved the capital to St. Petersburg, a new city that he built on the Gulf of Finland in a style that echoed the major European capitals. The capital remained there until necessity forced the Bolsheviks to relocate it back to Moscow in early 1918.

Peter's foreign policy focused on securing Russia's northern flank. He fought Sweden for over 20 years (1700–1721), defeating Charles XII, the most brilliant military commander of the early eighteenth century. The Treaty of Nystadt (1721) gave Russia control of the Gulf of Finland—its maritime route to the West—and the Baltic provinces of Estonia and Latvia. Henceforth, Russia, not Sweden, was to be the foremost power in northern Europe.

Peter's successors added to this legacy, especially Catherine the Great (1762–1796), who expanded Russia's southern and western borders by defeating Ottoman Turkey and Poland, respectively. Catherine's humiliating defeat of

Turkey and the consequent Treaty of Kuchuk Kainardji in 1774 advanced Russian territory to the Black Sea and led to the absorption of the Crimea, whose Muslim Tartars had previously relied on Turkish protection. Even more impressive was its role in effecting the successive partitions of Poland, which in 1795 ceased to be an independent state, until it was recognized again as such by the Provisional Government that succeeded the toppled tsarist regime in February 1917. Poland's internal weakness had left it incapable of resisting the rapacious appetites of its neighbors Russia, Prussia, and Austria.

At the beginning of the nineteenth century, Russia was one of the great powers of Europe, its empire "an accomplished and firmly established fact. Even at that time it was by far the largest state in Europe. It had spread all over the east-European plain from the Baltic and the Arctic Ocean in the north to the Black Sea and the Caspian in the south; in Asia it possessed the whole of Siberia. Further expansion during the nineteenth century made the territory of the Empire equal to one sixth of the surface of the globe."[3] After the defeat of Napoleon in 1815, Russia's foreign policy in Europe followed a course that was shaped more by imperial ambitions than by security concerns. Friendship with Prussia and Austria—which had been since 1795 Russia's neighbors in the west—would have ensured stability and security. However, expansion at the expense of the weak Ottoman empire caused friction with Austria in the Balkans and with Britain in the Middle East. Still, Germany (as the expanded Prussian state was called after 1870) under Chancellor Otto von Bismarck managed to keep the peace between the Hapsburgs and the Romanovs. But with his dismissal in 1890 the high-strung young Kaiser Wilhelm II decided to support Austria against Russia, thus turning Russia to an alliance with France, its long-time adversary.

Russia's interests in the Balkans had nothing to do with security. Its pressure on the Ottoman Turks for concessions on the Straits (the Dardanelles and the Bosporus) was likewise dictated by historical, economical, and religious impulses that had little to do with security—Russia's defeat of the Turks in 1833 had already turned the Black Sea into a Russian lake. Under the Treaty of Unkiar Skelessi, access was forbidden to Turkish warships, and a weak Turkey, which Tsar Nicholas had in 1844 dubbed the "sick man" of Europe, was certainly no threat.

By then, however, imperial rivalry with Great Britain had replaced Russia's traditional friendship with England, which dated back to the 1550s when Ivan IV had granted the English special trade concessions on Russian raw materials. The conflict extended along the rimland of Russia's southern border, from Ottoman Turkey to Iran, Afghanistan, and China. By 1907, however, fear of Germany led both powers to accommodation and a common alliance with France.

In the Far East, Russia took advantage of a weak China to extract additional real estate in the Amur-Ussuri region and de facto control of the provinces of Sinkiang and Mongolia. In northern Manchuria and Korea, the spread of Russian commercial interests precipitated a war with Japan, which was also bent on expansion into these areas. Russia's stunning defeat in the 1904–1905 war gave Japan a free hand and spurred the social unrest in St. Petersburg and other large cities that led to the revolution of 1905 that transformed Russia into a constitutional monarchy.

In August 1914, Russia entered World War I on the side of France and Britain, optimistic about the prospects for substantial territorial gains at the expense of Turkey. A year later, however, it had for all practical purposes been eliminated from the war. Its fate was sealed by Britain's failure to capture the Dardenelles, to knock Turkey out of the war, and to open a reliable supply route to help provision the poorly equipped Russian army. Faced with growing supply shortages and economic dislocation, the corrupt and inefficient tsarist regime proved incapable of stemming antiwar sentiment. The regime's last safety net collapsed in February 1917. Food riots in the capital brought out the usually efficient crowd-busting Cossacks; this time, in contrast to 1905, the regime's protectors joined the protesters. The tsar abdicated, and a caretaker provisional government was established to hold free and fair elections to a national parliament in January 1918.

The provisional government groped for a way of mitigating the domestic crisis while preserving Russia's commitments to its wartime allies. As part of its policy of liberalization, it permitted the return of political exiles including, among others, Vladimir Ilyich Ulyanov, better known to history as V.I. Lenin. His Bolshevik party was one of several hitherto illegal revolutionary groups. From the moment he arrived on April 16, 1917, in Petrograd (as St. Petersburg had been renamed in 1914 to make it sound more Russian), he hammered away at the need for immediate "Bread, Land, and Peace," a slogan that distinguished the Bolsheviks from all other political groups. As living conditions eroded, the rapidly waning popular support for the government was further sapped by an attempted military coup in September.

Lenin's political genius was never more apparent than in his insistence that the Bolsheviks should stage a coup d'état and seize power. On November 6–7 (October 24–25 of the old calendar), the Bolshevik forces seized key points in Petrograd and quickly found themselves in control as the government's support failed to materialize. In 1902, in *What Is to Be Done?* Lenin had written, "Give us an organization of revolutionaries, and we will overturn the whole of Russia!" On November 7, 1917, he did just that.

Following a bloody, three-year civil war, the Bolsheviks and their allies ultimately prevailed over the disorganized supporters of the provisional government, Lenin then focused all power in the hands of the Communist party; reaffirmed the preeminence of hierarchical and bureaucratic government institutions over society; foreclosed the emergence of a strong judiciary or any countervailing economic, social, or cultural institutions that might limit the power of the party; and made extensive use of the secret police to suppress any opposition.

Looking back, we can see that monarchy was responding, albeit slowly, to the impact of secularization and industrialization, and many historians speculate that had Russia somehow avoided entanglement in World War I it might well have become a full-fledged constitutional monarchy.[4] At the same time, however, certain characteristics of Russian political culture—the concentration of power in the hands of a few, the relative weakness of civil institutions independent of state control, the pervasive regulation of society by government bureaucracies, and a weak judiciary—suggested a continuity of outlook across tsarist, communist, and post-communist eras. Still, no nation is entirely defined by a single strand of political culture. Thus, it is also possible to trace throughout Russian history examples of civic and religious opposition to absolutism. These too persisted in the Soviet period, and no doubt contributed to the demise of the Soviet regime in December 1991.

There were always competing conceptions of how the country should move and develop. For example, in the mid- to late nineteenth century, a "debate" developed between two groups—the Slavophiles and the Westernizers—intent on influencing the course of autocratic rule. The Slavophiles believed in "the superior nature and supreme historical mission of Orthodoxy and of Russia."[5] At its best their vision was of a Camelot-like union in which all Slavs would live in harmony, governed by small civic assemblies; at its worst it expressed the cultural supremacist, messianic expansionism of writers like Nicholas Danilevsky, whose work, *Russia and Europe,* was published in 1869. However, such views had little effect on the actual policy pursued by the tsars, either in the Balkans, where Pan-Slavism was manipulated for imperial purposes, or in Central Asia, where Russification and Orthodoxy were not imposed.

The Westernizers, by contrast, argued that Russia was part of Europe, albeit at a less advanced economic and political stage of development, and they pressed for liberalization and a constitutional system modeled on the British experience. But their outlook, too, had little impact on the tsar in the 1890s, when he was assessing the relative foreign policy advantages of aligning with Paris or Berlin.

Key foreign policy issues were most often decided on the basis of regional and international configurations of power and the ambitions and skill of the individual tsar, and not according to any preconceived "ideological" blueprints. Periodically, attempts are made to equate the messianic Slavophile view of Russia's uniqueness, sense of mission, and commitment to the Orthodox faith with the "internationalism" of Marxism-Leninism, the leadership role of the Communist Party of the Soviet Union (CPSU), the incessant struggle against capitalism, and the inevitability of communism as the carrier of future civilization. However, whenever the security of Russia (or the Soviet Union) was at stake and "contradictions" between ideological postulates and national interests existed, decisions were usually made on the basis of the latter.

A number of generalizations relevant to understanding Soviet foreign policy up to the late 1980s can therefore be drawn from the tsarist experience.

First, much of Russia's expansion at the expense of other nations and peoples can be attributed to the quest for strategically defensible frontiers. The association of territorial depth with security was a conception of defense that came naturally to successive tsars whose realm had no formidable mountain ranges, deserts, or sea barriers to deter its enemies. From Moscow west to the North Sea, east to the Ural Mountains, and south to the Black Sea and the Caucasus the terrain is flat or gentle, a tempting course for invaders and restless nomadic peoples. Once the Mongols had been subdued, Russia was threatened mainly from the west. After defeating Sweden and acquiring the eastern shore of the Baltic in 1721, its subsequent expansion was always against weak and anachronistic regimes. Often attacked after the eighteenth century, Russia was just as often the aggressor as the aggrieved.

Second, as with other European monarchies of the time, foreign policy decisions were the domain of the few and the powerful. They were made, wisely or not, unencumbered by public opinion or moral considerations; the purpose was to preserve and strengthen the empire. Tsarist regimes moved in the international arena according to variants of traditional balance-of-power politics. The record shows that when there was advantage to be gained tsarist rulers were usually willing to negotiate, especially with whomever was the greatest threat. Their historically rooted approach was unsentimental, strategically coherent, and quintessentially pragmatic, irrespective of the personality or ideology of the adversary.

Finally, Russia's political elite rarely questioned the wisdom of expansion. Ambition reinforced the quest for security and the attachment to the empire, whose increasingly multinational character, in turn, deepened the perceived need for strong, centralized, autocratic rule. By the early twentieth century there was less and less need to cloak expansionism in universalistic or pious cant.

PERSPECTIVES ON THE SOVIET PERIOD

During the first seven decades of Communist rule in Moscow, Western analysts offered frequently contradictory interpretations of Soviet foreign policy. Some claimed that "communism was tsarism in overalls"—that Soviet foreign policy was essentially a continuation of traditional tsarist objectives and attitudes, which fused a concern for security with a covetous drive for real estate, resources, and international influence. Given the logic of geographic determinism, the quest for strategically secure borders had led to the expansion westward toward Central Europe and to an urge to gain access to the Baltic, the Mediterranean, the Yellow Sea, and the Persian Gulf.

Others believed that after 1917 ideology drove policy, that adherence to Marxism-Leninism impelled the USSR to seek *Pax Sovietica*, with Moscow as the center of authority of a network of Communist countries and parties having close links to tactical allies in the Third World. They saw in Marxism-Leninism a foreign policy of unremitting hostility toward the non-Communist world and a dangerous insularity and resistance to long-term accommodation. The ideology, they argued, gave rise to policies that were in turn deemed threatening by the objects of these policies, the opponents of Soviet hegemony, whose efforts to counter Soviet ambitions resulted in tensions that created the very conflictive situation originally forecast by the ideology. According to this view, an already strong and historically conditioned Russian paranoia, predisposed Soviet leaders to view the non-Communist world in the worst possible light and to proceed accordingly. When, during his visit to Britain, Khrushchev was told that his harsh anti-British sentiments were defeating his own purpose, he remarked: "I know this is true, but I cannot stop myself. We Russians have lived surrounded by dangers in a state of siege for a generation. So we are apt to be afraid, and to say and do the wrong things."[6]

There were also those who saw Soviet policy as motivated by a relentless opportunism. Whether as a response to perceived threats or to the prospects for gain arising from the changing international system, the result was an active search for advantage, a policy of continual pressure on adversaries, and a disposition toward exploitation of regional conflicts. According to this view, the Soviet Union was unable to cooperate for long with other governments, or to build lasting friendships based on mutual respect and mutual self-interest. Others saw in the USSR's post-World War II behavior in the world arena a stubborn insistence on recognition from the United States of coequal status in the management of the evolving international system, a determination to be accorded the prestige and role in world affairs consonant with its power and resources. Still others argued that the USSR was a totalitarian system, whose rulers required an external threat and an assertive foreign policy in order to justify the monopoly of power by the CPSU and the mobilization of the population in a state of perpetual military readiness and subordination to the demands of a command economy.

One of the most oft repeated explanations for Soviet behavior came from Winston Churchill. In remarks regarding the Soviet Union's collusion with Nazi Germany to dismember Poland, broadcast on October 1, 1939, he said: "I cannot forecast to you the action of Russia. It is a riddle wrapped in a mystery inside of an enigma; but perhaps there is a key. That key is Russian national interest."[7] Those wishing to convey the image of an ideologically driven relentlessly expansionist, difficult-to-comprehend Soviet leadership frequently omit the last twelve words from that quotation.

Admittedly, the term *national interest* seems imprecise and infinitely malleable, yet it conveys concrete situations in which leaders respond to the constraints placed on them by domestic and international pressures and considerations, and not in ways that reflect what individual leaders might really like to do. The term *national interest* places foreign policy behavior in a specific context and requires that we make detailed examination of the actual nature of the threat or challenge, the range of options, the dilemmas, and the probable reasons for the choice that emerges. It does not provide answers to all questions, but it shows the continuity of concerns and aims. Above all, it sheds light on the limitations—military, political, or economic—that must be considered in evaluating Soviet policy. In this approach there is a link that helps clarify Gorbachev's departure from the policies of his predecessors, as well as the even more radical transformations of Russian foreign policy we have seen since the collapse of the USSR.

THE GORBACHEV REVOLUTION

Seldom has the nexus between domestic and foreign policy been more evident than in the changes that Mikhail S. Gorbachev introduced after he came to power in March 1985. His position that foreign policy was a function of domestic policy elicited skepticism, because such statements had been made before by Soviet leaders who then proceeded to act abroad in ways that bore little relationship to internal needs or public opinion. As a member of the CPSU Politburo since 1978, Gorbachev must have known of the systemic problems: the slowdown in economic growth, the burden of military expenditures, lagging technological development, an infant mortality rate more than twice that of the United States, declining life expectancy, and pervasive alienation, alcoholism, and corruption at every level of society and government. Still it took a catastrophic event for Gorbachev fully to appreciate the magnitude of the problems his country faced.

On April 26, 1986, the Chernobyl nuclear power station, north of Kiev in the Ukraine, exploded sending tons of radioactive contamination into the atmosphere and forcing the evacuation of hundreds of thousands of people. The official death toll was listed as 31; unofficial estimates are much higher. Subsequent data indicate that the harmful fallout has been far more widespread, that well over 1.5 million people have been continuously subjected to high doses of radioactivity, that the food chain has been affected, that forests have been contaminated, that the clean-up has been inadequate,[8] and that costs related to Chernobyl for the 1990–1995 period alone will be at least $26 billion.[9] Subsequent investigation exposed gross mismanagement, bureaucratic incompetence, poor reactor design, lack of trained personnel and adequate safeguards, and ministerial indifference to ecological and environmental concerns. From what we know today, Chernobyl was the Soviet Union writ large.

Gorbachev realized that before he could even hope to begin dismantling and reforming the old Stalinist centralized command economy he would first have to secure his power and undermine the conservative opposition entrenched in the party, government, KGB, and military. Insisting on the necessity for "new thinking" (novoe myshlenie) to implement perestroika (restructuring) and glasnost (openness), he put on a dazzling display of tactical infighting and maneuvering, ramming through far-reaching reforms of the political system, including:

- the creation of a new legislative body, the Congress of People's Deputies, out of which a streamlined Supreme Soviet was elected;
- on February 7, 1990, an agreement by the CPSU leadership to end its nearly seventy-year monopoly on power, enshrined in Article 6 of the constitution, which held the party to be "the leading and guiding force of Soviet society and the nucleus of its political system, and of all state organizations and public organization";
- the establishment of a strong presidency, to which Gorbachev was elected in March 1990 by the Congress of People's Deputies. Gorbachev initiated an unprecedented structural transformation of the Soviet political system. While committing himself publicly to demilitarizing the society and the economy, to nurturing the rule of law, and to introducing a market-type economy, however, he continued to view the ultimate purpose of his reforms as "strengthening socialism."

Gorbachev concentrated even greater power in his own hands in the field of foreign policy. Within months of coming to power, Gorbachev had moved to gain more effective control of the foreign policy decision-making process. In July 1985, he appointed Eduard Shevardnadze to replace Andrei Gromyko as Foreign Minister and to undertake a major reorganization and personnel shake-up of the Ministry of Foreign Affairs (MFA). Although the MFA was the formal governmental body responsible for the conduct of foreign policy, it had in the past been subservient to the CPSU's Politburo and International Department (ID), and to the

Ministry of Defense, an influential bureaucratic actor. In July 1988, at a conference of the MFA, Shevardnadze cataloged some of its past shortcomings and introduced measures to strengthen its professionalism and responsiveness to legislative oversight. This behavior was part and parcel of Gorbachev's strategy of building up the legislative branch of government at the same time that he was maneuvering to diminish the party's role in governing the country. By reporting regularly to the Foreign Affairs Committee of the Supreme Soviet, Gorbachev (and the MFA) sought to broaden the base of popular support for his foreign policy and in the process outflank the entrenched party and military oligarchs who exercised so much influence in the past. His control of foreign policy was perhaps greater than that enjoyed by any individual Soviet leader since Stalin.

Russian society responded to Gorbachev's liberalization by organizing itself politically. Increasing social tensions and frustration with Gorbachev's policies (within the communist party he was accused of going too fast, within the populace for going too slowly) made the domestic constraints on Soviet foreign policy loom larger than ever before. Popular reluctance to send troops to quell unrest in the republics of the Soviet Union severely hampered Gorbachev's efforts to exert pressure on the Baltic States and on Georgia to prevent them from seceding. By mid-1990 seven of the fifteen republics of the USSR had declared their "sovereignty": Armenia, Georgia, Azerbaijan, Kazakhstan, Estonia, and Latvia, with Lithuania going so far as to declare "independence" (but it suspended its initiative under coercion from Moscow). Later that year even Russia, led by charismatic and popularly elected President Boris Yeltsin declared its sovereignty, albeit within the framework of a revised union. Gorbachev increasingly resembled a shadow monarch—popular abroad, but politically irrelevant at home.

These new political realities crystallized in the aftermath of the August 1991 coup attempt. Although Gorbachev was nominally restored to his former position, he served at Yeltsin's sufferance. In early December 1991, Russia, the Ukraine, and Belorussia signed an agreement to establish a new union, subsequently known as the Commonwealth of Independent States (CIS). With the exception of the Baltic States all the former Soviet republics have since affiliated themselves, to one degree or another, with this new entity. On December 25, 1991, the last Soviet leader, Mikhail S. Gorbachev, resigned, thus inaugurating the first noncommunist political leadership in Russia in more than seventy years. With Marxism-Leninism discredited, the world waited anxiously to see what the new Russia's foreign policy priorities would be.

SOME UNDERLYING ASSUMPTIONS FOR THE POST-SOVIET ERA

In any analysis of Soviet or Russian policy, whether it interprets past actions or speculates about future ones, the assumptions of the analyst are crucial. These, however, are rarely specified; instead they usually lie hidden in a line of analysis or advocacy, and the boundary between the two is not always clear to the reader. Making them explicit clarifies not only the assessment, but also the salience of the data, the suitability of the methods, and the rigor of the argument.

We believe that facts do not speak for themselves; they are construed by well-intentioned analysts who seek, reasonably, to rely on evidence that conforms to and buttresses their own predilections. Assumptions are omnipresent in political analysis: obscured in the interstices of formulations and arguments, they inexorably determine the choice of alternative explanations for policy outcomes.

Soviet foreign policy over the years and in different regions provides us with a solid record of what the Kremlin leaders did. But it does not supply the reasons for any specific Soviet action. Nor does it necessarily serve as a sure guide for what course of action the post-Soviet Russian leadership might choose. Mindful of the uncertainties that plague prognostication, we shall here briefly identify some of the principal assumptions that guide our approach to synthesizing past behavior and speculating about what the Russians are most likely to be up to in the future.

First, despite economic collapse and pronounced isolationist sentiments among the Russian populace, the urge to acquire influence and play an important international role—hallmarks of any great power—will continue. The Soviet Union paid dearly for its status as a military power: successive generations sacrificed and suffered to modernize the country and to expand its borders in search of strategically secure frontiers.

In the post-Soviet era, however, reduced capabilities necessitate a paring down of foreign policy objectives. New domestic constraints will mean that the Russian government must devote greater attention to accommodation with its neighbors and other powers rather than to their domination. Having driven itself to the center of the world stage, Moscow is not likely to retire to the wings soon, though new domestic constraints will force the government to embrace a much less ambitious foreign policy role for the foreseeable future.

Second, specific foreign policy initiatives will be undertaken in response to concrete threats to security and opportunities for gain. Contrary to the generally accepted view, Soviet diplomacy was flexible, adaptive, open to deals, and alert to "contradictions" in the noncommunist world. It is likely that post-Soviet leaders will continue to respond pragmatically to events and opportunities, weighing the risks and rewards, the difficulties and dilemmas, and, in this period of domestic turmoil, the costs and internal implications. With the gradual establishment of political pluralism in Russia, the cost of unpopular political decisions (such as the war in Chechnya) must also be factored in by decision makers.

Third, state-to-state relations will be determined not only by strategic and political calculations, but increasingly by economic considerations as Russia integrates into the world economy. Despite the conceptual shift away from reliance on military power to achieve political or economic objectives, however, the current generation of Russian leaders still believes that military power is essential for preserving the territorial integrity of the Russian Federation and promoting their foreign policy. Although Russia's military power has declined substantially since 1991, it will not be allowed to fall below the threshold needed to maintain Russian security interests in the "Near Abroad" (the former Soviet republics) and bordering regions. Analysts have dubbed this the Russian version of the Monroe Doctrine.

Fourth, the USSR will not be reconstituted, although economic and political efforts to forge closer ties between the republics will most likely continue and may eventually lead to close foreign policy and even military alliances. Any reintegration is likely to proceed slowly and through mutual accommodation, since Russia lacks both the will and the capacity to reconquer any of the other former Soviet republics. The territorial expansion of the USSR into the Baltic region and Eastern Europe during and at the end of the Second World War is therefore not likely to be repeated.

Fifth, the economy is in crisis, severely limiting Russia's foreign policy options. Although rich in raw materials and scarce minerals, the economy requires reforms that increase production and productivity; make better use of available land, labor, and capital; foster innovation; and attract foreign investment. These structural changes entail overcoming the resistance of vested political and bureaucratic interests, and permeating the system with new attitudes of accountability and entrepreneurship—in sum, a new work ethic. An essential step in this is resolving the fundamental dilemmas of who will wield political and economic power, and what kind of power they will wield.

The continuing, albeit slowing, decline in economic production continues to threaten political instability. At the same time, the "shock therapy" advocated by some economists could lead to armies of unemployed, while just "muddling through" merely enhances public frustration and encourages voter sympathy for demagogues like Vladimir Zhirinovsky. In any likely scenario, therefore, Russia's economic turmoil will leave little opportunity and scarce resources for an expansionist foreign policy.

Sixth, ethnic nationalism is an intensifying threat to regional stability. The Soviet Union was composed of fifteen union republics divided along major ethnic and linguistic lines. It had a population of about 290 million, less than half of whom were Russians, and a quarter of whom were non-Slavic in language, nationality, culture, or tradition.

With the breakup of the Soviet Union, the challenges of nationalism have increased. Russia proper has had to deal with separatism in Tatarstan and Bashkiriya (by negotiation) and Chechnya (by force), ethnically the Russian Federation is now much more homogeneous as an independent state (now 75% Russian) than it was as part of the Soviet Union.

In many other former Soviet republics the situation is even more dire than in Russia. Sergo Mikoyan has aptly characterized the process of independence as being accompanied by the transfer of imperial consciousness from the center to the republics. In Georgia, Moldova, the Ukraine, Tajikstan, Kyrgyzstan, and Kazakhstan new governments have moved quickly to squash dissidents and separatists. In the Baltic States restrictions on the rights of those not of Baltic ancestry (even though born there) have led to Russian claims that ethnocratic regimes are being established there.

With nearly one out of five Russians residing in the "Near Abroad," the status of ethnic minorities will remain a prominent Russian foreign policy concern. How the new nations of the Former Soviet Union treat their minorities will greatly affect the prospects for peaceful and stable relations within the CIS.

Seventh, Russian (as distinct from Soviet) nationalism is resurgent, with unpredictable political consequences. Long suppressed as antithetical to the internationalism and class solidarity exalted by the official ideology of Marxism-Leninism, it has reemerged as a popular movement seeking to reclaim Russia's pre-1917 heritage.

Russian nationalism can embrace patriotic values and be channeled into activities and institutions that support democratic and market reforms, or it can turn chauvinistic and xenophobic, manifesting hostility toward the West and modernization. Inevitably, it will be a major factor in defining the new Russian national interest.

Finally, there is the putative role of ideology in shaping Soviet foreign policy, a subject that goes to the very heart of one's assumptions about the motivations and aims underlying the USSR's behavior. Even though the Soviet empire ended in 1991, assumptions regarding the role that Marxism-Leninism played in shaping Soviet foreign policy continue to haunt our expectations regarding modern Russian foreign policy. To put it simply: if the Soviet regime subordinated Russian national concerns to Marxist-Leninist doctrine, then the removal of that doctrine opens the door for an entirely new Russian foreign policy agenda. By contrast, if Marxism-Leninism was so thoroughly Russified that, as Adam Ulam former director of Harvard's Russian Research Center once put it, "'Soviet patriotism' today is an ideological veneer over good, old-fashioned Russian nationalism,"[10] then there is little reason to expect any major rethinking of Russian foreign policy objectives after the collapse of communism.

There is evidence for both positions. On the one hand, it is clear that at critical moments throughout Soviet history (the Treaty of Brest-Litovsk, the Molotov-Ribbentrop Pact), the security and survival of the Soviet state took precedence over the spread of communism and revolution. Soviet leaders frequently manipulated their ideology to justify the course of action they wished to pursue.

Yet, the view that Soviet foreign policy can be entirely explained in terms of the national interest fails to take seriously Soviet definitions of what was so unique about Marxism-Leninism. The founders of the Soviet state chose this ideology as the best vehicle for achieving power and for the realization of a global proletarian revolution. They saw these two objectives—the establishment of communist rule in Russia, and the extension of communist influence throughout the world—as inseparable.

The argument that caution and pragmatism always take precedence over ideology in Soviet decision making ignores history. The construction of socialism, Lenin and his followers insisted, was not undertaken in the best interests of the nation, but in the best interests of the international proletariat. As British economist Peter Wiles points out, the Soviet leaders regularly conducted ideological experiments on their populace, such as the collectivization of agriculture, that were both difficult and disagreeable. "No one is forced to perform them; no one in his right mind would want to perform them. Yet they have been achieved. . . . The reason is of course that the Communist leaders are not in their right mind; they are in Marx's mind."[11] Should we expect foreign policy to be any different?

But why would Soviet leaders adhere to an ideology that ran counter to Russia's national interest? The question itself implies a distinction between the expansion of communist influence abroad and the domestic fortunes of the regime that may not, in fact, have existed. Even under Gorbachev, the Soviet leadership always took pains to ensure that the ideology of the party and the geopolitical concerns of the state always seemed mutually reinforcing. The influence of Marxism-Leninism on policy decisions, therefore, should be seen as a symbiotic relationship.

Part of the confusion regarding the role ideology played in Communist Party states may stem from the notion that an ideology must be believed to be influential. There was clearly a great deal of skepticism about Marxism-Leninism in the former Soviet Union, even among the Soviet elite. But while the writings of many highly placed defectors from communist regimes indeed confirm the widespread cynicism, they all stress the ideology's importance as a tool of public policy. The reason for this is that Marxism-Leninism was not just a set of abstract principles, but also a code of behavior. As such it served many important Soviet foreign policy interests: identifying and perpetuating the notion of an external threat to socialism, offering a broad and consistent rationale for foreign policy actions before both foreign and domestic audiences, and establishing the parameters for Soviet actions in times of crisis. To quote the late Oxford Sovietologist R.N. Carew Hunt:

> It is significant that whenever the leaders feel themselves in a tight corner—as in the recent aftermath of de-Stalinization and intervention in Hungary—their invariable reaction is to intensify indoctrination in an attempt to refocus public attention on first principles. As hard-headed men they would certainly not attach such importance to indoctrination if they did not know that it paid dividends—and experience has proved that the persistent repetition of a body of ideas which are never challenged is bound to influence the minds of their recipients.[12]

Soviet military interventions in Hungary in 1956, Czechoslovakia in 1968, Afghanistan in 1979, and Georgia and the Baltic States in 1991 have reaffirmed the resilience of these "first principles." The profound importance of the policy changes initiated by Gorbachev can be understood only against this background.

During the latter years of perestroika, the need to undertake sweeping policy changes in relations with the United States, in arms control negotiations, and in critical Third World areas prompted a call for "new political thinking," at the heart of which was a far-reaching deideologization of foreign policy. Such traditional Marxist-Leninist tenets as the preeminence of the "class struggle" and the inevitability of enmity between capitalism and communism were abandoned, and in their stead greater attention was paid to the "bourgeois" concept of national interest. These changes could occur only after Soviet Foreign Minister Eduard Shevardnadze had openly complained that past Soviet foreign policy had been conducted "against our own national interests," and charged that "dogmatism," "missionary zeal," and a hostile portrayal of the United States had "drastically limited the possibilities for rational and controlled action."[13] The Soviet Ambassador to the United Nations, Aleksandr Belonogov was even more specific: "The super ideologization [*sverkhideologizatsiia*] of foreign policy in the past often strongly prevented us from seeing where our interests lay in the international arena."[14]

One of the main questions for the future is, What is going to replace the former ideology? Since before the collapse of the Soviet Union, thoughtful commentators have been trying to develop a historiography of Russian foreign policy that would connect the present with traditional, pre-1917 Russian foreign policy objectives. Without such a broad-ranging discussion of Russia's historical mission as a nation, they say, it is unlikely to remain a great power. Some of the central themes of this discussion will be discussed in the final chapter.

The noted political scientist Barrington Moore once commented that Soviet foreign policy behavior becomes more readily understandable if one thinks of it as a complicated dance:

> Quite justifiably, international relations has been compared to a quadrille, in which the dancers change their partners at a definite signal. But no two dancers execute the steps in precisely the same fashion. Some, who are new to the steps, may try to stop the dance altogether, or call for a new tune. For this they may be sent to the corner (behind a cordon sanitaire), to emerge later as seeking and sought-after partners.
>
> The several phases of Soviet foreign policy in Europe and Asia represent in their essentials a single, continuous pattern. In this pattern the Soviet Union has reacted to the shifting distribution of power in international politics. Sooner or later the Soviets have danced the power political quadrille, throwing the weight of their force against any grouping of powers that showed signs of threatening their security. They have always aligned themselves against their "natural" antagonists in the balance of power at a given time. The choice of antagonist or allies had been determined not primarily by ideological factors, but the structure of the balance-of-power system itself.[15]

Since Moore penned these words, more than four decades have passed, and there have been dramatic changes inside Russia that affect how the Russian leadership defines its place in the world, and how Russian foreign policy is conducted. To what extent this new, postcommunist Russia will continue the foreign policy traditions of the past (and which past?), or depart from them, is the question we seek to answer in this book.

SELECTED BIBLIOGRAPHY

Danilevskii, Nikolai. *Rossiia I Evropa.* Moskva: Kniga, 1991.

Geyer, Dietrich. *Russian Imperialism: The Interaction of Domestic and Foreign Policy 1860–1914.* New Haven: Yale University Press, 1987.

Hammond, Thomas T. *Soviet Foreign Relations and World Communism: A Selected, Annotated Bibliography of 7,000 books in 30 Languages.* Princeton, NJ: Princeton University Press, 1965.

Jelavich, Barbara. *A Century of Russian Foreign Policy, 1814–1914.* Philadelphia: Lippincott, 1964.

——. *Russia's Balkan Entanglements, 1806–1914.* New York: Cambridge University Press, 1991.

——. *St. Petersburg and Moscow: Tsarist and Soviet Foreign Policy, 1814–1974.* Bloomington, IN: Indiana University Press, 1974.

Lenin, V.I. *What Is to Be Done?* Translated by S.V. and Patricia Utechin. Oxford, England: Clarendon Press, 1963.

Kennan, George F. *The Fateful Alliance: France, Russia, and the Coming of the First World War.* New York: Pantheon, 1984.

Lederer, Ivo J. (ed.). *Russian Foreign Policy.* New Haven: Yale University Press, 1962.

MacKenzie, David. *Imperial Dreams, Harsh Relaities: Tsarist Russian Foreign Policy.* Fort Worth, TX: Harcourt Brace College Publishers, 1994.

Madariaga, Isabel de. *Russia in the Age of Catherine the Great.* New Haven: Yale University Press, 1981.

Malozemoff, Andrew. *Russian Far Eastern Policy 1881–1904.* Berkeley: University of California Press, 1958.

Mikoyan, Sergo, "Understanding Ukraine," in George Ginsburgs et al., *Russia and America: From Rivalry to Reconciliation.* (Armonk, NY: M.E. Sharpe), 1993.

Mitchell, R. Judson. *Ideology of a Superpower: Contemporary Soviet Doctrine on International Relations.* Stanford, CA: Hoover Institution Press, 1982.

Nowak, Frank. *Russian Imperial and Soviet Foreign Policy.* Boston: Boston University Press, 1956.

Ragsdale, Hugh (ed.). *Imperial Russian Foreign Policy.* New York: Cambridge University Press, 1993.

Seton-Watson, Hugh. *The Russian Empire 1801–1917.* Oxford: Clarendon Press, 1967.

Tarsaidze, Alexandre. *Czars and Presidents; the Story of a Forgotten Friendship.* New York: McDowell, Obolensky, 1958.

Vernadsky, George. *Political and Diplomatic History of Russia.* Boston: Little, Brown, and Company, 1936.

Woodby, Sylvia. *Gorbachev and the Decline of Ideology in Soviet Foreign Policy.* Boulder, CO: Westview Press, 1989.

NOTES

1. Robert O. Crummey, *The Formation of Muscovy, 1304–1613* (New York: Longman, 1987), p. 137.
2. S. F. Platonov, as translated and edited by Joseph L. Wieczynski, *Moscow and the West* (Hattiesburg, MS: Academic International, 1972), p. 5.
3. Michael Karpovich, *Imperial Russia, 1801–1917* (New York: Henry Holt, 1932), p. 4.
4. See the works of Michael Karpovich and Michael Florinsky, as well as, more recently, the works of post-Soviet Russian historians Vladimir Shishkin, "The October Revolution and Perestroika," *European History Quarterly,* vol. 22, no. 4 (October 1992), pp. 526–546.
5. Nicholas V. Riasanovsky, *A History of Russia,* 3rd ed. (New York: Oxford University Press, 1977), p. 401.
6. Lord Taylor, "Deep Analysis of the Russian Minds," *New York Times,* January 7, 1962.
7. Winston S. Churchill, *The Gathering Storm* (New York: Houghton Mifflin, 1948), p. 449.
8. David Marples, "Chernobyl—Summer 1990," *Report on the USSR,* vol. 2, no. 26 (June 29, 1990), pp. 14–17.
9. *The New York Times,* April 28, 1990.

10. Adam Ulam, "Russian Nationalism," in Seweryn Bialer, *The Domestic Context of Soviet Foreign Policy* (Boulder, CO: Westview Press, 1981), p. 14.

11. Peter Wiles, *The Political Economy of Communism* (Cambridge, MA: Harvard University Press, 1964), p. 356.

12. Cited in "Garrett on Soviet-American Relations," *International Journal on World Peace*, vol. IV, no. 2 (April–June 1987), p. 17.

13. See the opening speech by Shevardnadze at the 19th All-Union confernce of the CPSU reprinted in *Mezhdunarodnaia zhizn'*, September 1988, p. 11. "Shevarnadze on Foreign Policy Prospects," *FBIS Daily Reports/Soviet Union* (FBIS/SOV), October 24, 1988.

14. "Glazami diplomata," an interview with Aleksandr Mikhailovich Bolnogov, *Pravda*, October 3, 1988, p. 6.

15. Barrington Moore, *Soviet Politics: The Dilemma of Power* (Cambridge, MA: Harvard University Press, 1950), pp. 351–352; 382–383.

Chapter
2

The Beleaguered Soviet State, 1917–1939

W hen the Bolsheviks seized power in Russia on November 7, 1917, they faced challenges for which their experiences as underground revolutionaries and exiled members of an obscure political movement had not prepared them. During their early days they were absorbed with consolidating the regime and had no real understanding of the nature of foreign policy. Leon Trotsky, in his autobiography, comments on the prevailing naiveté: the expectation was, he states, that on assuming the position of commissar of foreign affairs, "I will issue a few revolutionary proclamations to the peoples of the world and then shut up shop."

Burdened with the tsarist legacy of a dispirited and disorganized army, a population weary of war, and an internal order on the brink of collapse, the Bolsheviks considered that their first task in foreign policy was to take Russia out of the "imperialist" First World War. "Peace, bread, and land" had been a compelling slogan in their mobilization of popular support. The promise of peace represented a major political commitment—one that they neither dared nor desired to break. Furthermore, since they viewed World War I as an imperialist war started by rival capitalists seeking to redivide the world, they rejected traditional norms of international law and diplomacy as alien to a proletarian state. Accordingly, on November 8, 1917, the Bolsheviks issued the Decree of Peace, proposing "to all warring peoples and their Governments to begin immediately negotiations for a just and democratic peace," which they defined as "an immediate peace without annexations and without indemnities." They proclaimed the abolition of secret diplomacy and the firm intention "to carry on all negotiations absolutely openly before all the people" and to publish in full the secret treaties of the preceding tsarist government.

An appeal directed as much to the peoples and governments of Western Europe as to the people of Russia, the decree represented the first use by the Bolsheviks of what was later to be known as "demonstrative diplomacy." George F. Kennan described this as "diplomacy designed not to promote freely accepted and mutually profitable agreement as between governments, but rather to embarrass other governments and stir up opposition among their own peoples."[1]

The first step toward taking Russia out of the imperialist war was the preliminary armistice agreement signed with the Central Powers at Brest-Litovsk on December 15, 1917. At the time, some of the Bolsheviks balked at the Germans' insistence on detaching the parts of the Russian empire then under German control, notably parts of Lithuania, Poland, and the Ukraine. They procrastinated in expectation of the coming revolution in Germany. Remember: these revolutionaries, who had emerged so suddenly from obscurity, lacked any experience in foreign affairs and shared the belief that world revolution was imminent, that the success of the revolution in Russia depended on the spread of the revolution to highly industrialized Germany, and that all capitalist states were committed to the destruction of the newborn socialist state.

BREST-LITOVSK: THE FIRST FOREIGN POLICY CRISIS

The Bolsheviks' unorthodox delaying tactics at the Brest-Litovsk negotiations irritated the Germans, who were eager for a speedy conclusion of peace. Only then would they be able to transfer the bulk of their formidable army from the Eastern front to the West and hope to knock out the Allies before significant American reinforcements arrived. The impatient German military commander, Major-General Max von Hoffmann, presented Trotsky with alternatives: sign a peace treaty on German terms or face an immediate resumption of the German offensive.

Now began the first momentous debate on foreign policy. The Bolsheviks had to face up to the realities of an international system of which they were inextricably a part. They had hitherto assumed that after appropriate agitation and propaganda, the German troops would revolt against their imperialist masters, thereby sparking a revolution that would spread to the rest of Europe. As committed (and still doctrinaire) Marxists, they believed that the loyalty of the proletariat of all countries was to class, not country. Despite this, and despite Lenin's espousal in the years before he came to power of the principle of national self-determination, their own expansionist aspirations impelled them to oppose a peace with Germany that would require dismantling the Russian empire and granting independence to non-Russian peoples. At heart, most Bolsheviks remained attached to their tsarist patrimony, not because of any fondness for Russia's past, but because they believed that consolidating the empire offered the best vantage point for future expansion. The onrushing German advance confronted them with serious dilemmas and stark options.

Ever the realist and tactician, Lenin argued that a revolutionary outlook was not incompatible with *realpolitik*. He insisted that the preservation of the revolution (that is, the Bolshevik retention of political power) must outweigh other considerations; that for the immediate future at least, the interests of world revolution and the international proletariat must be subordinated to the task of consolidating the new Soviet state; and, most importantly, that the best way to ensure the eventual success of world revolution was first to safeguard and strengthen the socialist state in Russia. In any event, the Russian army was absolutely in no condition to undertake a revolutionary war; therefore, Lenin called for an immediate end.

Long-held and deeply felt beliefs were, however, difficult to shed. Those in the Central Committee who opposed Lenin's harsh decision (which amounted to giving over a third of European Russia to German control) hoped to prolong the negotiations and give the revolution time to spread. They adopted Trotsky's formula of "no war, no peace," but agreed that should the Germans resume their advance, a peace treaty would be signed. Lenin felt that delay would be costly, but reluctantly concurred, adding facetiously that "for the sake of good peace with Trotsky, Latvia and Estonia are worth losing."

On January 30, 1918, Trotsky returned to Brest-Litovsk. He found the Germans in a far less patient mood and in the process of recognizing as spokesman for the Ukraine a splinter anti-Bolshevik group, with whom they signed a separate peace treaty on February 9, thereby obtaining badly needed grain and raw materials.

On February 18, the Central Powers launched a general offensive and advanced rapidly against virtually nonexistent Russian resistance. In Petrograd the Central Committee hurriedly convened and, after some heated discussion, voted to sue for peace, as the Germans rolled onward. (In March the Bolsheviks moved the capital to Moscow and renamed themselves the "Communist Party.") Lacking any alternative, the Bolsheviks quit the war. On March 15, 1918, Soviet leaders ratified this "Pyrrhic" peace with the Central Powers and agreed to the loss of a third of Russia's population, cultivated land, and industry, illustrating just how much the new communist leadership was willing to sacrifice in order to retain their grasp on power.

The Brest-Litovsk crisis served as a crucible from which emerged the outlines of a foreign policy. First, Soviet leaders recognized that military weakness left them prey to foreign attack and increased the likelihood of their deposition. To secure the gains of the revolution and its leaders, therefore, no domestic sacrifice could be deemed too great. Second, the absence of expected revolutions in Germany and Western Europe meant that they could not depend on world revolution to strengthen the socialist revolution in Russia; therefore, though continuing to anticipate world revolution as their only ultimate security, they undertook the creation of a Red Army to provide for the short-term defense of the revolution. Finally, the policies both of the Central Powers and of the Entente buttressed their conviction that the capitalist world, irrespective of its internal rivalries, was basically hostile and would undermine communism whenever it could. Only world revolution could guarantee the success of the socialist revolution in Russia; yet the success of socialism in the new Soviet state was also deemed a prerequisite for the advancement of world revolution. Thus, Soviet leaders identified their own political survival with the good of the international proletariat. This dualism—the furthering of revolution abroad and the quest for national security—remained a salient feature of Soviet foreign policy to the end.

THE BIRTH OF AN UNCONVENTIONAL DIPLOMACY

The assumption concerning capitalist hostility was ominously confirmed by the Allied intervention, which started with the landing of Japanese troops at Vladivostok on April 5, 1918. Before it ended, British, French, American, and Japanese troops would be involved, a bitter civil war would run its course, and communism would be entrenched in Russia. Confused and contradictory motives prompted the halfhearted, inept intervention in Russia's internal turmoil: The Japanese sought to carve out a sphere of influence from Russia's Far Eastern territories, the Americans wanted to check Japanese ambitions, and the British landed at Murmansk to prevent the Germans from capturing stores of arms. The Western powers also sought to use the Czech Legion—50,000 prisoners of war from the Austro-Hungarian army—as pawns in an effort to weaken the Bolsheviks and encourage anti-Bolshevik forces. Allied strategists thereby hoped in some unspecified fashion to recreate an eastern front against the Germans.

Whatever military rationale the intervention originally had was no longer valid when World War I ended on November 11, 1918. But American inertia, Japanese persistence, and British and French commitments to anti-Bolshevik forces precluded any immediate disengagement. Fear of bolshevism spread quickly to the rest of Europe. French resentment over the Bolshevik repudiation of the prewar tsarist debts, and sympathy for the Whites (the anti-Bolshevik resistance) in Western capitals all hardened the hostility of the interventionists, who sought, in Winston S. Churchill's words, "to strangle the infant bolshevism in its cradle."

Not all foreign intervention in the Russian civil war, however, was on the side of the Whites. In fact, throughout the war "internationalists," soldiers from Latvia, Poland, China, Czechoslovakia, and Finland far exceeded the number of capitalist "interventionists." Early on they constituted the main, battle-hardened fighting forces of the nascent Red Army; as late as the summer of 1920 international units numbered nearly a quarter million.[2] Ultimately, the ambivalent and indecisive intervention of foreign governments succeeded neither in retaining Russia as an ally, nor in ending Bolshevik rule.

On November 13, 1918, seeing that the tide of the war was turning toward the Allies, the Soviet government unilaterally abrogated the Brest-Litovsk Treaty. Under Leon Trotsky's driving leadership, the new Red army eventually overcame the smorgasbord of armies and leaders that constituted the White opposition. A centralized military command, a compact geographical base and internal lines of communication, effective appeals to patriotism against foreign armies, and the inability of the Whites to coordinate their military activities or agree on a common political program worked to the Bolsheviks' benefit. In addition, the Bolshevik promise of national self-determination, including the right of secession, induced nationalists in Armenia, Georgia, and Central Asia to resist attempts by the White armies to reimpose Russian domination. However, once the civil war was won, the Communists proceeded to reincorporate the non-Russian nationalities in the Caucasus and Central Asia into the Soviet state and suppressed all separatist movements.

The year 1919 was crucial. At Versailles, a punitive treaty was summarily handed to the Germans. With it were sown the seeds of the next war in a Europe that did not realize the extent to which it had been weakened. In Germany, revolution met defeat at the hands of the military, and the fledgling Weimar Republic started its tragic, short life. In America, Wilson's dream of a League of Nations was defeated in the Senate and soon gave way to a "return to normalcy"—a phrase symbolizing America's abdication of international responsibility for two decades. The

"Balkanized" area of central and southeastern Europe (the consequence of the collapse of the Austro-Hungarian empire) had not yet been linked with France in the unstable network of military alliances that was to give the French an illusion of security. And in Russia, after the excesses and suffering of "war communism," as the period is called in the Soviet Union, bolshevism emerged victorious.

In his military weakness Lenin relied heavily on the power of ideas and propaganda to defeat his enemies. Indeed, he was the first revolutionary leader in the twentieth century to sense the political potency of the mass media. In March 1919, at an ebb in Soviet fortunes, he established the Communist International (Comintern), nominally to further world revolution and to serve the interests of the Soviet state. Specifically, through a network of foreign Communist parties, the Comintern agitated against the Allied intervention and anti-Soviet activity by capitalist governments. It defended the weak Soviet state through revolutionary propaganda, labor strife, protest movements, and subversion. Soviet leaders probed the antagonisms within the capitalist world, and capitalized on the conciliatory, frequently sympathetic attitudes of bourgeois intellectuals toward the Soviet Union. In Lenin's words, "Our policy is to use the differences of the imperialist powers in order to make agreement [between them] difficult or to make such agreement temporarily impossible."[3]

A newly confident Lenin delivered the key address to the seventh All-Russian Congress on December 5, 1919.[4] The danger from the Allied intervention had been rebuffed and the civil war had passed its most acute phase with the defeat of the principal White armies. Moreover, the pressures for peace in war-weary Western Europe and for an end to the Allied intervention had increased, and nowhere more than among the small nations bordering on European Russia. In 1920, Finland, Latvia, and Estonia concluded formal peace treaties with the Bolshevik regime, which recognized their independence. Implicit in Lenin's analysis of the main stages of the capitalist intervention and civil war were two assumptions: first, that the capitalist world, though hostile, was divided and that these divisions could be exploited to consolidate the revolution and promote Soviet security; and second, that the unconventional diplomacy of propaganda, peace movements, and front organizations could be a valuable weapon, especially for a militarily weak Soviet Russia that had very limited options.

At the second congress of the Comintern in August 1920, a high degree of centralization and discipline was introduced. The twenty-one conditions for membership made certain that the Comintern would, in fact, be a single Communist party having branches in different countries. Moscow laid down the fundamentals of policy on all significant questions and disseminated them throughout the world, through a system of pro-Soviet Communist parties, whose subservience to the Soviet Union became total in the Stalin period.

Unconventional diplomacy was adopted as a characteristic feature of Soviet foreign policy. It included the establishment and manipulation of political front organizations in order to weaken the anti-Soviet policies of capitalist governments, the support for revolutionary movements abroad, the use of mass media and propaganda, the recruitment of disaffected foreigners to serve the Soviet state, the use of cultural and commercial organizations for espionage, and the fomenting of social and political unrest. At the same time, however, it presupposed the simultaneous pursuit of normal, government-to-government relations—subversion at one level; conventional diplomacy at another. Developed as an arm of Soviet diplomacy in a period of military weakness, these techniques were perfected, richly financed, and often skillfully utilized through the decades of growing Soviet power.

The Comintern congress ended on August 7, 1920, amidst great hopes for a revolutionary surge into Central Europe: Seeking to take advantage of Russia's turmoil, Poland's Marshal Pilsudski invaded the Ukraine in May and seized Kiev. By July, however, the Red Army, having already demolished the opposition of the Whites, defeated the Poles and sought to carry the war westward into Poland. Contrary to hopes in the Kremlin, the Polish proletariat did not revolt, but fought for their country against their historic enemy, Russia. With this defeat, the lingering Soviet belief in an imminent world revolution ended. An armistice negotiated on October 12, 1920, led to a peace treaty ~~March~~ 18, 1921, which governed Soviet-Polish relations until the partit[...] [...]ptember 1939 by the Soviet Union and Nazi Germany.

By 1921 the new Soviet regim[...] [...]twin threats of foreign intervention and civil war. It now turne[...] [...]ernal recovery, consolidation of power, and "coexisting" in a ho[...]

ADAPTATION AND ACC[...]N

The pariah Soviet state also ut[...] [...]diplomacy to coexist with the capitalist states. While insisting [...] [...]greater military preparedness, Lenin pioneered the concept of p[...] [...]ce with the capitalists "to utilize the differences between them i[...] [...]e it difficult for them to unite" against the Soviet Union. He needed time to consolidate Communist rule. The economy was in shambles, unrest was growing in the countryside, food shortages and industrial bottlenecks were endemic, and a revolt at Kronstadt in March 1921 by the same sailors who had been stalwarts of the revolution just three years ago, all indicated the need for a breathing spell. Moreover, by 1921 the revolutionary mood in Europe had subsided and capitalism had entered a period of stabilization. The Allied powers too needed to tend to domestic matters, and they lifted the blockade of Russia after reaching agreements on the repatriation of prisoners of war and on trade.

Recognizing that Russia's economic weakness seriously undermined the country's domestic stability and ability to defend its borders, Lenin instituted the New Economic Policy (NEP). It gave the peasants monetary incentives to produce, allowed a limited revival of free enterprise, and relaxed governmental controls on the economy. It also welcomed foreign capital and encouraged trade with capitalist countries to meet the urgent Soviet need for industrial machinery and credits. Lenin thereby sought to strengthen the Soviet state and safeguard it from a feared coalition of capitalist powers bent on its overthrow.

Diplomatic recognition and "normalization" of relations were key objectives, not only to ensure legitimacy at home and abroad, but also to discourage intrigue against the new Soviet regime, for example, supporting exile groups dedicated to the restoration of a noncommunist regime. The end of isolation was accomplished first in Europe, then in Asia.

The Anglo-Soviet trade agreement of March 16, 1921, was an important step toward gaining acceptance internationally, as was Moscow's acceptance of the country's new frontiers, which involved the loss of Finland, Estonia, Latvia, Lithuania, eastern Poland, Bessarabia (Romania), and Kars and Ardahan (to Turkey). But the most momentous development was the agreement with Germany in April 1922, ending the isolation of the two outcasts of Europe. Russia and Germany had been invited to the Genoa economic conference called by British Prime Minister David Lloyd George in an effort to stimulate Europe's economic recovery. On Easter Sunday, April 16, 1922, the Soviet and German foreign ministers— Georgii V. Chicherin (1918–1929) and Walther Rathenau—met at Rapallo, near Genoa, and signed an agreement. The rapprochement was the first significant diplomatic triumph achieved by the Soviets through traditional norms of bourgeois diplomacy and power politics. It immeasurably enhanced the bargaining position of each country, both of which had emerged from World War I as international pariahs. For Britain and France, though they were at the time unaware of this, it signified the end of an era of political preeminence on the continent of Europe.

Diplomatically, the Treaty of Rapallo brought the Soviet regime de jure recognition from Germany—the first major country to grant it. Economically, there was a mutual cancellation of existing financial claims and expansion of trade, with commercial relations to be based on the most-favored-nation principle, and a German promise of economic assistance. Psychologically, Moscow established close contact with a key European country. Rapallo also gave new impetus to the clandestine military collaboration that had already begun to develop a year earlier when Lenin had decided to seek German assistance for the reorganization of the Red Army. To accomplish this he had used the Comintern agent Karl Radek to hold secret talks in Berlin with the Chief of the German General Staff, Hans von Seeckt. Actual military cooperation began in the spring of 1921, under the umbrella of a commercial agreement in May 1921. The Soviets obtained valuable assistance for construction of an advanced arms industry, training for their troops, and experience in modern warfare. In circumvention of the Versailles Treaty the German army was permitted to conduct tank and air maneuvers on Russian territory. This mutually beneficial arrangement continued until the rise of Hitler in 1933.

The essentials of Soviet foreign policy that emerged during the interwar period were: the primacy of the preservation of the Soviet state over short-term revolutionary aspirations; the courtship of Germany; the normalization of relations with all capitalist countries and promotion of "peaceful coexistence"; the establishment of correct relations and nonaggression pacts with the bordering Baltic and East European countries; the quest for close ties with China to counter Japanese expansion in Asia; and finally, the use of the Comintern and other nongovernmental organizations to manipulate public opinion in support of Soviet policies and to foment trouble in capitalist and colonial countries. Not until 1939 and the radical shift in the European balance of power, would the USSR have the military capability and the opportunity provided by a changing diplomatic environment abroad to pursue an expansionist foreign policy, and the luxury of a choice from among potentially advantageous options.

In the succession struggle that brought Stalin to power after Lenin's death on January 21, 1924, differences over foreign policy played a decidedly minor role. In the ensuing years, foreign policy was primarily a function of domestic politics. Intent on consolidating his power, Stalin courted the country's new elite by disclaiming interest in world revolution and stressing the construction of "socialism in one country."

Diplomatic recognition, however, did not bring the expected surge in trade and investment credits. The Western countries were wary of Moscow's revolutionary doctrine. They rejected its official commitment to conflict between socioeconomic systems, and its unwillingness to settle prerevolutionary tsarist debts, and they were suspicious of the Comintern and its network of communist parties.

The two major foreign policy setbacks that Moscow experienced in the 1924–1930 period were the result of developments in the internal affairs of other countries. In Britain, the Labour party—which had established full diplomatic relations with the Soviet Union in January 1924—fell in elections in late October, on the heels of a "Red scare" triggered by the publication of a letter allegedly signed by Grigorii Zinoviev, the head of the Comintern, but since proven to be a forgery concocted by a group of anti-Soviet emigres. The Zinoviev letter called on the British Communist Party to intensify its revolutionary activity and infiltrate British army units. The Conservative government severed diplomatic relations, and not until 1930 did British-Soviet relations again move onto a normal track.

In China, Moscow's position was abruptly shaken by domestic turnabouts that were not directly attributable to Soviet policy, though the Comintern's espousal of world revolution created a climate of suspicion that undercut Moscow's efforts to promote better relations on a government-to-government level. The result was cynical disbelief in Moscow's policy of peace, which included signing the 1928 Kellog-Briand Pact outlawing war as an instrument of national policy, and concluding treaties of nonaggression with Poland, Romania, and Estonia. These measures were inadequate to overcome the broad antipathy that was felt everywhere in official circles in Europe. As a consequence, the great powers ignored Russia's traditional interests in Eastern Europe, and all major steps affecting the area in the interwar period were taken without Soviet participation.

In the 1920s no immediate threat to Soviet security was posed by any neighboring state in Europe, but the Soviet Union did have reason to fear a powerful and expansionist Japan. Japanese intervention in the Russian civil war and its attempt to detach the Maritime Province (containing the vital port of Vladivostok) had failed, largely because of Western pressure. Japan was induced to withdraw its troops at the Washington naval disarmament conference (November 12, 1921, to February 6, 1922). In a twist of irony—for which history is often noted—the Soviet Union, not invited despite its protest that as a Far Eastern power it should have a voice in matters affecting regional security, was the principal beneficiary of the conference. Thanks to Japan's withdrawal, in November 1922 Moscow greatly improved its military position vis-à-vis the Japanese.

To the south, China loomed large in Soviet thinking. The ripening revolutionary situation, a desire to see Japan exhaust itself in expansion against China, and harassment from anti-Soviet forces operating in adjacent Manchuria, Outer Mongolia, and Xinjiang (Sinkiang)—areas nominally part of China but long vulnerable to Russian influence—heightened Soviet interest in the region. In the early years when its military weakness was most evident, the Soviet state had disclaimed any desire for special privileges in China. For example, the Karakhan Declaration of 1919 renounced the former tsarist sphere of influence in Manchuria, including the Chinese Eastern Railroad (CER)—the trunk line across northern Manchuria that connected with the Trans-Siberian line to Vladivostok and extended down to Port Arthur at the tip of the Liaotung Peninsula. But as the USSR's military position improved, such manifestos were superseded by a quest for the very same kind of concrete privileges enjoyed by the preceding tsarist regime.

From the first, Moscow wanted diplomatic recognition from the internationally recognized but weak government in Beijing (Peking); every revolutionary regime seeks legitimacy as much to cripple counterrevolutionary elements as to entrench its own power. But the Beijing regime was pro-Japanese and until 1924 refused to deal with the Soviet Union. Elsewhere in China, the absence of a strong central government magnified the regional power of local warlords, who were generally hostile to Moscow and therefore were poor prospects for Soviet infiltration. Particularly worrying was the anti-Soviet activity in Manchuria, which was ruled by Marshal Chang Tso-lin, who followed a pro-Japanese policy until 1928.

Frustrated in these directions, Moscow in 1921 made contact through the Comintern with Dr. Sun Yat-sen, the founder of the revolutionary Kuomintang (KMT) Party, who had established a political base in Canton, in the south of China. Through the Comintern, Moscow supported Sun's aim of overthrowing the very same government in Beijing from which the Soviet government was seeking diplomatic recognition. In this way conventional Soviet diplomacy and unconventional Comintern activity pursued common goals by different routes.

By supporting the KMT, Moscow aligned itself with an emerging revolutionary movement and hoped to weaken the Japanese position in China. For the first time it cooperated with a bourgeois nationalist leadership, in accordance with a policy laid down by Lenin at the 1920 Comintern congress. Under this approach, when imperialism (in this instance, Japan) was the main threat, cooperation with a progressive stratum of capitalism (defined by its readiness to work with the Soviet Union and local Communists) was justifiable. Under the agreement entered into in January 1923 by Sun Yat-sen and Comintern representative A.A. Joffe (who was supposedly acting on behalf of the nongovernmental Communist International and not the Soviet government), both signatories acknowledged that China was not suitable for communism and that its "most pressing problems are the completion of national unification and the attainment of full independence." Joffe assured Dr. Sun "that Russia is willing and ready to enter into negotiations with China on the basis of Russia's abandonment of all treaties, and of the rights and privileges (conceded by China) under duress, secured by the Czarist Government from China," including treaties concerning the Chinese Eastern Railway—the key to control of Manchuria. Joffe declared that "it is not, and never has been, the intention or objective of the present Russian Government to carry out imperialistic policies in

Outer Mongolia, or to work for Outer Mongolia's independence from China."[6] However, only one year later Moscow showed that it intended to retain control, if possible, over both.

Nonetheless, the Sun-Joffe agreement brought immediate help to the Kuomintang, which remained the centerpiece of Soviet policy in China until 1927. Comintern advisers flocked to aid the Kuomintang: General Vasily K. Blucher helped found the Whampoa Military Academy outside Canton, and Michael Borodin, the most important of all the Comintern agents in China, reorganized the KMT along the lines of the CPSU. The agreement was also instrumental in persuading the Chinese Communist party (CCP), which was created with Comintern support in 1921, to join the KMT in 1923, albeit under conditions that permitted the CCP to retain its identity as a party within a party.

In May 1924, three months after London had granted the USSR diplomatic recognition, Beijing followed suit. The weak Chinese government, desperate for any help it could get, made far-reaching concessions. Not only did Moscow keep ownership of the Chinese Eastern Railroad and retain its special position in Manchuria, but it also secured Beijing's recognition of autonomy for Outer Mongolia, whose actual status since 1921 had been that of Soviet satellite. The consolidation of control over Mongolia (and Xinjiang province) and reaffirmation of privileges in Manchuria were further examples of Moscow's familiar amalgam of security considerations and imperialist ambitions.

Three years later Soviet policy and prospects in China suffered a series of sharp setbacks. Sun Yat-sen died in March 1925 and was succeeded by Chiang Kai-shek, who felt strong enough by March 1926, because of Comintern assistance in training his troops, to launch his northern expedition to unify China under the KMT. Within a year, sweeping all before him, Chiang turned on the Communists, whom he suspected of harboring secret ambitions. He also improved relations with the Western powers, seeing in them a more lucrative source of assistance against Japan and for China's economic development. Stalin finally broke off relations with Chiang in late 1927, but Soviet policy was not without some lasting benefit: though Chiang was ideologically hostile to Moscow, he was a nationalist whose anti-Japanese position became the basis for Sino-Soviet cooperation after Japan invaded the Chinese province of Manchuria in September 1931.

Strained relations with Great Britain and the disappointments in China and elsewhere in Asia made the Soviets more insecure than ever. Internally they intensified the drive to develop "socialism in one country," introducing five-year plans for accelerated industrial growth. International events continued to be interpreted within the Marxist-Leninist mode of analysis, but Moscow's behavior generally accorded with more traditional norms of balance-of-power considerations and alignments against the main enemies of the moment; its policy was primarily opportunistic. Regardless of what Moscow may have wanted, it was constrained by a weak military position, absorption with its succession crisis, and an international environment that offered little opportunity for expansion or political maneuvering.

While at the diplomatic level Stalin followed a cautious foreign policy, at the same time he set the Comintern on an ultrarevolutionary tack. At its sixth congress in September, the Comintern enunciated guiding principles for foreign Communist parties; specifically, it held that

1. The Soviet Union was the citadel of world revolution—"She is the international driving force of proletarian revolution that impels the proletariat of all countries to seize power. [S]he is the prototype of the fraternity of nationalities in all lands that the world proletariat must establish when it has captured political power";
2. The preservation of the Soviet Union must be the primary concern of the international proletariat—"In the event of the imperialist states declaring war upon and attacking the USSR, the international proletariat must retaliate by organizing bold and determined mass action and struggle for the overthrow of the imperialist governments"; and
3. All Communist parties owed exclusive allegiance to Moscow.

These principles were to be at the heart of the cleavages that beset the communist world in the period after World War II when national communism and Eurocommunism became divisive political phenomena.

In the 1930s Moscow faced serious threats to its security in Europe and the Far East. It maneuvered as best it could in an international system in which the significant decisions were made in Berlin, London, Paris, and Tokyo. Not until the spring of 1939 did Moscow become an important actor.

As Lenin had, Stalin preferred alignment with Germany, rather than Britain or France. Rapallo was insurance against the gnawing fear of a capitalist coalition's mounting another intervention; it provided much-needed economic and military assistance, and it forestalled isolation. The renewal of the Berlin treaty in 1931 signified continuation of the special Soviet-German relationship. In keeping with the hard line that he had imposed on the Comintern in 1928, Stalin identified the Social Democrats, not the Nazis, as the main enemy of international communism, and actually contributed to Hitler's rise to power in early 1933 and to the consequent destruction of the German Communist Party. During the years immediately preceding World War II Germany became the Soviet Union's largest trading partner, and the two countries had extensive official ties, including high-level exchanges among members of the military and internal security forces. Hitler apparently admired the efficient way in which Stalin rid himself of political adversaries and adopted a number of his ideas, such as the establishment of a labor camp system. Despite Hitler's public diatribes against the communist menace, Stalin too hoped that Germany and the USSR could do business. Machiavelli more than Marx, it seemed, inspired Stalin's foreign policy.

THE QUEST FOR SECURITY IN EUROPE

A militarily weak and politically stigmatized Soviet Union sought security in various ways. To ensure that the nations on its western border would not serve as a staging ground for an interventionist-minded capitalist coalition, the USSR negotiated treaties of nonaggression and friendship with the nations of Eastern Europe.

Aided by the fears that Poland's pretensions to great power status engendered among the Baltic countries, Moscow concluded a friendship treaty with Lithuania in 1926 and a trade pact with Latvia in 1927. But not until after the Kellogg-Briand Pact of 1928 were the Soviets able to induce Poland, Romania, Latvia, and Estonia to agree to treaties of nonaggression. In Moscow, on February 9, 1929, these nations signed the East Pact (often called the Litvinov Protocol). At the time Soviet diplomats considered it a signal achievement: it served to foreclose any possible anti-Soviet coalition of powers involving the USSR's immediate neighbors. But the pact proved to be more form than substance.

Prior to 1939, the countries of Eastern Europe were united in their mistrust and fear of bolshevism. Only Czechoslovakia, which had no border with the USSR, did not regard Soviet policy, ideology, and objectives as threatening. However, the Versailles system of economic and political fragmentation in Eastern Europe did little to encourage cooperative approaches to mutual problems, and, since the USSR posed no immediate military danger, the nations of the area took no important measures to improve relations with the neighboring colossus. Instead, ideological antipathy toward communism led them to look to France and its system of alliances for security. Trade between the USSR and Eastern Europe remained insignificant; political ties were weak and proved incapable of being strengthened when both were confronted by a resurgent and aggressive Germany. Russia's traditional interests in Eastern Europe were ignored in the councils of Europe, and all major steps affecting the area in the interwar period were taken without Soviet participation.

The Soviet Union continued to pursue friendly relations with Germany, initially viewing the Nazi movement with total misapprehension. As Max Beloff noted, "Communist theory made no allowance for a movement which was at once revolutionary and non-proletarian."[8] Nazism, with its virulent anticommunist appeal, was considered merely another manifestation of bourgeois ideology aimed at attracting the support of middle-class constituents shaken by the disruptive social and economic consequences of the worldwide depression, and Hitler was considered the tool of German big business. None of this, Moscow reasoned, should preclude continued good government-to-government relations in the spirit of Rapallo. But Hitler's policy, especially the termination of military cooperation at the end of 1933, foreshadowed trouble in Soviet-German relations.

Stalin waited in silence and with growing anxiety, refraining for almost a year from any comment about events in Germany and thus adding to the confusion of an already sorely bewildered Comintern, which was still echoing an essentially anti-Western line. At the seventeenth congress of the CPSU in January 1934, Stalin at last spoke about the developments in Germany, as well as the overall international situation. Throughout his speech, he proffered the olive branch to Germany and made unmistakable his desire for continued relations in the tradition of Bismarck and Rapallo:

> Some German politicians say that the USSR has now taken an orientation towards France and Poland; that from being an opponent of the Versailles Treaty it has become a supporter of it, and that this change is to be explained by the establishment of the fascist regime in Germany. That is not true. Of course, we are far from being enthusiastic about the fascist regime in Germany. But it is not a question of fascism here,

if only for the reason that fascism in Italy, for example, has not prevented the USSR from establishing the best relations with that country. Nor is it a question of any alleged change in our attitude towards the Versailles Treaty. It is not for us, who have experienced the shame of the Brest Peace, to sing the praises of the Versailles Treaty. We merely do not agree to the world being flung into the abyss of a new war on account of that treaty. The same must be said of the alleged new orientation taken by the USSR. We never had any orientation towards Germany, nor have we any orientation towards Poland and France. Our orientation in the past and our orientation at the present time is towards the USSR, and towards the USSR alone. And if the interests of the USSR demand rapprochement with one country or another which is not interested in disturbing peace, we adopt this course without hesitation.[9]

By late 1933, Moscow's concern over its relationship with Germany stimulated interest in closer ties with the West, especially with France, whom Moscow courted even while it continued friendly relations with Germany. At all costs, Stalin worked to prevent a Franco-German understanding that would neutralize France and give Germany the green light to expand to the east.

Faced with growing Nazi hostility and rejection of Rapallo (that is, of a special relationship), Moscow accepted the French-sponsored invitation and on September 18, 1934, joined the League of Nations, where it became the leading exponent of collective security. The address of Soviet Foreign Minister Maxim Litvinov (1929–1939) before the League on the occasion of the USSR's becoming a member set the pattern for subsequent Soviet disquisitions on the potential positive role of the organization. Litvinov acknowledged an early Soviet fear that the nations of the League "might give collective expression to their hostility toward the Soviet Union and combine their anti-Soviet activities," but called now for cooperation of all peace-minded states, in the face of growing threats to their security.[10] Repeatedly during the next few years the USSR called on the League of Nations to resist aggression in Ethiopia, Spain, China, Austria, and Czechoslovakia—to no avail.

Moscow's bilateral relationship with France foundered on a deep mutual suspicion of each other's motives and an ideological antipathy that blinded them to the common danger they faced. The two countries signed a treaty of mutual assistance on May 2, 1935, and the USSR signed a similar treaty with Czechoslovakia two weeks later. The purpose was to create an interlocking alliance system; the actual result was to give Stalin flexibility in responding to the German threat. Stalin effectively prevented any Franco-German agreement and avoided isolation in Europe. Under the Soviet-Czechoslovak treaty, the Soviet Union was committed to aiding Czechoslovakia, but only if France first took action in fulfillment of its treaty obligations. France's failure to live up to its commitment to Prague in September 1938 led to the dismemberment of Czechoslovakia, and freed the USSR from any obligation to act on Czechoslovakia's behalf. However, that time of testing was still in the future.

In 1935, to stiffen the resolve of the Western countries to resist Hitler, Stalin ordered the Comintern to press for a popular front and to cooperate with all bourgeois parties, regardless of past differences, in the creation of this anti-Fascist front. But from 1935 to 1938 the Western powers gave way before Nazi Germany's relentless pressure, fearful of precipitating a showdown for which they were ill prepared They hoped, ostrich-like, that each concession would be the last, and were reluctant to stumble into a situation that would entail really meaningful cooperation with a Soviet Union they detested and mistrusted. In this sense, ideological perceptions shaped the behavior of Western leaders as much as they did Soviet policy.

For his part, Stalin continued in secret to put out feelers to Berlin for a new Rapallo-type agreement. He secretly admired Hitler and "appreciated" warnings in early 1937 from the German secret service suggesting that his former chief of staff, Marshal Mikhail Tukhachevsky, was part of a plot to seize power. Stalin was especially appreciative since the allegations against Tukhachevsky had been planted abroad by the Soviet secret police on his orders, "in the hope—perhaps even the knowledge—that they would return to Moscow in a form which could be used to frame" Tukhachevsky and other revolutionary heroes whom Stalin was determined to destroy in order to consolidate his absolute power.[11] A speculation that has less to commend it is that Stalin's purpose was to get rid of all possible opposition to a deal with Hitler, and Tukhachevsky's fear of Nazi Germany and interest in recultivating close links with France were not shared by Stalin. What was paramount for Stalin in 1935 and 1936 was carrying through his revolution from above: He wanted to eliminate all the old Bolsheviks who might oppose the new totalitarian socioeconomic order he was intent on creating. In this he owed more to Peter the Great than to Marx or even Lenin. The purges of the 1930s were intended to leave Stalin undisputed master of the Soviet Union. However, the external threats, which were manipulated as symbols, soon became realities Stalin could not ignore.

On March 7, 1936, Hitler marched into the Rhineland in violation of the 1925 Locarno Treaty. France, beset with one of its perennial cabinet crises, did nothing. Hitler had won his great gamble: From German government documents captured after the war we know that the German army had orders to withdraw at once if the French gave any indication of opposition. How different the subsequent history of Europe might have been if France had acted! Hitler's move not only set Germany irrevocably on the path to conquest and war, but strengthened his power in Germany. The last potential restraint—the German General Staff—was cowed into silence and submission by his stunning success. In the Kremlin, the French paralysis was viewed with concern, for it highlighted the lack of determination of the West to resist German remilitarization and expansion. Moscow may also have begun to reassess the value of the alliance with France.

Events in Spain soon revealed further vacillation and feebleness on the part of the French and British governments, which feared to intervene lest they push Nazi Germany and Fascist Italy into permanent alliance and be required to increase defense expenditures at a time when this would have been unpopular with their electorates. The newly formed French Popular Front Government of Leon Blum was scarcely two months old when, on July 19, 1936, General Francisco Franco turned the army against the Spanish republic. The Spanish Civil War of 1936–1939 accelerated the disintegration of the Popular Front, provided the first European battleground for World War II, and split West European political circles. It confronted Soviet leaders with a serious dilemma. A victory of the fascist Franco might push Paris into more intimate ties with Moscow. On the other hand, a Loyalist victory achieved with open Communist support, though it would undoubtedly raise Soviet prestige, might paradoxically frighten France and lead it to view Hitler less belligerently. A different line of argument is suggested by General W.G. Krivitsky, then Chief of Soviet Military Intelligence in Western Europe, who contended that Stalin wanted to establish a Soviet-controlled regime in Spain in order to "command the respect of France and England, win from them the offer of a real alliance, and either accept it or—with that as a bargaining point—arrive at his underlying steady aim and purpose, a compact with Germany."[12] According to David Cattell, the rationale for this thesis is that Stalin, preoccupied at home with the Great Purge that decimated military and party cadres, "weak militarily, intensely adverse to and distrustful of the capitalist powers, had only the one alternative of negotiating a pact with Hitler. Stalin's problem was to show Hitler that Russia had something to offer and was a power of enough consequence to negotiate with Hitler as an equal."[13] But the evidence for this position is circumstantial and strained, whereas there are specific Soviet actions and statements suggesting that Stalin was still essentially committed to the rapprochement with France and support for collective action through the League of Nations.

The Spanish Civil War was one of the major tragedies of the twentieth century. Like any civil war, it involved great bitterness and bloodshed. The Spanish Communists took advantage of the situation to increase their influence in Loyalist circles. When it was evident that the republican cause would be defeated, pro-Moscow Communists initiated a purge of Communist and socialist elements critical of Stalin that was comparable to the one then going on in the Soviet Union, the net effect of which was to intensify French and British suspicion of the Soviets.

By 1938 Nazi Germany was a power to be reckoned with. After a lightning annexation of Austria on March 12, 1938, Hitler turned on Czechoslovakia. His ostensible objective was integration of the predominantly German-speaking Sudetenland region with Germany. Litvinov's repeated calls for "collective actions" to check "the further development of aggression," which now reflected Stalin's growing perception of danger, were ignored. Hitler's threat of war prompted a hurried British-French intercession that led to an agreement with Germany for the dismemberment of Czechoslovakia. The Munich Agreement of September 15, 1938, was signed without the participation of the victim or the USSR. The British and French dismissed Soviet expressions of a readiness to act in concert with them as meaningless: The weakening of the Red Army by purges, the absence of a common border between the USSR and Czechoslovakia, and the unwillingness of either Poland or Romania to grant permission to Soviet troops to pass through its country convinced Paris and London that Moscow was not a credible partner. The fact of the matter was that Britain and France were not ready for war and suspected, correctly, that Moscow hoped to see them embroiled in a conflict that it would avoid. Suspicion of Moscow ran too deep in the West for political cooperation to occur.

Stalin watched Hitler's success, the West's surrender, and the Soviet Union's growing isolation. Whatever hope he might have had for collective action to stymie Nazi aggression disappeared at Munich. After Munich, Stalin intended to let the bourgeois countries fight among themselves and ultimately destroy each other. In early March 1939, a few days before Hitler occupied all of Czechoslovakia (contrary to his solemn declaration at Munich that he had no further territorial demands), Stalin delivered a major address to the CPSU's Eighteenth Party congress. His ostensible objective was integration of the predominantly German-speaking Sudetenland region with Germany. Litvinov's repeated calls for collective actions to check the further development of aggression, which now reflected Stalin's growing perception of danger, were ignored. He derided France and Britain for their pusillanimity and Germany and Japan for their aggressive acts, and conveyed his belief that war was inevitable; that the nonaggressive states draw back and retreat, making concession after concession to the aggressors; and that a new situation was being created that the USSR could not ignore. He did not elaborate on his plans for the future, other than to say that the Soviet Union must be cautious and not allow itself to be drawn into conflicts by warmongers who are accustomed to have others pull the chestnuts out of the fire for them. The price for Soviet agreement with either coalition was left open for negotiation. For the first time in its young history, the Soviet leadership was in a strong bargaining position: It could come to terms with Hitler or join with a Britain and France now thoroughly alarmed by Germany's expansionist appetite. Stalin was waiting for the best offer.

Unimpressed by the British government's belated diplomatic activity (essentially a unilateral guarantee to Poland in March 1939), knowing Poland's anti-Soviet attitude and unwillingness to allow any Soviet troops on Polish soil even against the Nazi threat, eager to keep the USSR out of the new "imperialist" war that he sensed was imminent, and very much occupied with containing the Japanese in the Far East, Stalin let Hitler know that he was prepared for a deal. His clearest signal was the replacement on May 3, 1939, of Foreign Minister Litvinov, a Jew who had been the object of Nazi propaganda, by Vyacheslav M. Molotov (1939–1949, 1953–1956), one of Stalin's closet aides. This move signified the abandonment of efforts to work with the Western powers and the League of Nations—a policy Hitler associated with Litvinov—and the start of active talks with Germany.

The infamous Soviet agreement with Nazi Germany was signed on August 23, 1939. The ten-year nonaggression treaty obligated each party to neutrality in the event that the other became involved in a war with a third power. Actually, it was the green light Hitler needed to make sure that Germany could go to war without worrying about conflict on two fronts. Stalin knew of Hitler's plan to invade Poland, and the last article of the treaty stated that it was to "enter into force as soon as it is signed"—an unusual diplomatic provision. In addition, there were secret protocols attached to the treaty dividing up Poland and the Baltic States. (The Soviet government continued to deny their existence until August 1988, when they were published in the Estonian Communist Party newspaper; finally, in early 1990, official acknowledgment of their existence came when they were published in Russian in *Vestnik*, the journal of the Ministry of Foreign Affairs.) Stalin and Hitler agreed to a division of the spoils: Stalin's booty for signing the pact was eastern Poland, "bounded approximately by the line of the rivers Narew, Vistula, and San," Estonia, Latvia, Finland, and Bessarabia. The rest of Poland and all of Lithuania were initially assigned to Germany, though in a second secret protocol in late September Lithuania was given to the Soviet Union, "while the province of

Lublin and parts of the province of Warsaw fell to the sphere of influence of Germany." Stalin's delight at the turn of events may be inferred from the toast he made with the German foreign minister: "I know how much the German people loves its Fuhrer. I should therefore like to drink his health."

One eminent scholar has described the importance of the Nazi-Soviet pact for Stalin as follows:

> August 1939 represented the fruition of Stalin's whole complex conception of the means of Soviet survival in a hostile world and emergence into a commanding international position. It embraced the presumption of the inevitability of a great new war: the idea that, through divisive diplomacy in the Lenin tradition, Russia could both help to precipitate the conflict and preserve neutrality during its earlier stages, allowing the combatants to exhaust themselves whilst she grew stronger and stronger; and the notion that at some point Russia would be able to take over territories to which she had historical claim and contiguous countries whose ensuing Soviet-guided revolutions would advance the world-revolutionary cause while creating the "socialist encirclement" that would give Russia's revolution the still missing guaranteed security.[14]

Stalin looked to the coming war in Western Europe with equanimity. As he viewed the situation, the Soviet Union could sit out the European war, wait for a further weakening of the capitalist world, and prepare for the inevitable revolutionary situation that would offer new opportunities for the spread of Soviet power and the proletarian revolution. This accommodation with Hitler did not come without a price. Western communist parties were thrown into complete disarray, and lost all political influence until the Soviet Union joined the Allies.

THE QUEST FOR SECURITY IN ASIA

The Nazi-Soviet pact also contributed to Soviet security in the Far East. For Soviet leaders, even more than for their tsarist counterparts, there has always been a discernible relationship between security in Europe and security in Asia. Fear of attack from both directions had been a Soviet nightmare ever since the Allied intervention of 1918–1920. The threat from Japan in the 1930s, coming as it did at a time when relations with Germany were deteriorating, heightened Moscow's fear of involvement in a two-front war and greatly influenced Stalin's decisions in 1939, a consideration generally given too little attention in Western writings.

After Japan's invasion and occupation of Manchuria in 1931, the main Soviet problem in Asia was determining whether Japan would strike south into China, and eventually toward the raw materials of Southeast Asia, or north against Siberia. The ineffectiveness of the League of Nations and the unwillingness of the great powers to do more than protest Japanese aggression exacerbated Moscow's sense of isolation and danger. The threat from Japan brought the Soviet Union and China together again, and relations with Beijing were restored on December 12, 1932, to the detriment of Moscow's ties with the Chinese Communist Party, then being relentlessly attacked by the KMT.

Moscow's diplomacy was to encourage Chiang Kai-shek to resist Japan and simultaneously to appease Japan and encourage it to expand at China's expense. In this, the Soviet Union practiced the same kind of above-the-counter and below-the-counter diplomacy in the Far East that it did in Europe. On numerous occasions Litvinov proposed a nonaggression pact to Japan; he was repeatedly rebuffed. Japan was interested, however, in purchasing the northern trunk lines of the Manchurian railroad, which were still controlled by the Soviet Union. Negotiations began in Tokyo in June 1933 and continued intermittently for almost two years until, in March 1935, Moscow finally agreed—over bitter Chinese protests—to sell its interest in the railroad and grant fishing concessions in Soviet Far Eastern waters. This appeasement was due in part to concern over secret Japanese–German military talks and in part to a desire to remove all possible pretexts for a Japanese attack, which the USSR was not then in condition to repel.

The Japanese, satisfied in Manchuria, restlessly probed Soviet determination and defenses farther to the east. In an attempt to discourage Japanese expansion into the Chinese provinces of Jehol and Chabar in Inner Mongolia, Moscow revealed that a mutual defense treaty with the Mongolian People's Republic (MPR) had been signed in March 1936, despite Beijing's claim that the MPR was legally part of China. Since 1924, Moscow's control over the MPR had been such that it could have annexed the area, but it chose to encourage Mongol separatism from China and to use the MPR as a buffer state. By contrast, further to the east, in Xinjiang, where Soviet influence was also preeminent, the USSR did not detach Chinese territory but chose to deal with compliant warlords, possibly because it feared that an independent Turkish-speaking Muslim people's republic in Central Asia might act as a catalyst for separatism in the USSR's own Turkish-speaking subdivisions—the Kazakh, Uzbek, and Kirghiz republics.

As for the Chinese, their protests against these extensions of Soviet influence gave way to their urgent need for Soviet help following the full-scale Japanese invasion of July 1937. Concerned over the implications of the anti-Comintern pact among Germany, Italy, and Japan, Moscow had pushed for a popular front in China during the previous year. In December 1936, Chiang Kai-shek was dramatically kidnapped. His captors insisted that he stop the enervating punitive expeditions against the communists and devote himself to leading the struggle against Japan. Reluctantly, he consented. The cooperation (for the most part halfhearted) between the KMT and the CCP strengthened the resistance to Japan and thus helped promote Soviet security, and Moscow provided China with important, though limited, quantities of military supplies, particularly during the period before Hitler's invasion of the Soviet Union.

From 1931 on, Moscow had striven to counter the Japanese threat. Its army east of the Urals was expanded from 100,000 in 1931 to about 600,000 in 1939; thousands of tanks and hundreds of planes were deployed. Between 1934 and 1936 there were many small but sharp military clashes along the Manchurian-Mongolian-Soviet border. Japanese probes, often in great strength, were repulsed: in July–August 1938, in the Lake Khasan (Changkufeng) area of the Manchurian-Korean-Soviet border; in 1939, along the Amur River; and in the spring and summer of 1939, in the Khalkingol (Nomonhan) steppe region along the Halka River that generally delineated the Manchurian-Mongolian border.

The latter was a full-fledged war that sharpened Stalin's interest in a nonaggression pact with Nazi Germany that would insulate Moscow from involvement in a European war. Buttressed by intelligence information on Japanese military intentions from Richard Sorge, the USSR's master spy in Tokyo, the Soviets' superior generalship and weaponry bloodied the Japanese Kwangtung Army and deflected the war party in Tokyo from pushing a major war against the Soviet Union. (Purges in the forces in the Far East were nowhere near as extensive as those that wracked the Red Army's combat effectiveness in Europe. In 1941, when Western experts assessed the USSR's ability to resist the Nazi onslaught, they used as their standard the poor performance of the Red Army in the 1939–1940 Winter War against Finland—in which more than one million troops were required to overcome a Finnish army one fifth that size—and ignored the much better Soviet showing against Japan in the 1938–1939 battles.) After the signing of the Nazi-Soviet pact, which apparently caught the Japanese by surprise, an uneasy quiet settled along the entire border, and the USSR concentrated on affairs in Europe. Soviet victories on the battlefield set the stage for the Soviet-Japanese neutrality pact of April 1941.

Stalin's diplomacy and military power in the Far East showed a sure sense of balance-of-power realities. Ideology and revolutionary agitation took a back seat to the pursuit of tactical objectives whose aim was to dissuade Japan from striking the Soviet Union and induce it to move south for satisfaction of its imperialist ambitions.

THE MOLOTOV-RIBBENTROP PACT: PRELUDE TO WAR

On August 31, 1939, Molotov defended the decision to conclude a pact with Nazi Germany in a major speech to the Soviet parliament. Criticizing Britain and France for the "howling contradictions" in their professed interest in cooperating with the Soviet Union, he emphasized the willingness of Germany to reach concrete and immediate agreements that were in the national interest of the Soviet Union, irrespective of the differences in the internal systems of the countries: "The art of politics in the sphere of foreign relations does not consist in increasing the number of enemies for one's country. It is our duty to think of the interests of the Soviet people, the interests of the Union of the Soviet Socialist Republics." He stressed the importance of good relations with Germany and never alluded to the secret protocol:

> Is it really difficult for these [British and French] gentlemen to understand the purpose of the Soviet-German Nonaggression Pact, on the strength of which the USSR is not obligated to involve itself in war either on the side of Great Britain against Germany or on the side of Germany against Great Britain? Is it really difficult to understand that the USSR is pursuing and will continue to pursue its own independent policy, based on the interests of the peoples of the USSR and only their interests? If these gentlemen have such an uncontrollable desire to fight, let them do their own fighting without the Soviet Union. We will see what fighting stuff they are made of.[15]

The next day German troops invaded Poland. As the curtain rose on World War II the Soviet Union, like the United States, was on the sidelines. Stalin had become master of the Soviet Union, surmounting the enormous resistance from the peasantry to his revolution from above in the 1930s, the debilitation and reconstitution of key institutions of Soviet society, the political isolation that foreign powers had sought to impose on a distrusted Soviet Union, and the vulnerability resulting from military weakness during most of the interwar period. None of his past foreign policy blunders seemed to have been too costly: not the exaggerated fear that Britain and France were plotting another intervention to topple the Soviet regime; not the misjudgment of nazism's inherent dynamism and expansionist threat to the Soviet Union; not the detrimental effects that the Comintern, as an instrument of Kremlin diplomacy, had on cooperation with the Western powers. On the eve of World War II, it appeared that Stalin's duplicity in handling the Western powers publicly and Germany privately had been practiced with great skill. The pact with Hitler had yielded fruits—a return of former tsarist lands that added strategic depth to the USSR's western defenses, and a neutrality that seemed to guarantee the nation against involvement in a two-front war or in the European war that was to change the political complexion of the continent forever.

No top Soviet leader ever criticized Stalin for his deal with Hitler (or his attack on Finland in November 1939). Using the "national interest" argument, defenders of the pact say it was a necessary measure to give the Soviet Union strategic depth and time to prepare for possible war. For example, on November 2, 1987, in a celebratory speech commemorating the seventieth anniversary of the Bolshevik Revolution, Gorbachev said the West resorted

> to all sorts of lies to put the blame for World War II on the Soviet Union, alleging that the way to war was opened up by the Ribbentrop-Molotov nonaggression pact. . . .
>
> They say that the decision that the Soviet Union made by signing the nonaggression pact with Germany was not the best one. Maybe so, if one is guided not by harsh reality but by speculative abstractions divorced from the context of the time. And in those conditions the question stood in about the same way as it did during the Brest[-Litovsk] peace treaty. Would our country be independent or not, would there be socialism in the world or not?
>
> It is known from documents that the date for Germany's invasion of Poland, no later than 1 September, had been set as early as 3 April 1939, that is long before the Soviet-German pact. London, Paris, and Washington knew everything, down to the smallest details of the preparations for the Polish campaign, just as they knew that the only obstacle capable of stopping the Hitlerites could be the conclusion, no later than August 1939, of an Anglo-Franco-Soviet military alliance. Those plans were also known to the leadership of our country, and for this reason it tried to convince Britain and France of the need for collective measures. It also appealed to the Polish Government of the time for cooperation in order to end aggression.
>
> But the Western powers had other calculations: to lure the USSR with a promise of an alliance, and thereby to hamper the conclusion of the nonaggression pact which had been offered to us, to deprive us of the possibility of better preparing ourselves for the inevitable attack by Hitlerite Germany against the USSR.[16]

With glasnost, however, revisionist historians like Yuri Afanasyev, Vyacheslav Dashichev, and Mikhail Semiryaga were able to argue that if Moscow had not signed the pact, or if it had dragged out the talks, Hitler would not have risked attacking Poland in 1939 and the course of European—and Soviet—history might have been very different. All of this is part of the ongoing effort to fill in the "blank spots" (*belyye piatna*) in Soviet history.

SELECTED BIBLIOGRAPHY

Beloff, Max. *The Foreign Policy of Soviet Russia, 1929–1936.* Vol. 1. New York: Oxford University Press, 1947.

Brandt, Conrad. *Stalin's Failure in China 1924–1927.* Cambridge, MA: Harvard University Press, 1958.

Braun, Otto. *A Comintern Agent in China, 1932–1939.* Stanford: Stanford University Press, 1982.

Carr, Edward Hallett. *German-Soviet Relations Between the World Wars, 1919–1939.* Baltimore: Johns Hopkins Press, 1951.

———. *Twilight of the Comintern, 1930–1935.* New York: Pantheon Books, 1982.

Dallin, David J. *The Rise of Russia in Asia.* New Haven, CT: Yale University Press, 1949.

Dyakov, Yuri and Bushuyeva, Tatyana. *The Red Army and the Wehrmacht: how the Soviets Militarized Germany, 1922–33, and Paved the Way for Fascism.* Amherst, NY: Prometheus Books, 1995.

Eudin, Xenia, and Harold H. Fisher (eds.). *Soviet Russia and the West, 1920–1927.* Stanford, CA: Stanford University Press, 1957.

———, and Robert C. North (eds.). *Soviet Russia and the East, 1920–1927.* Stanford, CA: Stanford University Press, 1957.

———, and Robert M. Slusser (eds.). *Soviet Foreign Policy 1928–1934.* 2 vols. University Park: Pennsylvania State University Press, 1967.

Freund, Gerald. *Unholy Alliance: Russian-German Relations from the Treaty of Brest-Litovsk to the Treaty of Berlin.* New York: Harcourt Brace Jovanovich, 1957.

Haslam, Jonathan. *The Soviet Union and the Struggle for Collective Security in Europe, 1933–1939.* New York: St. Martin's Press, 1984.

Hochman, Jiri. *The Soviet Union and the Failure of Collective Security, 1934–1938.* Ithaca, NY: Cornell University Press, 1984.

Kennan, George F. *Russia Leaves the War.* Princeton, NJ: Princeton University Press, 1956.

———. *The Decision to Intervene.* Princeton, NJ: Princeton University Press, 1958.

———. *Russia and the West Under Lenin and Stalin.* Boston: Little, Brown, 1960.

Lazic, Branko M., and Drachkovitch, Milorad M. *Lenin and the Comintern.* Stanford, CA: Hoover Institution Press, 1972.

Lensen, George A. *The Damned Inheritance: The Soviet Union and the Manchurian Crisis, 1924–1935.* Tallahassee, FL: Diplomatic Press, 1974.

Thornton, Richard C. *The Comintern and the Chinese Communists, 1928–1931.* Seattle: University of Washington Press, 1969.

Warth, Robert D. *The Allies and the Russian Revolution, from the Fall of the Monarchy to the Peace of Brest-Litovsk.* Durham, NC: Duke University Press, 1954.

Whiting, Allen S. *Soviet Policies in China, 1917–1924.* New York: Columbia University Press, 1954.

Volkogonov, Dmitri. *Lenin: A New Biography.* New York: The Free Press, 1994.

NOTES

1. George F. Kennan, *Russia Leaves the War* (Princeton, NJ: Princeton University Press, 1956), pp. 75–76.
2. Mikhail Heller and Aleksandr M. Nekrich, *Utopia in Power* (New York: Summit Books, 1985), pp. 91–92.
3. V.I. Lenin, *Sochineniia,* vol. 26, 2nd ed. (Moscow: State Publishing House, 1930), pp. 8–14, excerpts. From a report presented by Lenin to the Eighth Congress of Soviets of the Russian Soviet Federated Socialist Republic on December 21, 1920.
4. V.I. Lenin, *Sochineniia,* vol. 30, 4th ed., (Moscow: Institute of Marx-Engels-Lenin, 1950), pp. 185–197.
5. John W. Wheeler-Bennett, *The Nemesis of Power: the German Army in Politics, 1918–1945* (New York: St. Martin's Press, 1954), pp. 127–128.
6. Conrad Brandt, Benjamin Schwartz, and John K. Fairbank (eds.). *A Documentary History of Chinese Communism* (Cambridge, MA: Harvard University Press, 1952), pp. 70–71.
7. The Comintern's 1928 *Program,* as quoted in the U.S. Congress House of Representatives Committee on Foreign Affairs, "The Strategy and Tactics of World Communism," 80th Congress, Second session (1948), House Document 619, pp. 121–140, excerpts.
8. Max Beloff, *The Foreign Policy of Soviet Russia, 1928–1941,* vol. 1 (New York: Oxford University Press, 1947), p. 61.
9. Joseph Stalin, *Problems of Leninism* (Moscow: Foreign Languages Publishing House, 1953), pp. 592–593.
10. League of Nations, *Official Journal:* Special Supplement to No. 125 (Geneva, Septermber 1934), pp. 67–69, excerpts.
11. Malcolm MacKintosh, *Juggernaut: A History of the Soviet Forces* (New York: Macmillan, 1967), p. 92.
12. W.G. Krivitsky, *I was Stalin's Agent* (London: Hamish Hamilton, 1939), p. 99. Krivitsky, who defected to the West in 1938, was murdered, presumably by the Soviet secret police, in a Washington hotel in February 1941.
13. David T. Cattell, *Soviet Diplomacy and the Spanish Civil War* (Berkeley: University of California Press, 1957), p. 36.
14. Robert C. Tucker, "The Emergence of Stalin's Foreign Policy," *Slavic Review,* vol. 36, no. 4 (December 1977), pp. 588–589.
15. U.S. House of Representatives Committee on Foreign Affairs, "The Strategy and Tactics of World Communism," 80th Congress, 2nd session (1948), House Document 619, pp. 160–165, excerpts.
16. *Foreign Broadcast Information Service/Soviet Union* (hereafter referred to as *FBIS/SOV*), November 3, 1987, p. 46.

Chapter
3

From Wartime Alliance to Cold War, 1939–1953

At dawn on September 1, 1939, German legions rolled into Poland. Two days later, Britain and France declared war on Germany. World War II had begun. Moscow expected the new "imperialist" war to be a replica of the first one, only this time the Soviet Union would be a spectator positioned to profit from the mutual exhaustion of the competing capitalist coalitions.

Stalin wasted little time in claiming his booty. On September 17 the Red Army occupied eastern Poland; soon thereafter Stalin pressured the Baltic States into permitting Soviet troops to be stationed on their territory, a prelude to their formal incorporation into the Soviet Union in August 1940. He also tried to intimidate Finland into surrendering territory that would strengthen the defensive position of Leningrad (concessions the Soviets had been seeking since April 1938). Upon the Finns' refusal, the Soviet Union unilaterally abrogated its treaty of nonaggression on November 28, 1939, and attacked the next day. Although resisting valiantly, the Finns found themselves without help from the West and finally capitulated, signing a peace treaty on March 12, 1940. Thus ended the first wave of Soviet expansion.

Hardly had the Soviets begun to digest these territorial chunks than the Nazi blitzkrieg in April and May of 1940 overran Norway, the Netherlands, Denmark, Belgium and France. Britain stood alone and virtually defenseless. Stalin again availed himself of Hitler's absorption elsewhere, this time to wrench Bessarabia from Romania and make demands on Bulgaria and Turkey that would have resulted in the Black Sea's becoming a Soviet lake and Moscow's having control of the straits. With evident reluctance, Germany accepted the Soviet annexation of Bessarabia, at the same time taking measures to consolidate its own influence in the rest of Romania. The expansionist appetites of both tyrants sharpened their rivalry in the Balkans and in Finland. Stalin's covetousness was a match for Hitler's, and convinced Hitler that the USSR would have to be subjugated if his conquest of Europe was to be safeguarded.

Although officially neutral as far as the war in the West was concerned, the Soviet Union had a pro-German tilt: German naval vessels were outfitted in Murmansk (though after the German occupation of Norway, the Soviet port was not needed); crucial raw materials were supplied as part of overall Soviet-German economic agreements; foreign Communist parties opposed the war on orders from Moscow, thus weakening the home front in the western countries and helping the Germans; and British ships were detained in Soviet ports because of the British blockade of Germany. Soviet deference to German needs in the prosecution of the war against the West did not, however, extend to areas of overlapping Soviet and German ambitions.

In the Far East, Stalin secured his rear against attack by signing a five-year treaty of neutrality with Japan on April 13, 1941. He obtained Japan's recognition of the USSR's preeminence in the Mongolian People's Republic, its pledge to settle all outstanding Japanese claims for concessions in the northern part of Sakhalin Island, and an end to border clashes. The treaty was also intended to encourage Japan to strike south toward Southeast Asia rather than against the Soviet Union.

Thus, from September 1939 to June 1941, Stalin took advantage of a world at war to expand against his weak neighbors. In the next four years, the Soviet Union was to pay a crushing price for his greed. But despite the enormous suffering of the Soviet people in that 1941–1945 period, Stalin's imperialism in 1939–1941 and 1945–1946 is no more to be condoned than is the crime of the man who murders his parents and then asks the court to excuse him because he is an orphan. In 1939 and 1940, Stalin deported and killed thousands from eastern Poland and the Baltic States for political and ideological reasons, and many more "unreliable" peoples from the Caucasus and Crimea. This bloodletting was a prologue to what he was to do in Eastern Europe after 1945, and it contributed greatly to the fear in the West that spawned the Cold War.

On May 6, 1941, Stalin tightened his grip on party and government and assumed the post of chairman of the Council of People's Commissars (equivalent to premier). This, his first formal government position since his rise to undisputed leadership in the USSR, revealed the Kremlin's growing uneasiness over German intentions. Outwardly, German-Soviet relations remained unchanged as the Soviet Union tried in every way to mollify Hitler. Time, however, had run out on the unholy alliance.

THE WARTIME ALLIANCE

Stalin's sense of accomplishment and security was short-lived. On June 22, 1941, German troops swept into the Soviet Union along an eighteen-hundred-mile front. So confident had Stalin been of Hitler's friendship that he refused to believe his own intelligence reports and Western warnings of an impending attack. Not until eight hours after the Germans had crossed the frontier did Stalin accept the reality of the onslaught.

Twice within a generation Soviet leaders were engaged in a struggle for survival. This time, however, they were to have allies. A common cause—the destruction of nazism—submerged ideological antipathies and political antagonisms. Winston Churchill, long an avowed opponent of communism, offered the Soviets friendship and alliance. On July 12, the British and Soviet governments signed a protocol in which both agreed neither "to negotiate nor conclude an armistice or treaty of peace except by mutual agreement" and "to render each other assistance and support of all kinds in the present war against Hitlerite Germany." Thus began the forging of the Grand Alliance against Hitler.

On July 3, Stalin overcame his shock at what had happened and spoke to the Soviet people. With rare candor, no doubt dictated by the extreme gravity of the situation, he admitted that the country was in mortal peril and that there was no time for comforting words. Sensing a need to justify his pro-Nazi policy orientation of 1939–1941, he said that it had given the Soviet Union time to strengthen its defenses. He made no mention of the territorial acquisitions of that period, emphasizing instead the initial German advantage from the treacherous attack and appealing to the people to unite to defeat the invader as their ancestors before them had triumphed over Napoleon and Kaiser Wilhelm II, both of whom had enjoyed a reputation for invincibility.

Stalin did not tell the Soviet people that he had erred in ignoring repeated warnings of the impending German invasion from his own intelligence community and from Winston Churchill, nor did he assume responsibility for the country's unpreparedness. According to Khrushchev's revelations about Stalin's shortcomings at the Twentieth Congress of the CPSU in February 1956, it was Stalin's refusal to heed well-founded and persistent reports of an imminent German attack that cost the Soviets so much and facilitated the rapid and extensive initial Nazi advances. Khrushchev noted:

> Despite these particularly grave warnings, the necessary steps were not taken to prepare the country properly for defense and to prevent it from being caught unawares.
>
> Did we have time and the capabilities for such preparations? Yes, we had the time and capabilities.
>
> Had our industry been mobilized properly and in time to supply the Army with the necessary material, our wartime losses would have been decidedly smaller. Such mobilization had not been, however, started in time.
>
> When the fascist armies had actually invaded Soviet territory and military operations began, Moscow issued the order that the German fire was not to be returned. Why? It was because Stalin, despite evident facts, thought that the war had not yet started, that this was only a provocative action on the part of several undisciplined sections of the German Army, and that our reaction might serve as a reason for the Germans to begin the war.
>
> As you see, everything was ignored; warnings of certain Army commanders, declarations of deserters from the enemy army, and even the open hostility of the enemy. Is this an example of the alertness of the Chief of the Party and of the State at this particularly significant historical moment?[1]

Further details came to light under Gorbachev: for example, that Stalin rejected as disinformation a warning about Hitler's imminent attack from Berlin's ambassador to Moscow, Count Friedrich Von Schulenberg. Von Schulenberg was a diplomat of the Bismarckian school who, believing that war with Russia was against Germany's interest, told Moscow the date of Hitler's attack. Since the opening of the Soviet archives, we know that Stalin deployed Soviet troops contrary to intelligence data, enabling German troops to make rapid advances early in the war and that war losses were actually closer to 26 million, not the figure of 20 million put out officially.

To return to the sequence of events, as the Nazis penetrated deeper into Russia, even to the outskirts of Leningrad and Moscow, the Soviets relied on their traditional scourges for any would-be conqueror—the vastness of their country and the severity of its winters. They also adopted a "scorched-earth" policy, leaving nothing of use to the invader. The Germans were at first greeted as liberators in many areas of the Soviet Union, an illuminating comment on a generation of Communist rule. But the Nazis, themselves captives of their racist ideology, came as self-proclaimed conquerors intent on colonizing the country and brutally exploiting its people and resources. They thus wasted, both politically and psychologically, the strong vein of anticommunist sentiment and by this blunder contributed greatly to their eventual defeat.

While the Nazis continued to advance into the Soviet Union, anticipating the victory that would make them masters of the Eurasian land mass, the newly formed Allied coalition sought to establish a firm basis for military cooperation. Churchill had promised to render all possible aid, but obviously only the United States could meet the enormous needs of the Soviet Union. In America, as in Great Britain, all hostility toward the Soviet Union was overshadowed by the determination to work together in the common interest. President Franklin D. Roosevelt extended lend-lease aid. This aspect of cooperation with the Soviets proved successful, though not without frequent difficulties. In 1942, though eager to take the offensive against the Japanese after their attack on Pearl Harbor on December 7, 1941, the United States delivered more than $1 billion worth of war material and supplies to the Soviet Union. Subsequently, other lend-lease agreements were concluded, and America eventually supplied the USSR with approximately $11 billion in vitally needed goods of every description, from tanks and trucks to shoes and food. So grave was the danger that Stalin, according to a memoir published in 1978 by former Politburo member Anastas Mikoyan, at one time even requested the presence of Western troops on Soviet soil.

Meanwhile, the German advance overran the Soviet economic and industrial heartland. It failed, however, to attain its principal strategic objective: the destruction of the Red Army. Kiev fell, but Moscow and Leningrad held firm, and by the beginning of December it was apparent that Hitler would not winter in the Kremlin. As in 1812, winter providentially came early. Furthermore, the Japanese surprise attack on Pearl Harbor meant that the Soviets no longer had to fear a two-front war. Nonetheless, the danger to the Allied cause was never greater than during the bleak winter of 1941–1942—a winter of successive defeats and disasters—and the summer of 1942. But when the Nazis and the Japanese had failed to attain victory by late 1942, their ultimate defeat was ensured. Time and resources favored the Allies.

On all fronts, 1943 marked the turning of the tide. Now political differences within the strange alliance between the Soviet Union and the Western democracies assumed added dimensions. All had shared the resolve to defeat the Axis powers, subordinating other war aims to this overriding objective. However, as military victory approached, the political dilemmas and disagreements over the postwar settlement sharpened. The post-1945 Cold War was rooted in the incompatible objectives of the wartime Allies. Each sought security against a possible German revival, but this meant different and conflicting things to each. Subsequent Soviet maneuvering for power, position, and economic advantage and insistence on ideological conformity from the elites under its military control increased Washington's suspicion and rendered the task of shaping a congenial postwar settlement impossible. Throughout the war, even during the darkest days of the Nazi advance, Stalin was more concerned with political issues than was Roosevelt or Churchill. Certainly he had a clearer idea of what he wanted as a victor, though for the time being military necessities superseded political differences.

From the first forging of the coalition, the Soviet Union pressed for the launching of a second front in Europe that would draw forty to sixty German divisions away from the east. Stalin broached the issue in his first direct communication to Churchill on July 18, 1941, and the oft-repeated demand was a constant source of discord. Stalin's xenophobia and memory of two trying decades of Soviet-Western relations were reflected in his complaints of Allied unwillingness to make military efforts comparable to those being made by the Red Army. More than any other single issue, this signified the uneasiness that existed within the alliance. The British tried to overcome such attitudes by signing a twenty-year treaty of alliance with the USSR on May 26, 1942. A vague promise by Churchill to expect a second front in France in 1942 was seized on by Molotov, who stated it as a promised certainty rather than an eventual intention, in his speech of June 18, 1942, which called on the Supreme Soviet to ratify the Soviet-British treaty. (Churchill had a compelling reason to promise all possible assistance to the Soviet Union, fearing that Stalin might make a separate peace with Hitler.)

Of the many political problems besetting Soviet-Western wartime relations, none assumed more dramatic proportions or proved more elusive of accord than that of the future of Poland. Since the Nazi-Soviet partition of 1939, there had been no diplomatic relations between the Soviet Union and Poland. As far as the Soviet government was concerned, Poland no longer existed. With the advent of the Nazi attack, however, Stalin adopted a conciliatory position with respect to the Polish question—a gesture designed to strengthen the newly formed bonds of friendship with the West. On July 30, 1941, an agreement was reached in London between the Soviet and Polish governments that was supposed to serve as a basis for future amicable relations. In a fundamental reversal of policy, the Soviets conceded that the territorial changes of 1939 were no longer valid. Diplomatic relations between Poland and the USSR were reestablished, and plans were made for training and equipping a Polish army on Soviet soil from among the thousands of Poles imprisoned after the 1939 partition.

Several days later, a portentous article appeared in *Pravda*. Although applauding the Soviet-Polish pact, it justified Soviet action in the 1939 partition on the grounds that Moscow was "duty-bound to give a helping hand to the Ukrainians and Belorussians who made up most of the population in the Eastern regions of Poland." *Pravda* also asserted that although the time was not suitable for discussion of final frontier lines, there was nothing "immutable" in the Polish-Soviet frontier as established by the 1921 Treaty of Riga: "The question of future Soviet-Polish borders is a matter for the future."

During British Foreign Minister Anthony Eden's visit to Moscow in December 1941, Stalin insisted on recognition for the Soviet frontiers as they existed in June 1941, which would sanction all Soviet territorial acquisitions since September 1939. Although evaded at the time, this frequently repeated demand became another source of discord. The Allies opposed Soviet claims to eastern Poland, as well as any prospective incorporation of the Baltic States into the Soviet Union.

Tension between the Polish government-in-exile and the Soviet government reached the breaking point over the Katyn Forest incident. After the partition of Poland, the Soviets had interned, among others, some 15,000 Polish officers and men, the elite of the defeated Polish army. By the spring of 1940 the whereabouts of these men was a mystery. With the resumption of Polish-Soviet diplomatic relations in July 1941, the Polish government-in-exile repeatedly requested information concerning their fate. Soviet officialdom maintained an ominous silence. On April 13, 1943, the Nazis reported the "discovery" of the mass grave of these Polish troops in the Katyn Forest and blamed the Soviet Union for the atrocity. The Polish government-in-exile in London proposed an impartial investigation of this allegation. Stalin's reply was quick and harsh: he severed diplomatic relations with the Polish government, claiming that Polish belief in the Nazi accusations indicated a lack of faith in the integrity of the Soviet government.

Although the ostensible cause of the breach was the Polish request for an investigation of the German charges, in the background was the continued insistence of the Poles on a restoration of their 1939 frontier with the Soviet Union. The Poles refused to settle for territorial compensation at the expense of Germany. The Katyn incident was most convenient for Stalin. Eager to ensure a pro-Soviet (communist) regime in postwar Poland, he announced the establishment of an organization known as the Union of Polish Patriots a few days later. This group subsequently served as the basis for the Soviet puppet Lublin government.

There is a postscript to the Katyn Forest controversy. A joint Soviet-Polish Commission was established in April 1987 to examine, among other issues in the tortured relationship between the countries, the Katyn massacre. In March 1989, without waiting for the commission to present its report, Polish authorities publicly placed the responsibility for the massacre on the KGB's predecessor, the Narodyni Kommissariat Vnutrennykh Del (NKVD). A little more than a year later, President Gorbachev formally acknowledged that in April–May 1940, Stalin had indeed ordered the execution of some 15,000 Polish prisoners of war (POWs) by the NKVD. In a gesture of reconciliation, in October 1992, Russian President Boris Yeltsin released documents to the Polish government showing that the number of POWs murdered at Katyn was, in fact, closer to 25,000.

The Soviet-Polish rupture seriously tried Allied unity. The growing complex of political problems convinced the heads of state that a meeting was essential. Accordingly, at a preliminary conference of foreign ministers—Cordell Hull, Anthony Eden, and V.M. Molotov—in Moscow from October 15 to 30, 1943, an agenda was prepared; and on November 28, 1943, Stalin, Churchill, and Roosevelt met at Tehran. A broad range of topics was discussed, but no final decisions were made, though Roosevelt did imply to Stalin that the United States would not challenge the Soviet position in Poland and the Baltic States.

Meanwhile, the military picture progressively brightened. Soviet offensives drained Nazi strength and drove the Germans from Soviet soil. By January 1944, the Red Army had crossed the former Polish frontier. On January 10, the Soviet news agency TASS contradicted Polish claims to the 1939 boundary and accused the Polish government-in-exile of deliberately aggravating the frontier question. No longer was Stalin prepared to accept only minor changes in the Soviet-Polish boundary as he had implied in 1941; now he demanded major territorial adjustment. The TASS statement declared that "the injustice committed by the Soviet-Polish Riga Treaty of 1921, which imposed upon the Soviet Union," was rectified in 1939 (after the Nazi-Soviet partition of Poland) when "the territories of the Western Ukraine in which Ukrainians from the overwhelming majority of the population were incorporated with the Soviet Ukraine, and the territories of Western Belorussia in which Belorussians form an overwhelming majority of the population were incorporated with Soviet Belorussia the rebirth of Poland as a strong and independent state must be through the restoration to Poland of lands which belonged to Poland from time immemorial and were wrested by the Germans from her."[3]

The year 1944 was one of Allied victories. On June 6, Anglo-American-Canadian forces landed in France, and the long-awaited second front was a reality. By the end of the year, France had been liberated and the final preparations for the invasion of Germany itself were under way. On the eastern front, Soviet armies crossed the border into Germany. With the approach of victory, the unresolved political problems could no longer be evaded. Agreements had to be reached on the future of Poland and of all Eastern Europe, the division of Germany, the role of the Soviet Union in the war against Japan, the coordination of the final assault on Germany, and the preparations for the establishment of the United Nations.

Stalin thought in terms of spheres of influence. Security through expansion was a principle that had motivated the Kremlin for centuries; expansion entailed control, and control meant regimes that would unquestioningly toe Moscow's line. However rational and understandable Stalin's search for security was—after all, the Soviet Union had been devastated and lost more than 26 million people—what he did in the name of security in time triggered Western reactions that decreased his security and that of the West as well.

Stalin knew what he wanted and was open to a deal. In Moscow on October 9, 1944, Stalin and Churchill reached a secret understanding allocating spheres of influence. Under their so-called percentages agreement, Soviet influence in Bulgaria and Romania would be 90% as against 10 percent for Britain; in Hungary, 80/20; in Greece, 10/90; and Yugoslavia was to be divided on a 50/50 basis. This was Churchill's attempt to obtain the best possible deal for the West in an Eastern Europe that was already falling mainly to Soviet forces: Sofia, Bucharest, and Belgrade were then in Soviet hands. Because of the agreement, Stalin said nothing when the British suppressed an attempted takeover in Athens by the Greek Communists in December 1944. (But in a letter to Stalin on April 28, 1945, Churchill was to express dissatisfaction: "I must say that the way things have worked out in Yugoslavia certainly does not give me the feeling of a 50/50 interest as between our countries. Marshal Tito has become a complete dictator. He has proclaimed that his prime loyalties are to the Soviet Union."[4]

However, the United States was unwilling, for moral and domestic political reasons, to countenance politically what it was not prepared to resist militarily, namely, a cynical division of Europe into spheres of influence. This disagreement between Churchill and Roosevelt confused Stalin, who was eager for such an arrangement, and it was to be a source of future American-Soviet discord.

THE YALTA CONFERENCE

To reach agreement on plans for the final defeat of Germany and Japan and to establish a framework for a postwar settlement, the Big Three met in the Crimean resort of Yalta. The conference was held in the former tsarist palace of Livadia from February 4 to 10, 1945.

Much has been written about the Yalta Conference. Some insist that Eastern Europe and China were here "sold out" to the Soviets; others argue that the agreements reached were the best possible given the military situation and political alternatives at the time. Any appraisal must consider that differences in the relative weights accorded the same "facts" will result in strikingly different final judgments. On the eve of the conference, most Western leaders firmly believed that it would be possible to extend the unity forged in wartime to the postwar period. While suspicion of Soviet intentions did exist among some professional diplomats, popular sentiment in the West favored continued cooperation with the Soviet Union. Admiration for the courage displayed by the Soviet people and sympathy for their suffering and sacrifice were widespread.

Briefly, the military and political picture was this: Western troops were at the Rhine; Soviet forces were prepared to cross the Oder and launch the final attack on Berlin, some forty miles away. The Red Army already controlled most of Eastern Europe; Tito's pro-Moscow Communists dominated Yugoslavia. In the Far East, despite major victories over the Japanese at Iwo Jima and Okinawa, American military leaders expected a difficult fight before Japan's final surrender and urged that the USSR be brought into the final assault. In November 1944, the Joint Chiefs of Staff had weighed the pros and cons of Soviet participation and concluded that

(a) We desire Russian entry at the earliest possible date consistent with its ability to engage in offensive operations and are prepared to offer the maximum support possible without prejudice to our main effort against Japan.

(b) We consider that the mission of Russian Far Eastern Forces should be to conduct an all-out offensive against Manchuria to force the commitment of Japanese forces and resources in North China and Manchuria that might otherwise be employed in the defense of Japan, to conduct intensive air operations against Japan proper, and to interdict lines of communication between Japan and the mainland of Asia.

The discussions between Western and Soviet military staffs went smoothly in their planning for the final drive on Germany. However, the political issues affecting the fate of postwar Europe did not fare so well. The most important political discussions at Yalta focused on the Polish and German questions, the conditions under which the Soviet Union would later enter the war against Japan, and the voting procedures to be used in the United Nations Security Council. The Polish question figured in seven out of the eight plenary meetings. Attention centered on four key aspects of this, perhaps the most vexing of all pending questions:

1. a formula for establishing a single provisional government for Poland;
2. how and when to hold free elections;
3. possible solutions to the future of Poland's frontiers, both in the east and the west; and
4. steps designed to safeguard the security of the Soviet rear.

The final communiqué issued on February 12, 1945, took note of these and other problems and sketched solutions that, if applied with fidelity and good faith, might have served the interests of all. But it was evident even before the war was won that Stalin intended to interpret the Yalta accords in a manner most apt to maximize Soviet security and power. A prime catalyst in the disintegration of the wartime alliance, the Polish question represented in a larger sense a barometer recording the perilous points of two incompatible conceptions of security.

Agreement on Germany's immediate future came more readily. All parties agreed that Germany must surrender unconditionally. On the termination of hostilities, an Allied Control Council was to serve as the top coordinating and policy organ of the occupying powers; three zones of occupation were established, a fourth later being allocated to France from the American and British zones; the Soviets agreed that the Western powers were to have free and unhampered access to Berlin, which was situated deep inside the Soviet zone of occupation; and the basic principles guiding reparations arrangements were reached. Accord was also achieved on the proposed organization of the United Nations and on the broad approaches determining future political actions in Eastern Europe and the Balkans. The stage was well set at Yalta to finish off Germany and manage its surrender.

The Far East played no part in the published formal deliberations at Yalta; it was the subject of a secret protocol. No mention of it, therefore, appeared in the public statement or the grandiloquent Declaration on Liberated Europe issued at the end of the conference. Throughout the war the Soviet Union had maintained formal relations with Japan in accordance with the 1941 neutrality pact. However, despite its official posture of neutrality, it associated itself with the Chinese government and signed the Four-Power Declaration of November 1, 1943, under which the United States, Great Britain, China, and the Soviet Union pledged themselves to cooperate against all their common enemies. More significant, as early as August 1942, Stalin privately assured U.S. Ambassador Averell Harriman of Soviet help in the war against Japan at the appropriate time, and he had specifically repeated this assurance in November 1943 and in September and October 1944. There had been some informal discussion at the Tehran conference of Soviet territorial objectives in the Far East, with Stalin expressing interest in a warm-water port and the return of southern Sakhalin and the Kurile Islands, but nothing definite was settled at the time. In October 1944, at the Moscow conference, Stalin reaffirmed to Churchill his willingness to enter the war against Japan three months after the defeat of Germany, subject to certain conditions, which were presented to the American government in December and served as the basis for the secret agreement on the Far East concluded at Yalta.

The agreement provided for (1) the preservation of the status quo in the Mongolian People's Republic; (2) the restoration of "former rights of Russia violated by the treacherous attack of Japan in 1904," namely, the return of southern Sakhalin, the internationalization of the commercial port of Dairen—"the permanent interests of the Soviet Union in the port being safeguarded and the lease of Port Arthur as a navel base of the USSR restored" (these were territories of China that were being disposed of)—and the restoration of former Russian economic privileges in Manchuria; and (3) the annexation of the Kurile Islands, which Russia had granted to Japan by the Treaty of St. Petersburg (May 7, 1875) in return for renunciation of Japanese claims to Sakhalin Island. These stipulations, made without Chiang Kai-shek's approval, were later accepted by China and incorporated into the Sino-Soviet Treaty of Friendship and Alliance, signed on August 14, 1945, which contained a Soviet promise "to render to China moral support and aid in military supplies and other material resources, such support and aid to be entirely given to the Nationalist government as the central government of China."

Was the price paid for Soviet participation excessive, considering the dividends expected? Would the United States government have accepted Stalin's conditions had it realized the imminence of Japan's surrender? Could it have prevented Stalin from seizing these territories on his own? Indeed, in view of traditional Russian Far Eastern objectives, would Stalin not have entered the war even without the Yalta concessions? Ironically, it was the American military—including Generals George C. Marshall and Douglas MacArthur and Admirals Ernest King and Chester Nimitz—with their estimates of another eighteen months of war after the defeat of Germany and anticipated heavy casualties in any invasion of the Japanese home islands, who convinced Roosevelt to grant the Soviet demands. Three months later, the strategic position of the United States in the Pacific was so vastly improved that the Joint Chiefs of Staff felt less need for Soviet participation, but the die had been cast. The concessions gave Moscow a commanding position on the Asian mainland, far greater than that it had held in 1904, on the eve of the Russo-Japanese war.

The intricate story of all the controversies, discussions, and compromises that marked the Yalta deliberations, and their implications for the postwar period, will long be debated. We who examine the record in retrospect would do well to ponder the afterthoughts on Yalta so eloquently expressed by Sir Winston Churchill:

> It is not permitted to those charged with dealing with events in times of war or crisis to confine themselves purely to the statement of broad general principles on which good people agree. They have to take definite decisions from day to day. They have to adopt postures which must be solidly maintained, otherwise how can any combinations for action be maintained? It is easy, after the Germans are beaten, to condemn those who did their best to hearten the Russian military effort and to keep in harmonious contact

with out great Ally, who had suffered so frightfully. What would have happened if we had quarreled with Russia while the Germans still had three or four hundred divisions on the fighting front? Our hopeful assumptions were soon to be falsified. Still, they were the only ones possible at the time.

On May 8, 1945, Germany surrendered unconditionally. Japan collapsed quickly thereafter. The dropping of the atomic bomb on Hiroshima on August 6 and the entry of the USSR into the war two days later, as Stalin had promised—though only by breaking his neutrality pact with Japan—sealed Japan's fate. It capitulated on August 14; the formal signing was aboard the battleship Missouri in Tokyo Bay on September 2.

The war was over. The challenge of peace remained.

THE IRON CURTAIN DESCENDS

Preparations for the conference to conclude peace treaties with the East European countries dragged on through the spring of 1946. Not until the end of July did representatives of 21 nations meet in Paris. Although no agreement was reached on Germany or Austria—both occupied by the four powers—the Soviet Union agreed to treaties with Italy, Finland, Hungary, and Romania in February 1947. The West got the treaties it coveted, but time quickly revealed how irrelevant they were. The Soviet government ignored the provisions guaranteeing democratic safeguards and entrenched its domination of Eastern Europe. Stalin eliminated all Western influence from the area with a singleness of purpose that became only too clear to the Western powers by early 1947.

The 1947 treaties legalized most of Stalin's territorial acquisitions in Eastern Europe: from Finland, the ice-free port of Petsamo and territory extending the Soviet frontier to Norway; 70,000 square miles of eastern Poland, including the Vilnius area, which was ceded to Lithuania; the province of Ruthenia from Czechoslovakia; northern Bukovina and Bessarabia (and control of the Carpathian mountain passes into Central Europe and the Danubian plain) from Romania; and a common border with Hungary. The USSR advanced westward by annexing land from each of the countries on its western border; indeed, its policy of expansion and annexation was designed specifically to give the Soviet Union a common border with every country in Eastern Europe, the more easily to manage military and political control.[7] Moscow's annexation of Estonia, Latvia, and Lithuania (which was never recognized by the United States) gave it control of the eastern shore of the Baltic Sea, and the incorporation of East Prussia from Germany was not recognized by the West until the Helsinki conference in 1975.

Of all the postwar problems, none contributed more to East-West hostility than that of the future of Germany. In a sense, the German problem was the European problem. Economic, political, strategic, and technological considerations all coalesced in the struggle over Germany; and the unchallenged position of the Soviet Union in Eastern Europe could not be permanently ensured as long as Germany, with its reservoir of skilled manpower, scientific expertise, and industrial strength, remained a potential opponent.

The Soviets at first favored an exploitative policy to weaken Germany industrially. However, the Kremlin soon realized the folly of this course and shifted to a more conciliatory policy. This was first expressed by Molotov at the July 1946 Paris meeting of foreign ministers. Asserting that the spirit of revenge could not underline negotiations with Germany, he acknowledged that it would be foolish to seek to destroy Germany as a state or to agrarianize it and deprive it of major industries. Molotov suggested instead that Germany be permitted to become "a democratic and peace-loving state but [one] which would be deprived of the economic and military potentially to rise again as an aggressive force." He proposed that the Ruhr, the key to German industrial power, be placed under inter-Allied control and that a single German government willing to fulfill all its obligations, particularly those concerning reparations to the USSR, be set up.

Secretary of State James F. Byrnes responded to this bid for German favor by making similar conciliatory comments in his Stuttgart speech of September 6, 1946. He also, significantly, threw American support behind Germany in the question of a return of the eastern territories. Before the Potsdam conference, the Soviet Union had unilaterally transferred to Poland all German territory east of the Neisse River, thus strengthening Poland's claim to the area that served to compensate it for the 70,000 square miles of eastern Poland annexed by the USSR, and not unintentionally making Poland dependent on continued Soviet goodwill for preservation of its new territorial configuration. Byrnes's strategy forced the Soviets to side with the Poles against the Germans, thus deflating Soviet prestige in West Germany. Less than eighteen months after the defeat of Germany the victors had fallen out among themselves and were courting public opinion in the former foe.

The chill of Cold War, already perceptible in the middle of 1945, penetrated to the core of East–West relations by late 1946. The steel in Stalin's policy may be gleaned from a generally overlooked interview given to CBS correspondent Richard C. Hottelet in June 1946 by Maxim Litvinov, then a sidetracked, isolated, pessimistic deputy foreign minister, a holdover from the days when Moscow pushed collective security with the Western powers and he was its prime spokesman. When asked how he viewed prospects for East–West cooperation, Litvinov replied, "The outlook is bad. It seems as though the differences between East and West have gone too far to be reconciled." He gave two reasons: first, "there has been a return in Russia to the outmoded concept of security in terms of territory—the more you've got, the safer you are"; and second, "the root cause is the ideological conception prevailing [in Moscow] that conflict between the Communist and capitalist worlds is inevitable."[8]

The inability of the victors to maintain their wartime cooperation—and the consequent division of the world into two hostile camps—overshadowed all else in the immediate postwar period. Within months after the defeat of the Axis powers, this tragedy was revealed in the fundamental disagreements over Eastern Europe, Germany, Turkey, Iran, and the Far East. An investigation into the causes of the Cold War would take us far afield, and besides, an enormous literature on the subject does exist. However, to understand Soviet policy, we need to keep in mind a few relevant considerations.

First, there are these constants: the survival of Soviet-Western suspicion, only partially mitigated by wartime collaboration; the Soviet search for security, which involved not only an extension of military power westward into the center of Europe but also a radical transformation of the existing social, economic, and political order; Stalin's paranoia led him to regard the West as an implacable enemy; and, the desire for territorial expansion, which went far beyond the demonstrable needs of national security.

We must also consider the unpredictable chance actions and perceptions that shape historical events. Stalin viewed power in military terms, witness his depreciation of the Vatican's role in world affairs with the query "How many divisions does the Pope have?" Considering remarks of American officials at Yalta, he may have expected a rapid American military withdrawal from Europe and felt free to use the Red Army with impunity to bring about desired political outcomes in Eastern Europe. One may also muse on the Kremlin's view of the precipitate American decision, prompted by domestic politics, to end all lend-lease aid in May 1945, and on its view of Washington's silence regarding its request in January 1945 for a long-term reconstruction loan. The effect may have been to dispel any fleeting hopes Stalin had of basing Soviet recovery on continued American assistance. This in turn may have diminished his interest in a more conciliatory line toward the West and the problems it faced. Moreover, America's development of the atom bomb intensified Stalin's attention to military expenditures and modernization and to the urgency of overcoming the USSR's technological inferiority.

Finally, the inexorable drift in 1945–1946 toward the Cold War can also be discerned in Stalin's xenophobia, brutal domestic tyranny, and absolutist conception of security, which entailed total hegemony over all of Europe east of the Stettin-Trieste line. For example, the Soviet Union was of course entitled to firm guarantees against another attack through Poland. But Stalin treated Poland more as an accomplice of nazism than as its victim. He was no more considerate or generous toward Poland than he was toward the former enemy states of Bulgaria, Hungary, and Romania. Tsar Alexander I's troops occupied Paris, as Stalin himself remarked, but no Tsar ever envisioned the expansion of power into the heart of Europe that Stalin pursued. For the first time in European history, one great power dominated the entire area between the USSR's western border and Western Europe, an area extending from the Arctic Ocean to the Black Sea. This expansion of Soviet military power was seen by the Western nations as a permanent threat to their security. The roots of the Cold War lay both in this fundamental conflict between incompatible conceptions of security and in the worst-case assessments that each side made of the other's moves and intentions.

Even before the war was over, Stalin showed signs of the implacable enmity that was to occasion a countervailing response of domestic anticommunism in the West. As soon as Stalin judged the defeat of Germany inevitable, he ordered communist parties abroad to purge those who advocated continued "peaceful coexistence and collaboration in the framework of one and the same world." To convey the new line, he had published an article in April 1945 in a French communist journal, *Cahiers du Communisme.* The Duclos Letter, so dubbed because the article was signed by the French communist leader, Jacques Duclos, was the signal for party organizations to purge as unreliable those members who were not prepared to follow Moscow's twisting political line and wage political war against the policies of the Western governments. The "defunct" Comintern was revived under a new imprimatur.

Why Stalin chose this moment to call attention to Moscow's control over foreign communist parties, thereby inevitably raising Western suspicions of international communism again, is unknown. There are a number of possible explanations, none mutually exclusive. It could have been the counterpart of the move toward ending the relative relaxation of the wartime period and reimposing repressive measures at home. Perhaps it was deemed necessary in order to justify autocratic discipline over the Communist parties coming to power in Eastern Europe. Then again, Stalin may not have believed that the West would acquiesce to his conquests in Eastern Europe and wanted the extra margin of leverage over Western policies that indigenous Communist and Communist-front organizations provided. Or perhaps it was merely a reflection of his normal mode of political operation, one that he could comfortably revert to once the war was over.

The postwar difficulties may conveniently be dated from the spring of 1945. Relations between the USSR and its Western allies deteriorated noticeably after Yalta. Discord centered on the Polish issue, the heavy-handedness of Soviet rule in Bulgaria and Romania, the disposition of Trieste, the reparations question, and Allied administration of Germany. Stalin saw no reason to compromise. Behind his inscrutability and gruffness lay a disdain for discussions about principles and a confidence that whatever his artillery could reach was his to keep. In a conversation in the spring of 1945 with Milovan Djilas, an intimate of Tito's, Stalin described his attitude thus: "This war is not as in the past; whoever occupies a territory also imposes on it his own social system. Everyone imposes his own system as far as his army can reach. It cannot be otherwise."[9]

The West provisionally accepted the Oder-Neisse boundary between Poland and Germany, but failed to insist on guaranteed land access to Berlin, and accepted Stalin's puppet creation in Poland. Disenchantment followed Moscow's installation of coalition governments in Eastern Europe, in which the communists were assured control of the all-important ministries of interior and of the courts. In a moment of candor, Stalin admitted that a freely elected government in any of the East European countries "would be anti-Soviet, and that we cannot allow." While conflicting interpretations of what constituted "democratic" government aggravated relations, America's rapid demobilization encouraged Stalin to act without fear of effective countermeasures.

The foreign ministers of the big four powers met in the fall of 1945, primarily to draft treaties with Finland, Italy, and the Balkan countries. Old problems remained unsolved, and new ones appeared, such as Soviet demands for a trusteeship over one of the former Italian colonies and for the establishment of an allied control council in Japan comparable to the one operating in Germany, which would have given Moscow a veto over U.S. occupation policy.

Against the background of these protracted, stalemated negotiations, Stalin delivered a speech on February 9, 1946, that signified repression at home and ideological and political conflict on the international level. He reaffirmed the fundamental postulates of Marxist-Leninist theory on the causes and nature of capitalist wars and blamed the West for World War II. He insisted that the defeat of Germany did not necessarily eliminate the danger of war and, lauding the superiority of the Soviet system, called for a "new mighty upsurge in the national economy" that would treble prewar production and guarantee the Soviet Union against another invasion.

The call for improving the standard of living could not disguise the implicit stress on developing the industrial strength on which military power was based. Stalin's gloomy outlook on relations with the capitalist world paralleled Moscow's toughness on the diplomatic front, and was interpreted in the West as an indication of Soviet hostility. The world was sliding toward bipolarity. One month later, on March 5, at Fulton, Missouri, Churchill called for a strengthening of Anglo-American ties in the face of growing Soviet expansion. Although no longer in power, Churchill was still a leader who commanded attention:

> From Stettin in the Baltic to Trieste in the Adriatic an iron curtain had descended across the Continent. All these famous cities and the populations around them lie in the Soviet sphere and are subject, in one form or another, not only to Soviet influence but to a very high and increasing degree of control from Moscow.

The Iranian crisis, the Allies' first major postwar confrontation, lent immediacy to his warning.

THE IRANIAN CRISIS

British-Soviet cooperation first developed in Iran, where events impelled the two nations to act to forestall an imminent pronazi coup in Tehran. They jointly occupied the country. In its note of August 25, 1941, the Soviet government justified the Allied action on the basis of the pertinent provision of its 1921 treaty with Iran, which held that

> if a third party should attempt to carry out a policy of usurpation by means of armed intervention in Persia, or if such power should desire to use Persian territory as a base for operations again the Russian Socialist Federal Soviet Republic, or those of its allies, and if the Persian government should not be able to put a stop to such a menace after having been once called on to do so by the Russian Socialist Federal Republic, the Russian Socialist Federal Republic shall have the right to advance its troops into the Persian interior for the purpose of carrying out the military operations necessary for its defense. The Soviet Government undertakes, however, to withdraw its troops from Persian territory as soon as the danger has been removed.[10]

By mid-September 1941, the Shah of Iran had capitulated and abdicated in favor of his son (who ruled until January 1979, when a revolution forced him to leave the country). The joint Allied occupation was followed by a treaty of alliance with Iran, signed on January 29, 1942, and Iran soon became a main Allied artery of supplies for the Soviet war effort. In addition to outlining Allied prerogatives, including the right to "maintain in Iranian territory land, sea, and air forces in such numbers as they consider necessary," the treaty assured Iran that the Allies would withdraw their forces "from Iranian territory not later than six months after all hostilities between the allied powers and Germany and its associates have been suspended by the conclusion of an armistice or armistices, or on the conclusion of peace between them, whichever date is the earlier."

In early 1946, however, Iran could not obtain the promised evacuation of Soviet troops. During their occupation of northern Iran, Soviet authorities had denied the central government in Tehran access to the area and at the same time strengthened the local Communist (Tudeh) Party. In September 1945, the Tudeh party sought increased autonomy for Azerbaijan, the Iranian province bordering on the Soviet Union. The central government refused Tudeh demands for fear of augmenting Communist influence elsewhere in Iran. In December 1945 the Communists announced the creation of a new government in Tabriz, capital of Iranian Azerbaijan, under Ja'far Pishevari, a veteran Communist and Comintern agent; they proclaimed a Kurdish People's Republic, with its capital in Mahabad, in western Azerbaijan; and they intensified their efforts to kindle an irredentist movement among the Kurdish tribes of northern Iraq and eastern Turkey, which further heightened Ankara's apprehension. Meanwhile, Iranian troops seeking to reenter Azerbaijan were turned back by the Red Army.

Despite Stalin's assurance that the Soviet Union had no designs, territorial or otherwise, on Iran, Soviet troops continued to occupy the northern provinces. Iran appealed to the United Nations on January 19, 1946, charging the Soviet Union with interference in its internal affairs and with endangering the peace. American efforts to effect a withdrawal of all foreign troops by January 1, 1946, were rejected by the Soviet government, which maintained that under the Iranian-Soviet-British treaty of 1942, it was entitled to remain in Iran until March 2, 1946. During the often acrimonious negotiations in the UN Security Council, a cabinet crisis in Tehran led the Shah to appoint Qavam Saltaneh, generally regarded by Western officials as pro-Tudeh, as premier. Qavam began direct talks with Soviet leaders and spent almost a month in Moscow attempting to negotiate a settlement. In the United Nations, Soviet tactics thwarted every effort at a solution—a portent of future Soviet behavior in the world organization. As the date for the departure of Soviet troops under the 1942 agreement came and went with no visible change in Soviet attitude, Western leaders grew profoundly disturbed, particularly in light of Stalin's February speech.

On April 4, the Soviet government agreed to evacuate Iran in return for Iranian concessions, including the formation of a joint-stock Soviet-Iranian oil company and a degree of autonomy for Azerbaijan. Westerners viewed this as a Soviet triumph and glumly awaited Iran's early disappearance behind the Iron Curtain. Although the final decision by the Soviet government to withdraw from Iran by May 9 is usually attributed primarily to President Harry S Truman's tough talk, pressure by the UN Security Council, and world public opinion, the credit, according to Richard N. Frye, should go mainly to the shrewdness of Premier Qavam.

The Soviet evacuation of northern Iran was the result of a number of factors; probably the most important was the belief on the part of the Russians that Qavam had been won over to their side. He had suppressed the anti-Soviet elements and had agreed to a joint oil company, subject to ratification of parliament. The rebel government in Azerbaijan was growing in strength and there was every reason to suppose that it would maintain its position and even gain at the expense of the Tehran government. The pressure of world opinion and the debates in the United Nations, although they may have been responsible in influencing the Soviet government to evacuate Iran earlier than had been planned, were probably of much less significance than the factors mentioned above. When the Soviet government did announce that it had evacuated all its troops on May 9, 1946, it seemed as though Iran had fallen on the Soviet side of the curtain.[11]

Late that year, the Iranian parliament rejected the proposed economic treaty with the USSR. Qavam had outfoxed Moscow, and by the end of 1946, the danger of a Communist coup had passed. Azerbaijan was once again under the control of the central government. Shortly after, in an ironic twist, Qavam was dismissed and all but exiled because of palace intrigue.

The Truman Doctrine and the Zhdanov Line

Stalin's policies gave rise to two developments—one American, the other Soviet—that institutionalized the Cold War and the division of East and West into mutually antagonistic blocs. The Truman Doctrine and the Zhdanov Line were the formal expressions of the superpower impetus toward a bipolar world. The former led to an economic recovery program and military buildup and the latter to a closed ideological and political system, the consequences of which were to reinforce the trend toward bloc exclusiveness.

On March 12, 1947, President Truman announced the decision to extend economic and military assistance to Greece and Turkey, and "to support peoples who are resisting attempted subjugation by armed minorities or by outside pressure," that is, international communism. The announcement was prompted by the inability of Great Britain to continue to bear the responsibility for defense of the eastern Mediterranean, and British power in the area gradually being replaced by that of the United States. Moscow branded the Truman Doctrine "a smokescreen for expansion." It described the policy as an example of America's postwar imperialism and circumvention of the UN, and dismissed the U.S. contention that the USSR threatened the Turkish straits or the provinces of Kars and Ardahan, insisting that "no one and nothing actually threatens Turkey's integrity. This 'assistance' is evidently aimed at putting [Turkey] also under U.S. control."

The Truman Doctrine was a watershed in U.S. postwar policy. Once committed to the proposition that no other European countries should be allowed to fall under Soviet control, the United States went beyond the Truman Doctrine with a more permanent and far-reaching program of economic assistance. On June 5, 1947, Secretary of State George C. Marshall, speaking at Harvard University, expressed America's willingness to help rebuild Europe and invited the European nations to draw up a list of their needs. Under the leadership of British Foreign Secretary Ernest Bevin and French Foreign Minister Georges Bidault, a conference of all European nations, including the Soviet Union, was convened in Paris on June 27. Discussions were at first secret. Then, on June 29, Moscow unexpectedly issued a statement denouncing the conference and the proposals. The thrust of the attack was at first largely economic, with Moscow alleging that the proposals entailed an integration of the various national economies that would require it to abandon its own plans for Eastern Europe's industrialization and incorporation into the Soviet five-year plans. It also intimated that the Marshall Plan, which provided economic assistance to promote Europe's recovery from World War II's destruction and dislocation, was intended to advance the economic, and hence political, expansion of American influence.

By July 2, Moscow had withdrawn from the conference and forced all the East European countries to follow suit. It is unlikely that the U.S. Congress would have appropriated any funds for the program had the USSR remained one of the possible recipients, and continued Soviet participation in the talks might well have sounded the death knell for the Marshall Plan and for European recovery, but Stalin was not prepared to run any risks where Soviet control of Eastern Europe was concerned.

The Soviet refusal to participate in the Marshall Plan program was a logical outcome of the crystallizing East-West estrangement and of Stalin's domestic priorities, which called for tightened controls, forced savings, cultural conformity, and isolation of the population from outside influences—in brief, a ruthless harnessing of the society for internal reconstruction and recompression. Stalin's interest in "Sovietizing" Eastern Europe made him doubly suspicious of any Western proposal that could interfere with this overriding strategic objective. To have permitted the East Europeans extensive economic access to the West would have politically strengthened the pro-Western elements still hanging on in the Moscow-managed coalition governments and complicated the process of full Sovietization.

Nor was Stalin interested in all-European recovery unless there was immediate and significant advantage to the USSR. This was understandable economically, given the Soviet Union's need to tend its own wounds. It was also sound politically, since an unstable Western Europe decreased the likelihood of interference with Soviet policies in Eastern Europe. Indeed, instability might further strengthen Communist parties, particularly in Italy and France, where the Communists had emerged from the war with enhanced prestige and broad electoral support. Thus, impeding Western Europe's recovery would not only keep the West from challenging Soviet hegemony in Eastern Europe, but might even help the aggravation of internal turmoil in Western countries.

Stalin also mistrusted American motives. He assumed that the United States had imperial ambitions that mirrored his own and that the flag would follow the funds, with the U.S. influence and military control accompanying its aid. After all, in 1945, the USSR had approached the United States for a long-term credit and been "misplaced."

Finally, Soviet participation would have required Moscow to divulge statistical data revealing its economic weaknesses. A xenophobic and secretive Kremlin would hardly be receptive to such a requirement.

Whatever the compelling reasons, during the summer and fall of 1947, East-West relations sharply deteriorated as Soviet attacks on the Marshall Plan intensified. On September 18, 1947, Andrei Y. Vyshinsky, the Soviet delegate to the United Nations, set the general tenor for official policy in a speech before the General Assembly:

> As is now clear, the Marshall Plan constitutes in essence merely a variant of the Truman Doctrine adapted to the conditions of postwar Europe. In bringing forward this plan, the United States Government apparently counted on the cooperation of the Governments of the United Kingdom and France to confront the European countries in need

of relief with the necessity of renouncing their inalienable right to dispose of their economic resources and to plan their national economy in their own way. The United States also counted on making all of these countries directly dependent on the interests of the American monopolies, which are striving to avert the approaching depression by an accelerated export of commodities and capital to Europe.

Moreover, this Plan is an attempt to split Europe into two camps and with the help of the United Kingdom and France, to complete the formation of a bloc of several European countries hostile to the interests of the democratic countries of Eastern Europe and most particularly to the interest of the Soviet Union.

Stalin completed the breach by organizing his satellites into a formal grouping of states subservient to the Soviet Union. The Comintern was resurrected as the Cominform (Communist Information Bureau) at a special conference of Communist parties in Polish Silesia on September 22 to 23, 1947. Only nine parties—from Bulgaria, Czechoslovakia, France, Hungary, Italy, Poland, Romania, Yugoslavia, and the USSR—were invited because Stalin's primary aim was to consolidate Eastern Europe, not to promote international communism or the parliamentary prospects of communist parties elsewhere in Europe.

By ending the policy that had encouraged West European Communist parties in 1944–1947 to enter into coalitions with bourgeois governments and by ordering them to oppose Marshall Plan programs, Stalin sought to intensify Western uneasiness over the revolutionary potential of their own Communist parties and thereby divert the West's attention away from Soviet policy in Eastern Europe.[12] Besides, Stalin turned his regional need into an international advantage: seeing that Communist movements in China, Vietnam, the Philippines, and Greece had already implicitly rejected Moscow's leadership by not waiting for the Red Army to "liberate" their countries, and by choosing the revolutionary rather than the evolutionary road to power, he used his about-face in Europe to reassert Soviet militancy and again place the USSR in the vanguard of world revolutionary activity.

To justify the establishment of the Cominform ideologically, the Kremlin formally revived the thesis of the capitalist menace and emphasized the enduring and irreconcilable antagonisms between the capitalist and Communist systems. Andrei A. Zhdanov's speech at the founding conference must be regarded as the most significant effort since the Comintern program of 1928 to formulate the position of international communism in the world and to integrate it into a unified whole. The importance of the speech lay not only in its ambitious scope, but in the powerful position of the man charged with its presentation. Zhdanov, who died the following year, was regarded as second only to Stalin.

Zhdanov began by announcing that the war had altered world power relationships:

The fundamental changes caused by the war on the international scene and in the position of individual countries have entirely changed the political landscape of the world. A new alignment of political forces has arisen. The more the war recedes into the past, the more distinct become two major trends in postwar international policy, corresponding to the division of the political forces operating on the international arena into two major camps: the imperialist and antidemocratic camp, on the one hand, and the anti-imperialist and democratic camp on the other. The principal driving force of the imperialist camp is the USA. Allied with it are Great Britain and France. The cardinal purpose of the imperialist camp is to strengthen imperialism, to hatch a new imperialist war, to combat socialism and democracy, and to support reactionary and antidemocratic profascist regimes and movements everywhere.[13]

Clearly, he identified the United States as the principal antagonist and castigated the economic, ideological, and military bases of its foreign policy, claiming that its underlying motif was expansionism. Justifying Moscow's opposition to the Marshall Plan and its determination to control Eastern Europe, he at the same time dropped an olive twig along the way:

> Soviet foreign policy proceeds from the fact of the coexistence for a long period of the two systems—capitalism and socialism. From this it follows that cooperation between the USSR and the countries with other systems is possible, provided that the principle of reciprocity is observed and that obligations once assumed are honored.

But this hint that the Kremlin was open to a deal formalizing the division of Europe into spheres of influence was lost in the hostility that flowed from the rest of the speech and that characterized the behavior of the Soviet Union and its communist agents in the months that followed. Zhdanov's call for all communist parties to act in concerted opposition to the Marshall Plan was interpreted in the West as a declaration of permanent Cold War. The tactical consequences of this militant policy soon emerged in France and Italy, where in November 1947 general strikes accompanied by labor violence were instigated in an attempt to paralyze the nascent Marshall Plan program, and in Southern Asia, where Communist parties split with bourgeois nationalist movements and attempted to subvert the newly independent governments in India, Burma, Indonesia, and the Philippines by direct revolutionary means.

In addition to mobilizing communist parties against the Marshall Plan and Western policy in Europe, the Cominform had other, longer-term Soviet-bloc-oriented purposes. Ideologically, it promulgated the line from Moscow and provided political guidance for foreign Communists. Organizationally, it facilitated the consolidation of Soviet power, ensuring Moscow's control over the various East European Communist parties. Politically, as a focal point for international communism, it not only crystallized opposition to the West, but symbolized communist unity and Soviet leadership of the international communist movement. The establishment of the Cominform was a turning point for Stalin. Henceforth, accommodation and cooperation with the noncommunist world—the official line during the 1941–1947 period—was dropped, and the focus was on antagonism between blocs.

Soviet belligerence sharpened in the United Nations, in Germany, and in Austria, but it was in Czechoslovakia in February 1948 that Stalin showed his hegemonic absolutism and dropped the last fig leaf of democracy in Eastern Europe. The communist takeover that ordained Czechoslovakia's disappearance behind the Iron Curtain shocked the West. After all, the Communists had been in control of most of the country's institutions since 1945; the first postwar elections in May 1946 had given them 38% of the vote (the largest percentage), and Czechoslovakia had pulled out of the Marshall Plan discussions on Stalin's orders. Moscow's preeminent and unchallenged influence was accepted as a fact of East European reality. Presumably, this should have satisfied Stalin's desire for a compliant imperial order in Eastern Europe that would ensure the security of his western border. But Stalin would settle for nothing less than total domination. Perhaps more than any other single Soviet-inspired move, the fall of Prague dispelled remaining Western illusions concerning Soviet intentions, heightened fears of new Soviet thrusts, hastened Western rearmament, and froze the division of Europe. The disappearance of Czechoslovakia as a middle ground in which democratic socialist and communist groups could coexist symbolized the end of possible cooperation between East and West.

Next, Stalin took steps to end the last vestiges of coalition government in Eastern Europe and to consolidate his empire—a process noticeably accelerated after the split with Tito. Through an intricate network of alliances, trade and economic agreements, joint-stock companies, and Communist Party and secret police connections, Soviet hegemony was entrenched throughout the region. Cultural and political ties with the West were eliminated, and economic transactions were reduced to insignificant levels. By June 1948, the Soviet Union had created a cowed empire from the Baltic to the Black Sea. To the West it seemed that only America's monopoly on atomic weapons barred Soviet domination of all Europe and prevented the Red Army from marching to the English Channel.

Two dramatic developments occurred in that month: the Berlin blockade and the expulsion of Tito from the Cominform. Each had an effect far beyond its immediate frame of reference.

THE BERLIN BLOCKADE

The Berlin crisis, the most dangerous crisis of the immediate postwar period, was made possible by the Western powers' failure to insist on a land corridor to Berlin in 1944–1945. At the Tehran Conference in November 1943, Roosevelt, Churchill, and Stalin had agreed on a three-power occupation of Germany, but had left the final zonal divisions undefined. In April 1944, the Allied European Advisory Commission in London fashioned a general agreement on the boundary of the Soviet zone, and a formal protocol allocating the three zones was signed on September 12, 1944, three months after Western armies landed in France. It did not contain any specific provisions for access to Berlin, which was located 110 miles inside the Soviet zone, nor did Roosevelt or Churchill consider the issues important enough to raise with Stalin. The details were left to the military. Prior to the Yalta Conference, the U.S. Joint Chiefs of Staff had proposed that "the general principle be accepted of freedom of transit by each nation concerned between the main occupied area and the forces occupying Berlin."[14] The Soviets were reluctant to discuss the matter and it was dropped, no doubt because the Americans wanted "to avoid raising any subject which might weaken Soviet desires to contribute to the overall Allied effort" or cause the Soviets to reconsider their promise to enter the war against Japan.[15]

On June 24, 1948, the Soviet Union imposed a blockade on the Western sectors of Berlin, saying that the Western powers were carrying out a separate currency reform in their sectors of the city without Soviet agreement. In the previous months, Soviet authorities had periodically interfered with Western access to Berlin, but had hesitated to impose a full blockade.

However, once the Berlin airlift started, the Soviets' decision in favor of a lengthy test of strength brought results that were almost diametrically opposite to their original expectations. The stakes were high, particularly for the United States. American willingness to pay the price of the airlift eventually convinced Stalin of the danger of his gambit, and a settlement was reached in May 1949, after months of trying negotiations. The blockade failed to drive the Western powers out of Berlin and also to prevent the establishment of the Federal Republic of Germany (FRG) on May 23, 1949. Moscow responded in kind by setting up the German Democratic Republic (GDR) in October 1949. This formalized partition of Germany was an ever-present reminder of the division between West and East and of the deep-rooted rivalry between them. As long as the West lacked guaranteed land access to West Berlin, it was captive to Soviet and East German squeezes. Berlin was a local sore in East-West relations, easily irritated and quickly swollen to international proportions.

The Berlin crisis accelerated the West's rearmament and gave impetus and a stamp of permanence to the establishment in April 1949 of the North Atlantic Treaty Organization (NATO). The Western alliance, which Moscow condemned as anti-Soviet and aggressive, epitomized the increasing polarization of the West and East.

We do not know what Stalin's aims were toward Germany. Experts disagree, and the evidence is episodic and fragmentary. It seems most unlikely, however, given Germany's humbling of Russia twice in a generation and Stalin's respect for German industry, technical skill, and energy, that he would have wanted a united Germany, especially one that was communist and could become Moscow's rival for leadership in the communist world. His probable preference, expressed in offhand fashion to a group of visiting East European Communists in early 1948, was that Germany remain divided. "The West will make Western Germany their own, and we shall turn Eastern Germany into its our state."[16]

TITOISM: THE END OF MONOLITHIC COMMUNISM

The world first learned of the deep fissure within the supposedly solid edifice of the world communist movement on June 28, 1948, when the Cominform announced the expulsion of the Yugoslav Communist party for "anti-Party and anti-Soviet views, incompatible with Marxism-Leninism." Yugoslav leaders were unwilling to turn their country into a colony of the Soviet Union.

Stalin would not accept Tito, his most faithful and "Stalinist" disciple in Eastern Europe, as an equal. He insisted on unchallenged political and economic control by the Kremlin and a privileged position for Soviet diplomats and advisers stationed in Yugoslavia. Irritated by his inability to bend the Yugoslav leadership to his will, Stalin invoked the ultimate weapon, excommunication, against his former protégé. He expected to overthrow Tito by waging an intensive propaganda campaign through the Cominform and by utilizing Soviet prestige to wean Yugoslav party members away from Tito. He used every means at his disposal, short of military intervention, in the belief that Tito would soon be replaced by a pro-Soviet leadership prepared to do Moscow's bidding.

However, Stalin underestimated the countervailing pull of nationalism (as had Karl Marx). Aided by the fortunate circumstance of not sharing a border with the Soviet Union, by the loyalty of party and military cadres whose bonds had been forged in the common struggle against Nazi overlordship and in the bureaucratic intrigues of Kremlin-prescribed compounds, and by his popularity as a national hero, Tito's leadership held firm. Stalin was to rue his boast that "I will shake my little finger, and there will be no more Tito. He will fall."

Frustrated by Belgrade's intransigence, Stalin launched a series of purges of possible Titos, intensifying the pace and character of Sovietization and Stalinization throughout Eastern Europe. Leading Communists—Gomulka in Poland, Rajk in Hungary, Kostov in Bulgaria, Slansky in Czechoslovakia, Pauker in Romania—were swept from power. The Stalinist pattern of society was imposed on Eastern Europe. Industry, foreign trade, and transportation were nationalized; centralized economic control and planning were introduced. Party organizations were purged and secret police ties with the Soviet KGB were expanded.

As long as Stalin lived, brutal repression ensured Soviet imperial control and compliance to Moscow's wishes by compliant and cowed satellites. At the same time though, it heightened Western feelings of insecurity, which were further aggravated by the USSR's detonation in the fall of 1949 of its first atomic bomb. The mood was somber, therefore, when Stalin gave the green light for aggression in Korea.

THE KOREAN ADVENTURE

Stalin's interest in neighboring Korea was strategic. Like Russian policymakers in the late nineteenth and early twentieth centuries, he recognized the importance of Korea, with its warm-water ports in the southern part of the peninsula and its strategic location vis-à-vis both China and Japan. Moreover, he aimed to undo the August 1910 Japanese annexation of Korea, thereby reversing one result of Russia's defeat in 1904–1905 and ending the Japanese threat to the USSR.[17]

During the Allied conferences in World War II, Stalin maintained a strategic silence on his aims in Korea, shrewdly permitting the absence of concrete arrangements to allow him maximum military and diplomatic flexibility. It was to his advantage that neither at Yalta, in the secret agreement of the USSR's entry into the war against Japan, nor at Potsdam in July 1945 were specific dispositions made for Korea. The Soviet Union entered the war against Japan on August 8, 1945, "contrary to what Stalin and other Soviet spokesmen had been consistently saying about the need to conclude an agreement with China before Soviet entry into the Pacific War."[18] But Stalin was not one to be hobbled by consistency.

Soviet troops could have occupied all of Korea, because U.S. forces were nowhere in the vicinity and in no position to establish a foothold. However, Stalin was not looking for a quarrel with the United States. Therefore, on August 15, when in General Order Number 1 the United States proposed a temporary U.S.-Soviet occupation of Korea divided along the 38th parallel, Stalin acquiesced. He did so in part because he hoped Washington would agree to his request for a Soviet zone of occupation in Japan (in cabling his acceptance on August 16, Stalin asked that Soviet troops also be permitted to occupy the northern half of Hokkaido Island), and in part because he assumed that an early withdrawal of U.S. and Soviet forces would leave political control of the Korean peninsula in the hands of well-organized Soviet-trained Korean Communists. Under the pro-Moscow faction of the Korean Communist Party (renamed the Korean Workers' party in August 1946), headed by Kim Il-sung, North Korea was quickly built up militarily and industrially. In contrast to what occurred under Soviet occupation of Manchuria, North Korea was not ravaged economically, since it was in Communist hands from the very beginning[19]; and in contrast to U.S. policy toward South Korea, Soviet policy in North Korea was a model of clarity and determination.

With the onset of the Cold War in Europe, Moscow blocked UN efforts to effect a peaceful reunification, and the division of troops withdrew, leaving the country divided at the 38th parallel. All prospects for a peaceful reunification vanished on June 25, 1950, when North Korean Communist troops invaded South Korea in a calculated attempt to settle the issue by force. Well equipped, having the advantage of surprise, and encouraged by the evident U.S. lack of interest and the widespread discontent with the Syngman Rhee regime that had appeared in the May elections, they came very close to victory.

The UN Security Council convened in emergency session on the very day of the invasion in response to a request by the U.S. government. The Soviet Union was not represented at this or any of the subsequent meetings of the council, having undertaken a boycott of the United Nations in January 1950 in protest against its failure to recognize the People's Republic of China (PRC) as the legitimate government of China. The Soviet delegate did not return until August 1. With the USSR absent, the Security Council passed another resolution calling for the immediate cessation of hostilities and the withdrawal of the North Korean forces to their side of the border. It also requested all UN members to help in implementing this resolution. President Truman immediately committed U.S. forces, abruptly reversing his previous view that Korea was indefensible and beyond the area strategically necessary for America's own defense.

Soon afterward, the Soviet government set its vast propaganda apparatus in motion and, relying heavily on foreign communist front organizations, condemned the United States for allegedly intervening in a civil war, carrying on an aggressive war, practicing bacteriological warfare, and perpetrating assorted atrocities. By October 1950, U.S. forces (fighting under the UN banner) counterattacked, crossed the 38th parallel, and advanced northward toward the Yalu River—and the Manchurian border. Once across the 38th parallel, they were no longer merely repelling aggression; they were seeking to unify all Korea by force of arms. This decision by General Douglas MacArthur was never explicitly sanctioned by the United Nations. The Chinese, apprehensive over the approach of a hostile army and insecure enough to fear invasion of the mainland by Kuomintang troops who had fled to the island of Taiwan, sent in "volunteers" in early November. The war took on a new dimension. After much bitter fighting, a stalemate developed, roughly along the 38th parallel. Truce negotiations and hard fighting dragged on for almost two years. An armistice agreement was finally signed in July 1953, and today an uneasy truce prevails in a divided Korea.

What were Stalin's motives in approving the invasion of South Korea? Two persistently argued hypotheses have generally been discredited: first, the revisionist New Left contention that South Korea had actually started the war (recently published Soviet documents show that it was the North that invaded the South); and second, the conspiracy theory, that the attack was planned by Stalin and Mao in early 1950. Research in the Russian state archives by Kathryn Weathersby strongly suggests that Stalin gave Kim Il-sung his approval for the invasion in early 1950. Kim finally convinced a reluctant Stalin of the project's feasibility, and Stalin gave the order for the delivery to Korea of arms and equipment required for the attack.[20] Kim persuaded Stalin that the fighting would be an internal affair involving only the Koreans themselves, that the South Koreans would turn against Syngman Rhee's dictatorship once the invasion began, and that the civil war would end quickly, precluding any outside intervention.[21]

The impending return of Port Arthur and Dairen to the PRC, agreed on in the 1950 Sino-Soviet treaty, must have lent added importance to the warm-water ports in South Korea and prompted Stalin to gamble on what seemed like a reasonably sure thing. Seeing an opportunity for seizing prime real estate at little risk, Stalin gave the go-ahead. After all, he had good reason to believe that the United Sates would accept a fait accompli and do nothing to save Korea. America's apparent lack of interest in South Korea had been dramatically highlighted by Secretary of State Dean Acheson's failure to include it in the U.S. "defense perimeter" in a major speech on January 12, 1950; and Kim Il-sung's persuasive assurance that the forcible reunification of Korea could be accomplished swiftly and by North Korean forces alone whetted Stalin's strategic appetite. Nor did Stalin expect that the UN would do anything other than pass some resolutions of admonitions, as the League of Nations had done in similar circumstances in the 1930s—hence the continued Soviet absence from Security Council deliberations. Even though he expected a quick victory, Stalin took elaborate precautions to keep Soviet advisers away from the fighting, so as not to give the United States an excuse for intervening. Ultimately, he was betrayed by Washington's unpredictability—by Truman's decision to fight for what Washington had previously declared not to be a vital interest for the United States.

Although thwarted militarily, Stalin benefited from the conflict in two important ways. First, the United States was required to commit a large part of its limited existing strength to a remote area, thereby rendering itself impotent in frustrating the establishment of the Soviet imperium in Eastern Europe. Second, the Korean War made Mao more dependent on Soviet weaponry and assistance, and thereby widened the split between the PRC and United States. For the next 15 years or so, the existence of a common enemy—the United States—induced the PRC to stay on reasonably close terms with the Soviet Union and enabled Moscow to strengthen its position in Europe and expand in the Third World.

STALIN'S POLICIES IN RETROSPECT

Stalin's foreign policy combined elements of conservatism and expansionism. Although his policies took advantage of Moscow's victory in World War II to advance Soviet power in Europe and the Far East and thereby improve the USSR's strategic line of defense—they were also pragmatic and geared to the avoidance of war with the United States. Stalin's gains in Eastern and Central Europe cost him his wartime alliance with the West, which viewed with deepening concern each entrenchment of Soviet power and influence on the doorsteps of Western Europe. Stalin did not try to overwhelm the West by force. His aim was to undermine its security and cohesion, and correspondingly to enhance the strength and stability of the imperial system he had created in Eastern Europe. Under this system, each country in Eastern Europe was permitted to retain its form as a nation-state (in contrast to the fate of Estonia, Latvia, and Lithuania, which in 1940 were incorporated into the USSR itself) but each had to be communist in character, which for Stalin meant that its leadership was to do exactly as Moscow ordered and that its institutions and developmental pattern were to imitate the USSR's. To Stalin, security was synonymous with a permanent Soviet military presence, unquestioned political control, ideological conformity, and economic subordination to Soviet needs. His imperial system (the "socialist camp") was an uninterrupted land mass extending from the Baltic Sea to the Sea of Japan.

Stalin was no openhanded patron of revolutions. He was fully prepared to exploit them where feasible, but stayed clear of committing Soviet forces to their advancement. He was not averse, as in Greece, to scuttling a Communist leadership if he thought its actions might jeopardize Soviet interests elsewhere in the region. In Western Europe he sacrificed the electoral prospects of the Italian and French communist parties by ordering them to take active measures against the delivery of Marshall Plan economic aid. His decision not to extend to Finland the Sovietization imposed everywhere else in Eastern Europe was surprising. He may have had second thoughts about the implications of further aggravating tensions with the United States or about the difficulties that he would have encountered; possibly, he misplayed a strong hand, witness Andrei Zhdanov's remark to Djilas in 1946, "We made a mistake in not occupying Finland"[22]; or perhaps he decided to settle for heavy reparations because he remembered that in joining Germany in attacking the Soviet Union, Finland had not pushed its advance beyond the 1939 border, thus enabling Leningrad to be supplied across Lake Ladoga and to survive the nine hundred-day German siege.

Although Europe was the scene of the greatest expansion of Soviet military power and political influence, Stalin appreciated the importance of the Far East and advanced Soviet interests there by obtaining handsome dividends at Yalta for

Soviet participation in the war against Japan and by reaching an early accommodation with Mao Zedong's new communist regime. Where Stalin erred, however, was in not keeping the North Koreans on a tighter leash. As with Europe in the case of Berlin, his misjudgment in the Far East resulted in a return of American military power that was to have enormous significance in the future.

Overall, Stalin had a sound grasp on the realities of the postwar international system and used Marxism-Leninism to serve his ends. The Bolsheviks had come to power believing that the capitalist world was uniformly hostile and that "imperialism" was dedicated to the destruction of "socialism." However, they quickly learned to differentiate among the imperialists: some were more threatening than others; all were targets for exploitation, one against the other. In the late 1920s and 1930s, Stalin's theory of "capitalist encirclement," served to justify the suffering and sacrifice demanded of the Soviet people by his decisions to industrialize, collectivize, and transform Soviet institutions and society radically.

In doctrinal terms, this theory reflected the pervasive fear of imperialist attack against the Soviet Union and implied a type of war quite distinct from Lenin's "inevitable" intercapitalist wars. According to Lenin, such "imperialist" wars would stem from the nature and contradictions of capitalism, impelled to expand abroad in search of markets and raw materials. No systematic attempt was ever made to link Lenin's theory of these inevitable competitive intercapitalist wars with the subsequent Stalinist corollary of the "inevitable" capitalist war against the Soviet Union. Thus, there were, in fact, two distinct communist doctrines on war, though the impression that they were one and the same was encouraged. First came the Leninist theory of imperialism, with its focus on war and rivalries between capitalist countries, and second was the theory of capitalist encirclement, with its focus on the inevitability of war between the capitalist and communist camps.

Shortly before the nineteenth congress of the CPSU in October 1952, Stalin published his *Economic Problems of Socialism in the USSR,* which contained an astute diagnosis of the international scene and of Soviet relations with the non-communist world. He held that as an aftermath of World War II, capitalism had suffered grievous wounds and no longer ruled the world. Economically, the world had split into two parallel and self-contained trading systems. Politically, the capitalist countries had lost much of their former awesome power and therefore were not likely to attack the Soviet Union, although the contradictions and antagonisms between the two systems would continue to exist. A capitalist attack on the Soviet Union was unlikely because

> war with the USSR is more dangerous to capitalism than war between capitalist countries; for whereas war between capitalist countries puts in question only the supremacy of certain capitalist countries over others, war with the USSR must certainly put in question the existence of capitalism itself.[23]

He perceptively foresaw the reemergence of Germany and Japan as powerful nations and their competition with the United States for shrinking world markets. (Remember, this was said at a time when the United Sates was preeminent in the world, and both its allies and its former enemies Germany and Japan were weak and very much under its influence.) Finally, while emphasizing the continued and fundamental ideological and political hostility between the Communist and capitalist systems, Stalin carefully implied that armed conflict between them was not probable. In this way he kept alive the possibility of a measured relaxation of tensions, though it remained for his successors to give substance as well as form to the policy of peaceful coexistence.

The year 1953 was a fateful one. Stalin had ruled the Soviet Union for more than a generation. One of history's most ruthless tyrants, he was, in the words of France's General Charles de Gaulle,

> possessed by the will to power. Accustomed to a life of machination to disguise his features as well as his inmost soul, to dispense with illusions, pity, sincerity, to see in each man an obstacle or a threat, he was all strategy, suspicion and stubbornness. His fortune was to have found a people so vital and so patient that the worst servitudes did not paralyze them, a soil full of such resources that the most terrible destruction and waste could not exhaust it.

Undistinguished as a theorist, Stalin was seldom deluded by the orthodoxy that he imposed in ideological and party affairs. He placed no store in the imminence of world revolution, but was quite willing to use revolutions abroad to improve the international position of the Soviet Union. He understood the nature of power and used it to advantage to expand the Soviet empire, in the process fusing the need of national security and his imperialist ambitions. At a terrible cost in human lives, he modernized the country's economy and institutions, and transformed the Soviet Union into one of the world's greatest industrial-military powers.

On March 5, 1953, Moscow announced the death of Stalin. An era had come to an end.

SELECTED BIBLIOGRAPHY

Abarinov, Vladimir. *The Murderers of Katyn.* New York: Hippocrene Books, 1993.

Alperovitz, Gar. *Atomic Diplomacy: Hiroshima and Potsdam.* Expanded and updated edition. New York: Penguin Books, 1985.

Churchill, Winston S. *The Second World War.* 6 vols. Boston: Houghton Mifflin, 1948–1953.

Davison, W. Phillips. *The Berlin Blockade: A Study in Cold War Politics.* Princeton, NJ: Princeton University Press, 1958.

Deane, John R. *The Strange Alliance: The Story of Our Efforts at Wartime Cooperation with Russia.* New York: Viking, 1947.

Dedijer, Vladmir. *The Battle Stalin Lost: Memoirs of Yugoslavia, 1948–1953.* New York: Viking, 1971.

Eubank, Keith. *Summit At Tehran.* New York: Morrow, 1985.

Feis, Herbert. *Churchill-Roosevelt-Stalin.* Princeton, NJ: Princeton University Press, 1957.

Goncharov, Sergei et al. *Uncertain Partners: Stalin, Mao, and the Korean War.* Stanford, CA: Stanford University Press, 1993.

Herz, Martin F. *Beginnings of the Cold War.* Bloomington: Indiana University Press, 1966.

Kacewicz, George. *Great Britain, the Soviet Union and the Polish Government in Exile 1939–1945*. The Hague: Nijhoff, 1979.

Kennedy-Pipe, Caroline. *Stalin's Cold War: Soviet Strategies in Europe, 1943 to 1956*. Manchester, England: Manchester University Press, 1995.

Korbel, Josef. *The Communist Subversion of Czechoslovakia*. Princeton, NJ: Princeton University Press, 1959.

Mastny, Vojtech. *Russia's Road to the Cold War*. New York: Columbia University Press, 1979.

McNeill, William H. *America, Britain, and Russia: Their Cooperation and Conflict, 1941–1946*. New York: Oxford University Press, 1954.

Nagai, Yonosuke, and Akira Iriya (eds.). *The Origins of the Cold War in Asia*. New York: Columbia University Press, 1977.

North, Robert C. *Moscow and Chinese Communists*. 2nd ed. Stanford: Stanford University Press, 1963.

Parrish, Scott D. and Narinsky, Mikhail M. "New Evidence on the Soviet Rejection of the Marshall Plan, 1947" *Cold War International History Project,* working paper no. 9. Washington, DC: Woodrow Wilson International Center for Scholars, 1994.

Ra'anan, Gavriel D. *International policy formation in the USSR: factional "debates" during the Zhdanovshchina*. Hamden, CT: Archon Books, 1983.

Rieber, Alfred J. *Stalin and the French Communist Party, 1941–1947*. New York: Columbia University Press, 1962.

Shulman, Marshall D. *Stalin's Foreign Policy Reappraised*. Cambridge, MA: Harvard University Press, 1963.

Taubman, William. *Stalin's American Policy: From Entente to Detente to Cold War*. New York: Norton, 1982.

Thomas, Hugh. *Armed Truce: The Beginnings of The Cold War, 1945–1946*. New York: Atheneum, 1987.

Tolstoy, Nikolai. *Stalin's Secret War*. New York: Holt, Rinehart and Winston, 1981.

Ulam, Adam B. *Titoism and the Cominform*. Cambridge, MA: Harvard University Press, 1952.

Westad, Odd Arne. *Cold War and Revolution: Soviet-American Rivalry and the Origins of the Chinese Civil War, 1944–1946*. New York: Columbia University Press, 1993.

NOTES

1. Nikita S. Khrushchev, *Special Report to the Twentieth Congress of the Communist Party of the Soviet Union* (February 1956).
2. *Pravda*, August 4, 1941.
3. *USSR Information Bulletin*, vol. IV, no. 7 (1944), p. 1.
4. *The Sunday Times* (London), November 24, 1968.
5. U.S. Department of Defense, *The Entry of the Soviet Union into the War Against Japan: Military Plans, 1941–1945* (Washington, DC: Government Printing Office, 1955).
6. Winston S. Churchill, *Triumph and Tragedy* (Boston: Houghton Mifflin, 1953), p. 402.
7. Huey Louis Kostanick, "The Significance of Geopolitical Changes in Easten Europe," *Education,* vol. 72 (February 1952), pp. 381–387.
8. Quoted in Robert G. Kaiser, *Cold Winter, Cold War* (New York: Stein and Day, 1974), pp. 12–13. For an overall evaluation of Litvinov's series of revealing discussions with

Western journalists between May 1943 and February 1947, see Vojtech Mastny, "The Cassandra in the Foreign Commissariat: Maxim Litvinov and the Cold War," *Foreign Affairs,* vol. 54, no. 2 (January 1976), pp. 366–376.

9. Milovan Djilas, *Conversations with Stalin* (New York: Harcourt Brace and World, 1962), pp. 153–154.

10. *USSR Information Bulletin,* no. 37 (August 26, 1941), pp. 6–7.

11. Lewis V. Thomas and Richard N. Frye, *The United States and Turkey and Iran* (Cambridge, MA: Harvard University Press, 1951), pp. 239–240.

12. William O. McCagg, Jr. *Stalin Embattled, 1943–1948* (Detroit: Wayne State University Press, 1978), pp. 261–284.

13. Andrei Zhdanov, *The International Situation* (Moscow: Foreign Language Publishing House, 1947), excerpts.

14. Jean Edward Smith, *The Defense of Berlin* (Baltimore: Johns Hopkins University Press, 1963), p. 31.

15. *Ibid.,* p. 32.

16. Djilas, *Conversations with Stalin,* p. 153.

17. Robert M. Slusser, "Soviet Far Eastern Policy, 1945–50: Stalin's Goals in Korea," in Yonosuke Nagai and Akira Iriya (eds.). *The Origins of the Cold War in Asia* (New York: Columbia University Press, 1977), p. 127.

18. *Ibid.,* p. 136.

19. Joungwon Alexander Kim, "Soviet Policy in North Korea," *World Politics,* vol. 22, no. 2 (January 1970), pp. 237–254.

20. Kathryn Weathersby, "New Findings on the Korean War," *Cold War International History Project Bulletin,* vol. 1, no. 3 (Fall 1993), pp. 14–18.

21. Edward Crankshaw (commentary), Strobe Talbott (trans. and ed.) *Khrushchev Remembers* (New York: Bantam, 1970), pp. 400–402.

22. Milovan Djilas, *Conversations with Stalin* (New York: Harcourt, Brace & World, 1962), pp. 155.

23. Joseph Stalin, *Economic Problems of Socialism in the USSR* (New York: International Publishers, 1952).

Chapter

4

The Crumbling of the Empire, 1953–1985

*B*efore his death, Stalin had forged the most complete totalitarian dictatorship the world had ever known up to that point. His death, therefore, was accompanied by great uncertainty as to the future direction of Soviet policy. The ensuing power struggle among his heirs was not resolved until late 1955, when Nikita Khrushchev emerged as first among equals in the new Soviet leadership.

Khrushchev was an ambitious man of humble origins and had, apparently, an abiding faith in the Marxist-Leninist cause. Recognizing that society and the Communist Party had suffered under Stalinism, he staked his political career on fashioning a new, more responsive image of the party. In his famous "secret speech" to the twentieth party congress in February 1956, he publicly acknowledged some of the excesses of the Stalin era, and pledged that the party under his leadership could correct them.

The ensuing years were ones of intellectual "thaw" and a modest amount of economic and social experimentation. In foreign policy, the "de-Stalinization" of society that he instituted helped bring a speedy end to the Korean War and an era of "peaceful coexistence" with the West. He inaugurated a new, more equal relationship with foreign communist parties. Ultimately, however, Khrushchev's attempts to manage a slow transition to a less repressive regime while extending Soviet influence abroad failed, and his ambivalent foreign policy legacy laid the seed for the stagnation and ultimate collapse of the USSR.

The de-Stalinization process that reached its apogee at the CPSU's twentieth congress in February 1956 developed slowly, varying in degree and scope from country to country but following a common pattern. Amnesties were proclaimed, forced collectivization halted, price cuts on consumer staples instituted, the more oppressive features of the labor and criminal codes changed, and the arbitrary power of the secret police curbed. The aim was to "return to Leninism." In Eastern Europe, those too closely identified as Stalinists were gradually replaced by "national communists," that is, communists who were popularly regarded as defenders of the country's interests against unreasonable exploitation by and abject subservience to the Soviet Union. Party and government apparatuses were separated, and modest economic reforms were introduced.

De-Stalinization left deep and, ultimately, unhealable wounds in the communist system. In Eastern Europe and the USSR it would give rise to the dissident movement and help to weaken the moral authority of communism. In China, which did not undergo a similar process until Mao's death in 1976, it deepened the rift between the world's two leading communist parties. In the West it raised expectations that the USSR would reform itself domestically and begin to see the benefits of international cooperation. These expectations would crystallize in the policy of détente.

The USSR did de-Stalinize, but only to a point, then it stagnated. During the long period of Leonid Brezhnev's reign (1964–1982), the country was ruled by a gerontocracy that thwarted all efforts at serious economic reform despite mounting evidence of the country's industrial and military decline. The Party's choice for Brezhnev's successors, Yuri Andropov and Konstantin Chernenko, illustrated the leadership's ambivalence about major structural reform. While the former urged the beginning of a serious dialogue on the problems ailing the Soviet economy, the latter continued on as before. This ambivalence lingered on well into the Gorbachev administration.

DOCTRINAL INNOVATIONS IN FOREIGN POLICY, 1953–1956

After Stalin's death, Moscow decided on a reconciliation with Tito. The USSR and Yugoslavia concluded a barter agreement in September 1954, ending the Cominform's economic blockade. The following May, party leader Nikita S. Khrushchev and other top Politburo members went to Belgrade and did penance for Stalin's sins against Yugoslavia. They signed a joint government declaration endorsing the principle of nonintervention in domestic affairs and implicitly recognizing Yugoslavia as a socialist state, although it is significant that a comparable accord on party-to-party reconciliation was not agreed on until Tito's visit to the USSR in June 1956. At that time Moscow formally acknowledged the principle of "many roads to socialism," which was to serve as the doctrinal basis for granting greater measures of autonomy to the members of the Soviet bloc.

Moscow hoped the reconciliation with Tito would be a first step toward the reconstitution of the formal unity of the communist world. It sought thereby to stem the appeal of Titoism—that is, full independence and equality for all communist states—and to reconcile loyalty to the Soviet Union with the modicum of national autonomy allowed by Moscow. The Soviet leadership also hoped that the rapprochement would weaken Yugoslavia's ties with the West and diminish the value of the Balkan pact that Belgrade had signed in 1954 with Greece and Turkey. The Soviet-Yugoslav second honeymoon, however, lasted only until late 1956, when, in the aftermath of the Hungarian revolution, Moscow's temporary turn from diversity to bloc unity and neo-Stalinism alienated Belgrade. But this time, in contrast to 1948, the quarrel did not result in a rupture.

Khrushchev's determination to carry out far-ranging reforms at home and to place Soviet-East European relations on a more truly fraternal basis required improved relations with the Western countries. Accordingly, in the spring of 1955, over the objections of Molotov and others, Khrushchev agreed to a peace treaty with Austria, thus reversing Moscow's previous insistence on linking the treaty with a settlement of the German problem. The state treaty ending the four-power occupation was signed on May 15, following Austria's pledge, written into its constitution, of perpetual neutrality. This treaty was significant because it marked the first voluntary Soviet withdrawal from an entrenched position in the center of Europe (in May, the USSR also officially returned Port Arthur to the PRC, and in September, it withdrew from the military base that it had been granted in 1947 at Porkkala-Udd, only 12 miles from Helsinki in Finland). Moscow's surprising amiability extended to other areas as well. For example, in 1953 the Soviet Union renounced all claims against Turkey, made overtures for closer relations with Greece and Iran, and began to participate actively in the economic development and technical assistance programs of the various UN organizations.

Moscow's previously unchallenged authority in the Communist world was seriously shaken after the damaging revelations in Khrushchev's secret speech at the CPSU's twentieth congress in February 1956, denouncing Stalin's crimes and self-deification ("cult of personality"). An outgrowth of the struggle for power among the Kremlin oligarchs, the speech had a powerful effect on developments in Eastern Europe, China, and the world Communist movement. It set in motion in Eastern Europe additional pressures for changes that threatened to unhinge the Soviet empire.

Even without Khrushchev's speech against Stalin and the impetus that it gave to de-Stalinization, the twentieth congress would have been important because of the significant doctrinal innovations that reflected the Kremlin's approach to world affairs. First, Khrushchev declared that "war is not fatalistically inevitable," thereby significantly revising both Lenin and Stalin. While acknowledging that Marxism-Leninism dictates that wars are inevitable as long as imperialism exists, he noted that it was formulated at a time "when 1) imperialism was an all-embracing world system, and 2) the social and political forces which did not want war were weak, poorly organized, and hence unable to compel the imperialists to renounce war." What was "absolutely correct" in that period was no longer true because of the radically changed international system. According to Khrushchev, "Now there is a world camp of socialism, which has become a mighty force. In this camp the peace forces find not only the moral, but also the material means to prevent aggression." In other words, the emergence of the Soviet Union (and by implication its possession of nuclear weapons) enabled the forces of peace in the world to find a champion and to rebuff would-be aggressors; the USSR's possession of nuclear weapons would deter any would-be capitalist aggressor. Moreover, if "all anti-war forces" cooperated with the Soviet camp, "the greater the guarantees that there will be no new war."[1]

Second, Khrushchev formally embraced the Titoist thesis that there are many roads to socialism, thereby providing doctrinal approval for diversity in the Soviet bloc and the theoretical basis for closer cooperation not only with Yugoslavia, but also with the socialist parties of Western Europe.

Third, Khrushchev held that under certain circumstances socialism (that is, communist parties) could come to power "by using parliamentary means." It existed, as a consequence of the USSR's success and establishment of People's Democracies in Eastern Europe, the growth of "the forces of socialism" and the weakening of capitalism, and the opportunity for "the working class in a number of capitalist countries to unite the overwhelming majority of the people under its leadership." But Khrushchev declared one condition to be essential: "Whatever the form of transition to socialism, the decisive and indispensable factor is the political leadership of the working class headed by its vanguard [that is, the Communist party]. Without this there can be no transition to socialism."

Finally, Khrushchev drew attention to the growing importance of the newly independent countries of the Third World and provided the ideological rationale for the emerging Soviet involvement there.

In bringing Soviet foreign policy perceptions and guidelines into line with emerging international realities, Khrushchev greatly disturbed the Chinese, who saw in his stress on peaceful coexistence and efforts to effect a limited détente with the United States a downgrading of the Sino-Soviet alliance, a shift in Soviet foreign policy priorities and methods, and a possible shelving of Beijing's quest for international recognition and for the overthrow of the Kuomintang regime on Taiwan. But the disruptive effects of de-Stalinization were most apparent in Eastern Europe. An unwary Kremlin had unwittingly released turbulent anti-Russian, anticommunist, and nationalist currents. The resulting uprising against Soviet rule shook the very foundations of the Soviet empire and led to a Stalinist revival and to serious reconsiderations of ways to ensure the permanence of Soviet strategic gains in Eastern Europe and avoid the perils of liberalization.

Riots broke out in Poznan, Poland, in June 1956 protesting shortages of food and consumer goods. Sparked by Khrushchev's revelations, the smoldering resentment of a decade of economic exploitation and Soviet domination flared into open denunciations of the Moscow-controlled government. The Poles' traditional hatred of Russia made for a volatile political situation. The Kremlin, realizing the gravity of the situation, grudgingly made concessions. It permitted the ouster of many known pro-Moscow Communists from the Central Committee of the Polish United Workers' (Communist) party and in October 1956 accepted the elevation of Wladyslaw Gomulka, who had spent several years in prison for supposed Titoist tendencies, to the post of party secretary. Moscow also publicly reaffirmed Poland's sovereignty and independence, agreed not to interfere in its domestic affairs, and withdrew Soviet Marshal Rokossovsky as head of Poland's armed forces. Trade and financial relations were adjusted to Poland's advantage, and the number of Soviet troops permitted by special agreement to remain in Poland pending a settlement of the German question was sharply reduced.

Events in Hungary, however, took a violent and tragic turn. Matyas Rakosi, a confirmed Stalinist and longtime party boss of Hungary, was deposed in June 1956, and his successor, Ernî Gero, was not up to the challenge of leading popular pressure for change. On October 23, an anticommunist and anti-Soviet revolution threatened to erupt in Budapest. The rebels wanted to disband the Communist Party, leave the Warsaw Pact organization, and liquidate all vestiges of Soviet rule. The party leadership had lost control of the situation. Confronted with the imminent loss of Hungary and possible disintegration elsewhere in Eastern Europe, Moscow violated a truce that led to the capture of key Hungarian leaders and hurled 250,000 troops and 5000 tanks against the Hungarians on November 4. Brute force and deceit precluded the need to negotiate and compromise.

The UN General Assembly called on the Soviet government "to desist from its intervention in the internal affairs of Hungary, to withdraw its forces from Hungary, and to cease its repression of the Hungarian people." Aided by the diversion of the UN's attention to the simultaneously occurring Suez crisis, the Soviets ignored UN and Western protests. As the Soviet steamroller crushed the revolt, the West watched, unwilling to intervene for fear of precipitating World War III.

But the Kremlin learned several bitter lessons. First, Soviet control in Eastern Europe could be preserved only if backed by the Red Army. Military force, not ideology, was the effective cement for cohesion. Second, nationalism remained strong, even among avowed Communists, and in Eastern Europe it was permeated with an anti-Russian coloration. Third, authority once weakened could not easily be reimposed. Fourth, the continued political and military adherence of East European countries to the Soviet-dominated Warsaw Pact military alliance depended on Soviet acceptance of a substantial measure of economic, cultural, and political autonomy for those countries.

Above all, Moscow realized that Eastern Europe could no longer be considered an unquestioned asset. The area represented a material drain on Soviet resources; the reliability of East European troops remained a continual question; and East European nationalism, a force too often slighted in the West, greatly complicated the process of Soviet rule. The intervention in Hungary cost Moscow heavily among influential West European intellectuals and in the consequent agonizing reappraisals that occurred in Western communist parties. African and Asian leaders expressed varying degrees of disappointment, but the remoteness of Hungary to them blunted their concern and indignation. They were far more outraged over the British, French, and Israeli attack on Egypt, a country only recently emerged from colonialism and one with which they felt intimate emotional ties. What the 1956 crises in Eastern Europe (and the 1968 crisis in Czechoslovakia) showed was that the Soviet Union regarded Eastern Europe as vital to its national security and that it was prepared to use force if necessary to preserve its hegemony there.

In November 1957, on the occasion of the fortieth anniversary of the Bolshevik Revolution, the leaders of international communism met in Moscow to repair the damage of 1956. They issued a "declaration of unity" reaffirming the solidarity of the communist camp "headed by the Soviet Union." This declaration implicitly acknowledged the disruptive consequences of national communism, emphasized the unity of the communist world, and attacked "revisionism" (the sin of going further than Moscow in doctrinal, internal, or international innovation). The Chinese gave lip service to Moscow's leadership for the last time and tried to nudge the Soviet Union back to Stalinism, especially as it related to Moscow's policy toward the United States and Western Europe. Throughout the meeting, Moscow groped for a way of reinstituting the Cominform, which had been disbanded in the heady days of de-Stalinization in 1956, and of reimposing bloc unity, particularly in Eastern Europe. But like Humpty-Dumpty, the Cominform could not be put back together again, largely because of Yugoslav and West European Communist opposition to any effort to forcefully reassert Soviet political and ideological authority within the bloc.

THE EROSION OF COMMUNIST INSTITUTIONS

By the time Khrushchev was deposed in October 1964, Soviet policy toward Eastern Europe had changed considerably. From the one-sided and callous exploitation of the Stalin era, it had moved to a more businesslike and sophisticated economic give-and-take. From day-to-day control by pro-Moscow satraps and resident KGB procurators, it had changed to allow considerable autonomy to national Communists in managing their internal affairs, as long as there was no threat to the communist character of the regime or its loyalty to the USSR. And from imposed conformity to Soviet norms in all things, Soviet policy had grown to tolerate diversity in most areas. From a classic type of colonial system, the Soviet-East European bloc evolved into an imperial system, in which the center placed preeminent importance on strategic and military control rather than on economic exploitation or cultural conformity. As long as each country remained communist and a member of the Warsaw Pact, and local power was exercised by a communist leadership that did not challenge Soviet strategic hegemony, Moscow tolerated experiments with the limits of diversity.

The duumvirate of Leonid Brezhnev and Alexei Kosygin altered the style—the ebullience of Khrushchev was replaced by the deliberateness of Brezhnev—but not the substance of Khrushchev's policy. They followed the trail he marked to preserve Soviet hegemony in Eastern Europe. Confronted with intensifying nationalism in Eastern Europe, worsening relations with China, and the end of the myth of international communist solidarity, the Soviet leaders tried to improve relations with the West and find a formula for asserting their authority within the bloc.

To promote bloc cohesion and integration, the Soviet Union relied on a number of multilateral institutions, most notably the Warsaw Treaty Organization (WTO, more commonly referred to as the Warsaw Pact) and the Council for Mutual Economic Assistance (Comecon). The Warsaw Pact was created on May 14, 1955, the day before the signing of the Austrian state treaty. Moscow decided that it needed a formal alliance binding the bloc together. In shifting from an exclusive reliance on bilateralism to a heavy emphasis on multilateralism, it was motivated by several aims. The first and most immediate, given the imminence of the treaty with Austria, was to find a way to legitimate the continued presence in Hungary and Romania of the Soviet troops, which had been until then justified on the basis of ensuring lines of communication for Soviet occupation for in Austria. The second, after Moscow had failed to prevent the FRG's rearmament and formal entry into NATO on May 9, 1955, was to carry through on its previously announced intention to have Soviet-bloc countries "take common measures for the organization of armed forces and their commands," and to create a counterpart to NATO. Third, Moscow wanted an effective instrument for safeguarding its interests in the area.

Although formally a military alliance protecting the bloc against external threats, the Warsaw Pact mainly served an intrabloc policing function. It was also used by Moscow to pressure a reluctant member to go along with the consensus view, to persuade bloc members to join with it in isolating a dissident member (for instance, excluding Albania from participation because of its pro-Beijing policies from 1961 to 1978), to rebut Chinese accusations that the USSR was a disintegrating rather than integrating influence within the communist world, to keep East European ethnic tensions in check, and to encourage a sense of common interest among members.

The military objectives of the Warsaw Pact, though subordinate, were substantial. They included using Eastern Europe to project Soviet military and political power against the West, extending the Soviet air defense system as far west of the Soviet homeland as possible, serving as an offensive prod against NATO in the event of a war in Europe, creating military forces loyal to the communist regimes, and promoting bloc unity through standardization of weaponry, tactical coordination, and interlocking command structures. A considerable professional interaction among the officer corps also reinforced their sense of community as members of an alliance system.

Another mechanism used to promote economic integration and thereby political stability among communist states was Comecon. Originally established in January 1949 as a symbolic facade to parallel the Marshall Plan and as an instrument of boycott against Yugoslavia, Comecon was for many years a moribund organization. Under Stalin, there was no necessity for an effective regional organization; the USSR was in physical control and preferred to maximize its exploitation on a bilateral basis. It felt no need to rationalize the Soviet-East European economic relationship.

Starting under Khrushchev in 1955, Comecon went through a period of gradual upgrading: information was pooled, economic agreements were placed on a five-year instead of a one-year basis, and an atmosphere of bargaining replaced that of acquiescence. On December 14, 1959, Comecon adopted a charter (heavily amended in December 1962 and June 1974) defining its purposes and organizational structure. Standing commissions deal with a wide range of subjects, from electric power and nuclear energy to financial problems and transportation. In institutional terms, Comecon came of age in the 1960s, but actual integration proceeded very slowly.

At Khrushchev's behest, in June 1962 a programmatic document, "The Basic Principles of the International Socialist Division of Labor," was adopted. In November Khrushchev pushed for a supranational entity capable of rationalizing and transforming the economies of the bloc:

> We must move more boldly toward establishing a single planning agency for all countries that belong to the Council for Mutual Economic Assistance. This planning

agency should be empowered to draw up joint plans and settle organizational questions so as to coordinate the development of the countries of the socialist system.[2]

But his optimism and drive were not enough to overcome the legacy of autarky-oriented economies that Stalin had imposed on the East European countries, or the opposition of the Romanians, who did not want to abandon major industrial projects. The technological backwardness that made most East Europeans feel that the plan for division of labor was intended to keep them in an inferior position to the Soviet Union was also a stumbling block. The kind of cooperation that Khrushchev envisaged implied a sense of genuine community, which never emerged.

There were many other reasons for Khrushchev's failure. First, the idea of a supranational organization was perceived in Eastern Europe as entailing a surrender of newly regained national prerogatives to the USSR. The countries of the area were still in the early stages of their existence as nation-states, and for them nationalism was a positive force. Second, bureaucratic vested interests resisted the retooling and dismantling of national economic institutions. Further, they lacked the sense of shared trust and commitment to rely on their counterparts for fulfillment of national economic targets. The East Europeans mistrusted not only the Soviet Union, but each other. There is no love of neighbors in the area, which remains a cauldron of ethnic animosities. Finally, the heterogeneity of Eastern Europe, with its different levels of economic, industrial, technological, and educational development, heightened protectionist attitudes and militated against meaningful multilateralism.

Moscow's determination to promote economic interdependence in the "socialist commonwealth" (a concept popularized by Khrushchev) did have some limited successes—the *Druzhba* (Friendship) oil pipeline, an electrical power grid system, and a pool of rolling stock—but basic planning, investment, production, and pricing patterns were not as easily reshaped. In derision of integration, this Hungarian joke made the rounds: The Comecon countries, wanting a common emblem to signify their unity and fraternity, adopted a flag with a red field in which there were seven lean cows milking one another.

In July 1971 Comecon adopted a twenty-year blueprint for integration, albeit within the existing sovereign nation-state system. Moscow was serious about the Comprehensive Program and insisted that it be accorded the status of a multilateral treaty, but fundamental problems remained: the absence of a supranational authority, the reliance on consensus-building, and the indefiniteness in the statutes about implementing recommendations.

In June 1984, at the first summit since 1969 of Comecon members (the USSR, Bulgaria, Czechoslovakia, the German Democratic Republic, Hungary, Poland, Romania, Cuba, Mongolia, and Vietnam), Moscow indicated a continued willingness to meet members' needs for imported energy and raw materials, but in return it stipulated that they provide consumer goods and machinery "of a high quality and world technical level," and that they contribute more investment and labor for the development of Soviet resources. It called for greater coordination of economic plans, especially in the fields of microprocessors, robotics, and energy conservation. Moscow wanted the East European countries to live up to their economic commitments—repaying debts and expanding exports to the USSR, thereby redressing the chronic imbalance that had existed in their trade relationships since the mid-1970s. The promotion of multilateral enterprises, which began late in the Brezhnev era, was inhibited by interference from central administrative bodies. Accordingly, the ambitious multilateralization implicit in the 1971 Comprehensive Program gave way to greater reliance on traditional bilateral relationships.

In a belated effort to reimpose a measure of authority over the Soviet bloc, Moscow used two types of forums: (1) the worldwide meeting, epitomized by the conferences of world Communist and workers' parties held in Moscow in 1957, 1960, and 1969 (and supplemented by frequent annual gatherings of the dozen or so leading Communist-front organizations in the fields of labor, education, science, and culture); and (2) the regional forum, intended primarily for European communist parties, exemplified by the meetings in 1967 in Karlovy Vary, Czechoslovakia, in 1976 in East Berlin, and in 1980 in Paris. Even more important were bilateral meetings between the CPSU and one other Communist Party.

In the wake of de-Stalinization and the revolutions in Eastern Europe, shock and disillusionment reverberated through Western nonruling communist parties. Italian Communist Party (PCI) chief Palmiro Togliatti called for the independence of all communist parties from Moscow and their right to determine their own strategy for achieving socialism (which he termed "polycentrism"). The 1957 conference sought to restore unity to the movement. The conference did fashion a unity of sorts, acknowledging the leading position of the Soviet Union in the struggle against imperialism and condemning revisionism, which meant the Yugoslavs. Moscow and Beijing closed ranks, leaving Yugoslavia out and the Italian and Polish Communists uneasy. However, Sino-Soviet relations soon worsened, and at an accelerating pace.

By the 1960 Moscow conference of eighty-one Communist parties, the cracks in the Sino-Soviet relationship could no longer be puttied over. The final document was more a collation of views than a compromise; its very "ambiguities and qualifications were so numerous that it could hardly serve as a guide for any of the Communist parties."[3] There was no agreement on the fundamental issue of authority within the world communist movement, and the seeming accord hardly outlived the conference. Moscow no longer held its former unquestioned sway.

An indication of how far the Soviet Union's authority had slipped can be seen in the difficulty Moscow experienced in trying to convene an international communist conference to condemn or excommunicate Beijing. Khrushchev was determined in late 1963 to hold such an ecumenical kangaroo court but encountered stiff opposition from the Yugoslav, Romanian, Polish, and the Italian party leaders. The PCI's secretary-general, Palmiro Togliatti, a highly respected veteran Communist—a survivor of the Stalin period—told his Central Committee in April 1964: "When talk arose of a new international meeting of all Communist parties to examine and assess the attitude of the Chinese comrades this was likely to end in another excommunication; and it appeared to us unnecessary and dangerous."

Togliatti died of a stroke while on vacation with Khrushchev in the Crimea in August 1964, but not before publishing an extraordinary memorandum on the problems of the world communist movement. In it he opposed an international conference as untimely, and urged a continual round robin of working groups to defeat and alter the Chinese views. He called for "the unity of all socialist forces in a common action, going also beyond ideological differences, against the most reactionary imperialist groups." Deploring "the old atheist propaganda" as counterproductive to reaching the Catholic masses and coming to grips with the challenge posed by a changing Vatican, he denounced the "cult of Stalin" and stressed the need to study "the political errors" that gave rise to it. He cited the worrying centrifugal tendency of nationalism among the socialist countries and noted that "in this lies an evident and serious danger with which the Soviet comrades should concern themselves." For all of these reasons, he said, "we would be against any proposal to create once again a centralized international organization. We are firm supporters of the unity of our movement and of the international workers movement, but this unity must be achieved in the diversity of our concrete political positions, conforming to the situation and degree of development in each country."[4] His warnings were prophetic.

At the time of Khrushchev's deposal in October 1964, Moscow could count on attendance by only some forty-six parties, not the seventy Khrushchev had originally claimed. Brezhnev postponed the December conference, convening instead a "preparatory meeting" in Moscow in March 1965, which was attended by only eighteen of the twenty-six parties invited. Faced with widespread resistance to the excommunication of the Chinese and to any return to the monolithism of the Stalinist period, Soviet leaders groped through subsequent meetings in 1967 and 1968 for a way to accommodate both the diversity demanded by foreign parties and the minimal unity the Kremlin could accept and still retain the authority necessary for promotion of foreign policy priorities.

Far from forging the movement's unity, the world conference finally held in Moscow from June 5 to 17, 1969, demonstrated conclusively the Balkanization of world communism. The very holding of the conference was a minor feat of sorts for Moscow. Seventy-five parties attended (five did not sign the final document). The final document, which did not mention China or the Soviet invasion of Czechoslovakia, was a bland melange of generalities. The conference left the movement pretty much where it had been before: polycentric, beset with divergences, wedded on paper to a common ideology that frayed badly when used, and firm in rejecting any attempt to restore the CPSU's former leading position in the movement.

Moscow fared no better in the regional conferences of European communist parties, the most important of which was held in East Berlin in June 1976.[5] Even the timing was a failure: Moscow had wanted the conference a year earlier, to link it to the Conference on Security and Cooperation in Europe, hoping thereby to

> lessen the effect of the concessions that the East Europeans would have to make in Helsinki with regard to "Basket 3" (the freer movement of information, ideas, and persons); at the same time, it would at least implicitly reaffirm the status of the CPSU as *primus inter pares* in the European Communist movement.[6]

The conference document finally signed by the twenty-nine participants, many with one or another reservation, was not what Moscow wanted. It stressed the voluntary cooperation of the participating parties "strictly adhering to the principles of equality and sovereign independence of each party, noninterference in internal affairs and respect for their free choice of different roads in the struggle for social change of a progressive nature and for Socialism."

After 1969, Moscow stopped convening world conferences of communist parties. It came to realize that even the regional conferences had serious shortcomings, but continued to support them in those areas in which its influence over the parties concerned remained high (especially in the Middle East and Latin America).

COMMUNISM IN CRISIS: CZECHOSLOVAKIA, 1968; POLAND, 1980

While Soviet relations with its East European neighbors were officially described as "fraternal," just below the surface discontent with externally imposed Soviet rule periodically exploded to reveal the truth.

In January 1968 a combination of disgruntled Stalinists and reformers ousted Antonin Novotny, Moscow's man in Prague, as general secretary of the Czechoslovak Communist Party. They brought in Alexander Dubcek, who became the rallying figure for all factions and groups seeking to liberalize Czechoslovak society and to assert a greater autonomy in domestic affairs. By mid-February, liberalization was occurring so rapidly that the skepticism among the population at large changed to hopeful anticipation. By late spring, Dubcek and the reformers in the Central Committee spoke of a parliament free from party control; they rehabilitated the victims of the Stalinist past, began to rid the party and trade unions of the front men for Moscow, and eliminated censorship. From early February to August 1968, Czechoslovakia experienced a rebirth of political, cultural, and social freedom. The secret police were stripped of their arbitrary powers, and their links to the Soviet KGB apparatus were exposed. Criticisms of the past and proposals for the future were aired with a candor and passion that disturbed the other ruling communist oligarchies.

The "Prague Spring" lasted only seven months. In the early hours of August 21, Soviet troops invaded Czechoslovakia. As with Hungary in 1956, Moscow responded with overwhelming force to a perceived threat to its strategic military position in Central Europe. Joined by Polish, East German, Hungarian, and Bulgarian (but not Romanian) troops in order to give the intervention a Warsaw Pact imprimatur, the Red Army quickly occupied the country.

The Soviet justification for the invasion of Czechoslovakia appeared in *Pravda* on September 26, 1968. Quickly dubbed the "Brezhnev Doctrine," it proclaimed the inherent right of the "socialist commonwealth" to judge when socialism was being threatened, and to intervene as it saw fit to preserve it. While reaffirming the principle of "many roads to socialism," it insisted that no action "should do harm either to socialism" in the country or party involved

> or to the fundamental interests of other socialist countries and of the entire working-class movement which is striving for socialism. This means that each Communist party is responsible not only to its own people but also to all the socialist countries and to the

entire Communist movement. Just as, in V.I. Lenin's words, someone living in a society cannot be free of that society, so a socialist state that is in a system of other states constituting a socialist commonwealth cannot be free of the common interests of that commonwealth.

The article warned that though every Communist party is free to apply the basic principles of Marxism-Leninism, it is not free to depart from those principles or to adopt a nonaffiliated attitude toward the rest of the socialist community:

> The weakening of any link in the world socialist system has a direct effect on all the socialist countries, which cannot be indifferent to this. Thus, the antisocialist forces in Czechoslovakia were in essence using talk about the right to self-determination to cover up demands for so-called neutrality and the C.S.R.'s withdrawal from the socialist commonwealth. The Communists of the fraternal countries naturally could not allow the socialist states to remain idle in the name of abstract sovereignty while the country was endangered by antisocialist degeneration.

Castigating those who "disapprove" of the actions taken by the Soviet Union, the article declared that world socialism "is indivisible and its defense is the common cause of all Communists and all progressive people on earth, first and foremost the working people of all the socialist countries."

In proceeding as they did, Soviet leaders demonstrated the paramountcy of Eastern Europe in their thinking about the defense of the Soviet Union. They used force even at the risk of jeopardizing many of their policy goals—for example, détente with the United States, including prospects for an agreement limiting strategic delivery systems; the weakening of NATO; and the support of foreign communists, many of whom publicly condemned the Soviet aggression against an ally and fellow-communist country.

But the most important single determinant may have been the Kremlin's fear that the virus of Czechoslovak liberalization would find a congenial breeding ground in the national consciousness of the Ukrainians and would stimulate demands in the Ukrainian republic for extensive reform and relaxation of Muscovite domination. After all, if the Slavs and fraternal communists of Czechoslovakia were permitted democratization, why not those of the Soviet Union?

A second major consideration in the Soviet decision to invade Czechoslovakia was the pressure of the military to safeguard the Soviet position in Central Europe against possible erosion; strategic imperatives transcended political risks. The Czech suggestion in July 1968 that the Warsaw Pact be revised raised the specter of another Hungarian crisis. The military argued that Czechoslovakia was too crucial geographically for Moscow to let it become neutral or succumb to instability. As it was, Warsaw Pact maneuvers in 1966 exposed glaring weaknesses along the Czechoslovak-West German border, and Prague's unwillingness to agree to the permanent stationing of Soviet troops on Czech soil was an objection the Soviet high command wished to override. Soviet marshals saw an opportunity to station troops permanently in Czechoslovakia, at that time the only Warsaw Pact member on the central front without such a deployment.

East German leaders strongly supported the Soviet military, arguing that if Czechoslovakia continued to liberalize, to open its economy to Western investment, and to follow its own way in dealing with the Federal Republic of Germany, as Romania had, the net result would be a severe weakening of the GDR, Moscow's ally in orthodoxy and most important economic partner. It is also possible that Soviet intelligence had assured the Politburo that the Czechs would not fight and that the incident could be handled swiftly and satisfactorily if massive power was applied.

A final consideration may have been the Politburo's sense that, as in Hungary in 1956, the Czechoslovak Communist Party leadership had lost control and there was no alternative to a military intervention if the USSR's strategic interests were to be safeguarded.

Nevertheless, elsewhere in the region during the 1960s and 1970s, Moscow eschewed military intervention and tolerated polycentrism. Its rapprochement with Yugoslavia, acceptance of growing autonomy for the East European countries within the framework of socialist internationalism, and quest for rationalization of economic relationships showed that Moscow was seeking support for its position in the quarrel with Beijing over the future of the world communist movement. Especially after the rupture with Albania in 1961, it permitted larger doses of autonomy in return for adherence to the Soviet line against China. Thus, desatellitization accompanied the end of monolithism in the bloc. The degree of polycentrism varied from country to country, with Romania's assertiveness in foreign policy perhaps representing the most dramatic example of the utility of the Sino-Soviet rift to the emergence of nationalism and political assertiveness. Romania's political independence, however, may have been more easily tolerated because it was accompanied by a brutal repression of all domestic dissent. In August 1980, another and potentially far more dangerous and complicated threat to the Soviet imperial system erupted in Poland.

Events in 1956 temporarily stabilized Soviet-Polish relations, but by the late 1960s, Gomulka's failure to generate economic growth and his crackdown on cultural and intellectual freedom led to new unrest. Steep increases in the price of food just before Christmas 1970 triggered a wave of strikes and violence at the Lenin Shipyard in Gdansk and elsewhere. Edward Gierek took over, as Moscow watched but did nothing because Soviet-Polish relations were not affected, the party (Polish United Worker's Party, or PUWP) remained in control, and discontent was directed inward and not against the Soviet Union or Poland's role in the Warsaw Pact.

Gierek kept power for a decade. His economic policy was to raise wages to mollify the workers, borrow heavily abroad to finance huge industrial projects that he hoped would produce goods for export to repay foreign loans, and tinker with cosmetic reforms in management-labor relations but retain firm party rule. By the mid-1970s, however, escalating costs of oil imports worsened the balance-of-payments situation; party privilege, corruption, and mismanagement of public enterprises alienated the working class; and poor grain harvests resulted in higher prices and a lower standard of living. In June 1976, strikes protesting the hike in food prices, especially of meat, resulted in arrests, repression, and further alienation of the proletariat from the party and government. Tensions simmered as the economic situation worsened. In mid-August 1980 price increases for meat again precipitated a wave of strikes, this time leading to major concessions—notably the government's agreement with the Gdansk shipyard workers led by Lech Walesa, an unemployed electrician who helped create Solidarity (the Independent Self-Governing Trade Unions) on August 31, 1980. In September, Stanislaw Kania, a moderate committed to "socialist renewal" and a political solution, replaced Gierek; in February 1981, General Wojciech Jaruzelski, the defense minister, was made prime minister. As the party lost ground to Solidarity, Jaruzelski gradually emerged as the regime's strongman.

Moscow viewed Solidarity as a threat. For the first time since 1956 it worried that Polish domestic turmoil might disrupt the Red Army's lines of communication to East Germany, spread to other parts of Eastern Europe, lead to escalated demands for reform and wrest control away from an indecisive party leadership, and even occasion serious disagreements in the Politburo over how best to proceed. At first, Moscow adopted a critical but cautious and multifaceted approach to Solidarity. Warning against "antisocialist" elements, it supported Kania's policy and extended more than $1 billion in credits and commodities, while taking steps within the bloc to pressure the Poles to keep their house in order. At the twenty-sixth congress of the CPSU in February 1981, Brezhnev ominously cited Poland as an example of how "mistakes and miscalculations" in domestic policy give rise to conditions in which "opponents of socialism, supported by outside forces are, by stirring up anarchy, seeking to channel events into a counterrevolutionary course." Though he gave no prescription for a solution, the possibility of a Soviet military intervention loomed large, as the parallels between Poland in 1981 and Czechoslovakia in 1968 became increasingly evident. Indeed, in a letter to Brezhnev, East German party leader, Erich Honecker, urged a Warsaw Pact invasion, warning, "Any hesitation will mean death—the death of socialist Poland."[7]

Throughout the spring and summer, Soviet and Polish officials met frequently as Solidarity and the Roman Catholic church coalesced into a national force for democratization and for national (as opposed to "socialist") renewal. The Soviet media denounced Solidarity and Western "interference" and called on the government to take a firm position.

Before the PUWP congress in July 1981, held against Moscow's wishes, the central committee of the CPSU warned that the forces of counterrevolution were actively disseminating anti-Sovietism and threatened to revive nationalist and anti-Soviet feelings at various levels of Polish society. This could, it warned, undermine the cohesion of the socialist commonwealth and the security of its borders.

At the congress, Kania changed personnel, introduced reforms to revamp the party, and gave repeated assurances of Poland's fealty to the Soviet Union and the socialist community.

In early September, at its national congress, Solidarity infuriated Moscow with a series of bold resolutions, especially one calling on the working class in other socialist countries to establish free trade unions. This resolution was passed by the militants, who ignored pleas for restraint from moderates such as Lech Walesa. A few days later, the Polish government made public an ominous Soviet note saying that anti-Sovietism had reached "dangerous limits," that Solidarity was inciting "hostility and hatred" of the Soviet Union among the Poles, and that it "has become in effect a permanent tribune from which slanders and insults sounded against our state. The so-called message to the working people of Eastern Europe has become a revolting provocation."[8] On October 18, General Jaruzelski replaced Kania as first secretary of the PUWP. The penultimate step toward banning Solidarity had been taken. On the very next day, Jaruzelski convened the Military Council at the Ministry of Defense and instituted measures that deployed military units throughout the country to cope with the threats "to the country's internal life." On December 13, 1981, martial law was proclaimed and Solidarity was banned.

Moscow surmounted the dangerous Polish crisis, skillfully avoiding an open military intervention and forestalling a complete breakdown of civil order. Its undoubted connivance and cooperation facilitated Jaruzelski's well-planned and surgically executed police operation. Strategic control and the integrity of its imperial system were preserved, but the price was high: a sullen population; indeterminate subsidies for Poland's ailing economy; perennial nervousness over a possible spread of Polish disaffection; economic bottlenecks elsewhere in Eastern Europe because of reduced Polish exports of coal, sulfur, and selected industrial goods; and reliance for the first time on a military, rather than a party, leadership.

Poland remained a problem for Moscow. However, it became more manageable and far less dangerous in its potential for bloc disruptiveness than it had been at the beginning of the 1980s. General Jaruzelski stabilized his rule and even acquired a measure of national acceptance, especially after the sweeping amnesty of September 1986. He divided the opposition, permitted cultural liberalization, and improved relations with the Catholic church, though not with the outlawed and much-weakened Solidarity movement. Still eluding him was a formula for revitalizing the economy and overcoming the widespread dispiritedness that permeated Polish society. Internationally, by 1987, he had normalized relations with the West (the United States lifted economic sanctions in February 1987) and gained Polish admission to the International Monetary Fund, an important step toward reestablishing credit-worthiness and rescheduling Poland's hard currency debt of more than $35 billion. In retrospect, there is reason to accept Jaruzelski's contention that his imposition of martial law prevented a Soviet military intervention. But in Poland the debate over whether he was a patriot or a puppet goes on.

RELATIONS WITH CHINA: FROM ALLY TO ADVERSARY

In Asia, Stalin did not expect Mao to emerge the victor from the Chinese civil war. In late 1945, shortly before the CCP guerrillas moved in, Soviet authorities stripped Manchuria of all usable industrial equipment, rolling stock, and valuables; they evidently did not foresee that within four years they would need to establish formal state-to-state relations with a fellow Communist and "fraternal" regime. Moscow was committed to Chiang's Kuomintang government; three times it agreed to his requests that Soviet troops remain in Manchuria until such time as the KMT could be present in sufficient force to forestall a Chinese Communist takeover of the area. (Soviet forces finally withdrew in May 1946.) Stalin may have been as surprised as the West at the shocking disintegration of the well-equipped, well-supplied Kuomintang forces and at the dramatic Communist military advances in 1947 and 1948, and perhaps he feared U.S. intervention to prevent a CCP victory. According to a Yugoslav official, Stalin had recommended to Mao that he reach an agreement with Chiang and enter into a coalition government. Supposedly Mao agreed, but on returning home went his own way and won. Stalin is also alleged to have had doubts about the extent to which the Chinese Communists were genuine Communists, more than once referring to them as "radish Communists—red on the outside but white on the inside."

The outcome of the Chinese civil war was not determined in Moscow. At best, Soviet leaders contributed only marginally to Mao's victory. The CCP's reputation for reform and efficiency, the purposefulness and honesty of Mao and his associates, and the appeal that a strong and united China had for all strata of Chinese society contrasted vividly with the Kuomintang's failure to cope with China's inflation, poverty, and socioeconomic collapse; the venality of KMT officials; and Chiang Kai-shek's insensitivity to the peasants' profound desire for an end to war.

On October 1, 1949, the People's Republic of China (PRC) was proclaimed in Beijing. An era of Far Eastern history had come to an end. China's destiny was no longer decided in Europe or Japan. For the first time in more than a century, all of mainland China was ruled by one Chinese elite. The century of weak central authority, civil wars, unequal treaties, economic subordination to foreign powers, and military helplessness was now past. Out of this crucible emerged a ruthless, dedicated, disciplined leadership—the Calvinists of Asia—intent on creating a powerful, industrialized, independent China. This development inevitably affected Soviet foreign policy and great-power relationships in Asia, relationships already greatly altered as a consequence of World War II and the unstable 1945–1949 interregnum.

In December 1949 Mao went to Moscow and for two months negotiated a new political and military relationship between China and the Soviet Union. Although distrustful of Stalin on the basis of their previous dealings, Mao decided against a Titoist alternative, which might well have created problems for him in the CCP, and succeeded in exacting significant concessions from the Soviet leadership. After tough bargaining, three agreements were signed on February 14, 1950. First, a thirty-year treaty of alliance directed against the United States (though formally it was directed against "Japan or any other State which should unite with Japan, directly or indirectly") was concluded. Second, an agreement was reached on Manchuria, whereby the Chinese Changchun Railway and the naval base at Port Arthur were to be returned to China "immediately upon the conclusion of a peace treaty with Japan, but not later than the end of 1952," and the commercial port of Dalny (Dairen) was recognized as China's, though its disposition was left in abeyance pending a peace treaty with Japan. (In case of war Port Arthur was to be jointly operated; because of the Korean War, its final transfer to China was postponed until 1955.) Third, the Soviets agreed to a $300 million credit, a niggardly amount that sealed Mao's coolness toward Moscow and prompted Khrushchev's observation in 1956 that "Stalin treated Mao Tse-tung like a beggar."

In retrospect, the Stalin era looms as the apogee of Sino-Soviet accord. Mao Zedong was prepared to accept a junior partnership and follow the Soviet lead in world affairs. All of this changed rapidly in the post-Stalin period.

In October 1954 Nikita Khrushchev led a Soviet delegation to Beijing to negotiate a series of political and economic agreements that would more accurately
reflect China's independence and growing stature within the Communist world.
Under the agreement of October 11, 1954, Moscow made a number of concessions, indicative of its desire to eliminate obvious past inequities and possible
sources of future friction. The naval base of Port Arthur was returned (formally in
May 1955), in accordance with the 1950 treaty; the Soviet share in the four joint-
stock companies that had been set up in 1950 and 1951 (to mine nonferrous and
rare metals, to extract and refine petroleum, to build and repair ships, and to
develop civil aviation) was transferred to the PRC, with appropriate compensation
to be paid in goods over a number of years; and the USSR provided an additional
long-term credit of $230 million and agreed to help build fifteen additional indus-
trial projects and participate in the construction of a railway line from Lanchow
through Urumchi (in Xinjiang) to Alma Ata, on Soviet territory, and of another line
between Timin in Chinese Inner Mongolia and Ulan Bator in the Mongolian People's Republic (MPR) to the USSR's Trans-Siberian Railroad. Moscow would not,
however, return Tanu-Tuva, which had been detached from Chinese Turkestan
during a time of maximum Kuomintang weakness and incorporated into the Soviet Union in 1944; nor would it agree to any questioning of Mongolia's independence or weakening of Soviet-MPR ties. Finally, it resisted Beijing's effort to con-
vert North Korea into a Chinese satellite, but agreed to a compromise whereby the
Yenan (Chinese) faction of the Korean Workers' (Communist) party was assured of
suitable minority representation.

The catalysts for Sino-Soviet disagreements came from Europe. Khrushchev's
reconciliation with Tito, his acceptance of the principle of "many roads to socialism," and his interest in better relations with the United States, Beijing's main
enemy, alienated the Chinese. His attack on Stalin at the twentieth party congress
and subsequent de-Stalinization policy was the final shock to Mao. An implicit criticism of his own rule in China, this policy forced Mao to launch his own equivalent
of de-Stalinization—the very short-lived policy in 1956–1957 of "let a hundred
flowers bloom, let a hundred schools contend." Mao, however, used this bogus liberalization to draw opponents into the open, destroy them, and reassert his authority against leading rivals. Mao's perceived need to respond to Khrushchev's disruptive policy initiatives may have forced him on to ideological and economic paths
that hastened the separation from Moscow. The animus between Khrushchev and
Mao was profound, as Khrushchev suggests in his memoirs and as their acrimonious exchanges confirm.

There was a lull in the gathering storm in late 1956, when, in the wake of the
Soviet repression in Hungary, Khrushchev assured the Chinese that "We are all
Stalinists"; and at the November 1957 Moscow conference of Communist par-
ties, when Mao backed Khrushchev's antirevisionist line, which was directed
against Tito and other national Communists. (The supreme irony was that Mao
himself had been communism's first "Titoist" in departing from reliance on
Moscow in the 1930s and fashioning his own strategy for making a revolution.)
But as Soviet policy explored the path of détente with the United States,
Moscow's relations with Beijing took a turn for the worse. The adhesive of Marx-

ism-Leninism, and the sharing of a common enemy, which had bound the Soviets and the Chinese in the Stalin period, loosened under the strain of divergent national interests. Khrushchev's ideological innovations and his stress on peaceful coexistence with the West contrasted with Mao's preference for doctrinal orthodoxy and the polarizing strategy epitomized by the 1947 Zhdanov Line. Mao saw Khrushchev's formulation that war was no longer "fatalistically inevitable" as the ideological rationale for Moscow's reluctance to use its nuclear arsenal on China's behalf. In August and September of 1958, during the crisis between China and the United States triggered by the Communists' bombardment of the Kuomintang-held offshore islands of Quemoy and Matsu, Moscow's restraint emphasized that it would not risk nuclear war with the United States in order to help Beijing liberate Taiwan. The Quemoy crisis demonstrated that neither the Sino-Soviet alliance nor the shared commitment to Marxism-Leninism was sufficient to overcome diametrically opposed national interests in a concrete situation.[9]

Whatever chances there were for a reconciliation probably vanished with Mao's mastery over his rivals, many of whom favored better relations with Moscow (and a more pragmatic approach to domestic problems) because they wanted to modernize the Chinese army with Soviet assistance or develop China's nuclear capability with Soviet expertise and have a common front in Asia against the United States.[10] Khrushchev's unwillingness to provide more substantial economic assistance and his refusal in 1959 to help China acquire a nuclear capability undermined the anti-Mao faction in the CCP. Adding insult to injury, Khrushchev expanded his relations with the United States, and his visit there in 1959 showed that he had no intention of helping China regain Taiwan. Nor was he going to play nuclear brinkmanship to please Mao. In response to Mao's derisory description of the United States as a paper tiger, Khrushchev retorted, "The United States may be a paper tiger, but [it is] a paper tiger with nuclear teeth."

The tensions increased with Moscow's criticism of the ideological pretensions that underlay Mao's "Great Leap Forward" campaign in 1958 to bypass socialism and move directly to communism through a system of communes, mass mobilization, and do-it-yourself backyard industrialization.

At a meeting of ruling communist parties in Bucharest in June 1960, Moscow made a number of concessions in an effort to find a formula for bridging the rift. However, no amount of ideological circumlocution could resolve the concrete policy differences that divided the two colossi of communism. Khrushchev's peremptory withdrawal in the summer of 1960 of all Soviet technicians (and their blueprints) from China, leaving dozens of incomplete Soviet-assisted projects, intensified Beijing's hostility. If Khrushchev's purpose was to pressure Mao into submission, he failed dismally.

By 1961, the seriousness of the rift had become a matter of public record, as Moscow and Beijing hurled charge and countercharge at one another.

The condemnatory attacks crescendoed throughout the remaining years of the Khrushchev period. Moscow called Mao "a megalomaniac warmonger," "an irresponsible scribbler," and "a dogmatist" of whom it could truly be said, "Blessed is he who chatters about war and does not understand what he is chattering about."

Beijing responded with comparable venom and vigor, referring to Khrushchev as "a Bible-reading and psalm-singing buffoon."

Khrushchev's removal did not substantially alter the frosty tenor of Sino-Soviet relations, which derived from rival interests and conceptions of security: each side viewed the other as a long-term threat, which geography has confirmed in perpetuity. Each sought to enhance its prestige by pointing out the backsliding of the other. The Soviet Union saw China as a competitor for leadership in the international Communist movement and among radical groups. The two sought influence in the Third World, though for different reasons—Moscow to undermine the United States, Beijing to undermine the USSR. They had serious border problems. Finally, both the Russians and the Chinese have deeply ingrained psychological, cultural, racial, and historical antagonisms that inevitably made reconciliation more difficult.

Even the death of Mao in September 1976, however, brought little substantive change in Beijing's policy, though the polemics somewhat abated. Indeed, the new Chinese leadership went out of its way to downgrade Soviet overtures. Even the messages of condolence from Soviet-bloc party leaders were rejected.

A technical agreement in October 1977, to which both sides deliberately gave no publicity, resulted in the lifting of the ten-year Soviet blockade of Chinese shipping at the heavily trafficked junction around Bear Island (Hei Hsiatzu, in Chinese), situated just below Khabarovsk. New navigation rules for this very limited sector of the Amur-Ussuri basin were negotiated as a matter of mutual convenience, to prevent recurring incidents that could create more difficulties than either country would like.

On April 3, 1979, Beijing informed Moscow that the alliance treaty, signed in February 1950, would not be renewed when it expired in April 1980. Although long regarded as an anachronism, the alliance did signify a certain ideological kinship and sense of shared antagonists. To Moscow, China's renunciation of the alliance, coupled with its rapprochements with the United States and Japan, left no doubt that in Beijing's eyes the Soviet Union had become the main enemy in Asia, and the Kremlin acted accordingly.

Moreover, by the late 1970s the USSR faced a China that was no longer diplomatically isolated. The normalization of Sino-American relations, the signing of the Sino-Japanese treaty of friendship and cooperation in August 1978, the seating of the PRC in the United Nations in 1971, and the ever-widening range of contacts with Western and Third World countries all mocked the Soviet effort toward isolating China and gave Beijing greater authority in its dealings with Moscow. China's opening to the West in particular necessitated continual Soviet reassessments of Beijing's military, economic, and political options, since the modern technology and expertise that China imported made it a more formidable adversary, and its diplomatic flexibility has in the main limited Soviet maneuverability. The Soviet-Vietnamese friendship treaty of November 1978 provided the USSR with some middle-range options for frustrating China's policies in Cambodia, Laos, and Vietnam, but at the same time it strained relations with the United States and forced Moscow to react to Chinese thrusts instead of making its own.

OBSERVATIONS

Although Leonid Brezhnev rose to power to restore the Soviet Union, his reign of nearly two decade have come to be known as "the period of stagnation." Domestically, efforts to improve economic performance through the gradual introduction of market incentives were consistently thwarted. Opposition to the regime, easily manageable in the early 1970s, became more widespread and more nationalistically inclined by the 1980s.

Stagnation was also apparent in foreign policy. The so-called Brezhnev Doctrine was clearly no solution to the aspirations of other communist states for greater autonomy, and only served to further divide the "fraternal" socialist parties. Détente, envisioned by the Soviet leadership as an opportunity to receive Western support for the ailing Soviet economy and explicit recognition of superpower parity with the United States, collapsed. Relations with China barely skirted war, and in 1979 the aging Soviet leaders embarked on a costly and highly unpopular war in Afghanistan that only further undermined Soviet diplomatic efforts in the Third World.

Clearly, the empire that Stalin had so painstakingly assembled was fraying, and the Soviet gerontocracy's unwillingness to relinquish power (by the early 1980s the average age on the Politburo was well over 70) was not helping matters. All hopes were pinned on the eventual succession to power of a new generation of leaders.

SELECTED BIBLIOGRAPHY

Anderson, Richard D. *Public Politics in an Authoritarian States: Making Foreign Policy During the Brezhnev Years.* Ithaca, NY: Cornell University Press, 1993.

Brzezinski, Zbigniew K. *The Soviet Bloc: Unity and Conflict.* rev. ed. Cambridge, MA: Harvard University Press, 1967.

Cynkin, Thomas. *Soviet and American Signalling in the Polish Crisis.* New York: St. Martin's Press, 1988.

Dawisha, Karen. *The Kremlin and the Prague Spring.* Berkeley: University of California Press, 1984.

Edmonds, Robin. *Soviet Foreign Policy: The Brezhnev Years.* 2nd ed. New York: Oxford University Press.

Felkay, Andrew. *Hungary and the USSR, 1956–1988: Kadar's political leadership.* New York: Greenwood Press, 1989.

Gati, Charles. *Hungary and the Soviet Bloc.* Durham, N.C.: Duke University Press, 1986.

Goldgeier, James M. *Leadership Style and Soviet Foreign Policy: Stalin, Khrushchev, Brezhnev, Gorbachev.* Baltimore: Johns Hopkins University Press, 1994.

Hutchings, Robert L. *Soviet-East European Relations: Consolidation and Conflict, 1968–1980.* Madison: University of Wisconsin Press, 1984.

Mandelbaum, Michael, and Talbott, Strobe. *Reagan and Gorbachev.* New York: Vintage Books, 1984.

Ploss, Sidney I. *Moscow and the Polish Crisis: An Interpretation of Soviet Policies and Intentions.* Boulder, CO: Westview Press, 1986.

Steele, Jonathan. *The Limits of Soviet Power: The Kremlin's Foreign Policy-Brezhnev to Chernenko.* Rev. and updated ed. Harmondsworth, United Kingdom: Penguin Books, 1985.

Stoessinger, John G. *Nations in Darkness: China, Russia and America.* 5th ed. New York: McGraw-Hill, 1990.

Strode, Dan Lee. "Soviet Policy Towards the People's Republic of China, 1976–1986: The Determining Factors." Dissertation, University of California at Berkeley, 1992.

Teague, Elizabeth. *Solidarity and the Soviet Worker: The Impact of the Polish Events of 1980 on Soviet Internal Politics.* New York: Metheun, 1988.

Valenta, Jiri. *Soviet Intervention in Czechoslovakia, 1968.* Baltimore: Johns Hopkins University Press, 1979.

Vali, Ference. *Rift and Revolution in Hungary.* Cambridge, MA: Harvard University Press, 1961.

Weathersby, Kathryn. "Soviet aims in Korea and the origins of the Korean War, 1945–1950: New evidence from Russian archives." Cold War International History Project, no. 8. Washington, DC: Woodrow Wilson International Center for Scholars, 1993.

Wozniuk, Vladimir. *From Crisis to Crisis: Soviet-Polish Relations in the 1970s.* Ames: Iowa State University Press, 1987.

NOTES

1. N. S. Khrushchev, "Report of the Central Committee of the Communist Party of the Soviet Union to the 20th Party Congress" (Moscow: Foregin Languages Publishing House, 1956), pp. 41–42. The full text of the speech was not published in the Soviet Union until early 1989.
2. *Pravda,* November 20, 1962.
3. Donald S. Zagoria, *The Sino-Soviet Conflict, 1956–1962* (Princeton, NJ: Princeton University Press, 1962), pp. 367–368.
4. *The New York Times,* September 5, 1964.
5. For the best account of the background and significance of the East Berlin Conference of European Communist and Workers' Parties, see Kevin Devlin, "The Challenge of Eurocommunism," *Problems of Communism,* vol. 26, no. 1 (January–February 1977), pp. 1–18.
6. *Ibid.,* p. 3.
7. Stephen Kinzer, *The New York Times,* January 12, 1993.
8. *The New York Times,* September 19, 1981.
9. John R. Thomas, "Soviet Behavior in the Quemoy Crisis of 1958," *Orbis,* vol. 6, no. 1 (Spring 1962), pp. 38–64.
10. See Donald S. Zagoria, "Mao's Role in the Sino-Soviet Conflict," *Pacific Affairs,* vol. 47, no. 2 (Summer 1974), pp. 146–48. See also Gerald Segal, "Chinese Politics and the Soviet Connection," *The Jerusalem Journal of International Relations,* vol. 2, no. 1 (Fall 1976), pp. 96–128.

Chapter
5

In Search of the Russian National Interest

Although the USSR claimed to be a federation of independent republics, in reality it was ruled as a unitary state. As Lenin frequently reminded his colleagues, "The entire legal and actual constitution of the Soviet republic is built on the basis of the Party's correcting, determining and building everything according to a single principle."[1] Attempts to secede were suppressed so that, in fact, Soviet-style federalism became nothing more than a mechanism that allowed the CPSU to administer the country more effectively.

Not surprisingly, there was little attention paid to the foreign policy aspirations of national minorities. Although nominally free to exercise independent foreign policies according to articles 72, 76, and 80 of the 1977 Soviet Constitution, in reality, all foreign policy initiatives were strictly supervised by the Soviet party-state. When the non-Russian nationalities did play a role in foreign relations, therefore, it was strictly choreographed by Moscow for the purposes of advancing Soviet strategic objectives. The Islamic peoples of Central Asia for example, "voiced their concern" for the plight of oppressed Islamic brethren throughout the Third World, and when the Afghan war erupted, the neighboring Tajiks were the first soldiers sent to the region. Perhaps the best example of how the Soviet leadership utilized their "nationalities card" to obtain international advantage is the deal that Stalin struck with Roosevelt to obtain two additional seats in the United Nations for "independent" Ukraine and Belarus.[2]

In the West a debate has long raged over whether Soviet foreign policy, dominated as it was by Russia, could be properly said to express the Russian national interest. The classic, conflicting views on this subject were expressed by Samuel Sharp and Michael Karpovich.

Writing less than a generation after the demise of Tsarist Russia, Karpovich, who came to America as a young attaché to the Russian Embassy and after the October Revolution remained to teach at Harvard University, argued that in its ambitions, style, and content pre-1917 Russian foreign policy expressed the classical ambitions of its European contemporaries. By contrast, Soviet foreign policy marked a sharp departure from this tradition. Under Stalin, Soviet foreign policy became a "global policy, persistently seeking to achieve a number of aggressive aims simultaneously in various corners of the earth." For Karpovich, Soviet diplomacy had an all-embracing political plan contained in the body of literature the Communists call Marxism-Leninism-Stalinism" which made it qualitatively different from Russian diplomacy.[3] Karpovich's views may be said to characterize the consensus of many analysts before (and after) the Second World War.

Sharp, by contrast, argued that in the forty years since the October Revolution a new consensus on the legitimacy of the Soviet state had emerged in Russia. The Soviet regime, he claims, clearly demonstrated its legitimacy by surviving Hitler's invasion and emerging strengthened from the war. The Soviet leaders might pay lip service to Marxist-Leninist ideology, but they did not conduct their foreign policy according to its tenets because "the term policy excludes aims, ambitions, or dreams not accompanied by action visibly and within a reasonable time capable of producing the results aimed at or dreamed of."[4] Purely pragmatic considerations had long ago forced Soviet leaders to abandon any real commitment to world revolution. Since it is not Marxism-Leninism that guides Soviet foreign policy, Sharp concludes that it is the Soviet national interest.

Although communist ideology's iron grip on Russian foreign policy ended in 1991, the question of what (and who) defines the Russian national interest remains of central importance to foreign observers. If Karpovich is correct, then a postcommunist Russian leadership should find foreign policy accommodation with the West relatively easy because the main obstacle to agreement—an ideology predisposed to viewing all other social systems as hostile—is now gone. If, on the other hand, Sharp is correct, then fundamental antagonisms between Russia and the West are bound to persist, regardless of the character of the Russian political system.

These first few years since the collapse of communism have seen both a rapid warming of Russian relations with the West as the Russian government redefines the mission of Russian foreign policy, and a rapid cooling of relations as policy differences have emerged. It is clearly no longer ideology alone, but also Russia's perennial ambition (retained through Tsarist and Soviet times) to be treated as a great power, that remains a source of tensions with the West.

THE SOVIET FOREIGN POLICY MECHANISM

The key characteristic of Soviet foreign policy making was the parallel and complementary nature of party and state institutions in the conduct of Soviet foreign policy. Unlike Western countries, where the locus of foreign policy decision making is located in the government ministries, in the Soviet Union it was the Communist Party that determined major initiatives in foreign policy and supervised their execution. This control was enshrined in article 6 of the USSR Constitution, which described the Communist Party as "the leading and guiding force of Soviet society and the nucleus of its political system, of all state and public organizations." The task of the Foreign Ministry and other government agencies was therefore conceived of as largely administrative.

The Party structures directly involved in formulating foreign policy priorities were the Political Bureau (or Politburo) and the Secretariat with its many administrative subdivisins. Although nominally subordinate to the Central Committee of the Communist Party, in fact from Stalin's time on the real lines of power were reversed. The Politburo and Secretariat designated their membership (as well as the person to be General Secretary of the Party) to be approved by a compliant Central Committee.

The supreme political power in the Soviet Union rested in these two institutions. During the Brezhnev years the Politburo consisted of roughly twenty members, drawn equally from the ranks of party secretaries and government officials. Traditionally, it included, in addition to the General Secretary, the premier and first deputy premier, the ministers of foreign affairs, defense, and the KGB, as well as the head of the largest party organizations (typically, Moscow and the Ukraine).

The Secretariat headed the administrative branch of the CPSU. Consisting of roughly a dozen members, many overlapping with the Politburo, it monitored all government operations (foreign and domestic) to ensure that they were in compliance with Party policy. Its chief function was to administer the *nomenklatura* system, a spoils-system of high-level appointments that included appointments of all ambassadorships and key personnel dealing in foreign policy issues (including think tanks, leading foreign affairs journals, etc.)

Since most members of these two bodies had little or no background in foreign policy matters, foreign policy issues were often decided among a smaller, "inner circle" of Politburo and Secretariat members that included the General Secretary, the Minister of Foreign Affairs, and the "power ministries" of defense, KGB, and perhaps Internal Security (MVD). The influence of these ministries was further enhanced within the Defense Council, a subcommittee of the Politburo charged with formulating Soviet military doctrine and deciding on military procurement decisions.

Looking beyond the very highest levels of policy formulation, the Party managed its control over foreign policy through the central committee apparatus under the Secretariat. This apparatus was organized into twenty departments and two "administrations," six of which were directly concerned with foreign policy. Of these, preeminence was given to two: the International Department and the Department for Liaison with Worker's and Communist Parties (DLWCP).

While nominally responsible for relations with Western Communist Parties, in fact the International Department exercised dominant influence in Soviet foreign policy toward Western Europe and many Third World nations.[5] The DLWCP, by contrast was responsible for the formulation and implementation of policy toward countries that were members of what the Soviets called "the Socialist Commonwealth," including China and Third World countries with ruling communist parties. Because party-to-party relations between these countries were more important than government-to-government relations, the DLWCP's importance in this area generally outweighed the foreign ministry's.

On the other hand, the government agencies involved in foreign affairs had many functional similarities to Western institutions. The lead role was played by the USSR Foreign Ministry, which was charged with the administration of state-to-state relations.

Another ministry that wielded great influence in the arena of Soviet affairs was the Committee for State Security (KGB). Its functions combined those normally performed by the CIA, National Security Agency, FBI, and Border Patrol in the United States. Although much of its personnel was devoted to the control of domestic discontent, including separate directorates for control over the armed forces (Second Chief Directorate) and of the dissident movement (The Fifth Directorate), KGB agents were also routinely assigned to Soviet embassies, trade missions, or as journalists. Post-coup documents reveal that during the Soviet period roughly two thirds of Soviet embassy staff abroad had been on the payroll of the KGB.[6] Their functions included gathering political and economic information, recruitment of foreign nationals to work for the USSR, industrial espionage, and monitoring the loyalty of Soviet personnel stationed abroad.[7]

The Ministry of Defense also wielded considerable influence on foreign policy mainly through its ability to pursue a tightly compartmentalized policy in isolation from the Foreign Ministry.[8] Not only was the administration of national security policy functionally isolated from foreign affairs, it was supported by several highly secretive defense ministries coordinated by the military-manned Military-Industrial Commission of the Presidium of the Council of Ministers. Within the Soviet economic planning structure, military production quotas had top priority, and the military could requisition the best resources from any other branch of the economy. By all accounts they were never subject to cost accounting considerations or any external civilian supervision.

Finally, a word should be said about the role of research institutes and the press. After 1960 the Central Committee apparatus made increasingly frequent use of the research institutes established under the USSR Academy of Sciences. These included:

- The Institute of World Economy and International Relations (established in 1956)
- Institute of Economy of World Socialist Systems (1960)
- Institute of the Far East (established in 1966)
- Institute of Oriental Studies (established in 1930)
- Institute of Africa (established in 1959)
- Institute of Latin America (established in 1961)
- Institute of the International Worker's Movement (established in 1968)
- Institute of the United States and Canada (established in 1974)

Each of these institutes published its own journal, whose contents were supervised by the International Department (ID), and provided background information and policy recommendations for the ID and the foreign ministry. During the Soviet period, individuals in these "think tanks" were expected to play a supportive role in explaining Soviet foreign policy decisions to the West and making these decisions more palatable. As we shall see, under perestroika these think tanks also served as incubators of even more radical innovations.

Until 1986 the role of the press in Soviet society can be characterized as one of transmission of party policy to the Soviet public and to the outside world. Under the careful watch of the Propaganda Department, which scrutinized all party publications for ideological content, the ID carefully controlled the contents of all printed discussions of foreign affairs. In the West, therefore, Sovietologists would examine such publications with care for any shifts in wording that might suggest a change in Party policy.

At the same time, the press could occasionally be utilized by members of the Politburo to undermine the authority of their opponents. Disgruntled members of the elite might air their disagreements publicly in order to suggest that the Party had not yet achieved a consensus in this area, as when Lavrenti Beria launched the idea of possible Soviet acceptance of a unified Germany, or when Khrushchev criticized Malenkov for sacrificing security with his proposals to shift resources from defense to consumer industries. In each instance, however, the press did not really act to influence policy choices but acted merely as a tool of one party faction against another in the process of consolidating political power. The emergence of the press as an independent voice did not occur until the Party renounced its claim to a monopoly on the truth in February 1990.

In conclusion, therefore, the conduct of Soviet diplomacy was characterized by extreme secrecy (both from the eyes of the outside world and from the eyes of Soviet citizens); extreme compartmentalization, which reinforced rivalry and suspicion among institutions that often performed the same tasks; and Party supervision over both the broad direction of foreign policy and its implementation on a day-to-day level through the appointment of all key personnel.

It has often been argued that this duplication of state and party apparatus was wasteful and inefficient. Such costs, however, were considered a worthwhile price to pay in order to maintain complete party control over the process. When Mikhail Gorbachev assumed the General Secretaryship of the party in March 1985 he began a sweeping reform of the way foreign policy was implemented. His ultimate objective was to minimize the party's role in the daily implementation of foreign affairs and shift this responsibility to the Ministry of Foreign Affairs, while retaining party supervision over the general direction of foreign policy.

FOREIGN POLICYMAKING UNDER GORBACHEV

Gorbachev's new political thinking differed from traditional Soviet foreign policy in three ways. First, while it had little immediate impact on the execution of foreign policy, official publications began to publish occasional pieces critical of the USSR's "internationalist" obligations in Afghanistan and the Third World. Second, by calling into question the notion that the "class struggle" drives relations between states, the door was opened to redefining Marxism-Leninism in less aggressive and hostile ways. Finally, by replacing communist internationalism with the more amorphous concept of "humanitarian internationalism," new political thinking tried to provide a conceptual alternative that, Gorbachev hoped, would permit a smooth transition away from dogmatic Marxist-Leninism, while avoiding the pitfalls of Russian nationalism.

New political thinking combined into a new and more attractive package—traditional Soviet concerns with enhancing the security and the international influence of the USSR. What distinguished it from all previous Soviet foreign policy initiatives was the downplaying of the ideology. According to Marxism-Leninism, Soviet foreign policy was bound by the notion that a state's interests ultimately reflect the dominant class interest in each state. Even during the heyday of peaceful coexistence and détente, Soviet leaders were adamant that the common interest among states in preventing nuclear war did not vitiate the ongoing class struggle between capitalism and socialism, which would eventually result in the demise of capitalism.

Under Gorbachev, however, the class struggle was explicitly subordinated to the common interests of humanity. As Gorbachev advisor Georgi Shakhnazarov put it, the Soviet Union now believes that "the struggle for survival is more important that the struggle for class, national, or any other interest."[9]

This new, "humanistic" emphasis led to a curtailment of Soviet support for communist and revolutionary parties around the globe. The most dramatic reductions came in the withdrawal of Soviet support for Third World regimes that were of no particular strategic value to the USSR: Iraq, Libya, Somalia, Yemen, Angola, Kampuchea, and Mozambique. Subsequently, even long-standing client states like Vietnam and Cuba were cut off from the Soviet purse strings. Finally, Gorbachev began the slow withdrawal that would eventually lead to the collapse of Soviet regimes in Afghanistan and Eastern Europe. While Soviet monetary subsidy of nonruling communist parties continued up until the seizure of the assets of the CPSU by the Russian government in September 1991, for all practical purposes any serious commitment to these parties had ended by late 1989.

To help administer this new foreign policy concept, Gorbachev replaced seasoned cold warrior Andrei Gromyko with a complete unknown, Eduard Shevardnadze, as Foreign Minister. At the time many interpreted his appointment as a signal that Gorbachev intended to set the foreign policy agenda personally through party institutions by having a weak and inexperienced foreign minister. In fact, Gorbachev did intend to exercise more personal control over the direction of foreign policy, but in order to do so he needed to overcome the resistance of the Soviet foreign policy establishment to change by placing an outsider at its head and giving him more authority that any of his predecessors.

At the nineteenth Party Conference in June 1988 Gorbachev unveiled his ambitious plans to enhance the stature of the Supreme Soviet and the Soviet Presidency. In September of that year he overhauled the entire senior party apparatus, reducing and simplifying its role in government administration. These changes included reducing the number of departments and administrations by two thirds. In foreign affairs this meant reducing the number of Central Committee departments responsible for foreign policy oversight from six to just two: the International Department and the International Policy Commission. The latter commission, headed by Gorbachev ally Alexander Yakovlev, was to be the conduit for policy recommendations from the Politburo.

In the process, the DLWCP was eliminated and responsibility for party relations with socialist states was given over to the ID. At the same time, a new section for relations with socialist states was created within the Ministry of Foreign Affairs. The direct result of this reshuffling was to diminish the status of the ID by saddling it with the ever less important function of relations with ruling communist parties, while shifting its policymaking functions to a new coordinating body and to the MFA. Although the communiqué establishing these new commissions reiterates that the departments of the Central Committee would still "guide" the work of the commissions, since its membership was diluted by new people, many of them regional party officials with little or no expertise in foreign affairs, this reorganization actually served primarily to undermine bureaucratic resistance to new political thinking.

Gorbachev's reorganization of the party apparatus also weakened the defense industry's privileged access to resources. He moved supervision of defense industries to a Commission on Social and Economic Policy, which was supposed to require these industries to compete on an equal footing with scarce economic resources. This change reinforced the reliance of the military-industrial complex on the military industrial commission of the Presidium of the Council of Ministers, thus further reinforcing the shift of power away from the party and toward the government.

Finally, party oversight of the KGB was given to a Legal Policy Commission, a body with the rather broad mandate of enhancing the party's adherence to the rule of law. Since the head of the KGB at the time, Viktor Chebrikov, was also named head of this commission, however, real oversight continued to be minimal.

All in all, Gorbachev's efforts represented a concerted effort to subordinate the party to certain general administrative principles, reduce the size of the Party bureaucracy, and shift the responsibility for daily administration from the Party to the government, Gorbachev believed that these changes would allow the Party to manage more effectively the tasks of broad guidance and supervision of society.

Meanwhile, on the government side of the equation, Eduard Shevardnadze undertook the most sweeping overhaul of the foreign ministry since Stalin's purges. Between 1986 and 1989 all nine deputy ministers and three out of four senior officials in the Foreign Ministry were replaced. New functional departments were created for disarmament, humanitarian issues, the nonaligned movement, and international economic relations. In addition, new administrative departments were set up to disseminate evaluation and planning information to Soviet embassies abroad. The MFA was streamlined, and a section was added for relations with the Socialist Countries of Europe, indicating that the MFA would assume new responsibilities in this area.

The press, too, gradually came to see its role in a different light. With *glasnost* ("openness"), far more criticism of past policies was tolerated, and by the end of 1989 the press had become more than simply a conduit for factional disagreements within the Politburo. Gradually, major journals and newspapers like *Novyi mir* and *Nezavisimaya gazeta* began to define their role as the disseminators of objective information, regardless of the constraints imposed by the party. In a number of instances, the local media actively supported the efforts of local informal political groups to run alternative candidates for election to the Supreme Soviet in 1989, and effectively circumvented the censorship of regional party leaders.[10] In foreign policy, the press had the greatest effect in revealing the impact of the Afghan war on Soviet soldiers, and in discussing the capricious and isolated process that had led to the decision to invade.

To sum up, Gorbachev asserted greater personal control over the direction of foreign policy, and he did so in the face of tremendous opposition within both the party apparatus and the foreign ministry to his new political thinking. He replaced the dominance of the Central Committee and its International Department in foreign policy with that of the foreign ministry, which was headed by his ally Eduard Shevardnadze, thereby undercutting the power of the foreign affairs bureaucracy.

Glasnost further undermined the party's authority by revealing the party's isolated decision-making process. As conflicting recommendations were leaked to the press and published, people came to view the party's policies less and less as an expression of consummate political wisdom, and increasingly as merely one possible interpretation of events. As party control eroded, society's pent-up frustrations were unleashed in the form of an extreme rejection of any efforts to retain or justify the Soviet political order. Paradoxically, the man who had done the most to transform the political system could not salvage his reputation—in the eyes of many Russians to this day he remains the last communist leader of the Soviet Union, rather than the first democratic leader of a new Russia.

FOREIGN POLICYMAKING UNDER YELTSIN

Like Gorbachev, Yeltsin sought to keep the reins of foreign policymaking (and with them the determination of what Russia's national interest should be) in his own hands. To this end, he needed a foreign minister who shared his views, and he found one in Andrei Kozyrev, who had resigned his post in the Ministry of Foreign Affairs during the Soviet period and joined Yeltsin when the latter was elected President of the Russian Republic in 1990 (when it was the largest, but only one of the fifteen republics of the USSR). Kozyrev became Yeltsin's key advisor on foreign policy, playing a role comparable in some ways to that Shevardnadze played for Gorbachev.

A crucial institutional change came in December 1992 when Yeltsin created an Interagency Foreign Policy Commission within the Security Council to replace Gennady Burbulis's personal supervision of Russian foreign policy matters. Removed from direct presidential supervision, Russian foreign policy began to flounder for a sense of direction. Critics charged that it not so much acted as *react*ed to Western objectives, generally by accession. Even Western diplomats, accustomed to dealing with intransigent Soviet negotiators, expressed a certain discomfort at the degree to which the Russian side now seemed eager to reach agreement on Western terms.

In response to Kozyrev's repeated requests for greater control over foreign policymaking, in March 1995 Yeltsin issued a new "Statute on the Russian Ministry of Foreign Affairs" that consolidates its authority over all aspects of foreign policy and made the foreign minister directly accountable to the President. The Russian press has interpreted this decree as sharply enhancing the foreign minister's role in coordinating both the strategy and implementation of foreign policy, but has voiced skepticism about how well it will be observed.[11]

As dramatic as the shift in attitude toward the West was, however, it was over-shadowed by the changes in relations among the former Soviet republics. The agreement signed by the heads of Russia, Ukraine, and Belarus at the hunting lodge at Belovezhskaya pushcha on December 3, 1991 dissolved the USSR and diminished its principal successor state—Russia—by a quarter of its territory and nearly half of its population.

The domestic and foreign policy consequences of this agreement were not widely recognized at the time. Foremost on Yelstin's mind seems to have been the desire to displace the political authority of Gorbachev. International recognition of the independence of the former Soviet republics, however, quickly moved relations with the "Near Abroad" to center stage in Russian foreign policy. During these early years, Kozyrev once remarked that 80% of his time was being consumed by CIS affairs. This meant that foreign policy toward the West, Japan, and the rest of the world had to occupy a lesser place in Yeltsin's foreign policy thinking.

As Yeltsin has tried to fashion a national interest for Russia, he has had to come to terms with the new geopolitical situation of the new Russia. Gradually, the realization of these geopolitical realities led to the demise of the "romantic euphoria" with the West and led to a new debate over what should constitute the Russian national interest. One side of the debate—the "Atlanticists"—argued that a close relationship with the West was essential for Russia. They argue that Western support and good will are crucial to the success of economic reforms and the maintenance of democracy, hence integration into the Western economic, political, and military alliance structure is of paramount importance to Russia. According to the Atlanticists, Russian foreign policy should prioritize the concerns of the West over those of other regions of the globe. Views in this group range from those who seem to suggest that almost no price is too high to pay for Western support for democratic reforms to those who strive for cordial but balanced relations with the West.

The other side, often referred to as the "Eurasianists," see Russia as being weakened by excessive dependence on the West. They feel that Russia must define its national identity on the basis of indigenous traditions, rather than as an imitation of the West. Their name comes from a school of historical thought popular among Russian émigrés in the 1920s and early 1930s.[12] The Eurasianists argue that Russia (both before and after the October revolution) reflected a distinctive historical and cultural tradition, separate from that of Europe and Asia proper. Its geopolitical position spanning eleven time zones give it a unique, integrative perspective on world politics. Russian foreign policy therefore should give priority to Russia's role as a global mediator between Europe to the West, Asia to the East, and Islam to the South. If she looks only to the West it will be only a peripheral and secondary actor on the world stage; whereas if it pursues its own destiny, Eurasianists say, it will be able to rely on its natural advantages and very quickly again become a major player on the world stage. Views in this group range from those who see Russia as merely needing to balance its excessive concern with the West with an equal concerns for the Middle and Far East to those who see the West as orchestrating an anti-Russian conspiracy designed to reduce Russia to a group of loosely connected city-states.

Despite important differences, there is considerable common ground among these two competing visions of the Russian national interest. This common ground has become the foundation for a new foreign policy consensus that is expressed in the "Key Tenets of the Concept of Foreign Policy of the Russian Federation" signed into law by President Yeltsin in April 1993.[13] The "Key Tenets" illustrate just how much Russian foreign policy has turned inward, even isolationist, in its new definition of what Foreign Minister Kozyrev terms "fundamental national interests."

Several domestic and international changes made this consensus possible. First, Western powerlessness in ending the bloodshed in Yugoslavia shook the confidence of the Atlanticists, who had argued that integration into the Western alliance system would guarantee domestic stability within Russia. Second, ethnic and political tensions in Georgia, Tajikistan, Moldova, Armenia, and Azerbaijan threatened to spill over to other regions inside Russia, and required immediate attention. Third, the defeat of the self-proclaimed "irreconcilable opposition" to President Yeltsin on October 4, 1993, ended the rhetorical stalemate between the hard-line nationalist opposition and the Yeltsin government. Since then, criticism of aspects of early Russian foreign policy have been more carefully listened to in the Russian Foreign Ministry.

The inward bent of Russia's new foreign policy is illustrated by the description of major threats to its vital interests. As the document puts it: "The vitally important interests of the Russian Federation are connected, first of all, with the development of its relations with the states of the 'Near Abroad.'"[14] These are nuclear instability in the region, the role and status of conventional forces and Russian troops in the region, safeguarding the human and civil rights of Russian citizens living in the region, and the resolution of potential territorial and border disputes.

According to the "Key Tenets," Russia's relations with other states should be shaped very largely by how they advance Russian interests in the Near Abroad. The basic tenets of this concentric foreign policy are said by Russian experts to be modeled on the Monroe Doctrine. They include the following principles:

- "[A]ll of the territory of the former Soviet Union constitutes a vital sphere within which Russia's interests cannot be denied or ignored."
- "Because of the deep historic, political, cultural and other links with the neighboring states, Russian [can] not and [does] not have a moral right to remain deaf to their requests to secure peace."
- The post-Soviet space is a "unique, sui generis geopolitical space, in which no one but Russia could bring peace."
- Russia will "actively oppose attempts from outside the CIS to increase tension between the former Soviet republics."
- Russia will "oppose any plans to increase armed forces in states bordering on the territory of the former USSR."
- Russia will "restrain" the "third" states from "attempts to use in their interests the instability" in the Near Abroad.

In addition, Russia will welcome peacemaking by the United Nations and the Conference on Security and Cooperation in Europe (CSCE), but only on the condition of the "nonpresence" of foreign troops and military bases on the territory of the former Soviet republics.[15]

What then would Russia ultimately like to see happen in the Near Abroad? According to public statements, an economic union (akin to the European Community) that facilitates trade, travel, and human rights; a regional collective security arrangement; and joint peacekeeping of trouble spots in the region that will prevent Russia from becoming politically isolated, yet allow for containing the conflict while minimizing the threat of war.[16] Finally, Moscow intends to accomplish this through an emphasis on economic incentives and voluntary reintegration, reasoning that coercive integration would be resisted, and that there are strong economic and cultural pressures favoring reintegration in any case.

At the same time that Russia lays claim to regional preeminence, the "Key Tenets" assert that its nuclear arsenal, natural resources, size, and population allow it to lay claim as well to an international role as a great power. As a result, Russia expects international acceptance of its "special status" when dealing with neighboring regions, as negotiations over the expansion of NATO in 1995 indicate. Despite its present weakness, Russia does not intend to relinquish its ambitions to be a major player on the world stage and to play a hegemonic role in the CIS. These ambitions continue to be a major impediment to better relations with the West.

In and of themselves, philosophical changes, no matter how radical, cannot alter a nation's foreign policy outlook. They must be accompanied by new institutions that allow the new approaches to be implemented. It soon became apparent that Russian foreign policy would differ substantially from even the Gorbachev era. Although officially it was not until December 18, 1991, that Yeltsin brought the Soviet diplomatic service under Russian control, after the August coup the Russian Republic's young Foreign Minister, Andrei Kozyrev, began to move forward on his new agenda. Just weeks after the August coup, Kozyrev pushed through three strategically inconsequential but symbolically important foreign policy initiatives. First, the Soviet training brigade in Cuba that had so incensed President Carter was removed, removing the last Soviet military presence on the island. Second, all arms sales to the Afghan government were halted, ending any pretense of concern for the fate of the Soviet puppet government there. Third, diplomatic relations with Israel were restored, twenty-four years after they had been broken off in the aftermath of the Six Day War of 1967.

The scope of the changes the new Russian Foreign Ministry undertook have dwarfed even those of the Gorbachev era. They remind one of U.S. Secretary of State Dean Acheson's phrase that taking over the conduct of foreign policy in the immediate aftermath of World War II, he felt as though he had been "present at the creation." All foreign ministry staff were forced to reapply for their positions, with professional competence and loyalty to the new regime being the chief criteria for the jobs. Through this mechanism, Kozyrev was able to effect a "big-bang" generational transformation within the foreign ministry, removing older-generation Soviet diplomats and active communists and replacing them with deputy ministers and heads of departments who were, like himself, in their late thirties or early forties.

At the same time, the Russian MFA (RMFA) was restructured into a more logical and hierarchical structure. The old regional administrations were transformed into seven departments: Europe, North America, Central and South America, Africa, the Near East, Asia-Pacific region, and South West Africa. In May 1992, a department for relations with CIS states was added, along with departments for International Organization and Global Problems of International Humanitarian Assistance and for Cultural Cooperation.

While these restructuring and personnel changes brought in a much needed generational change, in the short run it weakened the ability of the RMFA to elaborate and conduct a professional foreign policy.

In January 1996, President Yeltsin appointed the director of the Russian Foreign Intelligence Service (SVR), Yevgeni Primakov, to replace Andrei Kozyrev as Foreign Minister. From 1985 to 1989 Primakov served as director of the prestigious government think tank IMEMO (Institute for International Economics and International Relations). An expert on the Middle East, Primakov was reputed to be one of the architects of Gorbachev's "new thinking" in foreign policy and served as one of his senior foreign policy advisors.

In his very first press conference after assuming his new responsibilities, Primakov outlined his top four priorities. They included: (1) fostering external conditions that strengthen Russia's territorial integrity; (2) encouraging peaceful integrative processes among the CIS states; (3) stabilizing regional conflicts in the CIS and in the former Yugoslavia; and (4) preventing the spread of weapons of mass destruction.[17]

His first two objectives clearly indicate an intention to shift the foreign ministry's attention away from the West and toward relations within the CIS. Not surprisingly, therefore, his first foreign policy initiative was a tour of CIS capitals, during which he launched a new effort at shuttle diplomacy between Armenia and Azerbaijan aimed at resolving the festering conflict between those two nations; pledged to increase diplomatic support for Russian business ventures in the CIS; and reaffirmed Russian commitments to the governments in Tajikistan and Georgia, both engaged in their own civil wars.

While Primakov's appointment reflects a generational reversal, replacing the younger, less-experienced Kozyrev with a member of the former Soviet foreign policy establishment, in all likelihood it does not signal a radical departure from the immediate past. Primakov is merely continuing the process, already begun under Kozyrev, of making closer relations with the CIS the key objective of Russian foreign policy. By the end of 1995 Kozyrev's name had become a lightning rod for the political opposition in the parliament, so when he won election to the Duma from his home district of Murmansk, it gave him a graceful way to leave the cabinet.

As far as relations with the West go, Primakov is clearly skeptical of Western claims of benevolence and, like nearly all Russian political figures, opposes NATO expansion eastward. At the same time, however, he has urged ratification of the SALT II treaty and stressed that Russia would continue to seek an "equal, mutually beneficial partnership with the West."

Primakov is expected to bring to Russian foreign policy the stability and professionalism that critics say it lacked under Kozyrev. As head of the SVR, Primakov is given credit for elaborating an analysis of Russia's position in the world that clearly outlined its geostrategic interests, something the foreign ministry failed to do. His clear, if not terribly innovative views should afford considerable predictability to Russian foreign policy, so long as he is foreign minister.

The Presidential Administration

The most significant of these new government bodies is undoubtedly the Security Council, which according to the Russian constitution coordinates Russia's military strategy and must confirm the use of military forces outside Russia. The Security Council has some dozen members representing the key ministries involved in matters of national security: the Minister of Foreign Affairs, the Minister of Defense, the head of Foreign Intelligence Service, the head of Federal Counterintelligence, the Minister of Interior Affairs, the Minister for Nationalities and Regional Politics, and the Minister of Civil Defense and Emergency Situations. As a concession to the legislature, after the Chechen invasion the heads of both the upper and lower houses of Parliament were added to this group.

The real power of the institution, however, apparently resides in its ten interdepartmental commissions, which prepare the reports and policy recommendations for the intermittent meetings of the entire Council. Originally designed to provide a forum within the executive branch where political and economic interests could be balanced against military and security concerns, the unpopular war effort in Chechnya has made it the center of political controversy. The popular Duma representative Yuri Chernichenko has attacked it for being a "secretive, illegal, dictatorial body"; columnist Fyodor Burlatsky has compared its decision-making process in Chechnya to Joseph Stalin's decision to start the Korean War and Nikita Khrushchev's decision to place missiles in Cuba.[18]

After the bungled rescue attempt in Budyonnovsk, where guerillas had seized several hundred hostages in southern Russia and obtained safe passage back to Chechnya, seven ministers tendered their resignations at the Security Council meeting of June 29, 1995. In a concession to parliament and to an outraged public opinion, Yeltsin accepted the resignations of the Director of the Federal Security Services (the successor to the KGB), the Minister of Internal Affairs, and the Deputy Prime Minister. Although the Security Council retains wide-ranging authority to manage areas ranging from combating organized crime to the review of national security policy, in the aftermath of harsh criticism of its conduct in the Chechen war its influence may be curtailed by more careful media and legislative scrutiny.

Despite an unrelenting barrage of press criticism, the disastrously managed retaliatory strike against the hostage takers in Kizlyar in January 1996 did not result in a similar shake-up of senior ministers although after the crisis, new chief of staff, Nikolai Yegorov, announced a reconsolidation of the President's administrative apparatus into six departments, cutting subdivisions from forty-three to nineteen and staff from twenty-one hundred to fifteen hundred employees.[19] Foreign policy issues would be combined with domestic policy issues in one of the six departments, fueling speculation that responsibility for foreign policy would now return to foreign minister Primakov.

The botched rescue effort also served to revitalize public efforts to end the war. Boris Nemtsov, the popular governor of Russia's third-largest city, Nizhnyi Novgorod, collected more than a million signatures in his region on a petition to end the war. Regional legislatures have also passed resolutions calling for an end to the fighting. On the eve of announcing that he would seek a second term of office, Yeltsin candidly acknowledged that the war in Chechnya must be ended before the June elections, or "it would make no sense to seek re-election."[20]

Another institution that wields considerable influence within the executive branch are the intelligence services, which are now divided into two branches. The first, the Federal Security Service (FSK) is responsible for domestic security and has a mandate comparable to that of the FBI in the United States. The second, the Russian Foreign Intelligence Service (SVR) deals with external threats to security and, like the CIA, prepares analytical recommendations on international threats to Russia. The FSK is currently headed by Col. General Mikhail Barsukov, a veteran of the KGB's Ninth Directorate, which was responsible for protecting Communist Party leaders, while the SVR is headed by Yevgeni Primakov's former first deputy, Vyacheslav Trubnikov.

The Parliament

In the new Russia, the executive branch represents only one, albeit the most significant, voice in the foreign policy formulation. Two other areas that also help shape Russian foreign policy are the legislature and independent civic institutions such as the press and think tanks. On the parliamentary side, both the upper and lower houses have set up permanent committees to review foreign policy matters. In the Duma (the lower house of the Russian parliament), these include the Committee of Foreign Affairs, headed by former Russian ambassador to the United States Vladimir Lukin; the Security Committee, headed by Viktor Ilyukhin; and the Committee on Geopolitics, headed by Viktor Ustinov. By far the most influential of these is the Committee on Foreign Affairs, whose head has been active in advocating the need for a distinctive Russian foreign policy agenda since January 1990.[21] His expertise, and centrist policies have allowed him to work quite effectively in forging coalitions among the ordinarily fractious Duma factions. The Committee on Geopolitics, in contrast, by all accounts was created specifically to prevent Vladimir Zhirinovsky's party from laying claim to the chairmanship of foreign affairs. The communist gains in the December 1995 elections saw no major shifts in the composition of the Duma committees dealing with foreign policy. As before, Vladimir Lukin of the centrist Yabloko bloc remains at the head of the foreign affairs committee, the Liberal Democratic Party's Aleksei Mitrofanov retains control of the geopolitics committee, and Lt. General Lev Rokhlin of the progovernment "Our Home is Russia" chairs the defense committee, which is currently reviewing the START II Treaty.

In the upper house of parliament, the Federation Council also has a Foreign Affairs Committee and a Security and Defense Committee. Whereas the leaders of key committees in the Duma have tried to appreciate the government's position and forge a consensus on foreign policy, the Federation Council has been extremely critical of the government, particularly after the invasion of Chechnya. It viewed the use of troops in the region without its consent as a direct challenge to its own authority in matters affecting Russia's autonomous regions. The Federation Council has consequently blocked Yeltsin on a number of regional peacekeeping initiatives by lifting the state of emergency Yeltsin imposed on neighboring regions in the Caucasus and opposing the use of Russian peacekeepers in Abhkazia. Several members of the upper houses Foreign Affairs Committee have called for the resignation of those responsible for ordering the invasion.

In the future the upper house of the Russian parliament may seek to play a more significant foreign policy role, since its avowed agenda of encouraging regionalism may force it to pay greater attention to strengthening ties with borders regions of the CIS. In any case the new speaker of the Federation Council, Yegor Stroyev, a Yeltsin ally, has repeatedly called for strengthening the supervisory functions of the upper house. The next Russian President may well move in this direction in order to counter legislative opposition from the Duma.

Occasionally, though infrequently, the Parliament will pass a resolution that is opposed by the RMFA. Such resolutions are similar to "sense of Congress" resolutions in the United States in that they have no binding effect, but do indicate potential trouble spots in the future. One example was the passage by the State Duma of a resolution on January 21, 1995, calling for Russia's representatives at the United Nations to start a campaign to end sanctions against Serbia, and expressing the Duma's concern over possible NATO bombings of Bosnian Serb targets. In the wake of actual NATO air strikes in September 1995, the foreign ministry position eventually came much closer to that of the Duma.

The Chechen war has also severely undermined relations between the Duma and the executive branch. In April 1995 the Duma took the unusual step of passing a law (by a vote of 286 to 1) forbidding the use of the armed forces unless Russia is invaded by a foreign country, and instructing the government to begin ceasefire talks with Chechen commanders immediately and without preconditions. Several Duma deputies then requested the Constitutional Court to rule on the constitutionality of the government decrees that initiated the military intervention in Chechnya. On July 30, 1995, the court did so, ruling that the President did have the authority to act. At the same time, however, the court struck down two provisions, one restricting media coverage of the event and the other calling for deportation of "dangerous individuals" from Chechnya.[22] Although this conflict between the legislative and executive branches may, ultimately, have had little perceptible impact on the fighting, it has put pressure on the government to pursue negotiations with rebel commanders in Chechnya more seriously.

The Media

The conflict between the executive and legislative branches is exacerbated by the new role being played by the Russian media (particularly the elite press). Today's Russian media seems as uncompromisingly hostile to the government as the Soviet press was subservient to it. Among its favorite targets are corruption among high officials (especially in the army), bureaucratic bloat and incompetence, and the

Chechen war. Despite the dependence of significant segments of the media on continued government subsidy, and even the murder of prominent journalists like Dmitry Kholodov and Vladimir Listyev who sought to expose corruption, the mass media continues to play a key role in shaping public opinion.

Its impact is reflected in the fact that nearly all key ministers and government appointees now hold public press conferences. It has become difficult, if not impossible for the government to maintain secrecy in its deliberations, as classified documents are commonly leaked to the press, which publish them with impunity. In the early stages of the Chechen conflict the government tried to prevent the Russian media from communicating with Russian soldiers in the region, but quickly abandoned this in favor of trying to put its own "spin" on events. The overwhelmingly negative public reaction to the use of force in the region is no doubt due to the consistently hostile coverage of the conflict.

Given the widespread coverage given to the Russian press in other CIS countries, the Russian media can also have a perceptible influence in other regions of the former Soviet Union. The media's outcry over the arrest of the head of the Russian Society of Northern Kazakhstan, Boris Suprunyuk, described in the Russian press as the first political trial of a Russian citizen in independent Kazakhstan, is widely credited with gaining his release on a suspended sentence.[23]

Think Tanks.

A new role in the foreign policy process is being carved out by independent think tanks. While most survive on contracts from various ministries of the Russian government, a few are supported by private Russian entrepreneurs or receive funding from the West (like their counterparts in the West). They very often include prominent journalists, political analysts, and former government officials.

Among the most influential think tanks dealing with foreign policy issues are Club '93, the Suzdal' Club, the Council for Foreign and Defense Policy, and the Gorbachev Foundation. Frequently, membership in these groups overlaps. Yeltsin advisor Sergei Karaganov, for example, belongs to both the Council for Foreign and Defense Policy and to Club '93; Gorbachev Foundation staffers Alexei Salmin and Viktor Kuvaldin are also members of the latter group.

Since the end of the Soviet Union, such groups have become a popular way for the broader foreign policy community to influence the choices made by public officials. The recommendations of the best-known institutes and authors receive wide dissemination in the media, and offer the public (and the legislature) an alternative set of policy options.

Civic and Religious Organizations

Lastly, the Russian foreign policy establishment must now deal with a variety of disparate interest groups that lobby central authorities for changes in policy, or that ever more frequently conduct their own foreign policies. One of the greatest threats here to foreign policy decision making is increasing regional autonomy. Dissatisfied with the perceived "Euro-Atlantic" orientation of the foreign ministry attention in 1992 and 1993, Far Eastern regions have increasingly taken to negotiating their own trade and customs arrangements with their Chinese and Japanese neighbors. The incompetence manifested by Moscow officials during the Chechen conflict has led regional governments in southern Russia to coordinate relief efforts on their own, and has encouraged regional efforts to aimed at altering Moscow's policy in the region.[24]

The Chechen conflict has also spawned new and old civic action groups to oppose the war. Among the more active new groups is the "Soldier's Mothers Committee," headed by Maria Kirbasova, which has received considerable attention in the press and support from leading attorneys like Sergei Alekseyev, former chairman of the Soviet Committee for Constitutional Surveillance, and Valery Savitsky, twice nominated by Yeltsin to a position of the Constitutional Court.

Another important civic organization that is carving out a new role for itself in a democratic Russia is the Russian Orthodox Church. During the Soviet era, the Moscow Patriarchate served as a pliant tool of Soviet diplomacy in international forums. This policy continued, more by inertia than intent, throughout the Gorbachev period. But since 1989, when the Russian Supreme Soviet passed landmark legislation that finally shielded religious institutions from state intrusion, the Church has gradually abandoned political advocacy, while at the same time expanding its missionary activities in Russian society and abroad. In 1994, Patriarch Alexei II signed agreements with both the Ministry of Defense and the Ministry of Internal Affairs on cooperation in enhancing the "spiritual health" of Russian society. As a result, Orthodox priests will be encouraged to visit garrisons and organize educational and religious conferences.

The Church has also actively participated in efforts to establish an Interparliamentary Assembly of Orthodox, which would bring together Orthodox parliamentarians from all CIS states, the Baltic nations, as well as Romania, Bulgaria, Serbia, Montenegro, and Greece. In addition to serving as a forum to "help overcome national and religious conflicts through the unifying spirit of Orthodoxy," the Assembly intends to "use the special role of Greece and Russia in the European Union and the UN Security Council" to increase the visibility of pan-Orthodox concerns. Some political analysts have interpreted this initiative as laying the foundations for a Russian-Greek axis that will seek to promote common objectives in the Balkans.[25]

HOW DIFFERENT WILL RUSSIAN FOREIGN POLICYMAKING BE?

Of the many challenges that face a newly conceived foreign policy, perhaps the greatest is the proper attitude to adopt toward the legacy of the past. Russian foreign policymakers now argue that Soviet foreign policy was deformed by excessive secrecy, compartmentalization, party supervision, and attention to ideological dogmas. Still, over the course of three generations it did develop certain routines that facilitated the conduct of day-to-day affairs and provided an overall direction to foreign policy that post-Soviet Russia is still sorely lacking.

Of course, it is scarcely surprising to find, just three years after the collapse of the USSR, that significant elements of the old foreign policy system still remain in place. Charles Fairbanks has identified four such "legacies of the Soviet operational code": the persistence of collective decision making; the weakness and arbitrariness of the laws; the "shapelessness" of bureaucratic institutions, which encourages widely overlapping responsibilities; and finally, the lingering importance of personal connections. Nor is it surprising to find, as he does, that these patterns work poorly in today's more pluralistic Russian political environment.

But it would be a mistake to overlook how much has changed. Three crucial characteristics of the way Soviet foreign policy was conducted—secrecy, compartmentalization, and Communist Party/ideological interference—have all seriously eroded. Russia national security and foreign policy is now routinely scrutinized in the press. Parliamentary oversight, while still weak, is enhanced by the considerable visibility of individual parliamentarians. Finally, there are now autonomous think tanks as well as civic and religious organizations that seek to mold the opinions of both the elite and the public at large.

Collective decision making as it was practiced in the Soviet Union is a thing of the past. By all accounts the Security Council votes on decisions, with a simple majority being sufficient to carry resolutions. Decisions made by a single-vote majority are not unknown.[26] Finally, while the noted shapelessness of overlapping jurisdictions is indeed a problem in preserving strict accountability, some officials see certain advantages to it. Minister for Nationalities Policy Sergei Shakhrai, for example, seems to view this as a mechanism for guaranteeing that only "the most dynamic and competent institution will survive in the competitive struggle."[27]

The most significant change, however, has been the gradual consolidation of civil society. When one considers the public outrage that ensued after the Chechen debacle, and President Yeltsin's attempts at damage control by broadening the council to include representatives of the legislature, it becomes apparent that the Security Council cannot be equated with the Soviet-era Politburo. Although both have very broad mandates (the Security Council is tasked with the fight against organized crime and drugs, the reorganization of key ministries, as well as the approval of national security strategy) and a penchant for secrecy, within weeks of the Chechen invasion, members of the President's own Analytical Center had published a report in the press critical of the government's decision-making process. The Council's press secretary has repeatedly complained to reporters about the widespread use of anonymous sources and leaked documents by the press.[28]

In retrospect, even foreign policy analysts known for their sympathies toward the West acknowledge that the youthful enthusiasm and "infatuation with the West" of the new personnel at the RMFA was a bit naive, and led to what George Breslauer has termed a "concessionary foreign policy."[29] Some Russian analysts have even gone so far as to reminisce about the usefulness of a guiding ideology.[30] They miss not the rigidity of an imposed dogma, but the practical benefits of a commonly shared higher purpose. Their motto, to paraphrase Voltaire seems to be: "if an ideology does not exist, we shall have to invent one." The days of a doctrine as all-encompassing as Marxism-Leninism, however, are gone. It does appear though that new consensus about Russia's foreign policy prioritiesis slowly replacing it.

The guiding tenet of this new foreign policy consensus is realism. In the often acrimonious debate between Russian nationalists and the Russian foreign minister, it is worth noting the remarkable similarity of the "Key Tenets" to the agenda of opposition Russian nationalists during the Soviet era: the rejection of any mandatory ideology or dogma, and a strong preference for isolationism. These two guiding principles are reflected in former Foreign Minister Kozyrev's recommendation that Russia "should be as far as possible from the conflicts between nations where our direct interests are not engaged."[31] This realism is reflected in the recognition of the limits on Russia's ability to influence events distant from it.

Writing in 1992, Sergei Rogov, the deputy director of the USA and Canada Institute, described Russia's geopolitical priorities as a series of concentric rings. The first and most important ring comprises the states of the former USSR. The second ring includes areas of political, economic, and strategic importance slightly more distant, such as Eastern Europe and the Middle East. The third and least important ring are the distant states of Western Europe, North America, and Japan.[32] As Russia's interests have turned inward, so has the potential for conflict between Russia and other major international actors. Today, all major Russian foreign policy and security issues intersect in the Near Abroad, making it one area of the world where Russian interests could potentially lead to a confrontation with the West. Western policies designed to offset Russian influence in this region and prevent any reintegration of the former Soviet states will no doubt be perceived as direct intrusions on vital Russian interests. These intrusions are all the more threatening because they now occur on the territory of the former Soviet Union.

Yet, while Russia still seeks to exercise hegemony within the CIS, it does not strive to isolate this region from the rest of the world, as the Soviet Union did. Indeed, Russia's new foreign policy establishment welcomes Western involvement in CIS states in both public and private projects that support stability, and economic development, so long as these are pursued with sensitivity to Russia's concerns for human rights and security in the region.

Despite the intense philosophical debates within Russia over its future direction, a greater realism is now apparent in Russian foreign policy than during the first two years after the collapse of communism. That this realism comes at the expense of downgrading relations with the West and especially the United States is less a reflection of the rise of anti-Western sentiment (although that too plays a part) than of the new geopolitical realities that Russia now faces.

SELECTED BIBLIOGRAPHY

Arbatov, Alexei (ed.). *The Security Watershed: Russians Debating Defense and Foreign Policy after the Cold War: Disarmament and Security Yearbook 1991/1992.* Langhorne, PA: Gordon and Breach Science Publishers, 1993.

Aron, Leon, and Jensen, Kenneth M. (eds.). *The Emergence of Russian Foreign Policy.* Washington, DC: United States Institute of Peace, 1994.

Bialer, Seweryn, and Mandelbaum, Michael. *Gorbachev's Russia and American Foreign Policy.* Boulder, CO: Westview Press, 1988.

Bialer, Seweryn. *The Domestic Context of Soviet Foreign Policy.* Boulder, CO: Westview Press, 1981.

Blum, Douglas W. *Russia's Future: Consolidation or Disintegration.* Boulder, CO: Westview Press, 1994.

Clark, Susan L. *Gorbachev's Agenda: Changes in Soviet Domestic and Foreign Policy.* Boulder, CO: Westview Press, 1989.

Connor, Walter D., et al. *Foreign Area Research in the National Interest: American & Soviet Perspectives: Essays.* New York: IREX occasional papers, vol. 1, no. 8, 1982.

Felshman, Neil. *Gorbachev, Yeltsin, and the Last Days of the Soviet Empire.* New York: St. Martin's Press, 1992.

Miller, Robert F. *Soviet Foreign Policy Today: Gorbachev and the New Political Thinking.* New York: Unwin Hyman, 1991.

Murray, John. *The Russian Press from Brezhnev to Yeltsin: Behind the Paper Curtain.* Brookfield, VT: Edward Elgar, 1994.

Nelson, Lynn D. *Radical Reform in Yeltsin's Russia: Political, Economic, and Social Dimensions.* Armonk, NY: M.E. Sharpe, 1995.

Rumer, Eugene B. *Russian National Security and Foreign Policy in Transition.* Santa Monica, CA: Rand, 1995.

Sakwa, Richard. *Gorbachev and His Reforms, 1985–1990.* New York: Prentice-Hall, 1990.

Shearman, Peter (ed.). *Russian Foreign Policy since 1990.* Boulder, CO: Westview Press, 1995.

Shtromas, Alexander, and Kaplan, Morton. *The Soviet Union and the Challenge of the Future,* vol. 4 of *Russia and the World.* New York: Paragon House, 1989.

Staar, Richard F. *Foreign Policies of the Soviet Union.* Stanford, CA: Hoover Institution Press, 1991.

Vachnadze, Georgii N. *Secrets of Journalism in Russia: Mass Media under Gorbachev and Yeltsin.* Commack, NY: Nova Science Publishers, 1992.

Wettig, Gerhard. *Changes in Soviet Policy towards the West.* London: Pinter Publishers, 1991.

Woodby, Sylvia. *Gorbachev and the Decline of Ideology in Soviet Foreign Policy.* Boulder, CO: Westview Press, 1989.

Zacek, Jane S. (ed.). *The Gorbachev Generation: Issues in Soviet Foreign Policy.* New York: Paragon House, 1988.

NOTES

1. Sergei Maksudov, "Prospects for the Development of the USSR's Nationalities," in Alexander Shtromas and Morton A. Kaplan (eds.). *The Soviet Union and the Challenge of the Future,* vol. 3 (New York: Paragon House, 1989), p. 331.
2. See the discussion in Herbert Feis, *Churchill, Roosevelt, Stalin; The War They Waged and the Peace They Sought.* (Princeton, NJ: Princeton University Press, 1967).
3. Michael Karpovich, "Russian Imperialism or Communist Aggression?" *The New Leader,* June 4 and 11, 1951.
4. Samuel Sharp "The National Interest" in Alexander Dallin, (ed.). *Soviet Conduct in World Affairs,* (New York: Columbia University Press, 1960), p. 53.

5. Alex Pravda, "The Politics of Foreign Policy," in Stephen White et al. *Developments in Soviet and Post-Soviet Politics* (Durham, NC: Duke University, 1992), p. 258.

6. Richard Sakwa, *Russian Politics and Society*, (New York: Routledge, 1993), p. 288.

7. Peter Zwick, *Soviet Foreign Relations: Process and Policy* (Englewood Cliffs, NJ: Prentice Hall, 1990), pp. 150–151.

8. Edwina Moreton recounts the famous story of how at the SALT I talks then General Nikolia Ogarkov, the representative of the Soviet General staff, took an American delegate aside and asked that the specific characteristics of Soviet weaponry not be discussed in front of the civilain members of the Soviet negotiating team, since they were not cleared to know them. Cited in Curtis Keeble, *The Soviet State: The Domestic Roots of Soviet Foreign Policy* (Boulder, CO: Westview Press, 1985), p. 131.

9. Richard Sakwa, *Gorbachev and His Reforms, 1985–1990* (Englewood Cliffs, NJ: Prentice Hall, 1990), p. 334.

10. Nicolai N. Petro, "Perestroika from Below: Voluntary Socio-Political Associations in the RSFSR," in Alfred J. Rieber and Alvin Z. Rubinstein (eds.). *Perestroika at the Crossroads.* (New York: M.E. Sharpe, 1991), p. 124.

11. "Yelstin Decrees Enhance Foreign Ministry's Role," *Current Digest of the Post-Soviet Press,* vol. 47, no. 11, 1995.

12. See Alexei Arbatov, "Russia's Foreign Policy Alternatives" *International Security,* vol. 18, no. 2 (Fall 1993), pp. 5–43; and Andrei and Sergei Kortunov, "From 'Moralism' to 'Pragmatism': New Dimensions of Russian Foreign Policy," *Comparative Strategy,* vol. 13, no. 13 (July 1994), pp. 261–269.

13. The discussion of the "Key Tenets" is based on the description provided by Leon Aron in "The Emergent Priorities of Russian Foreign Policy" in Kenneth Jensen and Leon Aron (eds.). *The Emergence of Russian Foreign Policy* (Washington, DC: US Institute of Peace, 1994), pp. 17–34.

14. Jensen and Aron, *The Emergence of Russian Foreign Policy,* p. 25

15. *Ibid.,* p. 29.

16. As Defense Minister Pavel Grachev remarked, "In our view the most probable scenario is not a direct armed invasion of Russia but its gradual entanglement in conflicts in neighboring nations and regions." Cited in Jensen and Aron, *The Emergence of Russian Foreign Policy,* p. 24.

17. Scott Parrish, "Primakov on Russian Foreign Policy," *OMRI Daily Digest* February 16, 1996.

18. Robert Orttung, "Burlatsky: Egorov initiated Chechen War," *OMRI Daily Digest,* January 31, 1995.

19. Robert Orttung, "Yeltsin Consolidates Administration into Six Departments," *OMRI Daily Digest* January 31, 1996.

20. January 30, 1996 (Interfax-Eurasia). Laura Belin, "Nemtsov Asks Yeltsin to Withdraw Troops from Chechnya," *OMRI Daily Digest* January 30, 1996.

21. V. Lukin, "Sovetskaya vneshnaya politika: russkii aspekt" *Izvestiya* (January 18, 1990), p. 5.

22. Scott Parrish, "Details of Constitutional Court Verdict," *OMRI Daily Digest,* August 1, 1995.

23. Bess Brown, "Defender of Russian Interests Sentenced in Kazakhstan," *RFE/RL Daily Report,* September 8, 1994.

24. Robert Orttung, "Regional Leaders to Meet," *OMRI Daily Digest,* Janury 24, 1995; and Robert Orttung, "Irkutsk Considers its Relations with Moscow," *OMRI Daily Digest,* August 4, 1995.

25. Vladimir Socor, "Pan-Orthodox Forum Established," *RFE/RL Daily Report,* November 7, 1994.

26. Suzanne Crow, "Shumeiko Added to Security Council," *RFE/RL Daily Report,* June 7, 1994.
27. Cited in Charles Fairbanks, "The Legacy of Soviet Policymaking in Creating a New Russia," in Aron and Jensen (eds.), *The Emergence of Russian Foreign Policy* (Washington, DC: US Institute of Peace, 1994), p. 63.
28. Laura Belin, ". . . and Vice Versa," *OMRI Daily Digest,* March 7, 1995.
29. Arbatov, "Russia's Foreign Policy;" and George Breslauer, "Selling a Concessionary Foreign Policy" *Post-Soviet Affairs,* vol. 10, no. 3 (July–September 1994), pp. 277–291.
30. Paul Goble, "Kozyrev Advisor sees Special Path for Russia," *Prism,* part 2, July 28, 1995.
31. Jensen and Aron, *The Emergence of Russian Foreign Policy,* note 38 on p. 34.
32. Dr. Mark Smith, "Russia and the Far Abroad: Aspects of Foreign Policy." A Report prepared for the Conflict Studies Research Centre at the Royal Military Academy Sandhurst, England, May 1994, p. 1

Chapter
6

Russia and the Commonwealth of Independent States (CIS)

With the collapse of the USSR, Russia faces the need not only to define its own national interests differently, but to distinguish those interests from those of the nations formerly under its control.

The nature of relations between Russia and the other newly independent states is further complicated by the reluctance of many Russians (particularly of the older generation) to see their neighbors as "others," and by the fact that one of every five Russians now lives outside of its borders.

In the wake of economic chaos and nationalist strife throughout the territory of the former USSR, in many of these new states rampant separatism has given way somewhat to efforts aimed at preserving the ties with Moscow that made good economic sense. Economic linkages between any two republics very often involve transportation over Russian territory or the use of Russian made goods. To stave off its own economic collapse, Russia has provided subsidies on oil and natural resources to its neighbors, who simply cannot afford to pay world market prices.

Yet, closer economic ties come at a price. By fostering economic integration, Russia clearly hopes to reassert its dominance in an area that it considers to be of vital security interest. While some states in the region might be willing to bow to what they deem to be inevitable, others will seek external support in order to counteract the reassertion of Russian hegemony. All of this makes the future of the region potentially volatile.

RUSSIA AND THE NEAR ABROAD

By abandoning the ideological explanation that had for three generations justified Soviet foreign policy decisions, Gorbachev unwittingly called into question the very

113

need for CPSU guidance. By 1990, it seemed that few, if any, Soviet republics even agreed on the need for a single, overarching definition of the national interest.

The first attempts to forge distinctive foreign policy agendas and apparatuses among the Soviet republics began well before the actual break-up of the USSR. In the Baltic States, for example, the first significant step in this direction was the formation of the Baltic Assembly in 1989, an attempt by the leadership of the Popular Front movements in Estonia, Latvia, and Lithuania to coordinate their political activities better.

Two other regions that expressed an early interest in establishing independent foreign policies were Georgia and Armenia. In the case of Armenia, Moscow's heavy-handed attempts to assume direct control over the Nagorno-Karabakh region and ambivalent policies in the region fostered so much resentment that they eventually led to calls for national independence despite the fear of a "pan-Turkic" influence in the region. In the case of Georgia, the tragic deaths of April 9, 1989, when Gorbachev ordered Interior Ministry troops to clear the main square of the capitol, Tbilisi, radicalized the Georgian intelligentsia and led them to call for secession.

Russia, however, was not far behind its neighbors in reasserting national sovereignty and putting more of a "Russian spin" on Soviet foreign policy. Still, for Russian nationalists opposed to the communist regime, foreign policy was not a major issue, compared to domestic reconstruction and eliminating Marxism-Leninism's pernicious influence. To the extent that foreign policy was discussed, there was virtual unanimity on what Russian foreign policy priorities should be: (1) the withdrawal of troops from Afghanistan; (2) the cessation of all military and economic assistance to Third World regimes supported by the Soviet government; and (3) the reduction of the burden of military expenditures. Advocates for an isolationist Russia, like the returned exiled novelist Aleksandr Solzhenitsyn, believed that simply by turning inward, Russian relations with the rest of the world, and particularly the West, would improve rapidly.[1]

While the efforts of Russian political opposition groups were not as successful as those in Eastern Europe, their ideas did resonate among certain official circles, and helped to provide a receptive environment for the emergence of a distinctive Russian foreign policy agenda by the end of the 1980s. One early champion of the creation of a distinctive Russian foreign ministry was Vladimir Lukin, the first post-communist Russian ambassador to the United States, and subsequently chairman of the International Affairs Committee of the State Duma. Back in January 1990 he wrote a provocative article in *Izvestiya* in which he complained that Russian interests had never received more than token attention in Soviet diplomacy. He goes on to cite a number of areas in which Russia (as distinct from the USSR) should take the foreign policy initiatives, including the Far East, where he advocated closer ties with the countries of the Pacific Basin, and the United Nations, where he says Russia should strive to obtain its own seat, like the Ukraine and Belarus.

In his campaign for a seat in the first democratically elected Russian Supreme Soviet, Boris Yeltsin was also quick to spot the popular appeal of a distinctive Russian foreign policy. He called frequently for high-level direct relations between the Russian Federation and leading Western countries and, as president of the Russian Federation before the August 1991 coup attempt, went out of his way to recognize the independence of the Baltic States and sign treaties of nonaggression with the three Baltic heads of state.

Since the collapse of the USSR, Russia has sought to reverse the process of disintegration and to strengthen the ties that bind the other CIS states to Russia. In his New Year's address to the Federation Council in 1994, President Yeltsin remarked that "it is Russia's vocation to be the first among equals" in its relations with the CIS. Russia clearly hopes that it can bind these nations closely to itself with interpenetrating military, economic, and political ties. The key to success in the strategy, according to Foreign Minister Kozyrev, is transforming Russia into a "locomotive of reform" that will become irresistibly appealing to its neighbors.[2]

The Russian approach has been to lead the former Soviet states to accept Russian leadership through a carrot-and-stick approach. The "carrots" are security under Russia's nuclear umbrella, domestic stability and territorial integrity guaranteed by CIS peacekeeping forces, and access to the trade opportunities and natural resources of Russia. The "sticks" are the possibility of economic sanctions against those who refuse to cooperate, emphasis on the civil rights of the large Russian diaspora, and tacit encouragement of opposition and secessionist forces within the republics.

The mechanisms for fostering integration are the series of interstate and interministerial treaties being worked on within the framework of the CIS. The key CIS documents signed to date are the CIS Charter, signed by the heads of state at a summit in January 1993; the collective security agreement, concluded in Tashkent in May 1992; and the Treaty on Economic Union signed in Moscow on September 24, 1994, by nine of the former Soviet republics. The Charter outlines the various cooperative structures established by the CIS states since December 1991 and also prescribes rules for interaction among member states. By 1994 it had been signed and ratified by nine states. The Tashkent treaty outlines the structures and mechanisms for collective self-defense of CIS states. As with NATO, an attack on one member is to be regarded as an attack on all. Levels of commitment to this treaty range widely, from strong support (Armenia, Belarus, Russia, and Tajikistan), to conditional support (Azerbaijan, Georgia, Kazakhstan, Uzbekistan, and Kyrgyzstan), to rejection of the agreement (Moldova, Turkmenistan, and the Ukraine).

The Treaty on Economic Union provides a framework for the gradual creation of a common economic space on the basis of market relations. It envisages the gradual reduction and eventual abolition of all customs tariffs, a payments union, and a multicurrency clearinghouse to be run through an Inter-State Bank, which would eventually lead to a currency union.

In September 1995, President Yeltsin issued a wide-ranging decree on "The Establishment of the Strategic Course of the Russian Federation with Member States of the CIS," which laid out the major objectives of Russian policy in the region.[3] According to this decree, the goal of Russian relations with the states of the CIS should be to "create an economically and politically integrated alliance of states capable of achieving a worthy place in world society." As the dominant power in this alliance, Russia should take the lead in forging "a new system of inter-state political and economic relations over the territory of the post-Soviet expanse."

A major portion of the decree is devoted to enhancing economic cooperation among the CIS states by encouraging three types of unions: an Economic Union, a Customs Union, and a Payments Union. By integrating all the CIS states into a customs union, Russia hopes to bind them closely to the Russian economy and to strengthen the "strategic partnership between these states. The normative aspects of this economic integration are to be left to the Interparliamentary Assembly of the CIS. The final stage of economic integration, the Payments Union, will establish common foreign currency regulation and exchange rates, make each currency within the CIS mutually convertible, and encourage the use of the Russian ruble as a reserve currency. Other major sections of this decree deal with national security (section 3) and humanitarian cooperation and human rights (section 4) and emphasize the familiar goals of safeguarding the interests of Russian citizens (both in Russia and in the Near Abroad) through closer integration with Russia.

Although it is too early to predict whether Russia's attempts to forge a closer union under the aegis of the CIS will be successful, it seems safe to predict that, whatever its aspirations, Russia will be forced to accommodate to the foreign policy aspirations of the new countries on its borders. Although these foreign policies are being developed from scratch in countries still struggling with the concept of independent nationhood, as these states establish themselves as independent actors in world affairs, some notable differences with Russia are bound to emerge.

These differences will reflect not only vastly different cultural heritages, but also differing geostrategic interests. For the sake of simplicity, they may be divided into four groupings: The Transcaucasian states of Armenia, Azerbaijan, and Georgia; the Central Asian states of Kyrgyzstan, Tajikstan, Turkmenistan, Uzbekistan, and the Kazakh Republic; the Slavic states of Belarus, the Ukraine, and its neighbor Moldova; and the three Baltic States—Estonia, Latvia and Lithuania.

THE TRANSCAUCASUS: AZERBAIJAN, ARMENIA, AND GEORGIA

The three former Soviet republics in the Transcaucasus—Azerbaijan, Armenia, and Georgia—sit at the crossroads of the Christian and Islamic worlds and are therefore subject to a variety of conflicting pressures. In addition, unresolved ethnic and territorial disputes in each country have contributed to an increasing dependence on Moscow since independence.

Azerbaijan and Armenia have been battling for control of the Nagorno-Karabakh Autonomous region since a majority of the Armenians in the region expressed a desire for greater autonomy from Azerbaijan in 1988. Initially they demanded only autonomy, but after this was rejected they proclaimed an independent Nagorno-Karabakh Republic and seceded. The Armenians, outnumbered more than two-to-one in population, looked to their traditional ally Russia for support against the Azeri-Azerbaijanis. In return for Russian military, political, and economic support, Armenia has been one of the strongest supporters of firm ties with Russia. It was one of the first states to ratify the CIS charter, and among the first to permit (along with Tajikistan and Georgia) the stationing of Russian military troops in its territory.

In July 1993 a military coup led by Colonel Suret Huseinov (who had providentially been left a huge stockpile of arms by the withdrawing Soviet forces) removed the nationalist government of Abulfaz Elchibey in Baku with former Soviet Politburo member Geidar Aliyev. Under Aliyev, Azeri-Azerbaijani foreign policy lost its pro-Turkish orientation and shifted noticeably toward Moscow. While Elchibey took Azerbaijan out of the CIS, in September 1993 Aliyev visited Moscow to correct "serious errors" that had derailed Russian-Azeri-Azerbaijani relations. As a first step, he announced that Azerbaijan would join the CIS.

Still, the improvement in relations did not prevent Aliyev from signing a ten-year Treaty of Friendship and Cooperation with Turkey in 1994 that includes a provision to provide mutual assistance in the event of aggression by a third party. The current Azeri-Azerbaijani leadership relies on expanded commerce and credit from the neighboring and kindred Turkey to play a major role in maintaining their independence from Moscow, and Turkish officials have encouraged this attitude.

By withholding its participation on CIS treaties on military cooperation and the sharing of intelligence, Baku has put pressure on Moscow to accommodate Azeri-Azerbaijani concerns. One the of the most important to the future of the region is the disposition of the rich oil reserves of the Caspian Sea. Azerbaijan has pursued its own course, signing a deal with an British-led consortium to develop the region's oil reserves. The Russian Foreign Ministry, however, has taken the position that the resources of the Caspian Sea should be treated as a common patrimony of the states in the region (an "internal sea"), and has even proposed economic sanctions against Azeri-Azerbaijan if it fails to comply with Moscow's wishes.

The Russian government, however, remains divided over how best to proceed, given its many competing interests in the region. As the largest country in the region, a key link between Europe and the Turkish world, and a gateway to three seas, Russia has a keen interest in anchoring Azerbaijan firmly into the CIS. Azerbaijan, however, has explicitly linked its participation to the successful resolution of the Nagorno-Karabakh dispute. On the other hand, Moscow does not wish to antagonize its long-time allies Armenia and Georgia by appearing to favor the Azeri-Azerbaijanis. Lastly, Russia must be wary of Turkey, which has been increasingly open about its desire to be seen as the leader of a pan-Turkish alliance of Central Asian states.

Moscow has found an unlikely ally in Iran, which sees Turkey as its main competitor in the region and which threw its weight behind the Russian designation of the Caspian as an "internal sea" after the United States pressured Baku to cancel a lucrative oil deal with Iran in April 1995.

Despite the prospect of more than $35 billion in oil revenues flowing into the country as a result of the agreements signed in 1994, Azerbaijan's foreign policy options in the near future seem limited. The country's current economic weakness was graphically demonstrated when Russia sealed its northern borders in order to isolate Chechnya. Russia can also decisively swing the course of the struggle with Armenia over Nagorno-Karabakh decisively against the Azeri-Azerbaijanis if it so chooses. Finally, since all the littoral states on the Caspian Sea have challenged

Azerbaijan's right to conclude unilateral agreements, it is not yet clear how the oil is to be delivered. The most promising alternatives to the existing pipelines that stretch through Chechnya is to ship the oil through the Georgian port of Batumi. Given the Russian naval presence in the neighboring Georgian port of Poti, however, this does not make the oil any less dependent on Moscow's good will. Russia's leverage over Azerbaijan, therefore, is likely to sharply condition the foreign policy options of both Armenia and Azerbaijan, as indicated by the security agreement signed between Azerbaijan and Russia in June 1995, which calls on all the former Soviet republics to join in enhanced security cooperation within the framework of the CIS.

Georgia's initial reluctance to join the CIS has gradually given way to a recognition that, as Georgia's Ambassador to Russia put it, "Georgia's independence depends to a great extent on Russia's position. Georgia will be independent if Russia wants it, and vice versa."[4] Weakened by separatist movements in Abkhazia and Southern Ossetia, and racked by internal civil conflict that ensued after the ouster of the country's first independent President, Zviad Gamsakhurdia, the current political leadership, headed by former Soviet foreign minister Eduard Shevardnadze has come to regard the 20,000 Russian peacekeepers in these regions as the price his country must pay to preserve Georgia's territorial integrity. The bilateral treaties signed by Georgia on February 3, 1994, allowed Russia to establish permanent military bases in the country and to station troops on the border with Turkey.

President Shevardnadze has argued that accommodating Russian interests in the region is a strategic necessity, given Georgia's multiethnic composition, lack of domestic energy resources, and the historical legacy of Persian (Iranian) intervention. He has even taken the highly unusual step of openly supporting Moscow's efforts to curtail "aggressive nationalism" in Chechnya, perhaps hoping that Moscow will in return allow him to reestablish authority over his own secessionist regions.[5] In return, Russia has rescheduled over $135 million in debts to Russia and has switched from supporting Abkhaz separatism to promoting autonomy for the Abkhaz with a federalized Georgian state.

As with Armenia and Azerbaijan, Russia's ability to manipulate separatism in Georgia has made Tbilisi dependent on Moscow, and has brought it so much into the fold of Russian security interests that the Russian Defense Ministry cites the Russo-Georgian base agreement as the model for other CIS countries.

CENTRAL ASIA: KAZAKH REPUBLIC, KYRGYZSTAN, TAKIJISTAN, TURKMENISTAN, AND UZBEKISTAN

Despite the fact that for a thousand years Central Asia has played a central role in the development of Muslim culture (Tamerlane had his capital in Samarkand and literary Persian was first used in Bukhara), the five republics—the Kazakh Republic, Kyrgyzstan, Tajikistan, Turkmenistan, and Uzbekistan—have been quite eager to participate in the non-Moslem CIS. In addition to signing on to the basic CIS treaties, each of these countries has signed bilateral treaties of Friendship and Mutual Cooperation with Russia. In the words of Uzbek President Islam Karimov,

Russia is the guarantor of "stability and peace in our region and preserving the integrity of our frontiers. . . . Uzbekistan cannot see its future without Russia."[6]

One major reason seems to be the determination of the region's thoroughly secularized and highly Russified political elite to hold on to power. The future of this region will thus be determined by whether the demise of communism spawns a modern, secular, Western-oriented state along the model of present-day Turkey, or whether those countries will instead embrace the pan-Islamic concept of a "Unified Millat" identified with fundamentalist Iran.

For now, the first priority for the states in the region is economic recovery. These nations, traditionally among the poorest in the USSR, have been deprived of many subsidies from Moscow, and must now seek to diversify their economy and industry. The end of Soviet economic support has led these countries to look to its southern neighbors for support, and in particular to the Economic Cooperation Organization (ECO). This council—which originally consisted of Iran, Turkey, and Pakistan—expanded On November 30, 1992, to include all five Central Asian republics. For the time being, however, the ECO has no funds, no permanent secretariat, and no credible political or economic agenda.[7]

Another major problem in the region is staunching the outflow of skilled specialists back to the European portions of the CIS. In Tajikistan—where since declaring independence a civil war has been raging between the communist-led government and the opposition Movement for Islamic Renaissance—only 80,000 Russians are left in a republic where they once numbered over 600,000. Since many local factories and government facilities were run by these European specialists, this loss represents an internal "brain drain" that has made Tajikistan and other states in the region receptive to Russian government demands for dual citizenship and guarantees protecting the rights of local minorities. On December 23, 1993, Turkmenistan and Russia signed an agreement permitting dual citizenship. By the end of 1995, similar treaties have been drawn up with Kyrgyzstan, Belarus, and Tajikstan, but they have not yet been signed.

The exception here has been Kazakhstan, where, despite a sharp decline since independence, Russians still constitute more than a third of the population. Together with Ukrainians and Russified Germans, non-Kazakhs comprise almost half the population. In addition, many ethnic Kazakhs speak only Russian, and only 37.2%, according to Abish Kekilbayev, the chairman of an official committee on nationality policy, "know their language well."[8] Under the leadership of its charismatic President, Nursultan Nazarbayev, Kazakhstan has tried to establish itself as the leader of the region. In July 1994, at the initiative of Kazakhstan, the leaders of Kazakhstan, Kyrgyzstan, and Uzbekistan agreed to form a Central Asian Union, building on the economic and customs union that had been agreed to just seven months before. According to communiqués, the union would work toward comprehensive defense and economic integration, under the guidance of an interstate committee headed by the prime ministers of each country. The committee will be tasked with standardizing laws, coordinating foreign affairs and defense, and establishing a Central Asian Bank for Cooperation and Development.

Nazarbayev has gone even further, repeatedly urging the creation of a "Eurasian Union" that should provide more effective guidance to the shape of the CIS. For Nazarbayev, this Union would not replace the current Commonwealth of

Independent States, but would rather resemble a body like the European Commission within the European Union. The idea has been received with lukewarm enthusiasm outside the region, although parts of it—such as an agreement on collective security that would broaden the existing Collective Security Treaty signed by Russia, Kazakhstan, Kyrgyzstan, Tajikstan, Uzbekistan, and Armenia on May 15, 1992—have been endorsed by Russia.

Moscow is likely to favor greater integration in the region for several reasons. First, it anchors the region even more closely to Russia, which already dominates the monetary systems of all states in the region except Kazakhstan. Further integration is likely to increase pressure on the lone holdout to join the "ruble zone." Second, because the political leadership of these states opposes the spread of Islamic fundamentalism, greater integration should better coordinate efforts aimed at reducing the penetration of Islamic militancy in the region, thereby stabilizing Russia's southern borders. President Nazarbayev, for example, has spoken with sympathy of Russia's need to create a security zone in the "belt of uncertainty" that stretches from Russia to India.[9] Third, the region's large Russian population is well represented in the Kazakh legislature; there will clearly be a need to accommodate the interests of Russians living in the region, and Russian interests generally. Lastly, Russia hopes that such regional integration will be but a prelude to greater integration into the CIS, as evidenced by Kyrgyzstan's desire to join the Russian-Belarus-Kazakh customs union established in January 1995 (indeed, by October 1995 Uzbekistan, Kyrgyzstan, and Tajikistan all indicated that they wished to join).[10]

On the other hand, the Kazakh Republic's decision not to join the ruble zone, the discrimination against non-Kazakhs in recent Parliamentary elections, the December 14, 1993, decision by the Kazakh Ministry of Justice to prohibit official registration on all Russian community organizations, and restrictions on the Russian Orthodox Church and Russian-language education have increased tensions with Russia.[11] It is also clear that President Nazarbayev sees himself as a leader both within the CIS and on the world stage, and is unwilling to take a back seat to Yeltsin. He envisions a Kazakhstan that serves as the heartland of Eurasia, and the true bridge between Russia and China. While maintaining close ties with Russia, he has encouraged the reopening of rail, air, and road links to China, where more than a million Kazakhs live just across the border in Xinjiang. He has also welcomed the interest of U.S. oil companies in the Kazakh Republic's economic development, pointing out that only about 1% of The Kazakh Republic's oil reserves have been exploited to date and that increased Western investment could reduce its dependence on OPEC.[12]

The Kazakh Republic's full geostrategic importance to Russia derives from the fact that its independence

- improves the prospects of Turkmenistan, Uzbekistan, Tajikstan, and Kyrgyzstan surviving as independent states;
- largely ends the likelihood that Moscow will soon resume an imperial-minded policy in Central Asia;
- strengthens the buffer zone between Russia and the Middle East; and
- eliminates Moscow as a threat to the flow of Persian Gulf oil or to the key oil-producers of the region—and, in the process, precludes a revival of a

major source of past tensions between Washington and Moscow during the period of the U.S.-Soviet Cold War.

An essentially indefensible borderland region, the Kazakh Republic faces many of the classic problems of nation building, including the need to stabilize relationships with its neighbors, develop a national identity, train native elites, and find a way of building institutions suitable to its political culture and economic potential. Solutions to these difficulties must be accomplished without triggering an interventionist response from Russia, on which the Kazakh Republic remains heavily dependent. Kazakhstan may, in time, emerge as a regional power in its own right. For the moment, however, it must forge a common identity for all inhabitants of the country and avoid polarization along ethnic lines.

Ultimately, the political survival and future economic well-being of the Central Asian leaderships are highly interdependent: no one of them can succeed without support from, or reliance on, the others. To this end, there is need for a network of meaningful (as opposed to symbolic) bilateral relationships, expansion of interrepublic trade, joint investment projects of mutual benefit, especially in the areas of water resources and conservation, energy, transportation, and communications, and finally, reassurance to Moscow that the civil rights of minorities are being protected.

It is perhaps too early to discern a pattern in the foreign policies of the Central Asian States. But the Kazakh Republic, Uzbekistan, and Kyrgyzstan seem to be prompted by a sense of what is important. All three, in varying degrees, have taken steps to establish close political and economic ties with Russia, as well as with Turkey and, to a lesser extent, Iran. All three have also been active in forging ties with China, India, the United States, and key Western European countries. They are also taking the lead in regional cooperation agreements, such as the twenty-one-point agreement on enhancing regional economic and security cooperation, signed in August 1995 in Bishkek by the five Central Asian heads of state, along with the Prime Minister of Turkey. By contrast, Turkmenistan and Tajikistan have been more cautious than their neighbors, either because of a greater sense of dependency on Moscow, or because of a desire to maintain a more neutral stance, for the time being.

Once again, oil is likely to be a prime factor in regional politics. If Russia can retain its position as defender of the Central Asia while the region becomes a major oil and gas producer, then its international stature will be improved. By contrast, if Russia fails to maintain its influence in the region, its relative importance in world affairs is likely to decrease.[13] This helps to explain Foreign Minister Kozyrev's remark, regarding Central Asia, that "We must not abandon those regions that have for centuries been spheres of Russian interests. And we must not be afraid to say so."[14]

UKRAINE, BELARUS, AND MOLDOVA

The three newly independent nations of Belarus, Ukraine, and Moldova now represent a new buffer zone between Russia and Europe. Their geostrategic location, close historical and cultural ties to Russia, and substantial Russian populations make them particularly important to defining Russia's relations with Europe.

The small country of Moldova, sandwiched between Romania and the now-independent Ukraine, shares no common borders with Russia, but given the presence of a sizable Russian and Ukrainian population that fears Moldova's reintegration into Romania, relations with Russia have not been smooth. In an effort to dilute the separateness of the region and tie it more firmly to the USSR, Stalin created the late Moldovan Soviet Socialist Republic by merging Bessarabia (which he had seized from Romania during World War II) with Ukrainian districts. Currently, nearly two thirds of the population is Moldovan (Romanian), and one third Russian or Ukrainian, concentrated in the region across the Dniester River. This side, which has never been part of Romania, fears that the Moldova will be reabsorbed into Romania and so since before the collapse of the USSR has been waging a civil war in the region to prevent reabsorption. Their efforts were supported, until 1994, by the presence of the Russian Fourteenth Army headed by the populist General Aleksandr Lebed.

Faced with the real possibility that the country might fragment, its leadership has come to terms with restoring close ties with Russia through the CIS. After intense fighting in early 1992 failed to resolve the issue, Yeltsin and Moldovan President Mircea Snegur signed an agreement setting a three-year term for the withdrawal of the Fourteenth Army in October 1994. In return, Moldova agreed to grant more autonomy to the "Dniester Republic." Following the electoral success of the more pro-Moscow Agrarian Party in the February parliamentary elections, Moldova rejoined the CIS in April 1994 and deemphasized its ties with Romania. In August 1994, General Lebed was removed from command of the Fourteenth army, and an accord was reached on the gradual withdrawal of Russian troops from the region.

Belarus faces an even more drastic identity crisis. Polls indicate that more than a quarter of the country's population considers itself Russian, and nearly two thirds favor having Belarus reabsorbed into Russia.[15] In addition, the 1994 Presidential elections in Belarus saw the upset victory of the strongly pro-integrationist Aleksandr Lukashenka. Although the two countries have not officially merged, they did sign a monetary and customs agreement on April 12, 1994, that goes a long way toward returning Belarus to the "ruble zone." In July 1995, Belarus and Russia eliminated customs controls, and simultaneously Belarusian president Aleksandr Lukashenka announced the suspension of the withdrawal of nuclear missiles from Belarus to Russia, arguing that the transport was no longer necessary since the countries may soon reunite. Belarus has also taken a very critical view of efforts to expand NATO eastward. Along with Russia, Moldova, and the Ukraine, Belarus has threatened that in the event of an expansion of NATO, it might be forced to review its commitments to reduce conventional forces under the CFE Treaty.[16] Georgia has also expressed its opposition to NATO expansion, saying that Russia should not be militarily isolated.

Clearly, the most strategically and psychologically important country in the region for Russia is the Ukraine. Roughly the size of France, both in size and in population, the Ukraine has a potentially rich agricultural base, has a well-developed industrial infrastructure, and is the world's third largest nuclear power.

Ukrainian national security and foreign policy is conditioned by the fact that 22% of its population, primarily concentrated in the heavily industrialized eastern third of the country and in the south, is Russian. In addition, the Ukraine is heavily dependent on Russian oil, which is now sold to it at world prices.

The new President, Leonid Kuchma, won election in July 1994, thanks to the overwhelming support of the Russian speaking population, which favors closer ties with Russia. Still, a number of issues remain that continue to hamper close relations with Moscow. The foremost among these has been the disposition of the Soviet Black Sea Fleet. Despite several tentative agreements, the fate of the 833 ships has not been decided in more than four years of negotiations. The Massandra agreement of September 1993 negotiated by former President Kravchuk would have restored the entire fleet to Russia in exchange for wiping out the Ukraine's debt, but was rejected by the Ukrainian Parliament. Despite the desire of the fleet to remain united, many Ukrainians see it as a matter of national pride to have their own fleet. A subsequent agreement, signed in April 1994 gives the Ukraine 15 to 20% of the fleet, but its implementation has been stymied over the issue of where to base them. Although obviously an important political obstacle, militarily the ships have become less and less significant as the negotiations have dragged on, since there is little money on either side to restation and refurbish it.

Another obstacle has been relations between Kiev and the island province of Crimea. In 1954 Soviet leader Nikita Khrushchev decided to transfer administrative jurisdiction over Crimea from the Russian Soviet Federated Republic to the Ukrainian Soviet Socialist Republic to commemorate the 300th anniversary of the union of Russia and the Ukraine. This transfer made no difference to the residents and, under Soviet rule, meant nothing. Early in 1991, however, the Crimean regional Soviet claimed the status of an Autonomous Soviet Socialist Republic, and since the Ukraine declared its independence in December 1991, it has sought to gain autonomy from Kiev. Perceived encroachments by the Ukrainian parliament on their autonomy have radicalized the Crimean Parliament, which declared Crimea's independence from the Ukraine on May 5, 1992. In March 1995, Kiev took the further step of formally dissolving the Parliament and placing Crimea directly under Ukrainian government control. The cause of Crimean independence has been supported by the Russian Duma, but disavowed by the Russian government and foreign ministry, who prefer to treat it as an internal Ukrainian matter. At the same time, it is a particularly sensitive issue for Ukrainian nationalists, who see it as a crucial test of Kiev's ability to impose a new sense of national allegiance and the dominance of Ukrainian culture in areas heavily populated by Russians. In August 1995, President Kuchma rescinded his decree and returned power to the Crimean legislature, now packed with officials loyal to Kiev. In this important test of will concerning regional separatism, Kiev has won.

While Belarusian foreign policy increasingly mirrors that of Moscow, the Ukraine has sought to preserve a certain distance from Moscow. To date this has not been excessively problematic for Moscow because in its dealings with the rest of the world, Kiev and Moscow rarely disagree. Moreover, Kiev appears to be content with the role of a nonnuclear regional power, supportive of collective security and economic cooperation within a general European framework.

Like the Kazakh republic, the presence of a large Russian population, along with the strong linguistic, cultural, and religious ties between the two countries, argues against major differences emerging between the two largest Slavic states of the former Soviet Union. The key to Moscow's satisfaction, presidential foreign policy advisor Sergei Karaganov has remarked, is a close relationship with Belarus: "Belarus is an absolutely crucial country for us. . . . Once we are in close alliance with Belarus, the problem of Ukraine will virtually be solved."[17]

THE BALTIC STATES: ESTONIA, LATVIA, AND LITHUANIA

By far the weakest link in the chain of political, military, and economic accommodations reached by Russia with the former Soviet republics are Baltic republics of Estonia, Latvia, and Lithuania. They have refused to join the CIS and have sought instead to ally themselves more closely with Western Europe and NATO.

As early as 1989, on the eve of the first session of the newly elected Congress of People's Deputies in Moscow, the leadership of the Popular Front Movements of Estonia, Latvia, and Lithuania issued a "Declaration of the Rights of the Baltic Nations" in which they reiterated their common aspiration for "independent cooperation with other nations and governments . . . [and] governmental sovereignty in a neutral and demilitarized Balto-Scandia."[18]

While the ultimate form that relations with the USSR should take was still being debated, there was broad agreement about the need for an independent foreign policy, particularly with regard to Scandinavia. To assuage Soviet security concerns, the Popular Fronts advocated that the entire Baltic region be transformed into a single economic market, demilitarized and neutral. Each state in the region would enter into its own diplomatic and economic accords, but would also maintain close consultation with its neighbors. Disputes were to be resolved on that basis on existing UN conventions, the CSCE, and international law.[19]

Today the foreign policies of all three states are based on the premise that Soviet occupation was illegal. Hence, the first priority was obtaining the withdrawal of Soviet forces stationed in the region (the last forces from Estonia and Latvia withdrew in August 1994, a year after they had left Lithuania). Even with the withdrawal of Soviet troops, however, the problem remained of how to treat the several hundred thousand nonnatives who emigrated to or were born in these countries during the years of their occupation. In Lithuania, where non-Lithuanians constitute only 11% of the population, this issue has been resolved by facilitating access to Lithuanian citizenship. In Estonia and Latvia, where nonresidents comprise nearly a third of the population, the government has taken a harsher position, actively encouraging nonnatives to leave. The Estonian citizenship law, for example, defines anyone not living in the country prior to 1938, or a direct descendant of such, as an immigrant. Immigrants who arrived prior to 1990 had two years to apply for residency, or Estonian or Russian citizenship, or face deportation. Although this deadline was extended under international pressure, only Estonian citizens are allowed to participate in elections, and many nonnatives have complained that their attempts to obtain citizenship have been made more cumbersome precisely to discourage their political participation.

The Russian Foreign Ministry has labeled these laws a variety of "ethnic cleansing," and appealed to the international community for support. In 1993, a CSCE commission did advocate certain changes in the law, which were adopted.[20] While the issue of establishing equal rights for all those who live in the Baltic states is not yet resolved, the March 1995 elections held in Estonia are evidence of some progress toward the integration of the non-Estonian community. A significant number of non-Estonian citizens of the republic participated, allowing the "Our Home is Estonia!" party to pass the 5% threshold and place seven members in parliament. The nationality law passed by the Latvian Parliament in June 1994, however, is still deemed by the Russian Foreign Ministry as making it extremely difficult for a Russian resident to become a citizen, and Russia has warned that the law undermines Russo-Latvian relations. In April 1995, Russian Foreign Minister Andrei Kozyrev added to the Baltic's suspicions when he remarked that "in some cases it may be necessary to use armed force as a means of defending our citizens and compatriots abroad."[21]

Another difficulty that continues to plague the region in its efforts to counterbalance Russian influence is the slow pace of cooperation among them. Understandably, the three Baltic nations do not wish to be simply lumped together indiscriminately, since each nation has its own distinctive history, language, and culture, which is only now again beginning to flourish. Historically, however, the three states have been slow to cooperate among themselves, competing instead for access to lucrative foreign markets. The most progress has been made in the coordination of mutual defense and foreign policy. In February 1995, the three nations agreed to establish more permanent funding for a Baltic Peacekeeping Battalion (BALTBAT) that is designed to participate in UN peacekeeping operations. In foreign affairs, the Baltic States have sought to avoid being lumped together with the CIS, and want instead to be considered a part of Central Europe. They have argued for a rapid expansion of NATO and the European Union eastward, arguing that failure to include the Baltic are a would lead to a "security vacuum" in the region.

Among the former Soviet republics, the foreign policy of the three Baltic States appears to be the most directly at odds with that of Moscow. The Balts seek the extension of European Union and NATO protection over them in order to guarantee their sovereignty, while Russia sees these extensions, if done in a manner that excludes Russia, as hostile and threatening. Russia's objective, by contrast, is to anchor the Baltic States firmly in Russia's sphere of influence, while preserving their distinctive role as Russia's window to the West. This would allow Russia to allay its security concerns and to safeguard the interests of the Russian minority in the region.

There is considerable Russian leverage that makes it likely that accommodation in the region will be reached on Russia's terms:

- The Baltic States remain dependent on Russia for natural gas and other energy supplies;
- Russia remains their largest trading partner, as well as a necessary partner in transit trade from any of the CIS states; if the Baltic states balk at Russian trade

contacts, then Russia can turn to Finland as an alternative. As a member of the European Union, trade with Finland become all the more desirable for Russia;

- The financial infrastructure of the Baltic region is still closely tied to that of Russia, as the collapse of Latvia's Baltija Bank in August 1995 has illustrated;
- The substantial Russian populations in the Baltic provide an additional source of pressure for Moscow;
- While supportive of Baltic independence, officials from both the European Union and NATO have made it clear that they do not want Baltic membership to be seen as an act of defiance and confrontation with Moscow, hence they have sought to dampen Baltic expectations of quick admission; and
- The geographic proximity of the Baltic States to Russia, their large Russian populations, and the presence of the heavily fortified Russian outpost of Kaliningrad on the Baltic Sea south of Lithuania, all add to the pressure that Russia is able to exert in the region.

Despite contrasting foreign policy objectives, agreements have been reached that bode well for the future. After protracted negotiations, all Soviet troops have been withdrawn. Estonia has also relinquished its insistence that the 1920 Treaty of Tartu, signed between Estonia and the USSR be the basis for future relations and all boundary demarcations. Negotiations over simplifying border crossing for local populations have been largely successful.

The sine qua non for good relations with Russia would appear to be explicit recognition of the independence of these three states. If this can be guaranteed, then realism would seem to dictate considerable accommodation to Russian foreign policy interests, a point recently acknowledged by Estonia's Foreign Minister, Riivo Sinijarv, when he said that in the future Estonian-Russian Relations should be modeled on those between Finland and Russia.[22]

REINTEGRATION OR SEPARATION?

Independence has been a mixed blessing for the former Soviet republics, including Russia. Shifting the burdens of statehood from Moscow to regional capitals has proved more costly and more difficult than anticipated. In addition, many of these new nations now face the challenge of separatism within their own borders. Lacking the resources of established armies and security forces, many have acceded to Moscow's desire for closer ties in return for help quashing rebellion and staying in power.

Every CIS state is thus torn between two paramount objectives. One, preserving its newly won independence; another, preserving its territorial integrity. Unfortunately, these objectives are often in direct conflict with one another. As Sergo Mikoyan, a former analyst for Latin America for the Soviet Foreign Ministry and the son of former Politburo member Anastas Mikoyan, has aptly remarked, the process of independence has in many instances been accompanied by the transfer of an "imperial mentality" from the center to the outlying regions—in Georgia, Moldova, Tajikstan, and the Caucasus new regimes have moved quickly to squelch dissidents and separatists. A number of others, such as the Kazakh Republic, Russia, Belarus, and Uzbekistan have become increasingly authoritarian, strengthening presidential authority at the expense of the legislature. These tensions have added to the economic and military dependence of these regimes on Moscow.

While technically, Russian relations with the Near Abroad fall under the category of foreign policy, they cannot truly be treated as any other foreign policy issue for several reasons. First, there is the matter of sheer numbers. Nearly 25 million former Soviet citizens of Russian ethnicity now reside in the Near Abroad. In countries like Estonia, Latvia, Kazakhstan, and the Ukraine noncitizens constitute a quarter or more of the population. Second, their legal status, including access to basic civil rights, has been restricted in many regions and become a source of contention between Moscow and its neighbors.

Third, Russia's industrial and economic infrastructure is still heavily integrated with that of its neighbors. Early efforts to simply cut those ties have proven too economically damaging, and have given way instead to efforts to restructure these relations along mutually profitable lines.

Fourth, Russia is still involved militarily in most of these states, in the form of peacekeeping forces or military bases. Indeed, the current national security strategy approved by the Security Council involves the retention of military facilities in at least thirty locations outside the Russian Federation, in what Defense Ministry officials call Russia's "zone of stability." A key aspect of Russia's new security concept is negotiating a common defense strategy among the former Soviet republics that strengthens mutual responsibility for the defense of the external borders of the CIS, while making the internal borders as transparent as possible.

Since independence failed to produce the anticipated economic well-being, a certain disillusionment has set in, and there is increasing talk of forging a closer integration of the CIS states. Such voluntary reintegration is in the air for several reasons.

First, economic necessity. It is now apparent that it will be many years before the countries of the former Soviet Union will have industries able to compete on the world market. Rather than competing against each other, therefore, some economists argue that it would be preferable to give preferential treatment to trade and commerce within the CIS, where established economic ties merely need to be rationalized and revived.

Second, cultural ties. Over the course of several centuries there has been extensive cultural intermixing among the many peoples of the former Russian Empire and the Soviet Union. As Ronald Gregor Suny has pointed out,

> Russian intellectual culture also serves as an integrating force, remaining as influential and attractive to many non-Russian intellectuals as it has since the 18th century. For Central Asians, Transcaucasians, and the smaller nationalities of Siberia and the Volga, the Russian language has been a window to the West and the Russian intelligentsia a model of humanistic, cosmopolitan values. In more sober moments, non-Russians may appreciate that Russians are not all to be identified with the ruling party and government elite, but include people who share their interests in a freer, more democratic, and more tolerable life.[23]

Even today, some 17.4% of Russians live outside Russia, 15.3% of all Ukrainians live outside the Ukraine, 21% of Belarusians live outside Belarus,[24] providing a strong Slavic cultural presence in many of the newly independent states, particularly in the larger cities and industrial centers. While the leadership of these republics may wish to curtail the effects of "Russification" and promote indigenous cultures suppressed by Soviet rule, there is also a frank recognition that Russian remains the lingua franca of the CIS, particularly in matters of commerce and science. Rather than abandon this bond entirely (thereby alienating an important domestic constituency), most leaders say they would like to establish themselves as bridges between Russia and the outside world.

Third, there is the issue of military security. In addition to severe budget constraints, the newly independent states face the additional difficulty of having to fund an army and border patrol to defend their sovereignty. Moreover, with the possible exception of the Ukraine, the size and inexperience of that fighting force is not likely to provide a significant deterrent against aggression. In the belief that the absence of an agreement might serve to justify unilateral Russian action, therefore, at the 1994 CIS leader's summit, the prime ministers of all but two states (Azerbaijan and Armenia) agreed to long-term military integration, including a CIS collective security system and doctrine, joint defense of borders, joint peacekeeping operations, the formation of a CIS rapid deployment force, and cooperation in standardizing military equipment and production.[25]

Finally, there is the issue of international stature. As new members of the international community, these nations have numerous hurdles to overcome in gaining acceptance and stature. However, by supporting the Russian strategy of promoting the CIS as one of the world's larger and more critical international organizations, states with otherwise minor resources have a greater opportunity to voice their common concerns than any one of them singly. For now this strategy serves the interests of both Russia and its neighbors, as the recent example of the joint appeal by Russia, Kazakhstan, Kyrgyzia, Tajikistan, and Uzbekistan to the UN Security Council for full-scale peacekeeping operation in Tajikistan shows.[26] As these nations become more prosperous and self-reliant, however, it is likely that their interests will begin to diverge. On the other hand, if Russian policy is seen as excessively intrusive, or if economic improvements do not come about quickly enough as a result of greater integration, Russia's strategy of putting intense pressure on its neighbors to reintegrate is likely to encounter stronger resistance. In either instance, however, Russia will continue to play a very important role in the domestic and foreign policies of the former Soviet republics for many years to come.

SELECTED BIBLIOGRAPHY

Allworth, Edward (ed.). *Central Asia, 130 Years of Russian Dominance: a Historical Overview.* 3rd ed. Durham, NC: Duke University Press, 1994.

Atkin, Muriel. *The Subtlest Battle: Islam in Soviet Tajikistan.* Philadelphia: Foreign Policy Research Institute, 1989.

Cranston, Alan MacGregor. *Central Asia in Transition: A Report to the Committee on Foreign Relations, United States Senate.* Washington, DC: Government Printing Office, 1992.

Dailey, Erika. *Human Rights in Moldova: The Turbulent Dniester.* New York: Helsinki Watch, 1993.

Dannreuther, Roland. *Creating New States in Central Asia: The Strategic Implications of the Collapse of Soviet Power in Central Asia.* Adelphi paper no. 288. London: Brassey's for the International Institute for Strategic Studies, 1994.

Jawad, Nassim, and Tadjbakhsh, Shahrbanou. *Tajikistan: A Forgotten Civil War.* London: Minority Rights Group, 1995.

Joenniemi, Pertti, and Vares Peeter (eds.). *New Actors on the International Arena: The Foreign Policies of the Baltic Countries.* Tampere, Finland: Tampere Peace Research Institute, 1993.

Karimov, Islam A. *Uzbekistan: The Road of Independence and Progress.* Tashkent: "Uzbekiston", 1992.

Karklins, Rasma. *Ethnopolitics and Transition to Democracy : The Collapse of the USSR and Latvia.* Washington, DC: Woodrow Wilson Center Press, 1994.

Kis, Theofil I. *Nationhood, Statehood, and the International Status of the Ukrainian SSR/Ukraine.* Ottawa: University of Ottawa Press, 1989.

Kuzio, Taras, and Wilson, Andrew. *Ukraine: Perestroika to Independence.* New York: St. Martin's Press, 1994.

Kuzio, Taras. *Russia–Crimea–Ukraine: Triangle of Conflict.* London: Research Institute for the Study of Conflict and Terrorism, 1994. Conflict studies No. 267.

Lieven, Anatol. *The Baltic Revolution: Estonia, Latvia, Lithuania and the Path to Independence.* New Haven, CT: Yale University Press, 1993.

Malik, Hafeez (ed.). *Central Asia: Its Strategic Importance and Future Prospects.* New York: St. Martin's Press, 1994.

Mandelbaum, Michael (ed.). *Central Asia and the World: Kazakhstan, Uzbekistan, Tajikistan, Kyrgyzstan,and Turkmenistan.* New York: Council on Foreign Relations Press, 1994.

Motyl, Alexander J. *Dilemmas of Independence: Ukraine after Totalitarianism.* New York: Council on Foreign Relations Press, 1993.

Rubinstein, Alvin Z., and Smolansky, Oles (eds.). *Regional Power Rivalry in the New Eurasia.* Armonk, NY: M.E. Sharpe, 1995.

Senn, Alfred Erich. *Gorbachev's Failure in Lithuania.* New York: St. Martin's Press, 1995.

Smith, Graham (ed.). *The Baltic States: The National Self-Determination of Estonia, Latvia, and Lithuania.* New York: St. Martin's Press, 1994.

Taagepera, Rein. *Estonia: Return to Independence.* Boulder, CO: Westview Press, 1993.

Zaprudnik, Jan. *Belarus: At a Crossroads in History.* Boulder, CO: Westview Press, 1993.

NOTES

1. Nicolai N. Petro, "New Political Thinking and Russian Patriotism: The Dichotomy of Perestroika," *Comparative Strategy,* vol. 9, no. 4, 1990, pp. 351–370.
2. Dr. M.A. Smith "Russian Hegemony in the Near Abroad," A Report prepared for the Conflict Studies Research Centre, The Royal Military Academy Sandhurst, England (July 1994), pp. 3, 18.

3. English-language summaries are provided in *The Washington Times*, September 22, 1995, and in Kathleen Mihalisko, "Yeltsin Outlines Strategy for a Renewed Superpower," *Prism: A Bi-Weekly on the Post-Soviet States*, vol. 1, no. 21, part 1, October 6, 1995. All quotes are from the latter source.

4. Vladimir Socor, "Hardening Russian Line on Treaties with CIS States," *RFE/RL Daily Report*, September 29, 1994.

5. Victor Yasmann, "Shevardnadze Supports Russian Action in Chechnya," *RFE/RL Daily Report*, December 15, 1994.

6. Smith, "Russian Hegemony in the Near Abroad," p. 10.

7. Alvin Z. Rubinstein, "The Geopolitical Pull on Russia," *Orbis*, vol. 38, no. 4 (Fall 1994), p. 586.

8. David Nissman, "The Ethnic Factor in Central Asia," *Prism: A Weekly on Post-Soviet States*, August 11, 1995 (Part C).

9. Bruce Pannier, "Nazarbayev Calls for Eurasian Econmic Union," *OMRI Daily Digest*, June 9, 1995.

10. "Will Three More Countries Join CIS Customs Union?" *Monitor: A Daily Briefing on the Post Soviet States*, October 19, 1995.

11. Rubinstein, "Geopolitical Pull," pp. 581–82, 586.

12. Liz Fuller, "Nazarbaev Proposes 'Alternative' to OPEC," *OMRI Daily Digest*, January 31, 1995.

13. Robert V. Barylski, "The Russian Federation and Eurasia's Islamic Crescent," *Europe-Asia Studies*, vol. 46, no. 3 (1994), p. 12

14. Rubinstein, "Geopolitical Pull," p. 579.

15. Ustina Markus, "Belarusian Majority Favors Restoration of the USSR", *RFE/RL Daily Report*, March 25, 1994.

16. Doug Clarke, "Several CIS Countries Might Disavow CFE Cuts," *RFE/RL Daily Report*, No. 236, December 15, 1994.

17. Valdimir Socor, "Russian View on Policy on Europe," *RFE/RL Daily Report*, August 30, 1994.

18. Nicolai N. Petro, "The Nationalities and Soviet Foreign Policy in the 1990s," *Collection Choix*, vol. 21, 1990, p. 71.

19. *Ibid.*, p. 73.

20. "Moscow is Pressured to Defend Rights of Russians in Balitc States," *Boston Globe*, July 5, 1993, p. 5

21. "Fate of the Russian-Speaking Population of CIS and Baltic Countries," *International Affairs*, (May 1995), p. 133.

22. Reported by the Baltic News Service, May 24, 1995

23. Ronald Grigor Suny, "Nationalism and Ethic Unrest in the Soviet Union," *World Policy Journal*, vol. 6, no. 3 (Summer 1989), p. 524.

24. Lillia Shevtsova, "Post-Soviet Emigration: Today and Tomorrow" in Daniel Kubat (ed.). *The Politics of Migration Policies: Settlement and Integration, the First World into the 1990s*, (New York: Center for Migration Studies, 1993), p. 361.

25. "Military Decisions" *RFE/RL Daily Report*. In addition, Moldova ruled out participation in political or military undertakings; and the Ukraine agreed to participate within the framework of its internal legislation.

26. *Golos Rossii*, February 17, 1995.

Chapter
7

National Security in an Era of Flux

T here was a saying among Sovietologists that the Soviet Union does not have a military-industrial complex, it is one. This saying reflects the tremendous burden that military expenditures placed on Soviet society. After several years of placing Soviet military expenditures at 6 to 8% of the gross national product, in 1976 the CIA doubled that estimate to between 12 and 14%.[1] By the early 1980s, however, reform-minded economists in the Soviet Union like Abel Aganbegyan speculated that the true figure might be higher still. Of a work force of some 100 million they said, between 30 and 40 million worked for military industries, placing the percentage of income devoted to national defense at somewhere between 40 and 50%. By contrast, during this period the United States spent 6 to 7% of its GNP on defense.[2]

What made this emphasis on defense all the more burdensome were the steadily declining rates of economic production, summarized in the table below.[3]

In the face of these declining rates, known to Soviet leaders as early as the late 1960s, the political leadership decided to maintain growth rates in consumer goods production and military allocations and to sacrifice investments for long-term capital reconstruction. The result was a planned deterioration of the economic infrastructure, which temporarily preserved the size of the Soviet military but crippled it economically.

Table 7.1   AVERAGE ANNUAL RATES OF GROWTH OF SOVIET GNP

1951–1960	5.8
1961–1970	5.1
1971–1975	3.8
1976–1980	2.8

The full cost of prioritizing military expenditures is, however, only partially reflected in the numbers. The military also siphoned off priority raw materials, requisitioned the most talented individuals, and preserved distinct lines of production for military goods even in civilian factories. Moreover, since all this effort was shrouded in secrecy, the military had no incentive to reduce costs, contain waste and fraud, or to share the benefits of its research with other sectors of the economy. The stranglehold of military secrecy was so great that a member of the Soviet general staff at the Strategic Arms Limitations Talks (SALT) once even went so far as to ask the American delegation not to discuss the characteristics of Soviet weaponry in front of Soviet diplomats![4]

THE ROLE OF THE MILITARY IN SOVIET FOREIGN POLICY

In order to explain how the Soviet leadership could justify such massive military spending, one must look at the role of the military in Soviet foreign policy.

During the period from 1918 (when the Red Army was created) to 1939 (when World War II started), the key aims of military policy were the preservation of the Soviet state and defense against external threats. Between September 1939 and June 1940, the USSR incorporated Estonia, Latvia, Lithuania, part of Finland, and Bessarabia and Bukovina from Romania, all of which were temporarily disgorged as a result of the Nazi invasion on June 22, 1941. Following the period of annexations and expansion after World War II, the military was assigned the additional task of defending the USSR's imperial order in Eastern Europe and East Germany. Also, as a result of the direct assistance rendered by the Red Army, the People's Republic of China and North Korea consolidated their power in the Far East. In this way, the basic goals of Soviet foreign policy in World War II were realized: "The capitalist encirclement of the USSR and its isolation were broken, a belt of socialist states along Soviet borders was created, and the Soviet Union acquired the position of a world power."[5] Discouraging intrasystemic efforts to break away from Moscow's hegemony or a Marxist-Leninist political system, the Soviet armed forces suppressed rebellions in Eastern Europe in 1953, 1956, and 1968, and by demonstrating overwhelming military force and determination, they dissuaded the Western powers from any intervention. In addition to their deterrent function, they enabled Soviet diplomats to negotiate with NATO countries from a position of strength.

Finally, the Soviet military was an indispensable adjunct of Moscow's "forward policy" in the Third World. Soviet arms, advisers, and sheltering shields aided client states and undermined Western positions. In a number of instances, Soviet combat forces actively participated in engagements to defend and promote the interests of Third World clients. This international outreach was especially evident during the Khrushchev and Brezhnev eras.

Like other great powers, Russia pursues foreign policy goals by military and nonmilitary means. In the past, during periods of stability and strength, the military has served for deterrence, defense of the homeland, diplomatic clout in bargaining with adversaries, and power projection in the pursuit of influence. Its use varies depending on such considerations as the domestic situation, the nature of the external threat, and the opportunities available for strategic, political, and economic advantage.

By the 1980s, however, no amount of ideological commitment could erase the fact that military expenditures had become an excessive burden on society. Both Khrushchev and Brezhnev had alluded to this burden, and had attempted to alleviate it by negotiating arms control agreement with the United States. Faced with declining Soviet economic production, Gorbachev tried to reconceive the military's role so that it placed less of a burden on society. These attempts help to explain the priority given to arms control and disarmament in Soviet foreign policy. Under Yeltsin this process has continued and been accompanied by a far-reaching reexamination of what national security means for a reduced Russia.

ARMS CONTROL AND NUCLEAR NONPROLIFERATION

Whereas arms control entails placing limits on the quantity and character of weapons and on their deployment, *disarmament* refers to a process in which weapons are destroyed and not replaced. It was a subordinate but useful component of Soviet military and diplomatic strategy. Linked to the traditional imperial and Soviet Russian policy of maintaining a large standing army, in part to redress its technological backwardness relative to the sources of threat, disarmament was a political tool to offset military inferiority. It was Tsar Nicholas II who was instrumental in convening the first world disarmament conference in 1899. Throughout the 1920s and 1930s, when threats loomed from Japan and Germany and when Britain and France were seriously regarded as advocates of another capitalist coalition to destroy the Soviet state, the Soviet government was in the forefront of campaigns for universal disarmament—for example, Litvinov's proposal in 1927 to the League of Nations Preparatory Commission on Disarmament. From 1930 on, it pushed for the modernization of the Red Army.

What is important to keep in mind is that neither Russian nor Soviet leaders ever regarded disarmament as a panacea for ensuring peace; they have always used the appeal of disarmament for political ends. Thus, any detailed examination of Soviet disarmament policy reveals that Moscow exploited the theme as a means of compensating for military and technological inferiority, trying to induce a rival to offer unilateral concessions and limit its military programs, and gaining support internationally and among pacifist-minded groups whose domestic lobbying might affect their government's policies.

The disarmament issue became prominent in the United Nations at a very early stage. At the first meeting of the UN Atomic Energy Commission in June 1946, the United States made a comprehensive proposal for controlling the atom. The Baruch Plan called for the establishment of an international agency to control, own, and operate all nuclear facilities "from the mine to the finished product" and provided for the eventual destruction of existing nuclear weapons, but only after an adequate international inspection system had been set up. Molotov attacked the proposal as intended to guarantee the United States monopolistic possession of the atomic bomb, warning that

> no single country can count on retaining a complete monopoly. Science and its exponents cannot be shut up in a box and kept under lock and key. It must not be forgotten that atomic bombs on one side may draw a reply in atomic bombs, and perhaps something else to boot, from the other side.

(The USSR was then intensely engaged in its own effort to build a bomb.)

By 1947 the Cold War took over and disarmament became a dead issue. From then on, to block Western rearmament programs, the Soviet government regularly condemned NATO (established in April 1949) and launched a global propaganda campaign calling for "the unconditional abolition of atomic weapons and the branding of any government which first used such weapons against another as guilty of war crimes against humanity." Nevertheless, Soviet proposals were important for two reasons. First, they recognized the need to limit nuclear stockpiles and safeguard against surprise attack. Second, they encouraged further discussions. At the Big Four summit conference in Geneva in July 1955, President Eisenhower made his "open skies" proposal, under which each country would carry out aerial photography of the other to detect and thereby to discourage and concentration of military forces that might be used to launch a surprise attack. But Moscow was not about to expose the Soviet Union to such detailed intelligence reconnaissance (though within a decade or so the development of space satellites was to provide each superpower with exactly this type of information-gathering capability).

Over the decades, Soviet diplomacy sought to contain the areas of Soviet-U.S. competition in strategic weapons, reduce the danger of accidental war, and ensure the best possible bargaining environment for the USSR by giving particular attention to four additional nuclear-related issues: (1) limiting nuclear testing, (2) protecting against surprise attack, (3) restricting outer space to peaceful purposes, and (4) confining the proliferation of nuclear weapons.

Limiting Nuclear Testing

Moscow has been an advocate of a nuclear test ban since it was first proposed by Indian Prime Minister Nehru in 1954.

Before March 1958, the United States had rejected proposals calling for a cessation of nuclear tests unless they included a ban on the production of nuclear weapons. Moscow countered with the demand that the use of nuclear weapons be outlawed. It also argued that linking a test ban with an end to bomb production was not practical, for while a cessation of tests could be verified, a production cutoff could not. The United States modified its position and agreed to a moratorium on nuclear testing for one year, effective October 31, 1958; this agreement lasted almost three years.

On August 31, 1961, amid mounting tensions over Berlin, Laos, and the Congo, the Soviet government abrogated the informal moratorium without warning and resumed testing in the atmosphere the next day. This was done despite Khrushchev's statement to the Supreme Soviet on January 14, 1960, that the

> Soviet Government, prompted by the desire to provide the most favorable conditions for the earliest possible drafting of a treaty on the discontinuance of tests, will abide by its commitment not to resume experimental nuclear blasts in the Soviet Union unless the Western Powers begin testing atomic and hydrogen weapons.

It was also done despite the gathering in Belgrade of the first summit meeting of nonaligned Afro-Asian countries, a group opposed to all testing and the target of intensive Soviet diplomatic attention since the mid-1950s. Khrushchev justified breaking the moratorium on several grounds: the requirements of Soviet security, the inability to agree on a treaty, and the testing by France of its first nuclear weapon on February 13, 1960, in the Sahara desert, during the time of the moratorium and allegedly with NATO's blessing. What Khrushchev did not mention was the intense pressure from the Soviet military to test new weapons and catch up with the United States.

After the Cuban missile crisis, the Soviets redoubled their efforts to improve relations with the United States, at the same time that they gave top priority to overcoming their glaring inferiority in strategic weapons. The Treaty Banning Nuclear Weapons Tests in the Atmosphere, in Outer Space, and Under Water was signed in Moscow on August 5, 1963. This was the first concrete result to emerge from post-1945 disarmament negotiations. The treaty does not cover underground testing, ostensibly because of the inability to agree on an acceptable system of on-site inspections but more likely because of the possibility that seismic instruments would not detect all possible violations and because of the resistance from each country's military establishment, which wants to continue testing of low-yield weapons. The treaty is self-executory: it continues to be operative for as long as each signatory observes it. In the event of a putative violation, "each Party shall in exercising its national sovereignty have the right to withdraw from the treaty."

Increasingly reliable ways of distinguishing between natural seismic phenomena and weapons testing enhance the feasibility of further limitations on nuclear testing—the ultimate aim being a comprehensive test ban treaty (CTBT). In 1990, the US and the Soviet Union ratified two subsequent treaties: the Treaty Between the USA and the USSR on the Limitation of Underground Nuclear Weapons Tests (also known as the Threshold Test Ban Treaty), signed in 1974, which prohibits explosions above 150 kilotons (about eight times the explosive power of the bomb dropped on Hiroshima); and the Treaty Between the USA and the USSR on Underground Nuclear Explosions for Peaceful Purposes (commonly referred to as the Peaceful Nuclear Explosions Treaty), signed in May 1976, which limits peaceful nuclear explosions to 150 kilotons and provides for extensive verification procedures, including on-site inspections.

Gorbachev pushed a CTBT, as has Yeltsin since 1992. In July 1985 he announced a unilateral moratorium on all nuclear testing from August 6 until January 1, 1986, and invited the United States to follow the Soviet lead. Through 1986 he extended the moratorium, arguing that ending of nuclear testing "would accelerate the process of entirely eliminating nuclear arms. The logic in this is simple: without nuclear testing the nuclear weapons, which both sides have stockpiled in abundance, cannot be upgraded." To demonstrate its readiness to accept reasonable on-site inspection, Moscow allowed a group of private U.S. citizens (Natural Resources Defense Council) to set up seismic monitoring equipment at three sites that are two-hundred miles from a major testing center at Semipalatinsk, in Soviet Central Asia. However, in the absence of any reciprocal restraint from the United States, the USSR resumed underground nuclear testing shortly after ending its moratorium on February 28, 1987. By the end of the year, it had staged about twenty tests.

The United States opposed a CTBT on two grounds: without on-site inspection, it was impossible to distinguish between low-yield nuclear-weapons tests and natural seismic phenomena; and some testing was necessary in order to develop better nuclear weapons—and this was especially true for the development of nuclear-powered x-ray lasers as part of the "Star Wars" antimissile defense. Now, with the extensive inspection procedure mandated by the INF (intermediate-range nuclear forces) treaty and the greater sophistication of seismic detection, the "cheating" argument has lost much of its former cogency. Therefore, the case against a CTBT rests mainly on the need for continued weapons testing.

On June 2, 1990, at the summit in Washington, DC, Gorbachev and Bush reached agreement on verification protocols for the Threshold Test Ban Treaty (TTBT), but not for the Peaceful Nuclear Explosions Treaty (PNET). The TTBT permits underground nuclear testing up to the 150-kiloton limit, with the following inspection procedures: right to hydrodynamic measurements of nuclear-weapons tests with planned yields above 50 kilotons, on-site inspection for tests with planned yields above 35 kilotons, in-country seismic monitoring for tests above 50 kilotons, and special provisions for unusual cases. On the PNET, the two sides agreed to disagree: They agreed to observe the 150-kiloton limit, but were unable to agree on appropriate verification procedures.

Protecting Against Surprise Attack

As the military capability of the superpowers increased, there was an ever greater need to avoid any kind of war between them and to create safeguards against surprise attack. Such safeguards are difficult to build into a treaty. Advances in military technology inevitably give rise to conflicting national assessments of areas of possible compromise; in some instances they make agreement less imperative, in others, even more so. Thus, on the one hand, fear of surprise attack has been allayed by the development of space satellites and high-altitude photography, which permit reliable information to be gathered about troop movements, missile placements, and the military testing. These national technical means of verification reduce the need for international inspection.

Two other agreements designed to lessen the fear of surprise attack and the danger of nuclear war through inadvertence were signed on September 30, 1971. One is intended to prevent overreaction in the case of an accidental launch of a nuclear weapon; it calls on each party to notify the other immediately "in the event of an accidental, unauthorized or any other unexplained incident involving a possible detonation of a nuclear weapon" and for advance notification of planned missile launches "if such launches will extend beyond its national territory in the direction of the other party." The second agreement improves the hotline service by providing for a direct communications connection via satellite.

Under Gorbachev, a number of agreements were concluded to further lessen the likelihood of surprise nuclear attack: In 1987 Nuclear Risk Reduction Centers (NRRC) were established in Moscow and Washington. Unlike the hotline, which is reserved for communication between heads of state in times of crisis, the NRRCs are used often as a means of exchanging information related to the movement of missiles and developments that might lead to tension. In 1988 an agreement on Ballistic Missile Test Notification provided for prior notification of such tests, and in 1989 an agreement was signed to prevent incidents involving the entry into national territory of military forces from the other party. These have been further strengthened under Yeltsin.

Restricting Outer Space to Peaceful Purposes

In an age when humans have walked on the moon, lived in space for months at a time, and launched unmanned probes to Venus, Mars, and Saturn, the military implications of peaceful exploration of outer space are ever-present. In 1967, the Soviet Union and the United States joined through the United Nations in signing a treaty prohibiting nuclear weapons in outer space or on any celestial bodies. However, by the late 1970s, the Outer Space Treaty had not prevented an ominous race to develop an antisatellite capability.[6]

The Soviet Union had been testing antisatellite (ASAT) weapons since 1968. Such a weapon, designed to destroy communications, navigation, and intelligence satellites, "consists of a simple bomb maneuvered into orbit alongside its intended victim. When the bomb explodes, shrapnel riddles its target like a shotgun blast. No treaty prohibits placing such weapons of pinpoint destruction in orbit."[7] Efforts to negotiate a ban on ASATs were started and broken off during the Carter Administration. In August 1983, five months after President Reagan's "Star Wars" speech, Andropov called for a moratorium on the testing of such weapons, but the deterioration in Soviet-American relations that followed the USSR's downing of a Korean airliner a month later and the impasse over the Pershing II deployment at the end of 1983 temporarily eclipsed concerns over the arms race in space. During the Gorbachev era, the issue waned, as INF and START (strategic arms reduction talks) agreements took form. Under Yeltsin, the end of the Cold War, economic constraints, and skepticism of ASAT's feasibility have discouraged and kept a tight lid on research and development in this field.

Unlike an ASAT weapon, an antiballistic missile (ABM) system is designed to destroy incoming missiles carrying nuclear warheads. In answer to the view that the Strategic Defense Initiative (SDI) contravenes the provisions of the 1972 ABM treaty, which is of indefinite duration and which prohibits the development, testing, or deployment of "sea-based, air-based, space-based, or mobile land-based" ABM systems or components (Article V), Reagan argued in late 1985 that the testing of systems that were not in existence at the time the treaty was signed is not banned.

In calling for negotiations on all aspects of the U.S.-Soviet rivalry in space, Gorbachev stressed particularly the need to contain the SDI. On numerous occasions he warned that the SDI would accelerate the race in strategic offensive weapons and compel retaliatory measures in the field of both offensive and defensive weapons. He saw the SDI as "an instrument for ensuring U.S. military domination" and said that it could destroy strategic stability (that is, the current reliance on mutual assured destruction).

In trying to restrict the SDI, Gorbachev had several objectives: to prevent the United States from effecting a technological breakthrough that could diminish the USSR's security and degrade its offensive capability; to avoid having to divert scarce resources to a new and extremely costly phase of the arms race; to exploit the differences within NATO; and to use arms control to limit a possible U.S. military-technological advantage, as Moscow did in the early 1970s when it used the SALT I treaty to curtail the U.S. lead in ABM development. Whatever his primary goals, Gorbachev's opposition to SDI, coupled with his call for the elimination of all nuclear weapons by the year 2000, underscored the apparent shift in Soviet doctrine in the early 1990s to a strategy of greater reliance on general-purpose conventional forces and a lower level of nuclear deterrence.

Confining the Proliferation of Nuclear Weapons

Moscow's interest in limiting the proliferation of nuclear weapons goes back to 1957 and rearmament of the Federal Republic of Germany. In the early 1960s the USSR assailed the U.S. proposal to provide NATO with a multilateral nuclear force, which was intended to satisfy Bonn without actually permitting it to acquire an independent nuclear capability. The entry of China into the nuclear club in October 1964 and the growing number of countries on the threshold of acquiring a nuclear capability (India, Israel, Pakistan, Iraq, and Japan) raised the importance of nonproliferation in Moscow's overall disarmament policy.

In general, Soviet opposition to the diffusion of nuclear weapons stemmed from a number of pragmatic considerations involving its perception of national security and strategic interests, such as

> a) concern that further nuclear spread might eventually add Nth-power threats to the physical security of the Soviet Union; b) concern that proliferation would undermine the stability of the prevailing U.S.-Soviet nuclear dominance over the international arena by introducing less nuclear principalities led by men of questionable responsibility and rationality; c) fears that local use of nuclear weapons in regional crises might generate enormous escalatory pressures threatening to embroil the superpowers in an unwanted nuclear confrontation.[8]

A convergence of U.S. and USSR interests led to agreement on a nonproliferation treaty (NPT) in late 1967, and the treaty was offered for signature on July 1, 1968. The NPT was ratified and came into effect on March 5, 1970: the delay was dues to a stasis in East-West relations after the Soviet invasion of Czechoslovakia in August 1968. As one of the nuclear weapons states, the Soviet Union undertook not to transfer nuclear weapons or other nuclear explosive devices, or in any way to help a nonnuclear weapon state to develop a nuclear capability. It shared with the United States a desire to prevent the spread of nuclear weapons: in Moscow's case, the principal concern was to prevent West Germany from going nuclear. It was also a consistent supporter of the International Atomic Energy Agency (IAEA), which is responsible for the implementation of safeguards and timely inspections to ensure detection of the diversion of nuclear material from peaceful use. During the period of the Cold War (1945–1991), both superpowers restrained their non-nuclear allies and clients in their respective spheres of influence from developing nuclear weapons. When, in early 1993, tensions erupted between North Korea and the IAEA over Pyongyang's possible development of nuclear weapons and evasion of inspection procedures, Moscow upheld the IAEA's position.

In November 1994, in a speech before the United Nations General Assembly, Yeltsin pressed his efforts for an indefinite and unconditional extension of the Nuclear Nonproliferation Treaty even further, urging the UN to become more involved in coordinated regional security and disarmament issues. Aware of its diminished status as a superpower, post-Soviet Russia has become even more eager to internationalize issues of nuclear proliferation and conflict resolution.

In May 1995, Russia joined the other major nuclear powers, and the overwhelming majority of the NPT signatories, to extend the NPT for an indefinite period. This decision by the NPT review conference represents a vote of confidence in the underlying purposes and accomplishments of the treaty. However, with India, Pakistan, and Israel refusing to sign, continuing difficulties in the IAEA's relations with North Korea and Iraq, and U.S. reservations about Iran's nuclear intentions, the NPT's future is far from assured. Russia's cooperation is essential for success in curbing the ambitions of these regimes: for example, in preventing black market smuggling of weapon's-grade nuclear material, the transfer of nuclear-relevant technologies, and the spread of missile components for their manufacture. All of this, of course, presupposes continued Russian collaboration with the Western powers.

Another step to curtail nuclear proliferation has centered on barring the "emplanting or emplacing" of nuclear weapons on the ocean floor more than twelve miles offshore. The issue was originally raised in 1967 by Ambassador Arvid Pardo of Malta, who urged the United Nations to demilitarize the seabed "beyond the limits of present national jurisdiction and to internationalize its resources in the interest of mankind." The superpowers pushed the military aspect but showed little interest in the economic one. On February 11, 1971, the USSR, the United States, and Great Britain signed a treaty prohibiting "any nuclear weapons and launching installations or any other facilities specifically designed for storing, testing, or using such weapons" from the ocean seabed beyond a twelve-mile coastal zone. The treaty does not ban nuclear-armed submarines or the emplacement of submarine detection devices, items that the Soviet Union tried to include but that the United States forestalled because of the difficulties of verification and the military's interest in perfecting antisubmarine defenses.

There were hints of uneasiness among some Soviet officials over the threats to regional stability represented by well-armed and potentially nuclear-capable countries in the Middle East and South Asia. One article that attracted considerable attention in late August 1990, written by Major-General Vadim Makarevskiy, noted that with time "the source of military threat to the Soviet Union will be less and less the traditional 'possible enemy' [that is, the United States] and more and more the South."[9] This region has acquired even greater importance for Russia since the collapse of the Soviet Union, as venal mafias at home and incipient instability in Transcaucasia and Central Asia expose Russia to possible terrorism and nuclear blackmail.

FROM STRATEGIC INFERIORITY TO SALT

In view of the American nuclear monopoly (July 1945 to September 1949), Moscow placed a premium on maintaining a commanding conventional force capability in Central and Eastern Europe. Implicit in Stalin's strategy of neutralizing the U.S. nuclear advantage, by which the United States could strike targets in the Soviet Union without fear of retaliation, was the belief that the United States could be deterred by the USSR's deployment of substantial conventional forces in the European theater and by the impression that those forces would be used "for a rapid advance to the Atlantic" if America tried nuclear blackmail; moreover, these same forces "also provided insurance against defections in East Europe."[10]

The Soviet Union was the first to test an intercontinental ballistic missile (ICBM) successfully, in late August 1957, and it placed the first space satellite, Sputnik I, in orbit on October 4, 1957. These scientific achievements emboldened Khrushchev to seek political advantages—prematurely, as it turned out. Convinced that the balance of world forces was shifting to the Soviet camp, he precipitated a new crisis over Berlin in November 1958, hoping to wrest concessions from the West—at a minimum, its recognition of East Germany. The year 1959 proved to be an inconclusive one, notwithstanding Khrushchev's visit to the United States. Then on May 1, 1960, a U.S. spy plane was shot down while on a routine mission over the Soviet Union, an event that aborted the summit meeting that had been scheduled for mid-May in Paris. The incident revealed the hollowness of Khrushchev's strategic claims, which the Soviet military had known all along because this was the first U-2 they had been able to shoot down ever since the U.S. intelligence missions had started in 1955, and because they knew how few ICBMs were available (for technical and economic reasons) in the Soviet arsenal. In fact, the undeniable Soviet strategic (that is nuclear) inferiority to the United States was one of the considerations that had led Khrushchev to shy away from supporting Mao Zedong during the 1958 Quemoy crisis and to resist his pressure for a tougher stance toward the United States. At that time, writes Andrei Gromyko in his memoirs, Mao sought Soviet cooperation "for a plan to lure United States troops into the heartland of China, then attack them with Soviet nuclear weapons.[11]

In January 1960 Khrushchev proposed a far-reaching reform of the Soviet military establishment that called for reliance on nuclear-armed missiles to deter any would-be attacker and for a sharp reduction in military manpower to ease the severe labor shortage in Soviet industry. Elements in the military pressed for acceleration of the buildup of strategic forces beyond what Khrushchev thought necessary, as part of the revolution in Soviet military doctrine being formulated by the high command. With other domestic priorities attracting his support, Khrushchev sought an alternative that would minimize defense expenditures on strategic weapons systems and still satisfy the military. Accordingly, to strengthen the credibility of the USSR's nuclear deterrent, Khrushchev agreed in the spring of 1962 to implant short- and intermediate-range ballistic missiles (IRBMs) in Cuba. Not only would the success of this stratagem have enhanced Soviet prestige, punctured Chinese criticisms that Khrushchev was behaving timidly vis-à-vis U.S. imperialism, and demonstrated Moscow's credibility as a patron, but

> the force of some forty MRBM [medium-range ballistic missiles] and IRBM launchers dispatched to Cuba would have narrowed in one quick stroke the actual margin of the U.S. advantage in strategic forces, for it would have had the effect, as Raymond Garthoff has pointed out, of transforming readily available missiles of 1100 to 2200-mile range into "ersatz" intercontinental missiles. In terms of the Soviet Union's then-existing first-strike salvo capability against targets in the United States,

this would have meant an increase of 80%. (*Note:* At the time, MRBMs had a range of about eleven hundred miles; IRBMs, about twenty-four hundred miles. According to information later revealed by the Soviets, all the missiles in Cuba were then SS-4 MRBMs.)

According to Foreign Minister Andrei Gromyko, Khrushchev decided, shortly after returning from a visit to Bulgaria in late May 1962, to deploy a number of missiles in Cuba to protect it from another U.S. attack (in April 1961, there had been an abortive attempt by CIA-supported Cuban exiles to mount an invasion at the Bay of Pigs, in Cuba).[13] Gromyko and other Soviet sources maintain that Khrushchev had no intention of risking a nuclear war but probably expected to sneak in the missiles without being discovered. Had he succeeded, he would have pressed for major U.S. concessions in Europe. The argument that he merely wanted to protect Castro seems somewhat ingenuous. After all, Kennedy had not been willing to use force against Castro in April 1961; why, then, would he contemplate invading Cuba eighteen months later, by which time Moscow had more than 30,000 combat troops on the island? The answer, according to a former CIA Deputy Director for Intelligence, may be that Khrushchev's game was "strategic blackmail": Khrushchev surely meant to shock world opinion into thinking he had got the whip hand over the United States by his unprecedented and menacing deployment of missiles to Cuba. After all, forty-two missiles, the number actually delivered to Cuba, would have doubled the total first-strike capability available to the Soviet Union in the fall of 1962. Having immobilized Kennedy from resorting to nuclear retaliation as a result of this sudden jump to nuclear parity, Khrushchev then would have tried to cash in his chips in Berlin.[14]

Khrushchev's failure in Cuba strengthened his opponents in Moscow. An ever-larger percentage of Soviet defense expenditures was committed to an accelerated buildup of strategic forces, while Soviet diplomacy worked to slow down the U.S. program through a combination of disarmament proposals and extensive antiwar propaganda. When the Kremlin backed down during the Cuban missile crisis, the Soviet military was determined—as the Soviet UN delegate, Vasily Kuznetzov, warned his American counterpart—that this would be the last time the Soviet Union would bow to America's nuclear superiority.

Between late 1953 and 1960, as the leadership sought to adapt to the nuclear age, Soviet military doctrine and the composition of the military forces that served as the instruments of Soviet foreign policy underwent a searching review. The debate was started in November 1953 in the journal of the general staff, *Voennaia mysl'* (Military Thought), by its editor, Major-General Nikolai A. Talenskii. His arguments implicitly challenged Stalin's dogma that the Soviet Union was destined to win any future war by virtue of the advantage of "permanently operating factors," such as a stable, loyal home front; high morale of the army; quality of leadership; and the quantity and quality of military units. Talenskii eventually convinced the Khrushchev leadership that the principles of military science needed revision and that they operated with equal validity for both sides in a conflict. Once freed from the confines of Stalin's dogma, Soviet theorists proceeded to dispute the contention of "some Western ones," who argued that the start of a nuclear war would itself end the war; they insisted that "the success of the nuclear campaign could mean ultimate victory." This put "unprecedented emphasis on the importance of surprise" and on the conditions under which a "pre-emptive war" might be initiated "in order to forestall an attack that is believed to be imminent."[15]

The result of this debate soon became apparent. By January 1960, when Khrushchev unveiled the essentials of a new military doctrine, the Soviet high command had embraced Talenskii's basic argument and moved far beyond it. Henceforth Soviet military writings made it clear that since nuclear war was possible, it had to be analyzed and prepared for like any other war. The USSR's military doctrine and strategic concepts were constantly modified and refined, in keeping with the development of a burgeoning arsenal of sophisticated and varied delivery systems and nuclear weapons.

Starting in 1960 (before the 1962 Cuban missile crisis), the Soviet leadership embarked on a buildup of its Strategic Rocket Forces, which were established as a separate arm of the Soviet armed forces; on the development of theater nuclear weapons, in accordance with a general program of modernizing and upgrading all weapons systems; and on the strengthening of anti-air defense and civil defense. The aims were to improve the country's ability to absorb a possible nuclear attack and to enhance deterrence.

Moscow's determination to redress its inferiority to the United States in strategic weapons brought impressive results. During 1965–1969, the USSR tripled the number of ICBMs (in 1967 alone it more than doubled its force, from three hundred and forty to seven hundred and twenty) and greatly expanded the number of submarine-launched ballistic missiles (SLBMs). By the end of the 1960s, it exceeded the U.S. ICBM force (which had not been increased at all) of 1054 land-based ICBMs, 656 Polaris SLBMs, and approximately 400 to 600 long-range bombers that were deemed sufficient by Washington for an assured destruction capability. Having developed what President Richard Nixon and Secretary of Defense James Schlesinger were later to term "essential equivalence," Moscow agreed to enter into the Strategic Arms Limitation Talks (SALT) with Washington.

For a variety of reasons such as intra-Politburo differences over how to deal with the United States, and the USSR's invasion of Czechoslovakia in August 1968, negotiations did not start in Helsinki until November 17, 1969. These talks dragged on into 1970 and 1971, in an international environment of high U.S.-Soviet tension. In the spring of 1972, even though the United States was bombing and mining North Vietnamese ports, the Kremlin decided to conclude the SALT I agreement, for reasons of its own—whether from satisfaction at having completed its planned expansion of strategic forces, a desire to give impetus to its policy of détente with the United States and garner the long-term economic credits that were a likely part of the package, concern that further delay might jeopardize the entire process, or uneasiness over the Sino-American reconciliation, epitomized by Nixon's visit to China in February.

SALT I was signed by President Nixon and CPSU Secretary Brezhnev on May 26, 1972. It consisted of three agreements. The first is a treaty of unlimited duration on the limitation of antiballistic missile systems, entered into force on October 3, 1972. The treaty prohibits the development of an ABM system, but originally permitted each side to protect its national capital and one ICBM silo launcher area; a protocol was signed in 1974 restricting each side to only one ABM deployment. The second agreement was a five-year interim agreement that entered into force on October 3, 1972. It fixed Soviet ICBM and SLBM launchers at 2350 and American launchers at 1710, thus marking the first time in the nuclear era that the USSR and the United States had agreed to set up quantitative limits on their strategic delivery systems (that is, missiles capable of striking the other's homeland). Bombers were not covered by the agreement. Although it formally expired on October 3, 1977, both sides respected its provisions until a follow-up agreement was reached in 1979.

There were several immediate advantages to SALT I for the USSR. Politically, the Soviet Union was recognized by the United States as a full-fledged and equal nuclear superpower. In the decade since the Cuban crisis, it had moved from inferiority to strategic equivalence. Militarily, through the ban on ABM development, the USSR nipped in the bud the American deployment of a more technologically advanced ABM system, and it negotiated a quantitative edge in offensive delivery systems. This included provision for three hundred and thirteen heavy missiles, compared to none for the United States—a quantitative advantage that became qualitative with the deployment of MIRVed missiles, that is, those capable of carrying more than one nuclear warhead. Economically, the USSR avoided the strains that an ABM race would have brought and was able to concentrate on upgrading its offensive capability. SALT also enabled Moscow to invest heavily in research and development. Finally, Moscow's policy of promoting détente slowed up the U.S. defense efforts.

The 1972 Moscow summit also helped Soviet diplomacy in Europe, by facilitating the convening of the CSCE (Conference on Security and Cooperation in Europe) and the accompanying Western recognition of the territorial status quo in Europe and Moscow's sphere of influence in Eastern Europe—prime postwar Soviet objectives. However, the budding Soviet-American détente went awry in October 1973 over the Arab-Israeli war, in 1974–1975 over competition in Angola, and in 1977–1978 over the Horn of Africa. These regional quarrels, coupled with mounting congressional criticisms of SALT I and the Watergate affair, which forced Nixon to resign in August 1974, made a new agreement limiting offensive weapons more difficult to negotiate.

At Vladivostok in November 1974, President Gerald Ford and Brezhnev agreed to guidelines that established quantitative equality in strategic delivery vehicles; each side was to be permitted a limit of 2400 ICBMs, SLBMs, and heavy bombers as well as a ceiling of 1320 MIRVed missiles. Secretary of State Henry Kissinger exultantly reported that the Vladivostok accord (which was never ratified) put "a cap an the arms race," but closer examination revealed that it actually had raised the threshold of the number of deliverable nuclear weapons.

The Soviet government was prepared to sign an accord on offensive missiles based on the Vladivostok formula, but in March 1977 the new Carter Administration offered its own proposals for a sharp reduction in the quantitative limits. For substantive as well as procedural reasons, Moscow demurred, and the 1972 interim agreement on offensive missiles lapsed in October 1977. However, a month before, the two governments had stated their willingness not to take any action inconsistent with the provisions of the interim agreement, pending negotiation of SALT II.

After two years of protracted negotiations in an environment of deteriorating Soviet-American relations, the USSR and the United States reached an agreement that was closer to the Vladivostok proposals than the Carter Administration's original counterproposals. SALT II produced none of the euphoria of SALT I. On June 18, 1979, at a summit meeting in Vienna, Brezhnev and Carter signed an agreement stipulating that it would "remain in force through December 31, 1985, unless replaced earlier by an agreement further limiting strategic offensive arms." In its essentials, SALT II set a ceiling of 2250 strategic delivery systems, effective January 1, 1981 (prior to this, each party had been permitted 2400). It placed a limit of 1320 on the number of such delivery systems that could be MIRVed, that is, carry multiple warheads. The Soviet Union was permitted to retain a 308-to-0 advantage in heavy silo-based ICBMs (SS-18). The Backfire bomber, which it insisted was a medium bomber, was not included in the formal agreement, but Brezhnev gave assurances that the USSR "does not intend to give this airplane the capability of operating at intercontinental distances," nor does it plan "to increase the aircraft's present production rate. SALT II also placed limitations on the development of cruise missiles with a range in excess of six hundred kilometers. Compliance with the treaty would have been by national technical means of verification.

Although the Soviet government was ready to ratify the agreement promptly, the U.S. government was not able to do so. Carter wanted quick ratification but encountered increasing opposition from the Senate. First, critics of SALT argued that the treaty gave the Soviets too many advantages, including the already-mentioned capability possibly to destroy the entire U.S. land-based ICBM force in a first-strike attack by the mid-1980s. Second, in the summer and early fall of 1979, Carter himself fed the anti-SALT forces by initially magnifying the significance of the Soviet military presence in Cuba and then accepting the status quo when Moscow refused to make even token concessions to help him sell SALT domestically. Third, the anti-Soviet mood in the United States spread in the wake of Moscow's unhelpful position on the seizure of American embassy personnel in Tehran in early November 1979 by Iranian radicals demanding extradition of the shah. The final blow to early ratification was the Soviet invasion of Afghanistan in December. On January 2, 1980, President Carter formally requested the Senate to postpone considerations of the SALT II treaty indefinitely. The chill in Soviet-American relations put the SALT process into deep freeze.

When the Reagan Administration took office in January 1981, Moscow encountered a far more skeptical attitude in Washington toward arms control, as well as a determination to upgrade U.S. strategic and conventional forces and to press forward, in accordance with NATO's 1979 decision, with the deployment of modernized Pershing-IIs and GLCMs (ground-launched cruise missiles) in Western Europe, starting in December 1983. The principal Soviet aim in Europe was to forestall this deployment.

In November 1981, Moscow and Washington began two sets of negotiations: START (strategic arms reduction talks, the new name given to SALT by the Reagan Administration) and INF (intermediate-range nuclear forces, also known as theater nuclear forces or Euromissiles), which dealt with weapons systems having a range of between three hundred and thirty-five hundred miles.

Moscow directed far greater attention to the INF talks. It rejected Reagan's "zero option" proposal, which called for the dismantling of all the triple-war-head Soviet SS-20s (whose deployment had started in 1977 and prompted NATO's 1979 decision and response) in return for U.S. renunciation of its scheduled Pershing-II deployment. Moreover, while mounting an all-out propaganda campaign against the scheduled deployment, the Soviet leadership put an increasing number of SS-20s into operation, indifferent to the uneasiness this occasioned.

In an atmosphere of escalating recrimination, Moscow broke off the INF talks on November 23, 1983, as the first Pershing-IIs were deployed in West Germany and Britain, and on December 8, it recessed START, refusing to fix a date for the resumption of either. One week later, the negotiations in Vienna on conventional force reductions were also adjourned, with no time set for the next meeting. For the next eighteen months the matter remained deadlocked. There were no arms control talks and, amid worsening relations, both superpowers deployed modernized versions of their INF arsenals.

On March 10, 1985, Konstantin Chernenko (who had succeeded Yuri Andropov in February 1984), died, and, on March 12, the day following the election of Mikhail S. Gorbachev as the CPSU's new general secretary. U.S.-Soviet talks on nuclear arms control and weapons in space resumed in Geneva. Behind the Kremlin's decision to return to the bargaining table may have been, first, its realization that having failed to stop the U.S. deployment of Pershing-IIs through an aggressive campaign of propaganda and political intimidation, it had to find a way of neutralizing the military threat that they posed to the Soviet Command and Control Headquarters near Minsk; and, second, its concern over President Reagan's Strategic Defense Initiative (SDI) proposal (commonly called "Star Wars") of March 23, 1983, in which he embarked the United States on a quest for a space-based missile defense system. But far more fundamental considerations were at work.

NATIONAL SECURITY AND ARMS CONTROL UNDER GORBACHEV

Recognizing that the reform of the economy was closely linked to the reduction of military expenditures, Gorbachev set out to reconceptualize the country's national security agenda. First, however, he needed to curtail the military's influence. In 1984, Chief of Staff Marshal Nikolai Ogarkov, who had master-minded the Soviet deployment of SS-20s in Europe in the late 1970s, had been summarily retired. He was rumored to have harbored "unpartylike tenden-cies."[16] At the 1985 commemoration of the October Revolution, the number of Soviet top brass allowed to stand alongside the party leadership atop the Lenin mausoleum was reduced from ten to five, and the traditional procession of mil-itary hardware shortened by half. Most significantly, the new Defense Minister, Marshal Sergei Sokolov, was not upgraded to the full Politburo status held by his predecessor.

After less than a month in office, Gorbachev proposed a moratorium on the development, testing, and deployment of spaced-based weapons and a freeze on strategically offensive arms. What was new were the increasingly specific propos-als, the seriousness that was suddenly infused into arms control negotiations, and the scope of the topics that Moscow was prepared to discuss. There was no break-through at the first Gorbachev-Reagan summit in Geneva in November 1985, but Gorbachev's suggestion of a freeze on all INF deployments in Europe to be fol-lowed by reductions on both sides was suggestive of the flexibility to come. Report-ing to the Supreme Soviet on the summit, he said the arms race must be halted and the process of disarmament accelerated.

On January 15, 1986, Gorbachev issued a major statement on arms control, which, among other things, called for deep cuts in offensive forces, an end to nuclear testing, the development of appropriate verification procedures, and the elimination of Soviet and U.S. medium-range missiles in Europe, "as a first stage on the path to freeing the European continent of nuclear weapons." At the party congress the following month, he discussed the general problem of arms control and disarmament at great length and with considerable candor:

> The character of present-day weapons leaves a country no hope of safeguarding itself sole-ly with military and technical means, for example, by building up a defense system, even the most powerful one. The task of ensuring security is increasingly seen as a political prob-lem, and it can only be resolved by political means. Security cannot be built endlessly on fear of retaliation, in other words, on the doctrines of "containment" or "deterrence." Apart from the absurdity and amorality of a situation in which the whole world becomes a nuclear hostage, these doctrines encourage an arms race that may sooner or later go out of control.
>
> In the context of the relations between the USSR and the USA, security can only be mutual. . . . The highest wisdom is not in caring exclusively for oneself, especially to the detriment of the other side. It is vital that all should feel equally secure, for the fears and anxieties of the nuclear age generate unpredictability in politics and concrete action.

Although dismissing the policies that were pillars of Western security—con-tainment and deterrence—Gorbachev's implicit call for strategic stability and "mutual security" and his renewed interest in the SALT/START process elicited receptive reactions in many Western quarters. Still, the hurdles were formidable: disagreement over what constituted adequate verification and Moscow's insistence that an agreement on intermediate-range missiles be tied to U.S. readiness to forgo development of a space-based missile defense.

In late May 1986, the Reagan Administration, which was sharply divided over the issue of whether the Soviets were violating the 1972 ABM treaty by heavily encrypting, or encoding, information from their missile tests and by constructing a new network of defensive radars in Central Asia, announced that it would no longer be bound by the provisions of the (unratified) SALT II treaty, unless Soviet policy changed. When the Reykjavik summit five months later ended acrimoniously, arms control prospects were very dim.

On February 28, 1987, Gorbachev unexpectedly offered to sign an INF agreement, without any preconditions. We can only speculate on his reasons for decoupling INF from SDI: Perhaps his advisers argued that any advances in missile defense could easily and economically be countered by merely expanding the number of offensive missiles; perhaps it was the prohibitive costs of persisting in an unchecked nuclear arms buildup; perhaps it was the realization that the original Soviet deployment of SS-20s had been a mistake, the consequence of which had been a startlingly threatening U.S. response in the form of the deployment of modernized Pershing-II missiles capable of hitting key Soviet targets in a matter of six minutes; or perhaps it was a desire "to create an atmosphere of greater trust" that would improve Soviet-American relations and restore the USSR's prestige in Western Europe.

The third Gorbachev-Reagan summit, held in Washington, DC, in December 1987, was crowned by the signing of an INF treaty calling for the total elimination of all intermediate- and shorter-range missiles and GLCMs with a range of between three hundred and thirty-five hundred miles. The treaty includes provisions for on-site inspection, under which "each party shall have the right, for 13 years to inspect by means of continuous monitoring."

With this precedent-setting treaty in hand, the two superpowers intensified their quest for a formula that would result in deep cuts in strategic nuclear forces, that is, long-range ICBMs; also a problem were SLCMs (sea-launched cruise missiles) and ALCMs (air-launched cruise missiles).

But to gain control of the arms control agenda, Gorbachev had to reassert the Party's authority over the military even further by intruding into the sacrosanct area of military doctrine. In unusually frank language, the party program adopted at the Twenty-seventh Party Congress in March 1986 states explicitly that "policy in the sphere of defense and state security and Soviet military doctrine . . . are formulated and implemented with the Party playing the leading role."[17]

Thanks to this tutelage, there was evidence of significant doctrinal shift in military doctrine. Khrushchev had begun the transition to downgrading the importance of nuclear weaponry in 1956, saying that nuclear war was "not fatalistically inevitable," thus undermining Lenin's postulate that war between "capitalism and communism" was inevitable. In January 1977, in a major speech at Tula, Brezhnev had rejected "the allegation that the Soviet Union is going beyond what is sufficient for defense, that it is striving for superiority in arms, with the aim of delivering a 'first strike.'" ("First strike" was used in the Western sense of a unilateral all-out nuclear attack aimed at preventing the opponent from responding in a way that would inflict comparable damage on the initiating party.) He said that he accepted the "essential equivalence" that existed between the Soviet Union and the United States in the realm of nuclear weapons and rejected the possibility of strategic nuclear superiority. Yet at the same time the Soviet military started deploying MIRVed intermediate-range nuclear missiles (SS-20s) and continued modernizing its ICBM force, far beyond the requirements of "essential equivalence," leading influential Western analysts to argue that Moscow was following a war-winning strategy that would enable it to prevail should a nuclear war break out.

Gorbachev's first Chief of the General Staff, Marshal Sergei Akhromeyev, described the new Soviet military doctrine as emphasizing "the prevention of war . . . staving off aggression, and methods of conducting armed combat to defend the native land." A marked shift from Ogarkov's definition of military doctrine which had defined it as "a system of beliefs on the nature, objectives, and character of possible future war, preparation of the country and its armed forces for it and ways to conduct it." Instead of Ogarkov's notion of massive forward defense needed to prepare a blitzkrieg to preempt a NATO nuclear weapons strike, Gorbachev's military doctrine was described as "nonoffensive defense," stressing confidence-building measures, openness on military real defense expenditures, and the proposition of reducing all military forces to a level of "necessary sufficiency" to implement a defensive posture. These changes later received concrete affirmation in the revision of the Warsaw Pact military doctrine, which changed its major objective from victory to the prevention of war.

At the same time that the role of military force in national security was being reduced, its sociopolitical and economic components were being emphasized. A special military section was created in the CPSU Central Committee's International Department, and greater prominence given to Institute for International Economics and International Relations' (IMEMO's) and Institut S. Sh. A. I Kanady's (ISKAN's) efforts to emphasize arms control as a component of national security

The conceptual underpinnings of Gorbachev's "new thinking" about national security and military policy were set forth in a comprehensive fashion in his Political Report to the twenty-seventh congress of the CPSU on February 25, 1986 (the INF treaty proved to be the first tangible sign that he had been serious about major shifts in policy). Increasingly aware of the magnitude of the country's economic backwardness and of the military's excessive claims on the GNP, Gorbachev was driven to recast not just Soviet security but the USSR's role in the world as well.

Several ideological innovations transformed the Soviet Union's approach to foreign policy and military policy. Taken together they represented a major departure from the past.

Interdependency

Gorbachev noted that "as a consequence of the scientific and technological revolution," the "global problems affecting all humanity cannot be resolved by one state or a group of states." In effect, no nation could be an island unto itself:

> The realistic dialectics of present-day development consists in a combination of competition and confrontation between the two systems and in a growing tendency towards the interdependence of the countries of the world community. This is precisely the way, through the struggle of opposites . . . that the contradictory but interdependent and in many ways integral world is taking shape.[18]

With a declared commitment to participation in an interdependent world, Gorbachev stressed the need to solve the problems facing all humanity and our civilization. One consequence of the attention to the interests of mankind was the deemphasis on "class struggle" as the driving force for political change.

Mutual Security

Convinced that security could no longer be ensured by military means, that the destructive potential of modern weapons makes it impossible for any state to defend itself "with military-technical means alone," Gorbachev said that security "can only be mutual":

> The highest wisdom is not in only worrying about oneself or, even more, about damaging the other side; it is necessary for all to feel they are equally secure, because the terrors and alarms of the nuclear age give rise to unpredictability in policy and specific actions.

This position implicitly rejected the Brezhnevite view that "the stronger the Soviet armed forces, the more respect would the USSR receive abroad and the greater would be Soviet power to influence other nations." Quantity was no longer something that automatically translated into quality: More was not always better. Gorbachev recognized that for the Soviet Union to feel secure, the United States would also have to feel secure, and vice versa. "The Soviet Union," he said, "lays no claim to greater security, but will not settle for less."

Reasonable Sufficiency *(razumnaya dostatochnost')*

Although Gorbachev mentioned this concept only briefly at the party congress, he had used the term during a visit to France in October 1985. It signified a desire to reduce, even eliminate, nuclear arsenals in a way that would still provide the Soviet Union and the United States with "reasonable" assurance of security. At times Gorbachev was vague on the specific criteria that could presumably fulfill this requirement. Still, he approached the issue pragmatically, on a sector-by-sector basis—for example, agreeing to abolish all intermediate range nuclear missiles and, in November 1990, signing a major agreement that set limits on various categories of conventional weapons to be deployed in Europe (defined as the area between the Atlantic Ocean and the Ural Mountains).

As a result of these significant transformations in doctrine, the Soviet Union achieved a number of significant arms control breakthroughs, and a slight reduction in the influence of the military in Soviet society. In his speech to the United Nations on December 7, 1988, Gorbachev promised to reduce the Soviet army unilaterally by 10%, and withdraw 50,000 men from Eastern Europe. That same day Akhromeyev, Chief of General staff resigned, to be replaced by the 49-year-old Mikhail Moiseyev. Public debates began to appear in the Soviet press calling for reductions in Soviet forces of as much as 50%. Among the proposals now being heard were calls for the creation of a professional, volunteer army.

In June 1989, Prime Minister Nikolai Ryzhkov outlined plans to cut defense spending by half by 1995. At the same time it was publicly revealed by Soviet economists that the widely accepted CIA estimate of Soviet defense was actually more in the range of 20 to 25%.[19]

Gorbachev helped to achieve some remarkable breakthroughs in arms control, as well as a substantial reassertion of Party authority over the military. He failed, however, in his primary objective—that is, altering the underlying structural drain on the Soviet economy by curtailing military expenditures. The deeply entrenched ties between industrial managers and the Soviet military elite prevented any serious reduction in the percentage of GNP devoted to the military. Moreover, by undermining the privileged status of the military, and forcing it to submit to the Party even on matters of doctrine, he upset many of the senior officers and aroused their enmity.

This enmity deepened when Gorbachev made the mistake of involving the military in his unsuccessful efforts to preserve the collapsing Soviet empire: in April 1989 in Tbilisi, for the brutal occupation of Baku in January 1990, as well as the intervention in Vilnius in January 1991.

Gorbachev's legacy on military reform and national security is, like his legacy on economic reform, a mixed bag: his ambitious declarations were never followed through with sufficiently decisive action to truly alter the Soviet Union's predicament.

OPPOSING NATO

Until the 1980s and Gorbachev's reconceptualization of Soviet national security needs, the Soviet Union's military policy in Europe was distinguished by the following characteristics: avoidance of nuclear war; commitment to high conventional force levels and their strong forward deployment; substantial numerical advantage over NATO forces in tanks, motor-rifle divisions, armored personnel carriers (half of which have amphibious capability), and artillery; improved logistical support; and a high state of combat readiness of forward-deployed divisions, which were continually modernized and given enhanced deep penetration capability.

Several basic Soviet attitudes may help to illuminate this policy. First, massive military power was perceived as the best defense, not only against any NATO attack or attempt to intervene in Eastern Europe, but also against attempted national Communist defections or uprisings. Second, the Soviet leadership, like its tsarist predecessors, valued redundancy. As the saying went, "Russians feel more comfortable with three armies too many than with three divisions too few." Overinsurance was axiomatic in pre-Gorbachevian Soviet military doctrine. Third, if war came, Moscow wanted an overwhelming retaliatory capability. Finally, Moscow believed that the West would in time accept the forward Soviet deployment as the norm for a tolerable balance of power in Europe.

Occasionally, Moscow jeopardized its political goals by its continual force modernization and quest for military advantage. The resulting action-reaction syndrome in the military sphere heightened political tensions. Thus, starting in 1977, the Soviet leadership began to deploy the SS-20, an advanced, solid-fuel mobile missile that carried three nuclear warheads and was capable of hitting targets anywhere in Western Europe. In December 1979, NATO responded with a decision to deploy 108 new Pershing-II missiles and 464 GLCMs by 1988. These weapons have twelve hundred- and fifteen hundred-mile ranges, respectively. Realizing that the modernized Pershing-IIs had the ability to hit command and control targets in the western part of the Soviet Union, including Moscow, and therefore constituted a formidable first-strike weapon, and seeing that the intensive propaganda campaigns and sizable antinuclear protests failed to sow disunity in NATO and block the Pershing-II deployment, Moscow changed course. It embraced Reagan's zero option and eventually signed the INF treaty in Washington in December 1987.

By the end of the 1980s Gorbachev, urgently pressed by domestic crises to make sharp reductions in military expenditures, began to rethink his military options and strategy in Europe. In his speech at the United Nations in December 1988, he announced unilateral reductions in force levels and the beginning of a military pullback from Eastern Europe. A year later, given the sweeping political transformations in the Soviet bloc, he could no longer rely on the Warsaw Pact forces. In February 1990, Gorbachev agreed to President Bush's proposal for deep cuts in Europe, but only if the countries had equal levels; by the time of the agreement with Kohl in July permitting Germany's unification and membership in NATO, he had even accepted the principle of asymmetry in U.S. and Soviet conventional forces in Europe.

Following the collapse of the Soviet Union, the most immediate area of concern between Russia and Western Europe is how to guarantee peace and stability in Europe after the unilateral withdrawal of Soviet troops. The main threat to regional equilibrium, from Russia's perspective, are the efforts to enlarge NATO, which threatens to remilitarize what First Deputy Defense Minister Andrei Kokoshin has termed the "semi-demilitarized zone which has now emerged in Central and Eastern Europe."[20]

Yelstin and Kozyrev assumed, perhaps naively, that the end of the Cold War also implied the end of the Cold War alliance system. However, in late 1993, President Clinton, largely in response to domestic criticism of America's inability to resolve the crises in Somalia, Haiti, and Bosnia, came up with a proposal for extending NATO to Eastern Europe that has since come to be known as the Partnership for Peace (PFP). Formally proclaimed at NATO headquarters in January 1994, PFP held out the prospect of NATO membership for Eastern Europe, the Baltic States, and the former republics of the Soviet Union, including Russia. But trends in Russia, and the shift in Russian-American relations, have made PFP more source of tension than stability.

Although in June 1994, Russia signed the "Partnership for Peace" agreement, it would clearly prefer a pan-European security structure with Russia as a full founding member. By mid–1995, however, bowing to the reality that no other security organization existed that could immediately take NATO's place, and a new one was not soon in the offing, President Yeltsin recognized the inevitability of NATO expansion, with three caveats. First, that expansion should be gradual and in consultation with Russia. Second, that there should be strict conditions for admission. Third, and most important, that Russia eventually be allowed to join NATO's political structure.

The NATO response has been to pursue a slow, gradual expansion while seeking to allay Russian fears that it will be politically and militarily isolated. The French and Germans both support the notion of creating a "strategic partnership" with Russia, perhaps even culminating in a separate NATO-Russia treaty before any further expansion. The notion that Russia deserved special status "corresponding to Russia's size, importance, and capabilities . . . commensurate with its weight and responsibility as a major European, international and nuclear power" was explicitly recognized in the famework document for Partnership for Peace, signed on June 27, 1994.[21] Another idea often floated by senior Russian political figures is that Russia and other CIS states be allowed to join NATO simulatenously with the other Eastern European countries. While the present NATO members see any expansion that includes the CIS as making the alliance excessively cumbersome, and diluting its effectiveness, Russia has argued that it is the only guarantee that the alliance will not be directed against it.

Critics charge that expanding NATO by allowing early admission to Russia's neighbors, but not to Russia herself, is designed to isolate Russian from the rest of Europe. Instead, the Russian government has proposed either simultaneous admission, the creation of Organization for Security and Cooperation in Europe (OSCE) security structures as an alternative to NATO, or the creation of some as yet unspecified alternative security structure for Europe.

Sergei Karaganov, chairman of the Russian Council on Foreign Policy and Defense and an adviser to President Yeltsin has gone even further, suggesting that Russia pursue a strategy modeled on that of the late French President Charles de Gaulle. According to Karaganov, Russia should reject both isolationism and the rush to join NATO. Instead, it should seek a limited partnership based on the promotion of Russian interests.[22]

In this scenario, which Karaganov dubs "Gaullism without de Gaulle," Russia should seek closer strategic cooperation and full participation in the European security structure, but aggressively oppose the expansion of NATO for the following reasons:

- It would delay Russia's integration into Europe and create security subsystems which exclude Russia.
- It would erode Russian trust in the West, further isolating Russia and strengthening anti-Western political circles within Russia

- It will increase the tendency within Russia to develop an alternative security system, accentuating the division of Europe.
- Expanding NATO before a new security mechanism is in place would limit Russia's ability to participate in the international arena.
- Expanding NATO would make the Baltic States and the Ukraine permanent sources of discord with the West.

By staggering participation in NATO, Russia would lose its major benefit from the end of the Cold War: the de facto neutral buffer zone on Russia's western border.

Noting that there is considerable disagreement within NATO over how to proceed with expansion, Karaganov suggests that Russian diplomacy work together with leading political forces in the West that oppose expansion.

In June 1994, the Russian government formally signed the Partnership for Peace (PFP) Framework Document. However, within months, Russian leaders began to reverse themselves. With nationalism on the rise and disenchantment with the West growing, a broad consensus against any rapid NATO expansion has emerged. This opposition was reinforced by NATO air strikes against Bosnian Serb positions in the late summer of 1995, and led the Duma to call for a reconsideration of Russian membership in the PFP, a unilateral withdrawal from UN sanctions against the rump state of Yugoslavia, and further coordination on Yugoslav policy with Ukraine and Belarus.[23]

THE NEW ECONOMIC REALITIES OF NATIONAL SECURITY

Yeltsin's attitude toward the military burden were reflected early on, in a speech given on June 17, 1987, in Moscow, when he was still a candidate member of Gorbachev's Politburo. In an unprecedented harsh critique, Yeltsin singled out the military for wastefulness, gross incompetence, and utter absence of glasnost and self-criticism.[24] Since becoming President of Russia he has consistently called for reducing the size of the armed forces, cutting back on equipment purchases, and enhancing military effectiveness by emphasizing smaller, more mobile forces. In his May 1992 decree organizing the Russian Ministry of Defense, he even went so far as to stipulate that the size of the armed forces will not be allowed to exceed 1% of the population.[25]

Under Gorbachev, the Soviet army always accounted for the lion's share of government expenditures. Postcommunist government leaders, however, have made it plain that the military's budget will be reduced sharply. Russia's first post-coup Prime Minister, Yegor Gaidar, immediately slashed arms procurements by 70%. Much of this cutback affected the purchase of hardware, including: tanks (cut 97%), helicopters (cut 85%), self-propelled artillery (cut 90%), and ammunition (cut 70%).

The 1994 defense budget allocated 40.6 trillion rubles for defense, or approximately 3 to 4% of the gross domestic product. According to the London-based

Institute for International and Strategic Studies, this amounts to roughly $78 billion, a 40% decline in real military expenditures since 1989. Some Russian sources dispute this amount, saying that if one includes other, "hidden" categories such as troops assigned to the Ministry of Internal Affairs and the border patrol, the true amount is nearly double. Even so this represent a devastating and unprecedented reduction for the armed forces. In addition, in November 1994 the Finance Ministry publicly stated that it will be able to pay out only 70% of this allocation, since there is not enough money in the country's treasury.[28]

Reeling from these draconian cuts, the military has resorted to going into business for itself, expanding arms sales abroad and converting defense industries to civilian usages. The record on defense conversion has been mixed. While the government claims that 80% of military-industrial output has now been converted to civilian use, in fact by the end of 1994 only 35% of the defense industry's two thousand factories had been privatized. The state intends to own either a majority share or to exercise veto power over managerial decisions in another 42% and exempt 22% from privatization completely. The net result of cutting government orders has been another 40% decline in production from 1993 to 1994. While there has been some success in recapturing the Soviet position in the international arms market, now dominated by the United States, overall the military-industrial complex reflects the chaotic condition of the Russian economy.

The problem lies in the symbiotic relationship of the defense-related and private sectors—structural reforms in one are dependent on structural reforms in the other. Just as in the private sector, when Prime Minster Gaidar tried to curtail monetary emissions and free prices on goods and services, many managers of military factories decided to call the government's bluff by continuing to produce unneeded items, anticipating (correctly) that the Russian Central Bank would extend them unlimited credit. As a result, the government owes an estimated 441 billion rubles to defense suppliers for orders filled in 1993 alone, which it cannot pay. On the other hand, so long as the government refuses to close plants (and risk exploding unemployment), it is likely that managers will keep right on conducting business as usual.

Still, these massive cuts have had the salutary effect of concentrating the mind of the military elite on the need for a radically altered military doctrine, and has forced them to accept changes that, in other eras, would have been summarily dismissed. The cuts have forced a dramatic shift in Russian nuclear doctrine: the abandonment of any attempt to preserve nuclear parity with the United States. Even before the collapse of the USSR, in September 1991, Yeltsin had called for massive reductions in nuclear stockpiles, and suggested that Russia should begin by making a unilateral reduction of 5%. Bush and Gorbachev soon followed suit, announcing their intent to implement even deeper cuts—the removal from alert of heavy bombers and 500 strategic missiles and a reduction of armed forces by 700,000 men. Thus, the framework was set for the even more ambitious SALT-II treaty, signed by Bush and Yeltsin in Moscow on January 3, 1993. The START-II treaty marked the true end of the Cold War. Under this landmark agreement, over

17,000 nuclear warheads were to be destroyed (out of a combined total of 21,000) by the year 2003, less than half the total agreed to for START-I. This treaty confirmed that each side no longer viewed the other as the main nuclear threat.

In the field of conventional weapons, negotiations on confidence-building measures (CBMs) and arms reduction, the Conventional Forces in Europe (CFE) Treaty signed in Paris on November 19, 1990, continued to contribute to diminished tensions in the center of Europe. But problems loomed. The confidence-building measures included: (1) prior notification of land exercises involving over 13,000 troops or 300 battle tanks, amphibious landings of more than 3000 troops, or transfers of forces numbering more than 13,000 troops to areas where they might constitute a threat to signatory members; (2) invitations to observers from all participating states "to monitor exercises and transfers when they meet or exceed 17,000 troops, and amphibious and parachute activities at 5,000 troops"; (3) one year's prior notice of military activities in the field involving more than 40,000 troops; and (4) verification that allows each state to conduct an inspection of a suspect activity on 48 hours' notice, although no more than three a year need be granted by the same state.[29] These provisions are important because they provide for on-site inspections

The major provisions of the CFE Treaty limit the number of key types of conventional weapons that the countries of NATO and the former Warsaw Pact are permitted to maintain in Europe (defined as extending from the Atlantic Ocean to the Ural Mountains. The number of tanks, armored vehicles, artillery pieces, combat aircraft, and attack helicopters that NATO and the Warsaw Pact are allowed has since been broken down by country, with no one country permitted to have more than two thirds of the alliance's (or former alliance, in the case of the Warsaw Pact) total in most categories. The verification procedures are the most extensive ever incorporated into a disarmament treaty. All weapons in excess of the totals permitted are to be destroyed by November 1995. There is the rub.

In September 1993, under pressure from his military, President Yeltsin formally requested that the treaty's provisions regarding the flanks be revised or temporarily suspended so as to permit Russia to maintain larger numbers in the North Caucasus Military District (which includes the Chechen Republic). Yeltsin argued that the ceilings set in 1990 for the Soviet Union as a whole did not take into account the current reality, in which Russia faces instability and border threats all along its border in the northern Caucasus that were unknown during the Soviet period. The issue became an even greater concern for Moscow in late 1994, when large numbers of troops and armored vehicles were sent to suppress secession in the Chechen Republic. Yeltsin is under considerable pressure from the military to insist on a revision of the treaty (General Anatoly Kravshin, responsible for the North Caucasus, has been quoted as saying that "only a complete idiot would comply with the CFE Treaty's flank limitations.")[30]

In late October 1995, Secretary of Defense William J. Perry and Russian Defense Minister Pavel Grachev reached agreement on amending the CFE treaty. The changes will allow Russia greater flexibility, permitting it to redeploy about 4%

of its forces along its Baltic and Transcaucasian flanks. For the moment, CFE survives, but its future might be in doubt, should NATO expansion to the east proceed under the PFP.

OBSERVATIONS

Critics have blamed Yeltsin for the absence of a concerted military doctrine in 1992, and claim that he "gave away the store" as the Russian leadership waffled between supporting CIS institutions that would try to reintegrate the former Soviet Union, and setting up its own independent structures. Today, the President is the commander-in-chief and, according to the constitution, he is advised on military matters by the General Staff and the Security Council, the main body that coordinates Russia's defense establishment. Policy decisions are implemented by the Russian Ministry of Defense, and coordinated with other Ministries of Defense of the CIS by the CIS Defense Council of Ministers. The Federation Council, Russia's upper house of parliament, must confirm the use of forces outside Russia.

Russia's first Minister of Defense, Pavel Grachev, was appointed by Yeltsin in May 1992. He is on record as favoring reducing the armed forces to 1.9 million (from a high point of 4.5 million in the mid-1980s), and supports a mobile, professional volunteer army. Along with his First Deputy Minister, Andrei Kokoshin, the first civilian to be appointed to a position of military leadership since the 1920s, he has also undertaken a major revision of Russian military doctrine.

A draft prepared by the General Staff Academy in June 1992 cited the Near Abroad as the greatest possible threat to Russian security, implying that these areas should be part of Russia's natural sphere of influence. Foreign intervention in any of these states, as well as the positioning of troops at internal borders, would be deemed a threat to Russian security. After extensive public criticism, a revised version of the draft was approved by Yeltsin's Security Council in November 1993.

Russia's new military doctrine emphasizes smaller, more mobile forces to meet threats along Russia's borders, and promotes the establishment, through bilateral negotiations, of a series of thirty Russian bases in the Near Abroad that would form a "zone of stability" around Russia, enhancing Russian interests in the region, and serving to protect the rights of the 20 million Russian citizens in these states.

The document distinguishes between "potential military threats," such as "the expansion of military blocs and alliances damaging to the security interests of the Russian Federation," and "direct military threats," which include interference in the command and control functions of nuclear forces and the introduction of foreign troops into neighboring countries.

In the wake of the Russian military's debacle in Chechnya, Yeltsin has called for a sweeping overhaul of the military. Implementation of the entire program is expected to take nearly a decade, but the basic elements have already been approved by the Russian military establishment. Under the new organization, the minister of defense would be a civilian who would formulate both "military and military-technical policy" and provide financial and logistic support to the armed forces. Command and control of the armed forces would be vested in the general staff, and its chief would be directly subordinate to the president. The high command of the individual services would be eliminated entirely, and their functions taken over by smaller main directorates in the general staff. The armed forces as a whole would be reduced in size to 1.2 million men, and the number of military districts cut from eight to six. The Baltic Sea and Black Sea fleets would be eliminated entirely.[31]

Observing the collapse of the once mighty Soviet military, one is reminded of the phrase that those who live by the sword will one day perish by it. It was Soviet military might that established the country as a superpower, but at the cost of tremendous social and economic deformations. As economic accountability is slowly, painfully being introduced into Russia, a number of important obstacles will continue to hamper military reform, and weaken the military as an effective policy instrument.

First, there is a fragmented command and control structure, with an unclear and unreliable allocation of responsibilities between Russian and CIS command structures. Until this issue is resolved, the Russian military will continue to face the prospect of casual commitments in theaters of war like Moldova, Tajikistan, Abkhazia, and Chechnya.

Although, in the wake of the public outcry over the military intervention in Chechnya, the Security Council was expanded to include the heads of both houses of parliament, there is still no effective mechanism of civilian oversight over the military.

Second, the privatization of procurement and production, while necessitated by severe cuts in military resources, has also led to a proliferation of corruption up to the very highest levels. The corruption extends from the lowest ranks to the highest levels of the military. The Far East Military District has had to sell or lease over a hundred abandoned military garrisons, just to make ends meet. The First Deputy Defense Minister, Matvei Burlakov was removed in November 1994, in connection with pullout from Germany. Even the Minister of Defense, Pavel Grachev, has been implicated in corruption. Until this activity is curtailed the morale of the officer core is likely to remain extremely low, and the prospects for reform bleak.

Third, implementation of the draft has become increasingly difficult. In 1992 only 28% of Russians responded. According to one Russian study, the law now allows so many exemptions that 84% of draft-age men were able to avoid conscription legally in 1984.[32] The problem of new military personnel is compounded by the fact that many senior military officers remain in rank. Indeed, the staff at the Ministry of Defense has swollen to over 9000, twice what it was during the Soviet era.[33]

Finally, Yeltsin's extreme personal loyalty to certain military commanders and political allies makes the process of transformation more difficult. It has served him especially poorly in the case of Chechnya, where the Security Council, headed by Yeltsin's erstwhile ally Yuri Skokov (who was forced to resign in the wake of the Chechnya debacle) and Ministers Pavel Grachev and Viktor Barannikov rejected out-of-hand any dialogue with the Chechen opposition.[34] The destructive combination of lack of clear mission, inadequate resources, corruption, and political indecision, all graphically combined in the disastrous military adventure in Chechnya. As a result of this political and military debacle, in which Russian troops suffered over five thousand casualties, respect for the armed forces has fallen to an all-time low.

Russia remains a formidable nuclear superpower with global pretensions. Still, it will take many years for the Russian military to recover from its present weakness and humiliation. In such an environment the Soviet military may not have the capability to embark on foreign adventures, but it remains an exceedingly unpredictable force when considering the prospects of either domestic economic reform or international stability.

SELECTED BIBLIOGRAPHY

Allison, Graham J., et al. *Avoiding Nuclear Anarchy.* Cambridge, MA: MIT Press, 1996.

Blacker, Coit D. *Hostage to Revolution: Gorbachev and Soviet Security Policy, 1985–1991.* New York: Council on Foreign Relations Press, 1993.

Blank, Stephen J., And Kipp, Jacob W. (eds.). *The Soviet Military and the Future.* Westport, CT : Greenwood Press, 1992.

Bluth, Christoph. *Soviet Strategic Arms Policy before SALT.* Cambridge, England: Cambridge University Press, 1992.

Bunn, George. *Arms Control by Committee: Managing Negotiations with the Russians.* Stanford, CA: Stanford University Press, 1992.

Calingaert, Daniel. *Soviet Nuclear Policy under Gorbachev: A Policy of Disarmament.* New York: Praeger, 1991.

Currie, Kenneth M. *Soviet Military Politics: Contemporary Issue.* New York: Paragon House, 1992.

De Nevers, Renee. *Russia's Strategic Renovation: Russian Security Strategies and Foreign Policy in the Post-Imperial Era.* Adelphi papers no. 289. London: Brassey's for the International Institute for Strategic Studies, 1994.

Frank, Willard C., and Gillette, Philip S. *Soviet Military Doctrine from Lenin to Gorbachev, 1915–1991.* Westport, CT: Greenwood Press, 1992.

Garthoff, Raymond L., *The Great Transition: American-Soviet Relations and the End of the Cold War.* Washington, DC: Brookings Institution, 1994.

Holden, Gerard. *Soviet Military Reform: Conventional Disarmament and the Crisis of Militarised Socialism.* London: Pluto Press, 1991.

Holloway, David. *Stalin and the Bomb: The Soviet-Union and Atomic Energy, 1939–1956.* New Haven, CT: Yale University Press, 1994.

Leebaert, Derek, and Dickinson, Timothy. *Soviet Strategy and New Military Thinking.* Cambridge, England: Cambridge University Press, 1992.

Mackintosh, Malcolm. *The New Russian Revolution: The Military Dimension.* Conflict studies no. 247. London: Research Institute for the Study of Conflict and Terrorism, 1992.

Nation, R. Craig. *Black Earth, Red Star: A History of Soviet Security Policy, 1917–1991.* Ithaca, NY: Cornell University Press, 1992.

Nichols, Thomas. *The Sacred Cause: Civil-Military Conflict over Soviet National Security, 1917–1992.* Ithaca, NY: Cornell University Press, 1993.

Rumer, Eugene B. *The Building Blocks of Russia's Future Military Doctrine.* Santa Monica, CA: Rand, 1994.

Savelyev, Aleksandr G., and Detinov, Nikolai. *The Big Five: Arms Control Decision-Making in the Soviet Union.* Westport, CT: Praeger, 1995.

Vigor, Peter H. *The Soviet View of Disarmament.* New York: St. Martin's Press, 1986.

NOTES

1. Richard Pipes, *Survival is Not Enough: Soviet Realities and America's Future* (New York: Simon & Schuster, 1984), p. 117.
2. *Ibid.,* pp. 118–119.
3. Pipes, *Survival,* p. 112.
4. Edwina Moreton, "Comrade Colossus," in Curtis Keeble (ed.), *The Soviet State: The Domestic Roots of Soviet Foreign Policy* (Boulder, CO: Westview Press, 1985), p. 131.
5. Anton Bebler, "The Armed Forces' Role in Soviet Foreign Policy," *Delo,* March 20, 1976; translated by Zdenko Antic in *Radio Free Europe Research Paper, RAD Background Report,* no. 70 (Yugoslavia), March 25, 1976.
6. Herbert Scoville, Jr., and Kosta Tsipis, *Can Space Remain a Peaceful Environment?* (Muscative, IA: Stanley Foundation, 1978).
7. Ben Bova, "Soviet Space Offensive," *OMNI* (July 1982), p. 63.
8. Benjamin S. Lambeth, "Nuclear Proliferation and Soviet Arms Control Policy," *Orbis,* vol. 14, no. 2 (Summer 1970), p. 308.
9. Major-General Vadim Makarevskiy, "The Threat from the South," *New Times,* no. 34 (August 21–27, 1990), p. 12; see also Alexei Arbatov, *Moscow News,* no. 41 (October 21, 1990), p. 3.
10. Thomas W. Wolfe, *Soviet Power and Europe 1945–1970* (Baltimore: Johns Hopkins University Press, 1970), pp. 33–34.
11. Philip Taubman, *The New York Times,* February 22, 1988.
12. Thomas W. Wolfe, *Soviet Power and Europe 1945–1970* (Baltimore: Johns Hopkins University Press, 1970), p. 98; see also Raymond L. Garthoff, "The Meaning of the Missiles," *Washington Quarterly,* vol. 5, no. 4 (Autumn 1982), pp. 77–80, excerpts.
13. *Izvestiia,* April 15, 1989.
14. Ray S. Cline, "Commentary: The Cuban Missile Crisis," *Foreign Affairs,* vol. 68, no. 4 (Fall 1989), pp. 194–195.
15. Herbert S. Dinerstein, *War and The Soviet Union,* rev. ed. (New York: Praeger, 1962), pp. 11–12.
16. Donald D. Barry and Carol Berner-Barry, *Contemporary Soviet Politics,* 3rd ed. (Englewood Cliffs, NJ: Prentice-Hall, 1987), p. 310
17. Sergei Zamascikov, "Gorbachev and the Soviet Military," in Lawrence L. Lerner and Donald W. Treadgold, *Gorbachev and the Soviet Future* (Boulder, CO: Westview Press, 1988), p. 76.
18. All relevant quotes from the twenty-seventh congress are taken from *FBIS/Soviet Union: Party Congresses,* February 26, 1986.

19. Richard Sakwa, *Gorbachev and His Reforms, 1985–1990* (New York: Prentice Hall, 1990), p. 335.

20. Michael Mihalka "Kokoshin: Ending Buffer zone destabilizes Europe," *OMRI Daily Digest,* April 5, 1995.

21. Maurice Blin, "Partnership for Peace: A Preliminary Assessment," *Interim Draft Report of the Sub-Committee on Eastern Europe and the Former Soviet Union, NATO International Secretariat,* (November 1994), pp. 1—2.

22. "Karaganov: Gaullist Strategy will Lead to Western Concessions," *Prism* (July 14, 1995), Part 1.

23. Scott Parish, "Duma Council Calls for Yelstin to Sack Kozyrev," *OMRI Daily Digest,* September 8, 1995.

24. Zamascikov, "Gorbachev and the Soviet Military," p. 82.

25. Article XII of Yeltsin's directive of May 1992 establishing the Russian Ministry of Defense.

26. William Mazzocco et al. "Economic Reform and Defense in Russia: The Interplay," *Global Affairs,* vol. 8, no. 2 (Spring 1993), p. 191.

27. Doug Clarke, "Russia's Military Strength Put at 1.7 Million," *RFE/RL Daily Report,* October 12, 1994.

28. Doug Clarke, "Military to be Short-Changed in Budget," *RFE/RL Daily Report,* November 28, 1994.

29. John Borawski, "Confidence- and Security-Building Measure in Europe," *Parameters,* vol. 16, no. 4 (1986), pp. 69–70.

30. As quoted in R. James Woolsey, "Say Nyet to Russian Treaty-Breaking," *Wall Street Journal,* May 8, 1995, p. 6.

31. Doug Clarke, "Russia Sweeping Military Reform Outlined," *OMRI Daily Digest,* April 12, 1995.

32. *RFE/RL Daily Report,* January 30, 1995.

33. Doug Clarke, "Paper Says Yeltsin to Cut Defense Ministry," *RFE/RL Daily Report,* November 30, 1994.

34. *RFE/RL Daily Report,* February 7, 1995.

Chapter
8

Russia and Europe

*F*or generations, Russian leaders have seen Europe as "the most important peninsula in the Eurasian continent" and believed that it is their continent and "that they have the right to be politically predominant in the European area.[1] The expansion of Soviet military power into the center of Europe after 1945 gave rise to the Cold War and a permanent threat to the nations of Western Europe. Yet despite the USSR's sustained military buildup and forward deployment of conventional forces far beyond what might be presumed necessary to ensure control of Eastern Europe or deter an attack by NATO, Moscow was not aiming at all-out war.

In the early post–World War II years, Moscow's objectives in Western Europe were subordinated to its East European policy and the demands of internal reconstruction, even though in the process Stalin aroused a sorely weakened and vulnerable Western Europe and an America intent on returning to normalcy to undertake the collective defense that he had hoped to forestall. Stalin was especially interested in the future disposition of Germany. The Soviet Union initially favored an exploitative and Carthaginian solution to the German problem: extensive reparations, the cession of territory east of the Oder and Neisse rivers to Poland as compensation for the USSR's absorption of eastern Poland, the expulsion of 12 million Germans from Eastern Europe, and the establishment of a Moscow-controlled Communist Party in the Soviet-occupied part of Germany. However, by mid-1946 it had adopted a more conciliatory position, seeking to obtain a choice in the management of the Ruhr and to disrupt the West's decision to include Germany's economy in its effort to promote overall West European recovery.

During the tense years of 1947, 1948, and 1949, Stalin's imperial strategy crystallized in the establishment of the Cominform, the Communist takeover of Czechoslovakia, the Berlin blockade, and the Sovietization of Eastern Europe. Unable to prevent the creation of NATO, Moscow played on European fears of a militaristic and revanchist Germany, hoping to forestall the Federal Republic's rearmament under U.S. auspices. In a diplomatic note to the Western powers on March 10, 1952, Stalin went so far as to propose a peace treaty and Germany's reunification as a neutral state, but this was very likely a ploy to kill West Germany's integration into the Western military alliance rather than a serious proposal for fundamentally restructuring the polarized alignments that gave Moscow a hegemony in middle Europe.

Under Khrushchev, the Soviet leadership ushered in an era notable for its flexibility and differentiation. Comprising a mixture of blandishment, pressure, bargaining, and growing military power, Soviet policy showed persistence and continuity in its tactically versatile pursuit of key objectives. Until the late 1980s, it was seeking basically to induce docility in Western Europe rather than strike for domination. To this end the Kremlin tried

1. to sow and exploit discord between the countries of Western Europe and the United States and among the NATO members;
2. to enhance its security, which it believed lay in a weakened West and a preponderantly favorable balance of power;
3. to improve relations with the Federal Republic of Germany (FRG), while maintaining control over the German Democratic Republic (GDR); and
4. to increase the political, economic, and military leverage that it could bring to bear on specific issues.

If Moscow had an ideal of relations with the countries of Europe, it was encapsulated in the word "Finlandization,"[2] a term commonly understood to signify a process whereby the Soviet Union would influence primarily the foreign policy behavior of countries so that they accommodatingly would adopt policies congenial to the Soviet Union. It was a conciliatory policy of self-imposed constraints where Soviet interests and preferences were involved.

With the collapse of the Soviet Union, Russia finds itself more distant from Europe than ever before, and also a weaker player in continental politics than at any time in this century. Peace and stability in Europe remain absolutely vital to Russia, and Russia itself as key to that stability. Moreover, close economic integration with the European Union, Russia's largest trading partner, is essential to Russia's economic recovery. Russia will therefore do everything in its power to ensure that the buffer zone that has been provided by the emergence of the newly independent states of Eastern Europe remains neutral and susceptible to Russian influence, and not a rigid border isolating it from the rest of Europe.

MOSCOW AND THE FRG: 1949–1989

At the heart of the Soviet Union's strategy toward Europe was concern over Germany. For more than a century, Moscow has alternated between fascination with and fear of German discipline, drive, efficiency, and technology. The revival of German military power was a cause of constant Soviet concern.

From 1955 on, the Soviet Union sought Western acceptance of the territorial status quo in Europe, recognition of the division of Germany and the legitimacy of the GDR, a weakening of ties between West Berlin and the FRG, and a minimal level of rearmament by the Federal Republic. To prod the West on these issues, Khrushchev decided to aggravate the Berlin problem. On November 27, 1958, he provoked a minicrisis, insisting that West Berlin be set up as a "free" city, guaranteed by the four occupying powers and the two existing German states, and that the Western powers withdraw from the city. Khrushchev's pseudo-ultimatum was extended for almost three years; there was petty harassment of traffic from the Federal Republic to West Berlin, but no repeat of the 1948 blockade as the West held firm. Frustrated and in need of some visible sign of achievement to still his critics in the Kremlin—and to help East German party boss Walter Ulbricht, whose regime was hemorrhaging from the flight of refugees, most of whom were skilled workers essential to economic development—he agreed to a politically humiliating but extremely effective move. On August 13, 1961, without warning, workers put up the Berlin wall, physically sealing off the two sectors of the city. A monument to Communist weakness, it helped Ulbricht and permitted Khrushchev to save face. The crisis petered out, especially after the upturn in Soviet-American relations that followed the Cuban missile crisis of October 1962, and ended on June 12, 1964, when the Soviet Union and the GDR signed a twenty-year treaty of friendship. The treaty was reassurance for Ulbricht, who had feared a Soviet deal with Bonn at his expense. But more important, by ending the Berlin crisis, Moscow was able to proceed on a new tack toward Western Europe. Within hours after Ulbricht had signed the treaty and left Moscow, Khrushchev held a talk with the ambassador from the Federal Republic to discuss a proposed visit to Bonn. He believed that a major Soviet initiative could aggravate intra-NATO tensions and prevent the FRG from acquiring control of or developing nuclear weapons, and he hoped to use the specter of Rapallo to extract concessions from the FRG's allies, particularly France. His son-in-law, Alexei Adzhubei, traveled to Bonn in July, and in the following month Khrushchev announced his intention to visit. However, two months later he was deposed by his closest associates—some speculate because of his German policy, though more likely it was because of domestic issues.

By 1966, after having assessed the situation themselves, Khrushchev's successors adopted his line and explored ways of improving Soviet-FRG relations. They dropped the "demand" for a German peace treaty, kept Berlin quiet, stressed the need for a European security treaty without offering details, and permitted the repatriation of many Soviet citizens of German origin (a decision that had been made by Khrushchev). The matter dragged on inconclusively until after the Soviet occupation of Czechoslovakia in August 1968, when polemics in the Soviet media against the Federal Republic dropped sharply as Moscow hinted at a desire to continue the talks. The discussions were given new impetus in March 1969, when the Soviet ambassador in Bonn pointedly briefed the government about the Chinese "aggression" on the Ussuri River; faced with tension in the East, Moscow again signaled that it desired normalization in the West.

Soviet overtures met a cordial reception in Bonn with the coming to power of the Social Democratic Party (SPD) in October 1969. SPD Chancellor Willy Brandt's Ostpolitik meshed with Brezhnev's Westpolitik. Convinced that reunification was unlikely in the foreseeable future and desirous of easing the situation of West Berliners, reducing the hostility between the FRG and the GDR, and opening the way for better relations with Eastern Europe, Brandt abandoned Bonn's previous insistence on reunification and expressed a willingness to recognize the territorial and political status quo in Europe. On November 28, 1969, the Federal Republic signed the non-proliferation treaty, renouncing any right to acquire, develop, or use nuclear weapons. On December 7, 1969, at Brandt's initiative, talks opened in Moscow on renouncing the use or threat of force between the two countries; and on February 1, 1970, the FRG and the Soviet Union reached a major economic agreement under which the FRG agreed to provide 1.2 million tons of large-diameter pipes on favorable terms financed by a consortium of German banks, in return for which the Soviet Union was to deliver natural gas over a twenty-year period starting in 1973. Key Soviet military, political, and economic objectives were within reach.

The capstone of the Soviet diplomatic strategy was the treaty signed in Moscow on August 12, 1970, in which the USSR and the FRG agreed to settle their disputes by peaceful means. The treaty further stipulated that the two parties undertook to respect the territorial integrity of all States in Europe within their present frontiers, including the Oder-Neisse line, which forms the western frontier of the People's Republic of Poland and the frontier between West and East Germany. For Moscow, the treaty meant that the FRG accepted the division of Germany, the reality of the GDR, and the renunciation of nuclear weapons; it was the augury—and essential precursor—of what Moscow was to achieve at Helsinki five years later, namely, Western recognition of Soviet hegemony in Central and Eastern Europe; and it accelerated the acquisition of advanced technology and extensive credits from the FRG—an objective that was increasingly important for Moscow.

Brandt's only condition for satisfying Soviet desires was an acceptable arrangement improving the condition of the West Berliners. Unimpeded civilian transit traffic was ensured from the Federal Republic by road, rail, and waterways to West Berlin, which was situated one hundred and ten miles inside the GDR; West Berlin could maintain its special relationship with, but not be part of, the FRG; and the West Berliners were granted easier access to visit family in the GDR.

That Moscow was keen on Brandt's Ostpolitik was evident; in May 1971, it forced the old-guard and antiaccommodationist Walter Ulbricht to resign from the party secretaryship (he died on August 1, 1973) and replaced him with the more compliant Erich Honecker. By implication, the USSR eschewed the use of the city's vulnerability as a lever against the FRG.

Economic cooperation with the Federal Republic was also important to the Soviet Union (as well as to the GDR, which received about $4 billion from Bonn during 1971–1982 for the construction of new roads and bridges on the transit route from the FRG through East German territory to West Berlin). By 1978, the FRG had become the USSR's leading noncommunist trading partner and source of high technology imports.

However, a harsh tone entered the political relationship in December 1979, when Bonn agreed to the stationing of U.S. Pershing-II and cruise intermediate range missiles as part of the two-track decision adopted at the NATO ministerial meeting. The Soviet invasion of Afghanistan that month and the eruption of the Polish crisis the following summer exacerbated the situation. However, Bonn resisted U.S. pressure to curtail economic ties, rejecting the use of negative levers—particularly sanctions—against the Soviet Union; it was skeptical of linkage—attempts to use inducements in one sphere to extract concessions in another.

The political bitterness increased when the social democratic coalition of Helmut Schmidt, whose party had ushered in the Soviet-West German détente of the 1970s, was toppled in late 1982 by a center-right coalition headed by Helmut Kohl and his Christian Democratic Party; and when Moscow blatantly though unsuccessfully tried to affect the outcome of the March 1983 general elections by siding with the Social Democrats and the peace movement in an attempt to derail the scheduled delivery of the first contingent of missiles, which started arriving on schedule in December 1983. Moscow pulled out all the propaganda stops to help the peace movement, stoking old fears of German militarism and revanchism, raising the specter of a new arms race, and playing on West European uneasiness about West Germany's growing power—all to no avail. The failure to prevent the deployment was a major setback for Yuri Andropov, who had succeeded Brezhnev on the latter's death in November 1982.

GERMAN REUNIFICATION

The chill that permeated Soviet-West German relations did not end until July 1986, when Gorbachev received FRG Foreign Minister Hans-Dietrich Genscher. Moscow's renewed courtship of Bonn took on particular policy significance following Gorbachev's decision in March 1987 to accept Reagan's "zero option," which called for the elimination of all Soviet and American intermediate-range missiles. The conciliatory efforts that sought Chancellor Kohl's support for the dismantling and destruction of the recently deployed missiles also included a state visit in July 1987 by West Germany's president. In January 1988 Soviet Foreign Minister Shevardnadze visited Bonn, in October, Kohl went to Moscow, and in June 1989 Gorbachev made his first state visit to West Germany, where he received a tumultuous welcome and signed a political document setting out goals for arms reduction and reconciliation.

Nothing in the cosmetic changes, however, even suggested the strategic turnabout of late 1989–1990. Gorbachev's decision to agree to the unification of Germany came suddenly, without extensive discussion in the Politburo. It represented a radical reinterpretation of the Soviet Union's national interest; it also completely transformed the political map of post–World War II Europe and rejected the bipolar international system that Stalin had forged and his successors had perpetuated. The implications for foreign policy were as sweeping for the future of Europe and U.S.-Soviet relations as the division of Germany had been in the first instance.

In for a penny, in for a pound, the saying goes. Having permitted decommunization and de-Sovietization in Hungary and Poland (see Chapter Four), Gorbachev decided in October 1989 to allow the process to undermine the ultraconservative GDR regime that prior to 1989 had loyally followed the zigs-and-zags of the Kremlin's line ever since its creation by Stalin 40 years earlier. It is not clear what Gorbachev expected. If he thought that toppling Honecker and introducing reform and political pluralism would save the Communist system, then he sorely underestimated the power of German nationalism. In November 1989 the Berlin wall came down, followed by the institutional props that had kept the system under control—the party, the *Stasi* (secret police), and government. Stunned by the rapidity of events, Moscow was without a plan in late 1989–early 1990. Like the proverbial revolutionary leadership unexpectedly faced with a popular uprising, it raced about trying to determine the general direction of the revolution so that it could dash ahead to be in front.

Change forced Soviet leaders to adapt to circumstances they could no longer control. On December 9, 1989, Gorbachev admitted to a plenum of the CPSU's Central Committee that the situation in the GDR was "unconventional" and that "our friends" had largely lost their positions. However, he sought to allay his colleagues' understandable anxieties:

> We stress with the utmost resoluteness that we will see to it that no harm comes to the GDR. It is our strategic ally and a member of the Warsaw Treaty. It is necessary to proceed from the post-war realities—the existence of the two sovereign German states, members of the United Nations. Departure from this threatens destabilization in Europe.[3]

Clearly, Gorbachev did not understand the irreversibility of the forces he had unwittingly unleashed by undermining the stability of the puppet East German regime.

Developments in the GDR, however—the flight of hundreds of thousands of East Germans to the West across the newly opened border, the political unrest that hovered on the threshold of mass violence, the deteriorating economy, and the unbridled calls for unity—rapidly upset long-established Soviet policy, so that by January 30, 1990, Gorbachev was forced to acknowledge the theoretical possibility of reunification. On February 2, Shevardnadze's proposal of "a Europe-wide referendum" for settling the German question seemed more a play for time than a transition plan for a period during which the rising nationalist fervor could be mollified. After meeting with Gorbachev in Moscow on February 10, Chancellor Kohl reported that the Soviet Union had accepted "the right of the German people alone to decide whether to live together in one state," subject to acceptable guarantees for the security and territorial integrity of other states.[4] Three days later, at a meeting in Ottawa, the Soviet Union joined the United States, Britain, and France—the four wartime powers that had defeated Nazi Germany—in agreeing to a formula for reunifying Germany. Their "two-plus-four" formula stipulated that the FRG and GDR would first negotiate arrangements to merge their economies and hold all-German elections; then they would enter into talks with the four powers to confirm the territorial, military, and international status of a reunited Germany. Would a reunited Germany accept is post-1945 boundaries? Would it be a member of NATO, as the West wished, or neutral, as the USSR preferred? What would be its military strength? Moscow envisaged a process that would extend over a number of years. Once again, Gorbachev egregiously miscalculated.

In an interview with *Pravda* on February 20, 1990, Gorbachev stressed that "the unification of Germany concerns not only the Germans." Vital questions affecting security and stability in Europe had to be settled and a "new structure of European security" replacing the one based on blocs had to be established.[5] His admonition reflected the growing pressure on him at home: conservatives in the party, such as Yegor Ligachev, and in the military, such as Marshal Sergei Akhromeyev (Ret.), expressed grave reservations. Moreover, his controversial German policy came at the very moment he was alienating party oligarchs by ramming through changes ending the party's formal monopoly on political power, which had dated legally from Stalin's 1936 constitution. To allay one of the concerns about German unification, he stated emphatically, in an interview on March 6 over FRG television, that he would not accept any form of a united Germany's membership in NATO: "This is absolutely ruled out."[6] But within four months Gorbachev again reversed himself. On June 26, Shevardnadze defended Gorbachev's momentous policy changes toward Eastern Europe and Germany. Although empathizing with fears occasioned by the prospect of German unification, he asked:

> How long could the partition of Germany have continued? Years more, decades more, forever? How long would our soldiers have had to stand guard on the Elbe-years, decades, forever?
>
> Right away, people are worried about what will happen if Germany's planned membership in NATO takes place. Here we need to clarify a few things. First, the FRG has long been a NATO member. This means that it can only be a question of increasing NATO's potential by the addition of the GDR, when and if the latter becomes part of Germany. I by no means intend to say that the possible expansion of NATO does not concern us. We are by no means indifferent to Germany's future military-political status. But this question will probably be viewed differently, depending on the changes which take place in Europe.
>
> A united Germany will exist in a situation that will be significantly different—not least in military-strategic terms—from what existed yesterday or exists today.

The denouement came on July 17. In the mountain resort of Zheleznovodsk in the Caucasus, Chancellor Kohl and President Gorbachev signed an agreement that was as dramatic as the Rapallo agreement of April 1922 and as momentous for all of Europe as the 1939 Nazi-Soviet pact. On the face of it, Gorbachev made sweeping political concessions

1. accepting a united Germany that consisted of the FRG, the GDR, and Berlin;
2. recognizing the right of the united Germany, in exercise of its sovereignty, to remain in NATO if it so desired; and
3. agreeing to withdraw all Soviet troops from the GDR no later than the end of 1994 (50 years after they first entered, in the closing months of the Second World War).

For his part, Kohl agreed that a united Germany

1. would have no more than 370,000 troops, approximately 50% of the combined strength of the armies of the FRG and the GDR in 1990;
2. would renounce the right to manufacture, possess, and dispose of nuclear, biological, and chemical weapons, and would remain a signatory of the nuclear nonproliferation treaty;
3. would forswear any territorial claims and accept the Oder-Neisse line as the boundary between Germany and Poland;

4. would give generous economic assistance to the Soviet Union. It committed itself to helping defray the upkeep of Soviet forces still in the GDR, in 1990 alone having provided $750 million of an eventual total of more than $8 billion for that purpose. Kohl also agreed to help the USSR build housing for the returning Soviet soldiers and to ensure that trade commitments made by the GDR to the Soviet Union would be upheld. (Since more than one third of the GDR's trade was with the Soviet Union, this item could prove expensive over the next decade.)

On September 13, 1990, the Soviet Union and West Germany initialed a "treaty on good-neighborliness, partnership and cooperation" that affirmed previous pledges of peace and comity and "resolved to continue the good traditions of their centuries-old history"; the document was formally signed in Bonn on November 9 (five weeks after the two Germanies were officially reunified), during Gorbachev's visit to commemorate the breaching of the Berlin wall; it includes a nonaggression clause stipulating that neither party will ever be "the first to employ armed forces against one another or against third parties."

More than any other single event, the unification of Germany marks the end of the Cold War that emerged in 1945 and divided Europe. Gorbachev's astonishing policy reversal was symptomatic of his broader agenda of seeking to reconcile Russia to Europe. Moscow's receptivity to strategic accommodation with Germany was not new, but there were important differences from the past. First, by contrast with Stalin in 1939, Gorbachev was in a position of military superiority. Although facing a profound crisis at home and in dire need of Western investment, trade, and technology to modernize Soviet society, he could, since he possessed a credible nuclear deterrent, gamble away assets of declining utility (for example, a military presence in East Germany) without seriously jeopardizing Soviet security. Second, by contrast with 1939, Germany was not bent on war. It is a prosperous democratic society, a member of a Western military alliance that constrains its political-military options, and a partner in Europe's move toward economic integration. As such, it is in a position to emerge as Europe's leading economic and political actor, a circumstance that should facilitate Moscow's efforts to improve relations with the other nations of Europe who continue to harbor historically rooted fears of German nationalism. Third, Zheleznovodsk is not Rapallo, though Moscow saw certain similarities in that Germany could garner economic benefits from close relations with the USSR; that its natural inclination is to seek a middle ground between East and West; and that friendship with the Soviet Union, and enlightened Ostpolitik, would redound to Germany's advantage.[8] This time, however, by contrast with Rapallo, it was the Soviet Union alone that was the nation outside the European system. Moscow needed the bridge to Germany not only for goods and services but for its political normalization with the European Community as well.

Far from complicating matters, the stunning collapse of the USSR in December 1991 seemed to strengthen the determination of Moscow and Bonn to live up to the Zheleznovodsk agreement. By the end of 1992, more than 60% of Moscow's forces in East Germany had been withdrawn; and on August 31, 1994, Russia officially ended its military presence, completing the withdrawal of more than half a million troops and dependents from Germany. Aware of the poor conditions in Russia, Bonn had sweetened the Russian pullback with grants, aid, and investment credits totaling more than $71 billion in the period between 1989 and 1994. German Chancellor Helmut Kohl expressed confidence in Russian President Boris Yeltsin's ability to deal effectively with Russia's problems. He provided assistance, encouraged trade, and accorded Yeltsin full diplomatic honors, for example, during his state visit to Germany in May 1994. Economically, Russia remains an important trading partner for Germany, but with unification the trade turnover has decreased by half, largely because of the chaotic conditions prevailing in Russia's economy. The long-term prospects for Russian-German economic cooperation, however, are bright: Russia has the energy and raw materials Germany requires; Germany has the industrial and consumer goods Russia wants. For the moment, though, only about one quarter of Russia's total foreign trade is with Germany, a figure that accounts for only 2% of Germany's foreign trade.[9]

Russia's problems with Germany are a reflection of those that it has had with the rest of Europe. The erratic, uncertain domestic economy elicits caution among West European bankers and investors. Its unpredictable sociopolitical development discourages greater Western involvement in Russia's efforts to reform herself. Russia's expectations of a rapid inclusion into a "common European home" have been disappointed. Its ambivalence toward the Clinton Administration's Partnership for Peace proposal, which envisages eventual NATO membership for Moscow's former satellites in Eastern Europe (and even for Ukraine), and toward the broad issues of ensuring security in Europe, fosters unease in Western capitals. Russia's insistence on revising the CFE agreement to permit increased troop strength in the Caucasus worries many in the West, who see an incipient neo-imperial policy developing in Moscow. Russia also holds quite distinct views on the future of the Organization on Security and Cooperation in Europe (OSCE), the new name given to the CSCE in Budapest on December 5, 1994. Ultimately, what Russia wants in Europe remains a large strategic question mark in Western capitals.

THE COURTSHIP OF FRANCE

The complexity of Soviet policy toward Western Europe can be seen in Moscow's simultaneous courtship of France and the FRG/united Germany. With France, Moscow stresses the Franco-Russian alliance in two world wars and a common interest in maintaining an equilibrium of power in Europe. The dangers of German militarism are subliminally nurtured. With the FRG/Germany, Moscow suggests the mutual benefit of a relationship on the lines of Rapallo. Trying to attract the one, it often disturbs the other, hence limiting its effectiveness with both.

Wooing France has been a staple of Moscow's diplomacy since Charles de Gaulle returned to power in 1958. Khrushchev seized on opportunities to exploit de Gaulle's differences with Washington, London, and Bonn; and though Moscow had long castigated French colonialism in Southeast Asia and North Africa, Khrushchev did not permit his interest in penetrating the Third World to interfere with his European policy. de Gaulle's grant of independence to Algeria in 1962 was a welcome move, but it was his rejection of the U.S. proposal for a multilateral nuclear force, his opposition to Western European economic and political integration, his quest for a reduced American role in Europe, his acceptance of the Oder-Neisse boundary, and his readiness to improve relations with the Soviet Union that accounted for the Kremlin's keen interest in a strengthened French connection. Over the years, Moscow has seen France as the odd member out in NATO and liked the Gaullist preference for a Europe of cooperating but nationalistic and independent sovereignties, which conflicted starkly with the "Atlanticist" formulations so favored by American and British officials. As one Soviet writer noted,

> A powerful France holds no menace for the Soviet Union or its interests. On the contrary, the more France asserts its great-power independence, the easier it will be for us to work in common for solution of the pressing problems of Europe and the world.

President de Gaulle visited the Soviet Union during the halcyon stage of the Soviet courtship, in June 1966, scarcely three months after he had informed NATO of his intention to withdraw France's participation in the integrated military commands and indicated the desirability of a shift of venue for NATO's headquarters from Paris to Brussels. Moscow persisted in its efforts to strengthen the relationship, but after the Soviet invasion of Czechoslovakia, which coincided with the twilight of de Gaulle's political career, a certain disenchantment and constraint developed in Paris. Succeeding French Presidents Georges Pompidou, Valery Giscard d'Estaing, and François Mitterrand continued high-level visits and Soviet leaders regularly returned them, but the mood has never been quite the same as in de Gaulle's time.

Moscow is under no illusions that France can disengage itself from the Atlantic alliance and play a completely independent role in Europe, but it finds enough promise in the neo-Gaullist propensities that shape the outlook of French leaders and the tenor of French domestic politics to seek agreement with France on the convergent strands of the two countries' foreign policy. Moscow, like Paris, supports a nonnuclear Germany, a limited role for the United States in Europe, a NATO of modest size, and expanded East-West economic cooperation. Both countries retain vestigial uneasiness over the danger of resurgent German nationalism and militarism. Overall, France is useful to Moscow in the ongoing process of détente and integrating Russia into Europe. Its demands are few, and its sympathetic voice generally stresses Russia's strategic importance.

In the economic and technological realm, France led the way to the Soviet market. In October 1964, it extended to the USSR a seven-year credit for $356 million, which was used to finance chemical plants and equipment. A ten-year Franco-Soviet trade agreement was concluded in October 1971, during the first of Brezhnev's visits to France. In January 1982 the two governments signed an agreement calling for France to purchase about 280 billion cubic feet of Siberian natural gas every year for 25 years, starting in 1984, and for large-scale Soviet imports of French equipment. With this agreement—which France signed notwithstanding the crackdown on Solidarity in Poland the previous month, the continued Soviet occupation of Afghanistan, and President Ronald Reagan's imposition of sanctions on companies selling the Soviet Union equipment for the natural gas pipeline—French President François Mitterrand affirmed his belief that expansion of East-West trade ought not to become hostage to the vagaries in political relations between the USSR and the West.

In the 1980s, France was the USSR's second-most important West European trading partner—a distant second to the Federal Republic of Germany. In May 1990 the two countries concluded an oil exploration and production agreement—the first Moscow has signed with a Western company, the French state-owned Elf Aquitane. Many of the French partners operating in the approximately forty Franco-Soviet joint ventures have, however, experienced difficulty since late 1989 in obtaining payment for trade debts and repatriating profits.

In Mitterrand, a socialist who was elected in May 1981 and again in 1989, Moscow had a stern critic. It was annoyed by his sale of arms to China, his outspokenness on human rights issues, his staunch support of Atlantic solidarity, and his refusal to include French nuclear forces in the INF treaty negotiated between the Soviet Union and the United States in December 1987. Relations were also plagued by Soviet industrial espionage, focused on the high-tech field.

Like Gorbachev, who visited France soon after becoming General-Secretary of the CPSU, Yeltsin was feted on his visit to Paris in February 1992, less than two months after the collapse of the former Soviet Union, and historic Franco-Russian ties were emphasized. Like Gorbachev, who during his second visit in July 1989 had reason to welcome President Mitterrand's statement that "It is the duty of the Western democracies to contribute everything they can to the success of perestroika," Yeltsin hailed France's grant of credits and technical assistance as a reaffirmation of traditional ties. And like Gorbachev, who signed a treaty of friendship and cooperation in Paris in October 1990, Yeltsin concluded a broad treaty during his visit in February 1992.

RUSSIA AND BRITAIN

One of the interesting features of Gorbachev's diplomacy in Western Europe was his attention to relations with Prime Minister Margaret Thatcher, Britain's "iron lady." Except for the period of wartime alliance against Hitler, Anglo-Soviet relations had been adversarial in nature. Britain has been seen as a close ally of the United States and an advocate of a strong NATO.

In December 1984, when still a junior member of the Politburo, Gorbachev visited Britain and impressed Prime Minister Thatcher, whose observation, "I like him. We can do business together," took on significance a few months later on his elevation to the summit of Soviet power. During her visit to Moscow in March 1987 the two leaders held "thirteen hours of frank and private exchanges" across the spectrum of contemporary issues: "With this visit, not only was the political dialogue resumed, but official and unofficial exchanges of all kinds were revived."[10] In a bravura performance on Soviet television, Thatcher argued forcefully for a strong NATO and reliance on nuclear weapons as deterrents to counter the Soviet Union's military buildup in Central Europe. Gorbachev, of course, disagreed, but he found her helpful in persuading President Ronald Reagan to continue to abide by the terms of the 1972 Antiballistic Missile Treaty (ABM) and in persuading the West Europeans to approve the treaty eliminating intermediate-range nuclear forces (INF). Moreover, Thatcher was the first Western leader to laud him repeatedly for pushing glasnost, perestroika, and a more open society—all of which greatly enhanced his image in the West.

By the time Gorbachev visited Britain again in April 1989, Anglo-Soviet relations had improved significantly. Their main differences centered on security issues, especially Britain's determination to maintain and modernize an independent nuclear deterrent (deployed primarily on SSBNs—nuclear ballistic submarines), its lobbying within NATO for modernization of short-range missiles (those with a range of less than three hundred miles and not banned by the INF), and its opposition to Soviet power projection in the Third World. But their views dovetailed across a series of arms control issues, such as ABM, NPT, INF, Mutual Force Reduction (MFR), and limiting SDI. Their meetings—Thatcher returned to Moscow in September 1989 and June 1990—were notable for the in-depth character of the exchanges. Two tough-minded, pragmatic leaders engaged in sophisticated discussions is rare in international politics. The resignation of Prime Minister Thatcher at the end of November 1990 did not adversely affect Anglo-Soviet relations; her successor, John Major, continues her policy.

During Yeltsin's visit in November 1992, a number of agreements were signed, including one on economic cooperation, another establishing a "hot line" between the Kremlin and 10 Downing Street, and others involving bilateral Russian-British military contacts, civil aviation, and aid to help Russia ensure the safety of the transportation of nuclear weapons slated for dismantling. The visit to Moscow in October 1994 of Queen Elizabeth, the first British monarch to visit Russia since the October Revolution, was recognition of the era of good feelings that both parties anticipate.

EUROPEAN UNITY AND THE "COMMON EUROPEAN HOME"

Khrushchev and Brezhnev had been hostile to European integration, arguing in accordance with then-accepted canons of Marxist-Leninist scripture that it was a desperate measure by "monopoly capital" to stave off the inevitable collapse of capitalism and would ultimately lead to increased international tensions and a further deterioration in the condition of the "working class." In March 1972 Brezhnev did implicitly recognize the European Community, but he made little effort to interact with it until 1977, when he sent an official delegation to Brussels to get permission to engage in fishing in the territorial waters of the community's members. Gorbachev, on the contrary, sought access to the process of European integration as an essential step toward the modernization of the Soviet economy. Whereas his predecessors thought "the Europe of Trusts" (as the edifice of supranational institutions was called) limited the USSR's freedom of diplomatic maneuver and ability to play off one capitalist country against another for maximum commercial benefit, Gorbachev looked to it for facilitating trade and investment.

In February 1989, Moscow appointed an ambassador to the community, and in July, Gorbachev spoke warmly of it in his speech to the Council of Europe in Strasbourg, France. By December, Moscow had realized a major objective, the conclusion of a ten-year cooperation treaty with the European Community (EC), covering a spectrum of concerns from trade to tourism, banking to energy, and food processing to the environment. Signing for the Soviet Union, Shevardnadze said the agreement "raises the practical construction of the economic foundation of a common European home one step higher."[11]

The key to understanding Gorbachev's overall European policy was his emphasis on a "common European home," a notion Brezhnev used in 1981. The term was a prominent, if vague, construct in Gorbachev's speeches and programmatic formulations ever since his visit to France in October 1985. It encapsulated a vision of the kind of Soviet Union he would like to have led into the next century and a general sense of what needs to be done.

Like the late French President Charles de Gaulle, Gorbachev spoke of Europe as a single, "cultural historical entity united by a common heritage."[12] Without specifically attacking NATO, his rhetoric clearly suggested that in an era of reduced regional tensions NATO would become superfluous. Indeed, in a speech in Italy in December 1989, he said that the Soviet Union had abandoned any claims to regional hegemony in Eastern Europe, and foresaw a day when the deplorable schism between East and West in Europe might be overcome by what he called a "Commonwealth of Independent States."[13] As a first step in this direction Soviet diplomacy therefore called for a transformation of NATO and the Warsaw Treaty Organization (WTO) from military alliances into purely political coordinating structures. With time these structures would eventually dissolve into political and economic coordinating structures that would also be responsible for the security of all member states. The CSCE was to play a considerable role in facilitating the transformation of the current Europe into a system of collective security that stretched from the Atlantic to the Urals.

Ultimately, Gorbachev realized that an end to the Soviet Union's expansionism and hostile image was a prerequisite for admission to the European concert of powers. He allowed internal political groups to dismantle the Communist regimes in Eastern Europe, permitted Germany to reunify, began a pullback of Soviet forces, came to terms with the EC, and introduced sweeping political changes at home. Perhaps nothing was more symbolic of the end of the Soviet Union's post-1917 isolation from Europe and European culture than Gorbachev's meeting with Pope John Paul II at the Vatican on December 1, 1989. The first meeting ever between a Soviet leader and a pope, it brought a promise from Gorbachev of religious freedom for all Soviet citizens, heralding an end to Soviet communism's assault on the Roman Catholic Church. It was an implicit acknowledgment of the pope's enduring influence in heavily Roman Catholic Poland, Czechoslovakia, Hungary, and Lithuania, and the church's role in encouraging resistance to Soviet rule. Gorbachev's visit led to the establishment of diplomatic relations between the USSR and the Vatican in March 1990.

By boldly abandoning the constraints of Marxism-Leninism, Gorbachev was able to highlight the traditional Russian strategic and security concerns. By finally acknowledging that the costly goal of expanding the socialist system no longer enhanced Soviet security, Gorbachev and his foreign minister Eduard Shevard-nadze went a long way toward "rationalizing" Soviet foreign policy, reducing the inconsistencies between rhetoric and actions, reducing foreign assistance to for-eign communist parties, and ending the costly war in Afghanistan. This in turn greatly enhanced Soviet influence in international forums. The success of these efforts in eroding Western animosity and suspicion, as well as their consonance with the long-term national interest of Russia led them to be continued and expanded under President Yeltsin.

Russia's membership in the Council of Europe, though delayed, was finally approved in January 1996. Duma deputy Sergei Kovalev, Russia's preeminent human rights advocate in the Yeltsin period, has argued that though "the human rights situation in Russia . . . will not correspond for a long time yet—for years, perhaps, to the high European standards," Russia's admission to the council would give a much-needed boost to internal political and legal reforms. Moreover, mem-bership "would have a restraining influence and prevent Russian authorities from going too far in an infringement of human rights."[14] In the wake of Yeltsin's use of force in late 1994–1995 to quell a secessionist challenge in the autonomous region of Chechnya, his pleas had a difficult time in Strasbourg. By February 1996, how-ever, despite continued turmoil in Chechnya, the Council of Europe did finally vote to offer admission to Russia, citing progress in the areas of human rights and freedom of the press.

THE CSCE (CONFERENCE ON SECURITY AND COOPERATION IN EUROPE)

The central political objective permeating almost all Soviet diplomatic moves after 1945 was Western recognition of the post–World War II territorial and political status quo in Europe. To this end, and to forestall the European Defense Com-munity and West German rearmament, Moscow started to lobby for a European security conference as early as 1954. Soviet leaders raised the idea often in the 1960s, but the Western powers gave it a cool reception.

By 1970, the mood had changed in the West; interest in an accommodation with the Soviet Union and improved East-West relations was strong. The USSR was now acknowledged to be a superpower in every military sense of the term: It enjoyed essential equivalence with the United States in nuclear weapons and deliv-ery systems and a numerically commanding advantage in conventional forces. Moreover, though the Soviet Union remained solidly entrenched in Eastern Europe, it was allowing increasing measures of autonomy, and its own sociopoliti-cal system had relaxed since the Stalinist period. Washington's interest was evident in the unseemly haste with which it swept under the rug the Soviet invasion of Czechoslovakia and urged the Strategic Arms Limitation Talks (SALT), no doubt also hoping that Moscow's interest in a limitation on strategic weapons would have a salutary effect on U.S. efforts to reach an agreement with Hanoi for an end to the American involvement in Vietnam. With the 1970 Soviet-FRG treaty, the 1971 quadripartite agreement on Berlin, and the Soviet acceptance of American and Canadian participation, Western opposition to the CSCE weakened. Moscow overcame what was perhaps the last hurdle when in May 1971, Brezhnev challenged the West to judge the Soviet Union's peaceful intention by "tasting" the wine of negotiations, offering to meet NATO's demand for parallel but interrelated talks on the reduction of forces in Central Europe.

Deliberations on CSCE started in Helsinki on November 22, 1972. When the Final Act was signed by the heads of state of 35 countries on August 1, 1975, the Soviet Union realized a thirty-year ambition. Although officially only a political statement of intent and not a treaty or a legally binding document, the Final Act in effect ratified the existing frontiers in Europe. It was a political settlement of World War II and recognized Soviet hegemony over the Communist half of Europe. Still, the Soviet triumph was not unmixed. The Helsinki Conference gave the East Europeans ammunition to use against Moscow in their struggle for greater autonomy and expanded contacts with the West. The Final Act reiterated the general principles that are the staples of international summitry: sovereign equality of states, inviolability of frontiers, territorial integrity of states, nonintervention in the internal affairs of other counties, renunciation of force or the threat of force to change existing frontiers, and so on.

There are three sections, or "Baskets," to the Final Act. Basket 1, as the set of principles on security, confidence-building measures (CBMs), and disarmament is called, was of most interest to Moscow. It held that the "participating states regard as inviolable all one another's frontiers as well as the frontiers of all states in Europe, and therefore they will refrain now and in the future from assaulting these frontiers." At the time, the provision seemed a victory for Moscow because its effect was to ratify the political division of Europe. The Western powers had to content themselves with CBMs, such as prior notification of major military maneuvers. While voluntary in nature, the CBMs were operating often enough to merit attention as a technique of arms control (see Chapter Seven). Basket 2, which is also of interest to Moscow, deals with economic and technological cooperation. Basket 3, which constitutes a potpourri of political principles on the freer flow of people, ideas, and information, was included at the dogged insistence of the West Europeans and contains the fly in the CSCE ointment that Moscow sought to avoid.

As a multilateral forum for criticizing the Soviet record of human rights violations, CSCE inspired the formation of "Helsinki groups" demanding democracy throughout the Soviet bloc, including the Soviet Union itself. It enabled prominent dissidents such as Andrei Sakharov and Vaclav Havel to mobilize world opinion against Moscow. Despite this, on balance, the Kremlin was not dissatisfied with the record of the first decade. The Soviet leadership obtained agreement for a Conference on Confidence and Security Building Measures and Disarmament in Europe, which began in Stockholm in January 1984, concluded on September 19, 1986, with adoption of a document that creates procedures for verifying a variety of military activities in Europe, and led to the Conventional Forces in Europe Treaty in November 1990.

The accomplishments of the Helsinki Accords in the human rights field were notable, especially the Soviet Union's acceptance for the first time of a continuous monitoring mechanism to ensure Soviet compliance with the CSCE provisions on human rights. Under Gorbachev, some political prisoners were released, psychiatric abuses largely ended, and freer emigration permitted.

The CSCE process insinuated the USSR into the center of the discussion over the future of European integration. With the collapse of communism and the disintegration of the WTO and Comecon, the CSCE (renamed the Organization for Security and Cooperation in Europe [OSCE] in late 1994) has remained the one international organization with a relatively constant membership in the rapidly shifting patterns of East-West relations. As we shall see, this made it particularly congenial to Gorbachev's new vision of a "common European home," which was part of his broader vision for a new world order—the "new political thinking."

THE EUROPEANIZATION OF THE USSR

Gorbachev's unwillingness to act in a heavy-handed way fed a perception that his foreign policy lacked coherence. But Gorbachev did have a vision of the Soviet Union's role during the next century. The key to understanding his new thinking was the emphasis on creating a "common European home." His aims are in some ways rather like those of Charles de Gaulle: to foster close ties among the European powers and to reduce the prominence of the United States's role in Europe. Gorbachev sought a variant of the nineteenth century's European concert of powers—but that means he had to end the Soviet Union's post-1917 isolation from Europe and European culture. In sum, the de-Sovietization of Eastern Europe was essential for the Europeanization of the Soviet Union.

By presiding over the destruction of the communist fabric of East European societies, Gorbachev weakened the sinews of Soviet power; triggered political, economic, and social tensions; and risked widespread instability. He did not surrender to the implacable antichange coalition at home that thwarted Khrushchev's tentative moves at imperial decentralization in the mid-1950s and forced him to return to Stalinism. Moreover, Gorbachev not only acquiesced in decommunization, but he accepted eventual military withdrawal from the region as a mere matter of time. He said that he was prepared to accept noncommunist regimes in Eastern Europe provided they did not assume an anti-Soviet character. In a way, Gorbachev sought to "Finlandize" Eastern Europe—that is, East European states would be responsive to Soviet concerns in foreign policy and defense matters, in return for Soviet toleration of diversity and pluralism.

Reversing the decades-long emphasis on maintaining local communist parties in power at all costs. Gorbachev recognized that political pluralism was the indispensable handmaiden of a shift to a market-type economy. Further, the institutionalization of all of these developments was deemed essential for the success of Gorbachev's policy of reintegrating the Soviet Union and Eastern Europe into the rest of Europe.

The use of Soviet military force against any country in Eastern Europe, after all that Gorbachev had unleashed and tolerated, would have jeopardized his chances of making the Soviet Union part of the common European home. In addition, it would have doomed his efforts to obtain foreign capital and cooperation, and it threatened the prospects for reform and transformation in the USSR.

But avoiding the alienation of Western powers was not the only reason for Gorbachev's decreasing military involvement in Eastern Europe. Because nuclear weapons diminish the likelihood of another land invasion of the Soviet Union, it made sense to end costly commitments to an area that drained Soviet resources, required sizable deployments of forces, and contained an unreliable population.

At the same time, and as a corollary to the unilateral Soviet withdrawal from Eastern Europe, Gorbachev hoped to lessen the influence of the United States in Europe. Success in this would enhance the attractiveness, particularly to France, of full participation by the Soviet Union in a restructured and integrated European system. He also sought to ensure that Germany, whose unification he has made possible in dramatic fashion and with few conditions, would not again emerge as Europe's preeminent military power and threaten the Soviet Union. Thus, Gorbachev's policy had four separate but interrelated components—denuclearization, disarmament, decoupling, and development—and they were all bound up with the German problem.

SOVIET POLICY TOWARD EASTERN EUROPE

After 1945, the lodestar of the Soviet Union's European policy was strategic control of Eastern Europe in order to prevent that territory from ever again serving as the springboard for an invasion of the Soviet Union. Stalin's postwar objectives were relatively clear-cut: to eliminate Western influence from Eastern Europe and concomitantly establish Moscow's hegemony, and to develop a belt of submissive Communist regimes whose leaders governed at Moscow's discretion and depended for their survival on Soviet troops. From 1945 to 1953, the Soviet Union's draconian policy toward Eastern Europe was unmistakably Stalin's handiwork.

His successors, however, were faced with more subtle challenges: to preserve yet decentralize their empire, to obtain Western acceptance of the permanence of Soviet domination over Eastern Europe, and to expand Soviet power without jeopardizing the security of the USSR or its imperial system. They soon discovered that preserving an empire is more difficult than acquiring one. Not only do the techniques of rule differ from those of revolution, but the price of empire may prove so high that it weakens the structure of power within the metropolitan country itself. Stalin's successors alternated reform and repression in a never-ending search for a mix that extended the range of permissible autonomy within a framework that ensured loyalty, stability, and strategic control.

The Soviet leaders, eager to establish the legitimacy of their rule and to effect an orderly transition of power, revived the principle of collective leadership. Except for the purge and execution in the summer of 1953 of Lavrenti Beria, the head of the secret police, who posed a physical threat to their survival, shifts at the top were managed without recourse to the terror of the Stalin period, and the struggle for power has remained bloodless, a reflection of the changing, more sophisticated nature of Soviet autocracy.

Throughout most of 1953 and 1954 the Kremlin was occupied with problems within the Communist world, in Eastern Europe, China, and the Soviet Union itself. To decrease the likelihood of intrusive pressure from the West, Soviet leaders held out prospects of an easing of Cold War tensions, most immediately by accepting an armistice agreement in Korea on July 27, 1953. Thus began the effort to liquidate the liabilities bequeathed by Stalin. The armistice enabled the Soviet government to reduce the military drain on its economy, return the East-West conflict to the political and diplomatic arenas, and provide the Chinese Communists with time to consolidate their hold on the mainland; it also gave the government more leeway in tackling the succession problem and in meeting the expectations of the Soviet people for a better life.

Post-Stalin leaders, however, were never able to successfully to relax external controls in a manner that would maintain socialist unity. Time and again, when local communist authorities allowed a modicum of political and cultural freedom to emerge (in Hungary in 1956, in Czechoslovakia in 1968, in Poland in 1980), it was quickly followed by demands to end Soviet hegemony and withdraw Soviet troops. As a result, Soviet efforts in the region become primarily aimed at propping up increasingly ineffective and unpopular regimes. By the mid-1970s, the empire that the Soviet Union had established after World War II, and whose industries it had plundered in the early postwar years, had itself become a drain on Soviet resources, dependent on extensive subsidies from the USSR to maintain its standard of living.

At a time of shrinking resources, the added burden of maintaining Eastern Europe had become unbearable. Within the first few months after Gorbachev came to power, two "debates" surfaced, reflecting the Kremlin's uncertainty over how to deal with Eastern Europe: One related to nationalism versus proletarian internationalism, and the other to the Brezhnev Doctrine and the management of future intrabloc discords.

On June 21, 1985, and article in *Pravda* by O. Vladimirov (a pseudonym for a high-ranking party official) deplored the persistence with which the nationalism and national interests of individual East European states complicated the joint struggle against imperialism, which, he said, is attempting "to weaken the alliance of fraternal countries, to alienate and isolate them from the USSR, and ultimately to attempt to secure an erosion and even a change of social system.[15] It stressed the need for bloc unity, which required "a coordinated course" and "vigorous political cooperation"—euphemisms for Soviet-preferred options.

A month later, *Kommunist,* the official party journal, published a virtual rejoinder by Oleg Bogomolov, a leading economist and director of a major research institute, whose views reflected Gorbachev's. Bogomolov argued the need for a differentiated approach in which each country's own specific interests and priorities must be respected. He noted that individual socialist countries "are at different stages of economic development and have differing economic and political structures and traditions. As a result, the sum of their national and state interests cannot be completely identical.[16]

An even touchier problem was raised in September by Yuri Novopashin, a colleague of Bogomolov's. Writing in the journal *Rabochii klass i sovremennyi mir* (The Working Class and the Modern World), he questioned the validity "of the so-called Brezhnev Doctrine of the 'limited sovereignty' of the members of the Socialist community," noting that there is "no magic wand" that can eliminate "national egoism," on the one hand, or "great-power ambitions," on the other.[17] Three months later, on December 14, *Pravda* countered this view by drawing attention to the fifteenth anniversary of the Czechoslovak Central Committee's adoption of a document criticizing the "revisionist" and "counterrevolutionary" evils of the "Prague Spring" and upholding the principles underlying the Brezhnev Doctrine. The document, it noted, "reflects experience that goes beyond the bounds of what is specific and national," and is still valid.

THE COLLAPSE OF THE SOVIET BLOC

Gorbachev did not address the issue at the CPSU's twenty-seventh congress in February 1986, but in late June, at the Polish party's congress, he sounded a familiar Brezhnevian refrain: Asserting that socialism is irreversible, he said,

> it manifests itself as an alliance of countries closely linked by political, economic, cultural, and defense interests. To threaten the socialist system, to try to undermine it from outside and wrench a country away from the socialist community means to encroach not only on the will of the people, but also on the entire post-war arrangements and, in the last analysis, on peace.[18]

In his speech on November 2, 1987, commemorating the seventieth anniversary of the Bolshevik Revolution, Gorbachev lauded the socialist camp "in all its national and social variation" as "good and useful," and stressed that "we have become convinced that unity does not mean being identical or uniform." He set forth five principles for regulating relations among socialist countries:

> These are unconditional and total equality; the responsibility of the ruling party for affairs in its state, and for patriotic service to its people; concern for the general cause of socialism, respect for one another, a serious attitude toward what has been achieved and tried out by friends; voluntary and varied cooperation; and the strict observation by all of the principles of peaceful coexistence. The practice of socialist internationalism rests upon these.[19]

But public asseveration of principles is often a smokescreen for policy reversals and a necessary tactic for neutralizing domestic opponents. The following month, with Gorbachev's connivance, the removal of old-guard Communist oligarchs began in Czechoslovakia: Gustav Husak, installed after the 1968 Soviet invasion, stepped down at age 75 in favor of his deputy Milo Jake, who Gorbachev hoped would be more receptive to reform. But Jake's interest was in system maintenance, not system renewal.

In 1988 major changes took place in Hungary. Once the envy of the Soviet bloc, in the 1980s it was beset by a massive foreign debt, difficulty in selling its industrial products in Western markets, sagging agricultural prices, and flagging efficiency and technological innovation. "Kadarism" had reached the limits of what the system would tolerate. In May 1988, Janos Kadar (age 76) retired after more than thirty years in power. His successor as general-secretary of the Hungarian Socialist Workers [Communist] Party (HSWP), Karoly Grosz, though a conservative, accepted the necessity of revamping the economy and received the green light from Moscow for extensive reforms. Far more rapidly than expected, he purged the Politburo of long-time Kadarites, moved toward a market-oriented economy, and acceded to pressures of radical party reformers for a multiparty system and Western-style parliamentary democracy. In November the Hungarian Smallholders' party, which had won the 1945 elections, became the first noncommunist party to be legalized; others followed, ending the Communist monopoly on power.

In October 1989 the HSWP renamed itself "Socialist," and on October 23, thirty-three years after Moscow had squashed the revolution of 1956, parliament changed the name of the Hungarian People's Republic to the Republic of Hungary. (Poland and Romania made similar changes in December 1989.) Free elections in April 1990 brought a noncommunist coalition to office.

It does not minimize Hungary's achievement in 1988 to say that it was the changes in Poland in 1989 that presaged the end of Soviet domination and Communist power. After declaring martial law in December 1981, General Jaruzelski presided over a continually deteriorating economic and political situation. So serious was the labor unrest in the fall of 1988 that it prompted him, after consulting with Gorbachev in January 1989, to enter into talks with Solidarity. As a result, in April 1989, Solidarity was legalized; in June, it swept to a decisive electoral victory. By prearrangement, General Jaruzelski was elected to the post of president for a six-year term; Tadeusz Mazowiecki, with Solidarity's Lech Walesa's approval, became the first East European noncommunist prime minister in forty years. His economic reforms to introduce a market economy proved controversial and divided the country. In a surprise move, Jaruzelski stepped down after just a year in office—a final service to the restoration of democracy in Poland. In late 1990, Lech Walesa was elected president in a bitterly waged contest. In foreign policy, there was a major improvement in Soviet-Polish relations. Gorbachev's relationship with Jaruzelski was better than with any other East European leader.

Symptomatic of Gorbachev's policy of glasnost and desire to place Soviet-Polish relations on a firmer footing was his willingness to deal more honestly with the seamy side of Stalin's treatment of the Poles in 1937–1945. Particularly significant to the Poles was Gorbachev's establishment of a joint commission to examine, among other events, the massacre in 1940 of Polish officers in the Katyn Forest, outside Smolensk. On March 7, 1989, the Polish government formally blamed Stalin's secret police for the Katyn massacre. Intent on healing the wounds from the past that prevented full reconciliation, on April 13, 1990, Gorbachev turned over to Jaruzelski documents establishing the NKVD's responsibility: "It is not easy to speak of this tragedy, but it is necessary."[20] The admission of guilt opened the way for better relations—a circumstance both Moscow and Warsaw desire in light of Germany's reunification and the new attention to secure borders.

The democratization in Hungary directly affected the GDR. In July and August 1989, apparently with Gorbachev's tacit approval, Budapest permitted vacationing East Germans to seek asylum in the West German embassy, and on September 10, it announced they could leave for the West. Thousands more fled the country. The exodus was a political blow to East Germany and a major breach in Moscow's East European imperial system.

On October 7, Gorbachev visited East Berlin to participate in the celebration of the GDR's fortieth anniversary. Mass protest marches, which had appeared in Leipzig on October 2, spread to other East German cities. All demanded reform. Although seemingly supportive of Erich Honecker, the 77-year-old leader who had banned Soviet publications containing the words glasnost and perestroika, Gorbachev did say that Soviet troops would not intervene to suppress the protesters. The aroused populace, already heady with "Gorbymania," intensified their pressure on the regime. Honecker wanted to quell the demonstrations in Leipzig, perhaps thinking that he could do so quickly, as his predecessor Walter Ulbricht had done in East Berlin in June 1953 and the Chinese leaders had done in June 1989 in Tiananmen Square in Beijing. But his security chief told him, "Erich, we can't beat up hundreds of thousands of people."[21] On October 18 Honecker was forced to resign. His successor quickly made concessions—permitting free travel to the West, endorsing economic and political restructuring, and agreeing to free elections. However, the "revolution from below" would not be assuaged. On November 7 the government resigned and requested parliament to select a new leadership. The following day the Communist Party Politburo stepped down. On November 9, against the background of huge demonstrations, the Central Committee announced that East Germans could go freely to West Berlin—the Berlin wall was opened. In a matter of days its dismantling began, 28 years, 2 months, 27 days after it had been erected. The pace of events outdistanced all expectations— Soviet and Western.

Gorbachev welcomed the revolution in the GDR. Moscow watched developments unfold, but whereas in June 1953 Soviet troops had intervened to protect the East German Communist leadership from a popular uprising, in October–November 1989 the Kremlin left its clients to their fates. German unification, unthinkable since 1945, had now become inevitable.

The next dramatic sequence unfolded in Czechoslovakia. On November 17, emboldened by events in the GDR, Czechs and Slovaks took to the streets. Police suppression and Jake's call for negotiations were ineffectual and came too late. Under the leadership of the formerly imprisoned dramatist Vaclav Havel, a coalition of dissident groups known as Civic Forum pressed for democracy and reform. Sensing the ground swell of opposition to the regime, the Soviet ambassador in Prague acted as a go-between, seeking only assurances that there would not be a bloodbath against the Communists. On November 24 Jakes resigned. Alexander Dubcek, the Communist leader during the Prague Spring, returned to the capital from internal exile and addressed a huge crowd in Wenceslas Square, his appearance evoking the events of 1968. Under pressure, on December 1, 1989, the Communist Party of Czechoslovakia reconstituted the Politburo and condemned the 1968 invasion, declaring that "the decision to do so was wrong." A few days later, members of the Warsaw Pact, meeting in Moscow, officially apologized for that violation of Czechoslovakia's sovereignty, but none of this could save the Communist regime. A noncommunist cabinet took over, and on December 29, Vaclav Havel was made acting president; in June 1990 he was elected to a full term.

Czechoslovakia's "velvet revolution" proceeded smoothly without violence. It brought a return of free elections, a multiparty system, the shift to a market economy, an opening to the West, and dramatic changes in Soviet-Czechoslovak foreign relations: President Havel quickly terminated cooperation with unsavory Soviet activities; for example, he stopped the sale of Semtex (a plastic explosive) to terrorist groups and to Soviet client-states such as Libya and Syria, and he closed down terrorist training camps. He also normalized relations with Israel (as, subsequently, did all the other East European countries). In early 1990, Moscow agreed to his request for the withdrawal of all Soviet troops from the country.

In Romania, Nicolae Ceausescu was overthrown in December 1989 in a convulsion that was more coup d'état than revolution. The elections in May 1990 brought to power many holdovers from the party-military-*securitate* apparat. However, to avoid being isolated in the new Europe, the National Salvation Front, the post-Ceausescu movement that coopted and supplanted the Communist party, promised reforms. Thus far, however, old-style authoritarian politics have overshadowed the faint evidence of democratization.

In November 1989, Bulgaria began its lurch toward democracy. As in Romania, the upheaval was antiCommunist, but not anti-Soviet. Traditional pro-Russian sentiments are deeply rooted in Bulgaria. Under Yeltsin, relations have warmed even further. For example, during Russian Prime Minister Viktor Chernomyrdin's visit to Sofia in May 1995, he found a welcome reception from the Russian-educated Bulgarian Prime Minister, Zhan Videnov, a former communist who campaigned for closer economic and military ties with Moscow. Bulgaria's desire to renew its traditional ties to Moscow is no doubt prompted by the disintegration of Yugoslavia and the rising uncertainty in the Balkans.

Gorbachev may well have been surprised by the extent of the revolution up to and including its outcome in Germany (that is, the liquidation of the GDR and Germany's national unification), but his tactical adjustment to the new situation was nothing short of brilliant. At home, however, there was a price to be paid. The "loss of empire" helped galvanize conservative elements against glasnost and perestroika, with a consequent narrowing of Gorbachev's room to maneuver. The result was a strengthened position of powerful reactionary elements in the Soviet military and the resignation of the reform-minded Shevardnadze in December 1990.

Gorbachev was politically unable to deny to Eastern Europe the freedom to make hard choices, even though this entailed an end to controls over dangerous centrifugal forces—nationalism, revisionism, economic and ethnic unrest, and the rejection of Soviet-imposed institutions. The abdication of Soviet authority accelerated the process of imperial decline. It became apparent that the entire Soviet position in Eastern Europe was built on sand: individual communist parties lacked legitimacy and popular support; the army was unwilling to suppress mass protests, and the security forces wavered in the face of splits within the leadership; the intelligentsia was hostile; the governmental bureaucracies were corrupt and inefficient, unequal to the task of producing goods for a consumer society; and the working class—the proletariat and peasantry in whose name Communist systems purported to rule—hated their leaders and the system that they created.

It became apparent that a common ruling ideology had not succeeded in producing a common social outlook or a sense of cohesion. Whereas once it had legitimated Soviet policies and rationalized Communist rule, by the late 1980s Marxism-Leninism was shown to be no more than a fig leaf, a flimsy cover for pretended unity, not a value system to foster change or serve as a guide for political discourse and transformation.

Gorbachev's refusal to resort to force to suppress threats to "socialism" signified de facto repudiation of the imperial intervention that had officially been dignified as "socialist internationalism." Although Gorbachev himself did not explicitly denounce Brezhnev's interventionist policy, the Soviet government issued a statement on December 4, 1989, holding "unfounded" the bringing of Warsaw Pact armies into Czechoslovakia in 1968 and the decision itself "erroneous." During his visit to Finland on October 25, 1989, Gorbachev was as explicit as he could be when he stated:

> All disputes, including regional conflicts, must be resolved only by peaceful means and by political methods. There can be no justification for any use of force—whether by one military-political alliance against another, or within such alliances, or against neutral countries.[22]

Eight months later in speaking to the CPSU's twenty-eighth congress about the upheavals that toppled pro-Moscow Communist leaderships, Foreign Minister Shevardnadze said that Moscow had not been ignorant of what was happening "but we chose not to intervene."

With the Brezhnev Doctrine a relic of another age, communism passé as a source of political cohesion, and the two Germanies unified, the Warsaw Pact lost its former utility to Moscow. Certainly, it was no longer a viable military alliance: Gorbachev assented to the requests of Hungary and Czechoslovakia that Soviet troops be withdrawn by mid-1991; in the agreement concluded in July 1990 with Chancellor Helmut Kohl, he stated that Soviet forces in East Germany would be withdrawn no later than the end of 1994; under the treaty of unification between East and West Germany, East German forces were disbanded or absorbed into the West German army in October 1990. Under Yelstin, there are no longer any Russian troops in Eastern Europe, and the Warsaw Pact has been dissolved. In President Vaclav Havel's words, it was "an outdated remnant of the past."

The Comecon

Once the focus of Soviet thinking on regional integration of the "socialist community," the Council for Mutual Economic Assistance (Comecon) quickly followed the Warsaw Pact into oblivion. At the January 1990 meeting of Comecon, the Soviet Union announced that starting January 1, 1991, trading between the Soviet Union and the East European members would be done on the basis of convertible currency at world market prices. This sudden shift in terms of trade reduced Eastern Europe's purchasing power in the Soviet Union by an estimated 30%, "leaving the former satellites with a $10 billion trade deficit."[23] Eager to cover its own growing deficits in hard currency, Moscow has a strong interest in operating under a new system of settling trade accounts. Under Yeltsin, Russia is insisting that its raw materials be paid for in hard currency at world prices or with high-quality manufactured goods. The Russians are now balking at the shoddy goods they gladly accepted in the past.

Glasnost and democratization also exposed the environmental catastrophe that four decades of unchecked centrally planned investment in heavy industry brought to Eastern Europe. In Soviet-type economies, where planned targets were bureaucratically determined and accountability was nonexistent, polluting and inefficient plants proliferated. The costs of coping with acid rain that destroys the forests, cleaning up poisoned lakes and rivers, and redesigning Soviet-built factories and nuclear reactors will be enormous—upwards of $200 billion. Even greater, however, was the legacy of bitterness toward the Soviet period of Eastern Europe's history.

YELTSIN'S POLICY TOWARD EUROPE

For nearly half a century Europe was divided into two spheres of influence, one American and one Russian. Even though Russia abandoned its hegemony in Eastern Europe in 1990, the lingering impact of this division continues to affect thinking in the region. Postcommunist Russian foreign policy has embraced Gorbachev's concept of a "common European home." Today this means enhancing political and commercial contacts with all states in the region, while pursuing a Europe-wide collective security arrangement.

But with the disintegration of the USSR, Russia lost half of its deep sea ports on the Baltic and Black Seas, and is now separated from Western Europe by an additional zone of buffer states (Ukraine, Moldova, and the Baltic States). As Andrei Zagorsky of the Moscow State Institute of International Relations, has put it, the independence of the former Soviet republics places Russia farther away from Europe than ever before in its history. As a result, Russian analysts view relations with Eastern Europe (now more appropriately termed "Central Europe") as posing different geostrategic problems for Russia than they did for the USSR.

After World War II, Eastern Europe was largely taken for granted by Soviet diplomacy. Even Gorbachev's desire to build a "Common European Home" was clearly an effort to obtain economic and political support from Western Europe, not to address the concerns of the Warsaw Pact states. As a result, when the Berlin Wall collapsed and the communist regimes in Central Europe disintegrated, Russia had no clearly defined objectives in the region.[24]

The first efforts of Russian diplomacy, therefore, were aimed at dealing with the legacy of the Soviet era, first and foremost, the withdrawal of Soviet troops from all of the former Warsaw Pact Countries, a process completed by August 1994. The second objective was mending relations by publicly acknowledging the atrocities of the Soviet era. This included accepting responsibility for the Katyn massacres and apologizing for the Soviet suppression of the Hungarian uprising in

1956 and the Prague Spring of 1968. The third task was to reestablish vital commercial links between the former communist economies in order to stave off economic collapse in the process of economic transition.

Within weeks of the failed 1991 coup, President Yeltsin began to court his Central European neighbors, encouraging them to establish diplomatic relations with the new Russian Federation. Zhenyu Zhelev, President of Bulgaria was the first to do so on his visit to Moscow in October 1991. The treaty between the two countries promised to develop relations "on the basis of respect for the principles of sovereignty, territorial integrity, equality and noninterference in each others affairs, as well as mutually beneficial cooperation."[25] In December 1991 Poland and Russia signed a three-billion-dollar economic agreement which, among other things, stated that Russia would continue to provide Poland with oil and gas at subsidized prices, for which Russia would receive coal, sulfur, medicine, and food products.[26]

Despite these early successes however, little attention was paid to developing a strategy toward Central Europe as a distinct entity. A survey among Soviet diplomats published in the journal of the Russian Foreign Ministry *International Affairs* showed that Central and Southeastern Europe played only the most peripheral role in the concerns of foreign policy professionals. And even though at a meeting of the scientific council on Foreign policy at the RMFA on November 3, 1993, Foreign Minister Kozyrev declared Eastern Europe to be a priority region for Russian national interests, his words seemed contradicted by the very structure of the Foreign Ministry, which still had no section dealing with Central Europe as a whole.[27]

Now that relations with individual states are good and that commercial ties in the region are growing steadily, due in no small measure to the fact that goods from Central Europe are not competitive on the Western European market, Kozyrev claims that Russia is entering a "new phase" in relations with Central Europe characterized by four key objectives. (1) the implementation and expansion of existing bilateral accords; (2) the deepening of legal commercial ties so as to prevent the further expansion of criminal commerce and black marketeering; (3) the expansion of Europe-wide agreements and institutions that transcend the traditional divisions between east and west; and (4) enhanced cooperation on a subregional level within Europe, also with the intent of further eroding the "bloc mentality."

After all is said and done, however, Central Europe as a distinct regional entity is likely to remain an area of secondary importance to Russia. This is partly the result of attempts by states in the region to forge closer links with the West, which paradoxically makes Western Europe all the more important to Russia, but also the result of the region's own inability to act in a unified fashion. At the same time, Central Europe's importance as a buffer zone has been transferred to the westernmost CIS states. Today, Russia's primary Russian interest lies in enhancing regional stability and prevent another Yugoslavia-like ethnic conflict that might spill over into the CIS.

The "Drang nach Westen" that enthralled Central European leaders after the collapse of the Berlin Wall engulfed Russia as well, and for obvious reasons. The countries of the European Union are not only Russia's largest trading partner, but account for three fourths of all humanitarian assistance to Russia. In December 1992 the EC extended to Russia and the other CIS countries the same tariff preferences that it grants to developing countries. On December 9, 1993, the leaders of the EC signed a Joint Political Declaration on Partnership and Cooperation that set the terms for future agreements. Russia is to be granted "most favored nation" status along with other members of the General Agreement on Tariffs and Trade (GATT), and the application of anti-dumping procedures with regard to Russian goods is to be curtailed. By 1998 both parties have agreed to begin discussion the creation of a pan-European free trade zone that includes Russia.[28]

Still, the integration of the Russian economy into the European market has proceeded slowly, partly because of domestic difficulties accompanying reform, and partly because of the understandable reluctance of West Europeans to open their markets to cheap Russian goods that compete with their own. Despite grumbling about discriminatory trade practices, however, most Russian analysts realize that economic integration will have to be a slow process. Many Europeans already view the integration of Western Europe as proceeding too quickly, and there is little public support for expensive economic subsidies of Central and Eastern Europe.

While there has been progress in expanding Russian linkages with Western Europe, these relations are still not as intense as Russia would wish them to be. One reason for this is the European Union's preoccupation with German reunification. The need to bind a more populous and economically more powerful Germany more firmly into the European Union (EU) and dilute its growing continental influence, has given priority to Western European integration before those of other European regions.

The EU's second priority seems to be stabilizing Central Europe, the region most directly on Western Europe's border. The tragic consequences of the Yugoslav war have, if anything, reinforced the EU's preoccupation with preserving territorial integrity and social stability in Central Europe. The most compelling reason today for integrating the countries of Central Europe into the West European alliance structure is not to protect them from Russian invasion, but to mitigate ethnic and social tensions in this region by binding these countries more closely to the political and economic structures of the alliance.

Finally, there is the lingering historic ambivalence about Russia's position in European affairs. Should Europe extend, as de Gaulle thought, "from the Atlantic to the Urals?" Or, should it encompass only Central Europe and the Baltic States? Should it include Belarus and the Ukraine, but not Armenia and Georgia, two of the world's oldest Christian states? If it were to include Russia, would political and economic accords extend all the way to Pacific, or include only Russian regions west of the Urals? The practicalities of integrating a country as large as Russia into European structures must surely appear daunting to the current membership of the European Union.

ENVISIONING RUSSIA AS PART OF EUROPE

As Russia seeks to strengthen ties with individual countries in both the East and the West, its long-term objectives are border transparency across the entire European continent, a pan-European collective security structure, and a Europe-wide free trade zone. Ultimately, Russia's vision for Europe involves bringing an end to the conceptual and practical divisions between the eastern and western parts of the continent.

All this is consistent with the advent of a "greater Europe" heralded in the Charter for a New Europe, signed in Paris on November 21, 1990, by all OSCE member states. It helps to explain Russia's preference for OSCE structures over those of other regional organizations. Despite the fact that Russia's suggestion that NATO, the CIS, and other European regional security organizations be officially subordinated to the CSCE has gathered little international support, Russian diplomats continue to promote the OSCE as the logical successor to NATO in guaranteeing regional security.[29]

More recently, Russia has begun promoting regional cooperation within Europe as one way to encourage trust and confidence at the national level. The Russian Foreign Ministry has cited positively the agreements reached by the "Visegrad Four" (Poland, Czech Republic, Slovak Republic and Hungary), so-called after the venue of their regional summit on February 15, 1991. These four countries agreed to create a free trade zone, and to cooperate in a variety of areas, including military relations. In this context, Russia has sought to establish a closer relationship with Slovakia, even signing an interministerial Slovak-Russia military agreement that Russia hopes may serve as a model for future military cooperation between the former Warsaw Pact States.[30] Following Slovak President Meciar's comment that "Russia will guarantee Slovakia's borders," Moscow even implied in a letter to the leaders of the United States, France, Germany and the United Kingdom, that Russia was prepared to become the coguarantor of East Central Europe's security.[31]

The linchpin to Russia's strategy for Europe-wide integration is reshaping relations among the CIS states into something akin to the former European Free Trade Association. The split between the six nation European Common Market and the seven-nation European Free Trade Association (EFTA) originally arose over the reluctance of the latter to pursue the integrationist strategies set forth in the Treaty of Rome. At the time the notion of a "single Europe" seemed remote, and was opposed by many as an unwarranted derogation of national sovereignty. Russia would like ties within the CIS to begin to resemble those within the EFTA. Then, as relations and trust warranted, they would begin more and more to resemble those within the EU. Ultimately, distinctions between the EU and the CIS might dissolve, just as the EFTA is dissolving today.

If such a pan-European union seems unlikely at present, it is worth remembering that the CIS is already far more economically integrated than the states of Western Europe were thirty years ago. In addition, during the three decades between the signing of the Treaty of Rome and the ratification of the Maastricht Treaty, there were many times when the process of European integration was confidently pronounced dead.

However its long-term agenda for a pan-European trade and security structure works out, in the short term Russia will continue to play a dominant role in European affairs, particularly in Central Europe. Given the natural reluctance of Western Europeans to open their markets to low-priced goods from the east, Russia and the CIS will continue to be a major market for East European products for many years to come.

In the next century, if democratic institutions survive in Russia and the western CIS states, it is quite possible that Europe as a whole will gradually move away from the current bipolar legacy that pits West against East (with Central Europe as a convenient buffer zone) to a single, free trade and security zone envisioned by the Charter for a New Europe.

If it does, a key role will be played by Central Europe. As it becomes economically stronger, and the memory of Soviet occupation recedes, the geographic advantages of this region as the crossing point for trans-European trade will emerge. Similarly, Russia's obsession with security is likely to fade as the region prospers. Provided that Russia is not artificially isolated, the natural economic and political developments under way in the rest of the continent should do much to make Russia an integral part of Europe.

SELECTED BIBLIOGRAPHY

Baranovsky, Vladimir and Spanger Hans-Joachim (eds.). *In From the Cold: Germany, Russia, and the Future of Europe.* Boulder, CO: Westview Press, 1992.

Brzezinski, Zbigniew K. *The Grand Failure: The Birth and Death of Communism in the Twentieth Century.* New York: Scribner's, 1989.

Dawisha, Karen. *Eastern Europe, Gorbachev and Reform: The Great Challenge.* 2nd ed. New York: Cambridge University Press, 1990.

Gati, Charles. *The Bloc That Failed: Soviet-East European Relations in Transition.* Bloomington: Indiana University Press, 1990.

Gianaris, Nicholas V. *The European Community, Eastern Europe, and Russia: Economic and Political Changes.* Westport, CT: Praeger, 1994.

Ginsburgs, George, and Alvin Z. Rubinstein (eds.). *Soviet Foreign Policy Toward Western Europe.* New York: Praeger, 1978.

Heller, Agnes and Ferenc, Feher. *From Yalta to Glasnost: The Dismantling of Stalin's Empire.* Cambridge, MA: Blackwell, 1991.

Keeble, Curtis. *Britain and the Soviet Union, 1917–89.* New York: St. Martin's Press, 1990.

Lindahl, Ingemar. *The Soviet Union and the Nordic Nuclear Weapon Free Zone Proposal.* New York: St. Martin's Press, 1988.

Malcolm, Neil (ed.). *Russia and Europe: An End to Confrontation?* London: Pinter Publishers, 1994.

———. *Soviet Policy Perspectives on Western Europe.* London: Routledge, 1989.

Pravda, Alex, and Peter J.S. Duncan (eds.). *Soviet-British Relations Since the 1970s.* London: Cambridge University Press, 1990.

Remington, Robin A. *The Warsaw Pact.* Cambridge, MA: MIT Press, 1972.

Sodaro, Michael J. *Moscow, Germany, and the West From Khrushchev to Gorbachev.* Ithaca, NY: Cornell University Press, 1991.

Stent, Angela. *From Embargo to Ostpolitik: The Political Economy of West German-Soviet Relations, 1955–1980.* New York: Cambridge University Press, 1981.

Terry, Sarah (ed.). *Soviet Policy in Eastern Europe.* New Haven, CT: Yale University Press, 1984.

Tiersky, Ronald. *French Communism, 1920–1972.* New York: Columbia University Press, 1974.

Vigor, P.H. *Soviet Blitzkrieg Theory.* New York: St. Martin's Press, 1983.

Vloyantes, John P. *Silk Glove Hegemony: Finnish-Soviet Relations, 1944–1974.* Kent, OH: Kent State University Press, 1975.

Wolfe, Thomas. *Soviet Power and Europe, 1945–1970.* Baltimore: Johns Hopkins University Press, 1970.

NOTES

1. Malcolm MacKintosh, "Future Soviet Policy Toward Western Europe," in John C. Garnett (ed.), *The Defense of Western Europe* (London: Macmillan, 1974), p. 39.
2. For a discussion of this concept, see George Ginsburgs and Alvin Z. Rubinstein (eds.), *Soviet Foreign Policy Toward Western Europe* (New York: Praeger, 1978), chap. 1.
3. *FBIS/SOV,* December 11, 1989, p. 47.
4. *New York Times,* February 11, 1990.
5. *Pravda,* February 21, 1990.
6. *FBIS/SOV,* March 9, 1990, p. 27.
7. "O vneshnei politike," *Pravda,* June 26, 1990.
8. George Ginsburgs, "The Theme of Rapallo in Post-War Soviet-West German Relations," *Soviet Union,* vol. 13, no. 3 (1986), pp. 358–365.
9. Judy Dempsey, "Gone but Not Forgotten," *The Financial Times,* August 30, 1994, p. 11.
10. Curtis Keeble, *Britain and the Soviet Union, 1917–89* (New York: St. Martin's Press, 1990), p. 299.
11. *FBIS/SOV,* December 19, 1989, pp. 29–30.
12. Richard Sakwa, *Gorbachev and His Reforms, 1985–1990* (New York: Prentice Hall, 1990), p. 327.
13. *Ibid.,* pp. 397–398.
14. *FBIS/SOV/Russian International Affairs,* March 1, 1995, pp. 10–11.
15. *Pravda,* June 21, 1985.
16. Elizabeth Teague, "*Kommunist* Speaks out in Defense of East Europe's National Interests," *Radio Liberty,* RL 262/85 (August 12, 1985), p. 5.
17. Elizabeth Teague, "Soviet Author Repudiates 'Brezhnev Doctrine,'" *Radio Liberty,* RL 4/86 (December 20, 1985), 1.
18. *The New York Times,* July 2, 1986.
19. *FBIS/SOV,* November 3, 1987, p. 60.
20. *The New York Times,* April 14, 1990.
21. *The New York Times,* Ocotber 19, p. 1989.
22. *FBIS/SOV,* October 27, 1989, p. 41.
23. *The New York Times,* January 10, 1990.
24. "From Eastern Europe in to a United Europe," *International Affairs* (Moscow) (October 1991), p. 133.
25. S. Mushkaterov, "Diplomatic Relations Establisahed" *CDSP,* vol. 43, no. 43 (1991), p. 25.
26. N. Yermolovich "Russia and Poland Conclude $3 Billion Trade Agreement" *CDSP,* vol. 43, no. 52 (1991), p. 21.

27. "Eastern Europe and Russia" *International Affairs* (Moscow) (March–April 1994), p. 21
28. Boris Pichugin, "The EC and Russia in the All-Europe Context" *International Affairs* (March–April 1994), pp. 40–41.
29. Michael Mihalks. "OSCE as the Basis for New Security Order in Europe," *OMRI Daily Digest,* April 5, 1995.
30. Yutaka Akino and Adma Smith Albion, "Russia-Ukraine-Visegrad Four:The Kozyrev Doctrine in Action," Prague: European Studies Center Institute for EastWest Studies, 1993), pp. 11–12
31. *Ibid.,* p. 1

Chapter
9

Russia in Asia

Despite its long history of settlement east of the Urals, Russia has never thought of itself as an Asian power. Since early Muscovite times, when eastward settlement began, political authority always lagged behind the eastward movement of the population. Thus, it might be said of Russia, as one pundit said of Britain, that it gained its empire in Asia in a fit of absent-mindedness. This ambivalence, coupled with the relative sparsity of the population from the Urals to the Pacific Ocean, and the wealth of natural resources of the region, has often led to frictions between Russia and its Asian neighbors.

The apparent closeness of Stalin and Mao belied the underlying tensions over leadership of the world Communist movement. These tensions erupted publicly after Stalin's death. Although outright war was avoided during the Soviet period, border disputes have occasionally erupted into armed conflict costing several hundred lives. Oddly enough, it was left to the first postcommunist Russian leader, Boris Yeltsin, to put Russo-Chinese relations on a better footing. The fact that the two leaderships are no longer vying for ideological preeminence has helped to clear the way for accords on a number of substantive issues.

Meanwhile, in Japan the obstacle to closer ties with Russia—Russian ownership of the four islands seized after World War II—remains. In Korea, Russia has switched from supporting North Korea to forging close ties with the much more economically dynamic South. Likewise, Russia has all but abandoned its erstwhile ally Vietnam, and concentrated instead on cultivating relations with the successful market economies of Southeast Asia.

Postcommunist Russia's main objectives are the enhancement of regional stability, participation in any regional alliance structures, and cultivating access to lucrative regional markets. Despite a historical penchant for viewing Russia first and foremost as a European power, Russian analysts increasingly see that in the twenty-first century Russia must focus increasingly on developing its role as an Asian power.

THE SINO-SOVIET DISPUTE, 1957–1990

In retrospect, the Stalin era looms as the high-water mark of Sino-Soviet amity and cooperation during the Soviet period. From 1955 on, tensions mounted and relations deteriorated, as national interests overshadowed Communist ecumenism.

Although the Sino-Soviet dispute is often cast within an ideological framework, it was fundamentally a rivalry over power that mirrored the divergent strategies, interests, and objectives of the two countries during the period from the mid-1950s to the late 1980s. Briefly, the main source of discord were five broad issues.

First, as the senior and most powerful member of the world communist movement, Moscow believed it had the authority to establish basic strategy for the bloc, especially to decide on the best way to deal with the capitalist world. Khrushchev resented the pretensions to leadership of this newcomer to the international scene. He felt Mao was unfamiliar with global realities and did not appreciate the extent to which imperialism (in particular, the United States) could be weakened by non-military means. Moscow couched its political preferences in Marxist-Leninist formulations that it claimed it had the indisputable right to interpret. Thus, the struggle over ideology was also a struggle for control of the communist world's foreign policy agenda. This issue became increasingly difficult to reconcile after Khrushchev's de-Stalinization speech, which Mao considered a threat to his authority.

Second, the two nations disagreed over priorities: The areas and issues that were most important to Moscow were least important to Beijing, and vice versa. For example, if for no other reason than that the main military threat to the USSR came from the West, Moscow's primary political interest was drawn to European developments, to centrifugal tendencies in Eastern Europe, to the resurgence of West Germany, and to the impact of the Common Market. A power satisfied territorially, the Soviet Union was not prepared to go to war against the United States over the Taiwan question, an issue that was paramount in Chinese thinking. Thus did geography, history, and economics shape national priorities.

Third, Moscow and Beijing differed in their approaches to developing countries. While the differences were not as clear-cut as many in the West sometimes imagined, they did connote China's readiness to advocate militant policies that would have interfered with Moscow's courtship of key Third World countries and exacerbated relations between the Soviet Union and the United States. A major source of discord between Moscow and Beijing was Soviet assistance to India, particularly the military help given after the Sino-Indian war of 1962. Another was Moscow's program of extending considerable economic and military assistance to noncommunist nonaligned countries, whereas aid to China was brusquely terminated in 1960. By emphasizing the revolutionary path to power and opposing (more in principle than in practice) cooperation between local communist parties and bourgeois-nationalist parties, China directly challenged the Soviet strategy for spreading Communist influence in the Third World.

Fourth, Moscow's unwillingness after 1959 to help China to develop a nuclear capability and its signing of the limited nuclear test ban treaty in 1963 signified to China a Soviet desire to keep its communist ally a second-rate military power dependent on Moscow's nuclear shield. Ironically, the Chinese detonated their first nuclear explosion in October 1964, literally within hours of Khrushchev's fall from power.

Fifth, China had long-standing border grievances against the USSR. Under treaties imposed on imperial China by tsarist Russia in 1858, 1860, and 1864, China was forced to cede almost one million square miles of territory in central Asia and the maritime provinces of Siberia. Beijing argued that these "unequal treaties" should be renegotiated, a demand rejected by Moscow.

After Khrushchev was toppled, Brezhnev acted quickly to suspend the vitu-- perative exchanges with the Chinese. For a time the Soviets shelved their polemics and refrained from responding to Chinese gibes that they were practicing "Khrushchevism without Khrushchev." However, within the world communist movement, Moscow strengthened its ties. For example, it concluded a new treaty of alliance with the Mongolian People's Republic, which had long depended on Moscow and feared Beijing's ambitions; it supported the establishment of a rival Communist Party in Japan to compete with the entrenched pro-Chinese one; and in February 1965, Premier Kosygin visited North Korea and North Vietnam, which generally followed China's lead in intrabloc politics for geostrategic reasons but which were noncommittal in the dispute itself.

By late 1966 the grievances between the Soviet Union and China were unchanged. In October, Moscow ordered all Chinese students to return home, in retaliation for the expulsion of Soviet students from China. In November, it resumed open attacks on Beijing, charging that "experience shows that success is achieved by Communist parties that guide themselves unswervingly by Marxism-Leninism, while those espousing pseudo-revolutionary phraseology and dogmas inevitably suffer a fiasco."

On March 2, 14, and 15, 1969, border clashes erupted at the confluence of the Amur and Ussuri rivers below the Soviet city of Khabarovsk in the vicinity of a swampy, uninhabited, vaguely delineated area known as Damansky Island. For the first time, regular military units of one communist country fought against those of another. A common adherence to Marxism-Leninism was no automatic bar to conflict. Skirmishes in this area had been going on since 1959, and each side had cited thousands of violations by the other. The Damansky affair symbolized a dangerous deterioration in diplomatic relations;[1] it was followed in late spring and early summer by border clashes in Xinjiang and veiled Soviet threats of a preemptive strike against China's nuclear installation at Lop Nor. Realizing the gravity of the situation, Beijing reopened talks on October 20, 1969.

To make sure that the ideological militancy and economic disruptiveness of the Cultural Revolution would not tempt Mao to start new border incidents, *Pravda* issued a stern warning on August 28, 1969. Observing that "given goodwill, the necessary conditions can and must be assured to guarantee normal relations between the Soviet Union and the People's Republic of China," it called on China to cease "its absurd territorial claims on the Soviet Union" and warned that if a war broke out, "with the existing weaponry, lethal armaments, and modern means of delivery, it would not spare a single continent." This is as close as the Soviet Union has ever come to threatening the use of nuclear weapons against China. There is conjecture that Moscow was not only warning China but also trying to sound out Washington's reaction to a possible strike against the nuclear facility at Lop Nor in Xinjiang.[2]

The Soviet leadership's growing perception of implacable Chinese hostility prompted a major military buildup. Beginning in the mid-1960s, even before the Damansky Island crisis, Moscow increased the number of divisions in the Far East from fifteen in 1967 to twenty-one in 1969, thirty in 1970, and forty-five in 1980—about 25% of the entire Soviet army. The Soviet army possessed commanding superiority in tanks, artillery, combat aircraft, and, of course, nuclear-capable missiles. As a result of the Soviet-Mongolian treaty (renewed on October 19, 1976), Moscow significantly increased its combat forces in the MPR. Militarily, the Soviet army was more than a match for the numerically larger Chinese forces, whose level of modernization and firepower was far behind the USSR's. The Soviet naval buildup in the Far East in the late 1970s and 1980s, though an additional source of tension with Japan, served as a constant reminder to China of its vulnerability to Soviet military power.

Sino-Soviet tensions festered after the dramatic announcement in mid-August 1971 that Secretary of State Henry Kissinger had arrived secretly in Beijing and arranged for President Richard Nixon to visit China the following year. This completely new variable, a stunning turnabout, fueled Soviet paranoia over possible U.S.-Chinese collusion against the USSR. For Moscow there was bitter irony in Beijing's startling policy reversal, which was in its own way every bit as politically momentous as Moscow's deal with Berlin in 1939 had been.

Moscow's détente toward the West having failed to perpetuate the isolation of China, the Kremlin's policy of containing China had to be adapted to the new political situation. Soviet leaders declared that they were not in principle against the Sino-U.S. normalization of relations, provided that it was not used as a lever against other parties. Their worst fears were of secret arrangements designed against the USSR. After Nixon's visit to China in February 1972 (he was also scheduled to go to Moscow in May), Brezhnev continued to work for the containment of China through a combination of military and diplomatic means, while holding out the offer of improved ties and hoping that when Mao died his successors would prove amenable to a Sino-Soviet reconciliation.

For the next few years, Soviet policy in the Far East sought to offset Beijing's opening to the West with a campaign to strengthen Moscow's own ties with Mongolia, North Korea, and Japan; to undercut Chinese standing in the Third World by exposing its negligible ability to help national liberation movements or governments in need of military or economic assistance; to play on the fears of Chinese ambitions in Southeast Asian countries, including Vietnam; and to enhance the USSR's prestige through projection of its formidable military power.

GORBACHEV AND CHINA

By the early 1980s Soviet policy in Asia had become stagnant. Long-standing hostilities with China kept a sizable Soviet military presence in Mongolia and along the Chinese border. Relations with Japan remained stuck on the issue of returning the four southern Kurile islands claimed by Tokyo. On the Korean peninsula, Russia's traditional support for the Stalinist regime of North Korean communist leader Kim Il-Sung excluded the possibility of improving ties with the burgeoning economy of South Korea. Even Vietnam, Russia's strategic ally against "world imperialism" had decided to normalize relations with both Laos and China and diminish its reliance on Soviet economic assistance. As part of his "new political thinking, Mikhail Gorbachev decided to put renewed emphasis on improving relations with Asia, and most particularly with the neighbor with whom the Soviet Union shared the world's longest border—China.

In a major speech delivered in Vladivostok on July 28, 1986, Gorbachev spoke of "the need for an urgent, radical break with many of the conventional approaches to foreign policy."[3] Comparing the situation in the Far East with that in Europe—clearly, with the Soviet Union's two-front problem in mind—he noted that "the Pacific region as a whole is not yet militarized to the same extent as the European region," but the potential for this happening "is truly enormous and the consequences extremely dangerous." For the first time, he addressed directly "the three obstacles" raised by the Chinese as preconditions for an improvement in Sino-Soviet relations: Mongolia, Afghanistan, and Kampuchea. Gorbachev held out three conciliatory olive twigs, saying that "the question of withdrawing a considerable number of Soviet troops from Mongolia is being examined" by Moscow and Ulan Bator, that the Soviet government would withdraw six regiments from Afghanistan by the end of the year, and that the Kampuchean issue (that is, the USSR's subsidizing of Vietnam's occupation of Kampuchea) "depends on the normalization of Chinese-Vietnamese relations." He also called for expanded trade and hinted at concessions on long-festering border issues and the construction of a railroad linking the Xinjiang Uygur Autonomous region of China and Soviet Kazakhstan. It was his concrete proposal that "the official border could pass along the main channel" (particularly of the confluence of the Amur and Ussuri Rivers near Khabarovsk) that broke the logjam and led to the resumption of border negotiations in February 1987 after almost a decade.

Gorbachev's overture was impelled by a desire to change China from an enemy to a good neighbor, to shed the divisive legacy of Khrushchev and Brezhnev and to end the Soviet Union's isolation from the dynamic societies of the Pacific Basin, to reduce the arms burden, to attenuate the anti-Soviet alignments of China (and Japan) with the United States, and to expand economic interaction.

In a speech on September 16, 1988, in the Siberian city of Krasnoyarsk, Gorbachev addressed "the problems of untying the knots of conflict and confrontation and the curbing of militarization." Noting that "some people" had "tried to cast doubt on the sincerity" of his Vladivostok initiative, he called for ensuring security "not by means of the arms race but by political and economic means and by creating a climate which removes hostility, suspicion, and mistrust." Gorbachev said the USSR would abandon its naval base in Cam Ranh Bay in Vietnam if the United States withdrew from the Philippines, and again he called for a summit meeting. This time, in contrast with two years earlier, the Chinese responded positively, sending Foreign Minister Qian Qichen to Moscow in December with an invitation for Gorbachev to visit China. Journeying to Beijing in February 1989 to finalize arrangements for the upcoming summit, Shevardnadze confirmed Soviet plans to cut approximately 260,000 troops along the Sino-Soviet border, including more than 75% of the estimated 55,000 total still in Mongolia (the token withdrawal of 11,000 in 1987 had not impressed the Chinese).

The summit between Gorbachev and Deng Xiaoping, in Beijing from May 15 to 18, 1989—the first since Khrushchev went to meet Mao Zedong in 1959—symbolized an end to the Sino-Soviet Cold War and ushered in a time of incremental normalization. Unfortunately for Gorbachev, what should have been a singularly satisfying moment was marred by the Chinese leaders' distraction over the prodemocracy student demonstrations in Tiananmen Square. The demonstrations frequently disrupted the official program; moreover, "less than eager to endanger their carefully crafted series of relationships with the West by rushing to return Moscow's would-be ardent embrace, the Chinese chose to keep their distance."[4] For his part, Gorbachev, the international evangelist of glasnost, was uncharacteristically silent, not wishing to offend his hosts, but his mere presence during the civil unrest contributed to their acute embarrassment. The joint communiqué issued on May 18 contained no concessions by either side.

Despite Gorbachev's best efforts, there was no resumption of party-to-party ties; no new breakthrough on the key territorial issues, except that China quietly shelved its more extravagant claims; and no change in the preponderant military power that the Soviet Union deployed in the area. Beijing was disturbed by the upheavals in Eastern Europe and remained leery of glasnost and perestroika. Moscow was disappointed by the modest expansion of trade. Although Sino-Soviet trade more than doubled in the latter part of the 1980s and grew "more than 10 times as much as in 1981, before the process of normalization began," the USSR trailed "a distant fifth among China's trading partners, accounting for only 3.1 percent of China's total foreign trade [in 1916, Russia's share was more than 9 percent], while China accounted for less than 2 percent of Soviet trade."[5] The problems were mainly on the Soviet side—poor-quality goods, erratic deliveries, an absence of modern forms of business management and partnership, and a paucity of market information about China's capabilities.[6]

Still, Gorbachev made a promising start. He took steps to reassure the Chinese with a lower level of military deployment along the border; an increase in informal cross-border trade, based mainly on barter; and the promotion of a number of large-scale cooperative projects such as the railroad line connecting Urumqi in Xinjiang province and Alma Ata in Soviet Kazakhstan. A ten-year agreement on economic and scientific cooperation was signed in April 1990 and, in July, China opened negotiations "for the purchase of Soviet military technology" for the first time since the 1950s.[7]

Gorbachev's visit proved to be historic, not only because he was the first Soviet leader to visit China since the late 1950s, but also because his appearance before adoring throngs served as a catalyst for reform minded youth. Not long after his departure, the huge crowds gathered on Tiananmen Square to support the democracy movement were suppressed. General Secretary Zhao Ziyang was forced to resign, and as many as a thousand students were killed when the army moved against the remaining occupants of the square on the night of June 3–4.

The new Chinese leadership's resentment against Gorbachev was softened somewhat by the mission of Valentin Falin, hardline head of the Central Committee's International Department, to reassure Beijing of Soviet support and under-standing for the actions of the new leadership. In return, the Chinese chose not to protest the transfer of thousands of tanks, armored vehicles, and other military equipment east of the Urals in the fall of 1990, under the terms of the new Conventional Forces in Europe (CFE) Treaty. Two subsequent visits, by Foreign Minister Eduard Shevardnadze and Defense Minister Dmitry Yazov, paved the way for the signature of a Soviet-Chinese Border Accord (by then called the Russian-Chinese Border Accord) on May 15, 1991.

This accord now serves as the cornerstone of the ongoing Russian-Chinese rapprochement. It resolved numerous disagreements along the disputed (4300 km) Russian border with China that had led to armed clashes between the two nations in 1969. Gorbachev agreed to the Thalweg principle, according to which Russia would retain half of the islands identified by 1845 treaty in the Amur-Ussuri rivers. In return, the status of several islands around the city of Khabarovsk, although undetermined, would be left under Russian control. Finally, the agreement established a time frame for beginning the final demarcation of borders between the two countries. This accord, one of Gorbachev's most significant achievements in Asia, was a milestone in diplomatic relations between the two countries. The resolution of the territorial dispute between the two largest countries, even if only in principle, promised to shift the substance of relations from competition to active cooperation.

YELTSIN'S CHINA POLICY

The barely disguised Chinese support for the coup plotters in August 1991, however, threatened this rapprochement even before it had begun. The overarching importance of reducing military tensions with China, however, led Yeltsin to send Vladimir Lukin, then Chairman of the Foreign Affairs Committee of the Russian Parliament, to Beijing in December 1991 to reassure the Chinese leadership that political upheavals in Russia would not affect Sino-Russian relations, and that Russia would abide by all treaties and agreements signed by the Soviet Union.

When President Yeltsin made his first visit to China on December 17, 1992, he came, as he put it, "to usher in a new era in Russo-Chinese relations."[8] Building on the groundwork that had been laid by Gorbachev in the previous three years, Moscow and Beijing moved from limited cooperation to extensive cooperation. Of particular importance was the changed strategic context. For the first time in several centuries, Russia was in an intrinsically weaker position vis-à-vis China, and hence no longer a threat. Not only was its economy in shambles, its military demoralized, and its role in regional affairs drastically diminished as a result of the collapse of the USSR, but as a noncommunist country it is now also less of an ideological problem for China's aging oligarchy.

If pragmatism is the cement in the new relationship, then trade and a convergence of strategic interests are its key building blocks. After approaching $8 billion in 1993, trade with China fell back to 1992 levels in 1994, resuming steady growth in 1995. Experts expect that as the Russian economy revives, the total volume of trade between the two countries may double by the year 2000, possibly making

China Russia's largest trading partner. China has already become a major purchaser of Russian military equipment—$1.8 billion in 1992 alone. Strapped for cash, Russia's military-industrial lobby has so far been able to override any concern's about the long-term implications for Russia's security interests. The short-term attraction of hard cash has simply overwhelmed those who worry about Russia's readiness to upgrade China's military establishment, including radar-evading stealth technology for a new generation of Chinese fighter jets and a medium range strategic bomber that would substantially increase Chinese force projection capabilities.[9]

Cementing this new relationship, which Chinese Foreign Minister Qian Qichen described as "ruling out confrontation and at the same time not ruling out an alliance," was, Boris Yeltsin's visit to Beijing in December 1992 to sign a memorandum of understanding on military cooperation that declared Russia's willingness to "cooperate in all sectors, including the most sophisticated armaments and weapons." Going beyond what had been accomplished under Gorbachev, Russia and China now committed themselves not to enter into any "military-political alliance directed against the other party."[10]

In November 1993, Russia and China signed a five year agreement on military cooperation that provided a framework for the expanded transfer of advanced military technology and expertise from Russia. It also consolidates the close ties between the Russian military-industrial complex and their Chinese counterpart, dominated by the PLA (People's Liberation Army), which is likely to be a key player in the upcoming succession crisis in China.

The strategic concerns of the two countries are converging far more than they are diverging. They include a common desire for stability along their long and erratically delineated border; fear over Japan's growing regional influence; an interest in stability on the Korean peninsula; and the pursuit of good relations with the United States, which both countries wish to see playing a minor role in Asia. Certainly, by the time the Jiang Zemin visited Moscow in September 1994, the first visit by a Chinese head of state since 1950, the growing Sino-Soviet détente was showing signs of moving toward an entente of sorts.

Despite the initial reluctance on the part of the Russian Foreign Ministry and some of Yeltsin's closest advisors to forge closer ties with the brutal suppressors of Tiananmen square, the Russian leadership realizes that stability and good relations along the world's longest border are simply too important to hold hostage to differing ideologies. Moreover, as the Foreign Ministry has shifted to a more Eurasian view of Russia's role, initial concerns that a Sino-Russian entente might harm Russian relations with the West have evaporated.

To be sure, a number of problems still remain between the two nations, though for the moment they are largely quiescent: the difficult border negotiations; the flow of migrant Chinese workers into Siberia; rivalry in Mongolia and Central Asia; and espionage. There is also Russia's attraction to Taiwan, whose generous foreign assistance and economic achievements have created a powerful pro-Taiwan lobby in the Kremlin.[11] To allay Chinese concerns, Yeltsin took the unusual step of issuing a decree affirming Russia's "one China policy" and keeping relations with Taiwan on an "unofficial" level. As trade with Taiwan expands, however, the issue may again become a source of disagreement.

Another issue now much more prominent than in communist times is the Chinese government's violations of human rights. As a commentator in *Izvestiya* remarked, "those who crushed the student's revolt in Beijing can hardly expect the sympathy of Russian leaders." Following the West's lead, Russia has voted for the inclusion of Tibet on the agenda of the UN High Commission on Human Rights since 1991. In a March 1992 visit to China, however, Foreign Minister Kozyrev stated that while Russia would continue to criticize China's human rights record, this would not be allowed to undermine overall relations. In fact, Yeltsin's visit to China in late April 1996 demonstrated the new "climate of trust" between Russia and China, in its array of agreements on military-technical cooperation, economic issues, and delineation of Central Asian and Asian borders.

JAPAN'S RELATIONS WITH MOSCOW

At the time of the Korean War, Moscow regarded Japan as "the main American bridgehead in the Far East." Japan was the staging area from which the United States mounted its military operations in Korea and threatened the Soviet Union and China with long-range air power. The United States used the war to accelerate the transition of Japan from occupied ex-enemy state to passive participant and incipient ally. In September 1951, at the San Francisco conference convened to sign a peace treaty with Japan, Soviet aims toward Japan emerged. The Soviet delegate proposed Japan's neutralization: that Japan agree "not to enter into any coalitions or military alliance directed against any Power which participated with its armed forces in the war against Japan," and that it not permit any foreign power to have its troops or military bases on Japanese territory. There were other proposed amendments as well, including limits on Japanese rearmament, demilitarization of all straits leading into the Japan Sea, and acknowledgment of Soviet title to all the northern islands under Soviet occupation. The Soviet proposals were rejected; the peace treaty was signed, though not by the Soviet Union (or China), and Japan concluded a mutual security treaty with the United States.

After Stalin's death, Soviet leaders desired to establish diplomatic ties with Japan but were unwilling to accede to Japan's demand for the immediate return of Shikotan and the Habomai Islands off northern Hokkaido. They persuaded a weak Japanese government to agree to the Adenauer formula, which had led to the reestablishment of diplomatic ties between the USSR and West Germany, namely, "restoring diplomatic relations before the differences between the two countries were resolved"; and to accept the promise of the return of the above-mentioned islands "under certain conditions" after the signing of a formal peace treaty.[13] In the declaration signed on October 19, 1956, leading to the resumption of bilateral relations, Moscow recognized the right of Japan to enter into diplomatic and military agreements with any country and disengaged itself from a common approach with Beijing to Japan, thereby angering Mao.

Over the years, there has been a remarkable continuity in Moscow's objectives: to undermine the U.S.-Japanese mutual security pact, to keep Japan from acquiring nuclear weapons or rearming on a major scale (which would be contrary to a provision in the U.S.-imposed Japanese constitution limiting Japan to "self-defense" forces), to see the U.S. military presence in Japan reduced, and to expand economic relations.

A major impediment to better political relations has been Moscow's unwillingness to return what Japan calls the northern territories, which include Shikotan and a group of five islands called Habomai (all of which Moscow in 1956 had agreed to return) as well as Iturup and Kunashir, both of which Moscow insists Japan renounced in 1951 at San Francisco. In a reversal of its promise of 1956, the USSR linked the return of Shikotan and Habomai to Japan's renunciation of the U.S.-Japanese security pact. In November 1967, Politburo member Mikhail Suslov told a visiting Japanese Socialist party delegation that the USSR would never return any former Japanese territory as long as Japan's military pact with the United States was in effect.

In the early 1970s Soviet leaders found it expedient to hint at a possible compromise, without ever being really specific. This attitude was motivated by the beginnings of a Sino-Japanese rapprochement, which led China to support the Japanese claim to the northern territories as Sino-Soviet relations worsened, and by the Nixon visit to China in February 1972, which aroused Soviet fears of U.S.-Chinese-Japanese collusion against the USSR. High-level exchanges all faltered on the inability to reach agreement on a peace treaty, which in turn foundered on the territorial dispute.

The issue was further complicated in December 1976 when the Soviet government announced the establishment of a 200-nautical-mile fishing zone, effective March 1, 1977, that makes the ability of Japanese fishermen to operate in Soviet waters and in the vicinity of the disputed islands hostage to Soviet goodwill.[14] After the Soviet Union and Japan established diplomatic relations in 1925, Moscow used the fisheries issue to obtain diplomatic and political concessions from the Japanese government. Paradoxically, however, with the proclamation of the 200-nautical-mile fishing zone, it has lost much of its former leverage, because in reaction to restrictions placed on its own catches by other countries, Moscow reduced Japanese quotas.

> Based on the so-called "principle of equal quota," what Moscow and Tokyo have agreed upon since 1979 are total fishing quotas of 750,000 and 650,000 tons, respectively for Japanese and Russian fishermen within the other's 200-mile zone. Whereas the Japanese quota became about half of the previous one of 1,220,000 tons, the Soviet quota has remained the same or even increased above the former level of 500,000—600,000 tons. Furthermore, in an exchange of a 100,000 ton difference, the Japanese side has been paying the USSR a fee in foreign currency, which the Soviet Union badly needs. As these quotas have become a stable standard acceptable for both the USSR and Japan, the Japan-Soviet negotiations on fishing rights have recently become pro forma, almost ceremonial, lasting only about ten days. Thus, the fishing issue has ceased to be a serious source of dispute or a resource for manipulation by the Soviets.

The economic potentialities of Soviet-Japanese trade have been limited by Japan's political dissatisfaction, even though economic considerations generally play a very important role in Japanese foreign policy. Moscow courted Japanese investment to develop its rich oil, natural gas, and mineral deposits in Siberia and to discourage Japan's keen interest in the Chinese market. It hoped that a combination of economic inducements and pressure would influence Japanese foreign policy and that an innate pragmatism on both sides would keep economics fairly separate from politics. In this, however, its thinking was out of date. Japan's increasingly labor-intensive, high-tech economy "has resulted in a greatly reduced level of demand for Soviet raw materials, particularly in the energy, steel, and construction sectors that once absorbed the vast majority of Soviet exports to Japan."[16] Prospective Japanese investors are not as attracted to the proximity of the resources of Siberia as they were in the 1970s. Moscow wants Japan's high-technology equipment; some it can purchase, and some it tries to obtain by means of espionage and bribery (as in the mid-1980s when Toshiba and the Kongberg Vaapenfabrik of Norway surreptitiously sold computer controls for Japanese milling machines that were used by the Soviet military to manufacture better propellers for nuclear submarines).

In 1975 and 1976, Moscow proposed a Soviet-Japanese treaty of amity that would sidestep territorial issues—as did the prospective Sino-Japanese treaty that avoided any mention of the disputed Senkaku Islands—but the Japanese replied that the Soviet-Japanese territorial issue involved vital national interests. The Soviet government regarded the Sino-Japanese treaty as anti-Soviet, first, because of inclusion, at Beijing's insistence, of the antihegemony clause, which states that "the contracting parties declare that neither of them should seek hegemony in the Asia-Pacific region or in any other region and each is opposed to efforts by any other country or group of countries to establish such hegemony"; and second, because it reinforced Moscow's fear of a Beijing-Tokyo-Washington military alliance being formed against the USSR.

GORBACHEV'S FLAWED COURTSHIP

Although Soviet criticism of Japan's "militarism" and close ties to the United States continued during the months after the change of leadership in the Kremlin in March 1985, by the end of that summer a number of overtures signaled Gorbachev's desire to institute a new "common language" and improve relations.[17] They were not successful, however. The visit by Shevardnadze in January 1986, the first in ten years by a Soviet foreign minister, was a disappointment, because he brought no concessions on security or territorial issues, and Gorbachev's Vladivostok speech in July contained nothing to interest the Japanese. Also, his projected visit to Japan in January 1987, eagerly arranged by then-Prime Minister Yasuhiro Nakasone, failed to materialize, largely because of Nakasone's inability, politically, to accede to Gorbachev's insistence that the issue of the "Northern Territories" not be raised.

Gorbachev was surprised and stymied by Tokyo's obduracy. Aware of the strong anti-Soviet sentiment in Japan, he nonetheless kept thinking that the potential of the Soviet Union's market and resources would be sufficient to sidetrack, if not overcome, the territorial dispute, and that economic possibilities could be separated from political problems, as they had been in the Soviet-German relationship. Occupied with securing his power at home, establishing better relations with the United States, and coming to terms with the implications of "new thinking" in the European context, he had little time for attention to Japan. By mid-1988, however, with the growing importance of Shevardnadze and the Ministry of Foreign Affairs (MFA) in foreign policy decision making and the relative decline in influence of the International Department of the CPSU's Central Committee, signs of flexibility appeared on the Soviet side: Japanese officials were permitted to speak of the Northern Territories problem on Soviet television, and Soviet journalists and academics wrote about the dispute over the islands, acknowledging that it would exist "as long as Japan insists that it does."[18]

By Shevardnadze's second visit in December 1988, the Soviet government had abandoned its previous position that there was no problem, since the territories were clearly Soviet, and had agreed to discuss the issue. A joint Soviet-Japanese working group was set up to explore the negotiation of a peace treaty, which would officially settle all unresolved issues remaining from the Second World War and, in this context, would include the territorial issue. At the first meeting of the working group in March 1989, Soviet Deputy Foreign Minister Igor Rogachev's position was that the Kurile Islands, which were handed over to the Soviet Union by the Yalta accords, "are age-old Russian lands by right of first discovery, first annexation, first settlement, and first exploration"; and that Japanese arguments saying the islands of Iturup, Kunashir, Habomai, and Shikotan are not part of the Kurile chain are only "attempts to artificially manipulate the concept of the Kurile Islands" and have "no serious foundation."[19]

But there were also Soviet analysts who called for concessions and unilateral initiatives. Some proposals suggested the demilitarization of the islands, the establishment of joint economic ventures to exploit their natural resources, and even the leasing of some of the islands to Japan. Others emphasized the need to reduce Japan's fear of the Soviet Union and recommended that the government "withdraw troops from border areas, put an end to ostentatious patrols off the Japanese coast, notify Tokyo of military exercises in areas contiguous to Japan, and so on"[20]; and the reformist historian, and People's Deputy, Dr. Yurii Afanasyev, came out unequivocally for "the return of four of the Kurile Islands to Japan."[21]

When Aleksandr N. Yakovlev, a key Gorbachev confidant, visited Tokyo in November 1989 at the head of a delegation from the Supreme Soviet, the Soviet-Japanese dialogue took on a new importance. In September 1990 Shevardnadze arrived to complete the arrangements for Gorbachev's trip in April 1991. Seen as a landmark event at the time, the visit proved to be a show without substance. Gorbachev was, by this time, too weak at home to deliver the major concessions required by Tokyo for reconciliation.

YELSTIN AND JAPAN

At the urging of his advisers, who saw Japan as a possible major investor and supplier of foreign assistance to Russia, Boris Yeltsin visited Japan in January 1990 (five months before his election to head the Russian Supreme Soviet) and proposed an innovative five step process to re-open negotiations. The steps would include:

1. formal recognition of the existence of a territorial dispute;
2. demilitarization of the four southernmost Kurile islands;
3. an agreement creating a free enterprise zone, with preferential treatment for Japanese investment. At the same time, Russia and Japan would conclude a broad-ranging treaty of cooperation on trade, science, technology, economic, cultural, and humanitarian exchanges;
4. formal signing of a peace treaty; and
5. formal settlement of territorial issues.

Yeltsin envisioned the entire process as requiring roughly a generation to complete. After the collapse of the Soviet Union, in December 1991, Foreign Minister Kozyrev specifically mentioned that the 1956 joint agreement would be an acceptable starting point for negotiations. Japan has responded by altering its position that the territories must be returned before a peace treaty can be signed. It is now willing to delay transfer of the island if Russia formally recognizes Japanese sovereignty over them.

Despite some encouraging signs, the fate of the disputed islands remains a crucial stumbling block to better relations. The military has stated that Kunashiri and Etorofu must be kept because they control the access to the Sea of Okhotsk. The area around Habomais and Shitokan is also believed to be rich in manganese nodules and crusts as well as barite nodules and crusts, while Kunashiri and Etorofu are described as having large deposits of titanium and magnetite. Therefore, the loss of these islands could mean a substantial economic loss for Russia down the road.[23] In addition, a variety of other problems remain: low quotas for Japanese fishermen operating in Russia's two hundred-mile economic zone; Russia's seizure of Japanese fishing boats in disputed waters; Russia's reluctance to support a permanent seat on the UN Security Council for Japan; and Russia's dumping of nuclear waste into the Sea of Japan.

Further progress is also hostage to ambitious regional politicians like Valentin Fedorov, chief administrator of the Sakhalin region. Fedorov has publicly rejected the idea of transferring any territory under his control, and has pledged to refuse to implement any such decree. If Moscow returned the islands to Japan, Fedorov said the Far East region "would have to consider demanding full independence" from Moscow.[24] Fedorov and other regional leaders have been able to stir up concerns in the Russian parliament about "giving away" Russian land for momentary financial gains, thus effectively killing any deal.[25] Interestingly, in his recent memoirs Foreign Minister Kozyrev says that Japan did indeed offer Russia $28 billion for the four Kurile Islands, but the offer was rejected.[26]

Yeltsin caused a flurry of optimism in Tokyo on February 27, 1992, when, in a letter to Japan's prime minister, he referred to Japan as a "potential ally," and sent his foreign minister for talks.[27] It soon became apparent, however, that Kozyrev had no mandate to make the concessions expected by Japan. In addition, a long-scheduled trip by Yeltsin to Japan that was to help establish a new framework for Russo-Japanese relations was delayed twice. Although he attended a G7 ministerial meeting in Tokyo in July 1993, he did so only after receiving assurances that the islands would not be discussed.

When his long-awaited visit finally took place, in October 1993, a scant week after Yeltsin had used the military to crush his parliamentary opponents, Yeltsin did not offer any major concessions on the islands, but he did tell Japanese Prime Minister Morihiro Hosokawa that "the issue exists and must be resolved some day." Perhaps equally important, Yeltsin went out of his way to apologize for the "inhuman" treatment of Japanese prisoners of war captured by the Soviet Union during World War II.[28]

It has often been suggested that Japan, with its lack of resources but strong financial resources, and the Russian Far East, rich in resources but in dire need of investment, are ideal trading partners. Simply conceding the islands to Japan, it is said, would release a flood of Japanese direct investments in the region and do much to improve the confidence of investors from other Asian countries.

Other analysts, however, point out that Japanese investment has been directed largely toward regions of political stability. Forty-six percent of Japanese direct investments overseas went to North America, while only 0.8% went to its neighbor China. Given Russia's instability, they say, it is unlikely that return of the islands would result in any substantial increase in Japanese investment.

The main obstacle to resolving this issue, however, is undoubtedly psychological. Russian analysts have dubbed this dilemma the "Kaliningrad syndrome," after the small, isolated Russian enclave taken from Nazi Germany. The fear is that such territories will be sold back to foreign countries, and the Russians living there will be forced out. This is a time when public consciousness is still reeling from the loss of the Soviet republics, and Russians living in these border regions see themselves in danger of becoming second class citizens. Thus, it is highly problematic for any Russian government to agree to any further abandonment of Russian territory. Until the Russian government is perceived by its own population as sufficiently self-assured to withstand the temptation to exchange territory for monetary quick fixes it will not be in any position to take bold new initiatives toward Japan.

MOSCOW AND THE TWO KOREAS

One legacy of the Stalin era has been a divided Korea. Throughout the Korean War, and immediately thereafter, Moscow's hegemonic position was unchallenged in Pyongyang. But in 1956, the aftermath of the CPSU's twentieth party congress and de-Stalinization gave Kim Il-Sung the opportunity to purge most of the "Russian men," the so-called Soviet Koreans, from the party and government, and to build a political network loyal only to him,

From the late 1950s on, Kim Il-sung exploited the emerging Sino-Soviet rift, gaining for himself a growing independence, as Moscow and Beijing tried to offset the other's influence in the Democratic People's Republic of Korea (DPRK), more commonly referred to as North Korea, with generous economic and military assistance. For a time Kim sided with Mao against Khrushchev, then tilted toward Moscow in the late 1960s during Mao's destructive isolationist Cultural Revolution. He adapted adroitly to his two patrons, whose enmity continued through the 1970s and 1980s. Moscow's aims were to keep Pyongyang from slipping too close to China and to ensure that it did not start a new war to reunify Korea.

The Soviet-North Korean relationship took on an appearance of renewed health and durability in the mid-1980s, even as it was entering a period of major change. Kim Il-sung visited Moscow in May 1984, for the first time in seventeen years, in an international environment of high tension between the Soviet Union and the United States. Particularly worrisome to both Moscow and Pyongyang was the improving relationship between China and the United States. This prompted Moscow's hard-liners, headed by the infirm Konstantin Chernenko, to court Kim and reward his unrelenting anti-Americanism.

Moscow's aid package was substantial: extensive credits and deferral of North Korea's debt; advanced military equipment used to upgrade North Korea's air force and air defense capability; and technological assistance in the fields of nuclear and conventional power generation. The military part of the package included aircraft and SCUD surface-to-surface missiles capable of hitting the South Korean capitol of Seoul. The days of such largesse, however, were numbered.

The Gorbachev Era

When Kim Il-sung again visited Moscow in October 1986 to meet with Chernenko's successor, Mikhail Gorbachev, he obtained an assurance that Moscow would fulfill its earlier agreement. In return, Pyongyang permitted Moscow to use North Korean airspace for military flights to and from Vietnam and agreed to joint naval operations in the Sea of Japan and access to the port of Wonsan. The high level of military cooperation introduced during Kim's visit in 1984 continued throughout the Gorbachev era.

At the political level, however, Soviet-North Korean relations deteriorated rapidly after 1988, when the Soviet Union decided to participate in the Olympic Games in Seoul that year, and opened trade relations with the Republic of Korea (South Korea). Despite Moscow's efforts to reassure the North Koreans that trade links would not lead to diplomatic recognition, Kim Il-sung correctly perceived the threat to his regime inherent in Gorbachev's "new political thinking." One consequence was the acceleration of North Korea's nuclear program, notwithstanding Pyongyang's signing of the nuclear nonproliferation treaty (NPT) in 1985 at Moscow's behest.

In 1989, North Korea watched as Soviet-South Korean relations improved. Consular relations were established, permanent trade offices were opened in each other's capitals, a direct sea link was inaugurated between Vladivostok and Pusan. The Soviet press wrote positively about South Korea's economic accomplishments and prospects. Trade more than tripled in one year, and Kim Young-sam, the co-leader of the Democratic Liberal Party visited Moscow to explore the possibility of full political normalization.

During Gorbachev's visit to the United States in 1990, he met in San Francisco with South Korean President Roh Tae Woo and agreed to establish full diplomatic relations, though no time was set. As in his approach to West Germany, Gorbachev's policy toward South Korea was driven by great expectations of massive economic assistance for the troubled Soviet economy. It was at this time, too, that Soviet officials informed the Americans of the advanced stage of North Korea's nuclear programs. North Korea recalled its ambassador in Moscow in protest and denounced Gorbachev's "shameless flunkeyist" behavior.

On September 30, 1990, disregarding its previous assurances to the North, Moscow established formal diplomatic relations with South Korea. To strengthen economic ties—and doubtless a part of the price of such rapid recognition—Seoul established a $3 billion fund for South Korean exporters trading with the Soviet Union, and soon thereafter extended a $3 billion credit to Moscow.

Kim Il-sung, realizing his worsening isolation and the unreliability of Soviet treaty guarantees, applied for membership in the United Nations in May 1991, abandoning his long-standing position that the two Koreas should occupy a single seat in the United Nations. In September, the two Koreas entered the world organization.

The final curtain soon fell on the Soviet Union, as Gorbachev proved unable to master the new conditions he himself had helped to create. For the two Koreas, the end of the communist regime in Moscow meant a complete reversal from what had been traditional Soviet policy.

Yeltsin and Korea

From the very beginning, Yeltsin demonstrated far greater sympathy for South than for North Korea. In March 1992 he sent his foreign minister to China, Japan, and South Korea. The omission of North Korea was a pointed signal of Moscow's intentions.

With the end of the Soviet regime, the Russian government abruptly ended any pretense of support for communist North Korea. Kozyrev indicated that Moscow intended to end all military cooperation with Pyongyang as soon as possible and to put pressure on the North Koreans to end their nuclear program. Yeltsin described the Soviet-North Korean security treaty as existing only on paper, and his Minister of Information, Mikhail Poltoranin, advised the Japanese to stop paying reparations to the North, as it would only help to shore up a repressive and obsolete regime.[29] For their part, North Korean officials complained publicly that Russian oil deliveries to them had dropped to 10% of pre-1991 levels, and that Russia was demanding cash payments in hard currency.[30]

Although trade between Russia and South Korea was expanding slowly, the totals are nowhere near those projected in 1989–1990. Unlike Japan, South Korea has maintained a high profile in the Russian market, viewing the country as a promising prospect for long-term investment. One reason for the relatively higher degree of optimism may be the significant Korean cultural presence in Russia. The Korean community inside Russia numbers more than 600,000. Moreover, it has long been fashionable to earn advanced degrees in the Soviet Union. For example, the presidential candidate of the leading opposition party, the Democratic Party, obtained his doctorate from the Russian Diplomatic Academy.[31]

During a visit to Seoul in November 1992, Yeltsin told the South Korean leadership that Russia would no longer provide the North access to nuclear technology and that he planned to revise the 1961 treaty of friendship between the Soviet

Union and North Korea. Like Gorbachev eighteen months earlier, Yeltsin came as a supplicant, but with far less to offer. Strapped for hard currency and unable to pay the interest due on the South Korean loans extended in 1991, Moscow suspended debt repayments, and South Korea refused to extend new credits. Still, some progress was made after Yeltsin publicly apologized for the Soviet downing of the Korean Airline flight 007 by Soviet forces. The two countries signed a series of wide-ranging agreements on intergovernmental assistance, cultural cooperation, mutual tariff reductions, and exemptions from double taxation. The unwillingness of the South Korean government to purchase Russian arms and military technology further reduces Russia's ability to pay for Korean imports. In general, Seoul's shabby treatment of Moscow in 1993–1995 did much to dampen interest by the two parties in closer relations. It also strengthened the case, particularly among Russian nationalists and ultraconservatives, for retaining ties to North Korea. Still, some improvement may be visible in the two Russian-South Korean arms deals signed in April and July 1995, totaling over $650 million.[32] Under these agreements Russia would provide South Korea with tanks, light infantry, and defensive missile systems in return for offsetting some of its debt.

In its current weakened condition, Russia has modest but clear-cut objectives on the Korean peninsula. These objectives are no longer imperial but primarily strategic in character: the denuclearization of the Korean peninsula and adherence of both Koreas to the NPT and its inspection safeguards; reconciliation of the two Koreas and their eventual peaceful reunification; and the removal of all foreign troops from the peninsula. Given its continued ties with the North and expanding ties with the South, Russia will continue to be a significant, albeit more balanced, participant in regional developments.

VIETNAM AND THE ASEAN COUNTRIES

A very different set of priorities shaped Moscow's policy toward Vietnam. America's major intervention after 1964 prompted extensive Soviet economic and military assistance to enable Hanoi to prosecute its war: Aid rose from approximately $40 million in 1964 to almost $1 billion annually from 1967 to 1972. At stake was not only Soviet credibility as an ally and Soviet rivalry with China for influence among Asian Communists, but also a desire to embroil the United States in a quagmire that would reduce its capacity for decisive action in areas of greater concern to the USSR.

Soviet aims in Vietnam were ambivalent in the years after 1945 when Stalin refused to support Ho Chi Minh's bid for Vietnamese independence in order to avoid antagonizing France and compromising the strong position of the French Communist Party. Moscow established diplomatic relations with Ho Chi Minh's Democratic Republic of Vietnam (DRV) on January 30, 1950, soon after the communist triumph in China, but gave Hanoi little attention or aid. It served as co-chair of the 1954 Geneva Conference, which formally ended French rule in Indochina and recognized the two Vietnams, but despite a limited involvement in the 1962 Laotian crisis, Moscow did not urge intensification of "wars of national liberation" by Vietnam: it regarded Vietnam as a sideshow and did not want a communist insurgency in Laos or Cambodia to hamper its efforts to improve relations with the other nations of Southeast Asia. However, Ho Chi Minh had his own ambitions, which inexorably drew Moscow into the Vietnam conflict, as much because of its rivalry with China as because of that with the United States.

During the late 1960s and early 1970s, both Moscow and Beijing, though increasingly at odds on a wide range of issues, lent support to Vietnam. For its part, Hanoi sought to preserve an essential neutrality on the Sino-Soviet dispute. It benefited from the rivalry that impelled each party to accede to Hanoi's requests lest it be labeled defeatist and seem overly concerned about the United States. In 1972, when both Moscow and Beijing were courting Washington (the USSR, in order to reach an agreement on SALT I and promote détente in Europe, and China, in order to have the Nixon visit lead to diplomatic normalization) they still met the DRV's economic and military needs. Neither communist power was willing to pressure Hanoi to agree to a negotiated settlement, even in the interests of better relations with the United States.

Hanoi's victory in 1975 brought Moscow new problems. When Vietnam, now an unified nation of more than 66 million people, expanded into Laos and Cambodia, Moscow's support of this expansionism made the other nations of Southeast Asia leery of Soviet overtures for closer ties, which had been intended to offset China's diplomatic efforts in the region. Vietnam's economic and military reliance on the Soviet Union became even more pronounced after 1975 because of Vietnam's deteriorating relationship with China and poor prospects for normalizing relations with the United States: In December 1975, Le Duan, the head of the Vietnam Communist Party (Ho Chi Minh died in 1969) signed a long-term economic agreement with the USSR; in June 1978, Vietnam joined Comecon as a full member; and on November 3, 1978, the USSR and Vietnam signed a twenty-five-year treaty of friendship and cooperation. Although not a formal military alliance, the treaty calls for mutual consultations in the event of a military threat—an obvious allusion to China. When Vietnam overthrew the pro-Beijing Pol Pot regime in Cambodia (Kampuchea) in January 1979, it could count on the USSR's support.

The Soviet Union benefited in a number of ways. It acquired military privileges at the Cam Ranh Bay naval base and the Da Nang airfield, one of the largest in the region. This enabled the Soviet military to fly reconnaissance missions throughout Southeast Asia and virtually to double the length of time that the Soviet Pacific Fleet spent at sea. The cost of reinforcing the USSR's presence in the country was a sizable aid package, which in the 1980s exceeded $2 billion annually—half economic and half military.

By 1986 Gorbachev realized that support for Vietnam's occupation of Kampuchea was hampering Moscow's attempt to improve relations not only with China but also with ASEAN countries (the Association of Southeast Asian Nations, whose members are Indonesia, Malaysia, the Philippines, Singapore, Thailand, and Brunei). Shevardnadze's extensive promotional tour of the region in March 1987—the first by a Soviet foreign minister in almost three decades—had many purposes: to show the flag, to convey the desire of both Moscow and Hanoi for a peaceful resolution of the Kampuchean problem, and to encourage trade and establish "a regular dialogue" with the vibrant, free-market ASEAN economies.

Sustained Soviet pressure (which included the threat to reduce subsidies) combined with a reform-minded Vietnamese leadership under Nguyen Van Linh (who succeeded Le Duan in 1986 and sought to improve relations with the West) led Hanoi, on May 25, 1988, to announce that it would begin a phased withdrawal of its forces; by September 30, 1989, all the Vietnamese troops had pulled out, leaving in doubt the fate of the pro-Vietnamese Cambodian government of Hun Sen, which was under attack by the coalition dominated by Pol Pot's Khmer Rouge.

During the era of Cold War confrontation, Moscow viewed Vietnam merely as a convenient pawn in the global superpower rivalry. The speed with which Soviet relations with Vietnam eroded after Gorbachev made the strategic decision to court China illustrates just how little interest there was within the Kremlin for Vietnam per se.

The decision in January 1991 to move to hard currency trading with Vietnam did much to force Vietnam to open up its economy to foreign influences and to seek reconciliation with the United States. Prior to that time the Soviet Union accounted for 60% of Vietnam's foreign trade; by 1994 it accounted for only 3%.[33] Still, the possibility of a mutually acceptable arrangement to cover the $10 billion debt that Vietnam owed to the Soviet Union before 1991 was explored during a July 1995 visit by Foreign Minister Kozyrev to Vietnam. The deal would work like this: in exchange for some reduction of the debt, Vietnam has agreed to keep open the Soviet naval base at Cam Rahn Bay until the year 2004. Although Russia's military presence there is now less than a quarter of what it was during the Soviet period, apparently Russia hopes that it can in some way benefit from Vietnam's expanding trade with the outside world.

As Russia's economic interest in its former allies diminishes, its attention has shifted to the economically more dynamic countries of the Pacific Rim.

The ASEAN countries, especially Thailand, Singapore, and Malaysia have become favored destinations for postcommunist Russian entrepreneurs. The absence of any serious prior contact has led Foreign Ministry trade officials to tout the region as one where the "trade potential . . . is greater than Europe."[34]

Through numerous high-level political and economic summits, Russian officials have attempted to interest the newly industrialized countries of the regions (NICs) in the concept of an expanded free trade agreement, to include Russia. In 1993 trade with the region topped $2 billion in 1993, though most of this is military hardware sold to Malaysia and Thailand. For their part, countries in the region have expressed an interest in utilizing Russian talent in the fields of physics, engineering, and computer programming. Still, commodity turnover with Russia accounts for less than 1% of the region's total commodity turnover.

At the same time, Russian attempts to join multilateral initiatives have scored some tangible successes. In 1993 Russia joined the Pacific Economic Council (PEC) and the Pacific Economic Cooperation Council (PECC), both formed to promote business ties among states of the region. It has been unable, however, to join the more influential Asia-Pacific Economic Corporation (APEC) because of a moratorium on the admission of new members until 1996. At the 1994 regional forum on ASEAN security issues in Bangkok, Foreign Minister Kozyrev laid out a step-by-step proposal of an Asian-Pacific regional security mechanism, which received considerable support. Even Australia has voiced its support for Russian participation in the settlement of regional conflicts and in multinational security and economic arrangements. A Russian proposal to establish a regional center for conflict resolution was approved at that meeting.[35] Although Russia has made some progress in becoming a welcome participant in regional affairs, it is starting virtually from scratch, and it will be many years before significant economic and political ties are forged.

OBSERVATIONS

Given the level of military and foreign aid invested in the region, unequivocal Soviet accomplishments in Asia have been remarkably few. The USSR managed to establish itself as the preeminent military power on the mainland of Asia, but in the process it aroused the fears of its neighbors. Under Brezhnev, China reduced somewhat its anti-Soviet rhetoric, but fears stemming from China's potential to develop into a genuine superpower and from its own domestic turmoil and technological backwardness actually grew during the Gorbachev period.

Moscow could derive some satisfaction from the role that it played in bringing about a thinning out of American power in Asia. In contrast to the decade after World War II, in the 1990s the United States was not in a position to project significant military power (conventional, not nuclear) in the Far East in a way that could threaten Soviet clients or interests. The United States could deter Soviet expansion, but its capacity for generating threats to the USSR was limited.

Against this modest list of achievements can be juxtaposed difficulties produced by the counterproductive policies of Khrushchev and Brezhnev. The Soviet Union was still viewed with suspicion by China and Japan. Its image as a hostile and threatening actor will take time to dispel. Moreover, the Soviet Union remained only a marginal actor in the most dynamic sector of the global economy.

For most of its history (Soviet period included), Russian interest in Asia has taken a back seat to its interest in Europe. Although Asiatic Russia accounts for 80% of the country's territory and the overwhelming majority of its natural resources, less than a third of its population lives east of the Urals. For most Russians the Far East is still a distant, uncharted frontier.

This placid indifference to Asia is not likely to continue in the next century. As Russian analyst Alexei D. Bogaturov put it:

> No matter how much Foreign Minister Andrei Kozyrev is personally committed to "Atlantic"—one should rather say "Euro-Atlantic"—thinking, there are two hard facts he is unable to ignore: never since the Middle Ages has Russia's political space been so distant from Atlantic Europe, and never were Russian national interests so strongly tied with the challenging East."[36]

Trade opportunities are likely to increase much more dramatically in the East than in Europe, given the rapid liberalization of the region's economies and the resultant demand for natural resources. Second, Russia's regional governors are chomping at the bit for increased autonomy to conduct their own trade relations and to retain the lion's share of the profits for their regions. To date, there is little serious talk of secession, but if central authorities in Moscow six thousand miles away continue to try to dictate commerce from the center, discontent will grow. In the final analysis, regional economic and political autonomy may be the only solution to preserving Russian territorial integrity.

Still, many Russians remain ambivalent about this process of shifting attention to the East. Psychologically, they do not think of Russia as an Asian country. They have not forged the cultural ties with their Asian neighbors that they have with Europeans or, to a much lesser extent, with Central Asians. The fundamental laws of economics and geography, however, seem to lead inevitably to the conclusion that unlike the USSR, which saw itself as a global superpower with strategic interests in Asia, Russia will be forced to seek out a distinct role for itself as an Asian power.

SELECTED BIBLIOGRAPHY

Babbage, Ross (ed.). *The Soviets in the Pacific in the 1990's.* Canberra: Brassey's Australia, 1989.

Berton, Peter. *The Japanese-Russian Territorial Dilemma: Historical Background, Disputes, Issues, Questions, Solution Scenarios.* Cambridge, MA: Strengthening Democratic Institutions Project, John F. Kennedy School of Government, Harvard University, 1992.

Buszynski, Leszek. *Soviet Foreign Policy and Southeast Asia.* New York: St. Martin's Press, 1986.

Chung, Chin O. *Pyongyang Between Peking and Moscow.* University: University of Alabama Press, 1978.

Chung, Yung Il, and Chung, Eunsook. *Russia in the Far East and Pacific Region.* Seoul, Korea: Sejong Institute, 1994.

Ellison, Herbert J. (ed.). *The Sino-Soviet Conflict: A Global Perspective.* Seattle: University of Washington Press, 1982.

Gittings, John (ed.). *Survey of the Sino-Soviet Dispute.* New York: Oxford University Press, 1968.

Goodby, James E., et al. (eds.). *"Northern Territories" and Beyond: Russian, Japanese, and American perspectives. . . .* Westport, CT: Praeger, 1995.

Hasegawa, Tsuyoshi, et al. (eds.). *Russia and Japan.* Berkeley: University of California Press, 1993.

Hauner, Milan. *What Is Asia to Us? Russia's Asian Heartland Yesterday and Today.* New York: Routledge, 1992.

Il Yung, Chung (ed.). *Korea and Russia: Toward the 21st Century.* Seoul, Korea: Sejong Institute, 1992.

Jain, Rajendra K. *The USSR and Japan: 1945–1980.* Atlantic Highlands, NJ: Humanities Press, 1981.

Kap Young, Jeong (ed.). *Cooperation between Korea and Russia.* Seoul, Korea: Institute of East and West Studies, Yonsei University, 1993.

Kotkin, Stephen, and Wolff, David (eds.). *Rediscovering Russia in Asia: Siberia and the Russian Far East*. Armonk, NY: M.E. Sharpe, 1995.

Mandelbaum, Michael (ed.). *The Strategic Quadrangle: Russia, China, Japan, and the United States in East Asia*. New York: Council on Foreign Relations Press, 1995.

Nimmo, William F. *Japan and Russia: A Re-evaluation of the Post-Soviet Era*. Westport, CT: Greenwood Press, 1994.

Ross, Robert S. (ed.). *China, the United States, and the Soviet Union: Tripolarity and Policy Making in the Cold War*. Armonk, NY: M.E. Sharpe, 1993.

Singh, Bilveer. *Moscow and Southeast Asia since 1985: From USSR to the C.I.S.* Singapore: Singapore Institute of International Affairs, 1992.

Stephan, John J. *The Russian Far East: A History*. Stanford, CA: Stanford University Press, 1994.

Swearingen, Rodger. *The Soviet Union and Postwar Japan: Escalating Challenge and Response*. Stanford, CA: Hoover Institution Press, 1978.

Thakur, Ramesh, and Thayer, Carlyle (eds.). *Reshaping Regional Relations: Asia-Pacific and the Former Soviet Union*. Boulder, CO: Westview Press, 1993.

————. *Soviet Relations with India and Vietnam*. New York: St. Martin's Press, 1992.

Valencia, Mark J. (ed.). *The Russian Far East in Transition: Opportunities for Regional Economic Cooperation*. Boulder, CO: Westview Press, 1995.

Yu-Nam, Kim (ed.). *Soviet Russia, North Korea, and South Korea in the 1990s: Nuclear Issues and Arms Control in and around the Korean Peninsula*. Seoul, Korea: Dankook University Press, 1992.

Ziegler, Charles E. *Soviet Foreign Policy and East Asia: Learning and Adaptation in the Gorbachev Era*. New York: Cambridge University Press, 1993.

NOTES

1. For example, see George Ginsburgs, *The Damansky/Chenpao Island Incidents: A Case Study of Syntactic Patterns in Crisis Diplomacy*, Asian Studies Occasional Paper Series, no. 6 (Edwardsville: Southern Illinois University, 1973); and Rajan Menon and Daniel Abele, "Security Dimensions of Soviet Territorial Disputes with China and Japan," *Journal of Northeast Asian Studies*, vol. 8, no. 1 (Spring 1989), pp. 3–19.

2. Victor Louis, a foreign journalist alleged to have close ties to the KGB and Soviet officials, caused shock waves when he suggested that whether the Soviet Union attacked Lop Nor or not was only "a question of strategy," and that if the Soviet Union had intervened in Czechoslovakia to defend socialism, why should it not also apply the Brezhnev Doctrine to China? See *New York Times*, September 18, 1969. The Soviet government also circulated a note to its East European allies asking whether the USSR should launch a preemptive strike against China.

3. *FBIS/USSR National Affairs,* July 29, 1986, pp. R11–R18.

4. Coit D. Blacker, "The USSR and Asia in 1989: Recasting Relationships," *Asian Survey*, vol. 30, no. 1 (January 1990), p. 5.

5. "Trade on Track," *Far Eastern Economic Review*, May 25, 1989, 14.

6. This assessment comes from a member of the USSR Academy of Sciences' Institute of World Economics and International Relations: Alexander Salitsky, "Communist Economic Giants," *Far Eastern Economic Review*, May 18, 1989, pp. 20–21.

7. *Washington Post*, July 17, 1990.

8. Xue Wu Gu, "China Policy Towards Russia," *Aussenpolitik*, vol. 3 (1993), p. 288.
9. Bin Yu, "Sino-Russian Military Relations, *Asian Survey*, vol. 33, no. 3 (March 1993), pp. 310–311.
10. Hung P. Nguyen, "Russia and China: The Genesis of an Eastern Rapallo," *Asian Survey*, vol. 33 no. 3 (March 1993), p. 301.
11. Eugene Bazahnov and Natasha Bazhanov, "Russia and Asia in 1992," *Asian Survey*, vol. 33 no. 1 (January 1993), p. 95.
12. Maksim Yudin, "Moskva-Pekin: polosa ispytaniya," *Izvestiya*, March 24, 1992.
13. James William Morley, "Soviet-Japanese Peace Declaration," *Political Science Quarterly*, vol. 72, no. 3 (September 1957), pp. 373–374.
14. Robert Rand, "Sonoda's Visit to Moscow," *Radio Liberty Research Paper* (January 17, 1978), p. 2.
15. Hiroshi Kimura, "Soviet Policy Toward Japan," *Working Paper* no. 6 (Providence, RI: The Center for Foreign Policy Development, Brown University, August 1983), pp. 17–18.
16. Gordon B. Smith, "Recent Trends in Japanese-Soviet Trade," *Problems of Communism*, vol. 36, no. 1 (January–February, 1987, p. 58.
17. Bohdan Nahaylo, "Shevardnadze's Visit to Tokyo: Courtship in a Cold Climate," *Radio Liberty Research*, RL 22/86 (January 14, 1986), p. 6.
18. Bohdan Nahaylo, "Shevarnadze's Visit to Tokyo: Courtship in a Cold Climate," *Radio Liberty Research*, RL 22/86 (January 14, 1986), p. 6.
19. *FBIS/SOV*, March 29, 1989, p. 9.
20. Alexei Bogaturov and Mikhail Nosov, "How to Even Out the Lop-sided ~'Triangle'?" *New Times*, no. 18 (May 1989), p. 9.
21. *FBIS/SOV*, October 20, 1989, 6.
22. Andrei Krivtsov, "Russia and the Far East" *International Affairs* (January 1993), pp. 80–81.
23. Mark J. Valencia and Noel Ludwig, "Minerals and Fishing at Stake in Northern Territories Talks," *The Japan Times* (weekly international edition) February 25–March 3, 1991, p. 8.
24. Leszek Buszynski, "Russia and the Asia-Pacific Region," *Pacific Affairs*, vol. 65, no. 4 (Winter 1992–1993), p. 493.
25. On the eve of parliamentary debate on the territories in October 1991, the Russian foreign ministry released documents from its archives that showed that tsarist Russia had never viewed the disputed islands as Russian territory. Buszynski, "Russia and the Asia-Pacific Region," p. 494.
26. Robert Orttung, "Kozyrev publishes new book" *OMRI Daily Digest* February 28, 1995.
27. William F. Nimmo, *Japan and Russia: A Re-evaluation in the Post-Soviet Era* (Westport, CT: Greenwood Press, 1994), p. 124.
28. Stephen Foye, "Russo-Japanese Relations: Still Travelling a Rocky Road," *RFE/RL Research Report*, vol. 2, no. 44 (November 5, 1993), p. 33.
29. Bazahanov, "Russia and Asia," p. 98.
30. Buszynski, "Russia and the Asia-Pacific Region," p. 489.
31. Bazhanov, "Russia and Asia," p. 97
32. Doug Clarke, "Russian/South Korean Arms Deal Signed. *OMRI Daily Digest* July 11, 1995.
33. Thomas Sigel, "Kozyrev Visits Vietnam to Strengthen Economic Ties," *OMRI Daily Digest* July 27, 1995.
34. Buszynski, "Russia and the Asia-Pacific Region," p. 496.
35. Leonid Velekhov, "'Stal' v obmen na frukty'—ili nastoiashchee sotrudnichestvo?" *Segodnia* (July 29, 1994), p. 3.
36. Alexei D. Bogaturov, "Russia in Northeast Asia," *Korea and World Affairs*, vol. 17, no. 2 (Summer 1993), pp. 298–299.

Chapter
10

Russia and the Third World

*T*he emergence of the Soviet Union as a superpower was marked by its shift from a continental-based strategy to a global one and its penetration of the Third World. Between the mid-1950s and the late 1980s, it was in this arena, made up of two thirds of the world's nations, that the Soviet Union engaged the United States in a relatively low-cost, usually low-risk, multifaceted, highly intensive pattern of classical imperial competition—imperial, not imperialist, because the primary impetus underlying Soviet policy was to undermine the influence and position of the United States and not to seize additional territory or markets.

The regions of the Third World had special importance in an age of nuclear stalemate. Whereas Europe and the Far East had relatively stable political and military constellations that coincided generally with established territorial boundaries and spheres of influence shielded by security agreements, Southern Asia, the Middle East, Latin America, and sub-Saharan Africa were stamped with transient alignments and systemic instability that attracted Soviet attention. Moscow viewed any gains as a way of weakening the West; setbacks, on the other hand, were accepted with equanimity, since they did not threaten Moscow's own security position. After 1988–1989, Gorbachev's "new thinking" ushered in a less confrontational, even cooperative policy. Though Gorbachev's policy had many new characteristics, it also retained elements of rivalry that suggested residual national and imperial goals.

The collapse of communism has led to a retrenchment of former Soviet interests. Imperial competition with the United States is no longer as important to Russian leaders, who are trying to reestablish their relations with individual countries on the basis of national and commercial interests, rather than ideology or strategy. As a result, the Third World now plays a decidedly peripheral role in Russian foreign policy calculations.

SOVIET IDEOLOGY AND STRATEGY IN THE THIRD WORLD

Third World countries long occupied an important place in Soviet ideological formulations and long-term projections. The essentials on which Soviet strategy was predicated were set forth first by Lenin in his theory of imperialism: a belief that capitalist countries, impelled by their economic and government systems to seek cheap sources of raw materials and labor as well as outlets for their surplus production and capital, expanded into Africa, Asia, the Middle East, and Latin America in order to stave off their own decay and disintegration; and that this expansionist compulsion bred wars among capitalist countries that were competing for choice colonies and markets. Originally published in Switzerland in 1916, Lenin's *Imperialism: The Highest Stage of Capitalism* attempted to extend Marx's concept of the class struggle from the domestic to the international arena and to show thereby that World War I had stemmed from the avarice of monopoly capital and the big financial interests. Whereas Marx predicted that the downfall of capitalism would be brought about by the proletariat of the industrialized nations, Lenin's thesis was that this process could be hastened and the capitalist countries could be undermined and eventually toppled by detaching the colonies from the control of the capitalist rulers—in Leon Trotsky's words, "that the road to Paris and London lies via the towns of Afghanistan, the Punjab and Bengal"—and that revolution in the colonial world must inevitably redound to Moscow's advantage.[1]

Lenin, the revolutionary, advocated national self-determination. As a concept meaning "the political freedom of a people to establish and to function as an independent nation," national self-determination had but a brief and almost exclusively tactical significance in Russia during the period of War Communism, when some non-Russian peoples took advantage of the Bolsheviks' weakness to gain their independence. Once secure in power, the Bolsheviks interpreted national self-determination in such a way as to preclude any further secessions from the Soviet Union. However, outside of the Soviet Union, the concept was used to portray the Soviet Union as a champion of the liberation of all peoples from colonial rule and as an opponent of imperialism.

In the early years, the Soviets were engrossed with survival in European Russia, but as the situation stabilized, Lenin shrewdly perceived that the East could be used to improve Russia's military and political situation. Accordingly, he assigned colonial areas a more significant role in Soviet strategy. In July 1920, at the second Comintern congress, Lenin's "Preliminary Draft of Theses on the National and Colonial Questions" stressed the division of the world into oppressing and oppressed nations and enjoined the Comintern to promote the alliance between the proletariat of the advanced industrialized countries and the peoples of the economically backward colonial areas. As natural allies, the two would work toward the defeat of capitalism—the proletariat by weakening imperialist power at its home base and the colonial peoples by driving out the European rulers and thereby creating social and economic unrest in their home bases. Lenin acknowledged that nationalist movements in colonial areas would usually have a bourgeois character initially. Nevertheless, he endorsed temporary cooperation with them, provided that the communist movement, however rudimentary, maintained its sense of identity and independence of action. (The first Soviet experiment with such a coalition was in China in 1923–1927 and had disastrous results.)

In April 1924, as part of the quest for Lenin's mantle of legitimacy, Stalin embraced his position of the intimate connection among the vitality of national-liberation movements, the success of the proletarian revolution in Europe, and the preservation of socialism in the Soviet Union. Stalin lauded Lenin for expanding the national question to include all the oppressed peoples of Asia and Africa, and he expressed the view that, though it was but one aspect of the world proletarian revolution, "the road to the victory of the revolution in the West lies through the revolutionary alliance with the liberation movement of the colonies and dependent countries against imperialism.[2]

Events elsewhere, however, soon left Stalin with little time for the colonial question. During the period from 1934 to 1945, with the exception of the brief Nazi-Soviet honeymoon, he sought to develop better relations with the ruling imperialist powers and hence was quite circumspect about Comintern activities in colonial areas. Soviet national interest demanded accommodation and cooperation with the West. Generally speaking, the entire 1922–1945 period was one in which Soviet diplomacy centered on European and Far Eastern developments. The paramount problem was ensuring the security of the Soviet Union. Internal troubles (such as the intraparty struggle for power after Lenin's death, the agricultural crisis occasioned by Stalin's decision to accelerate industrialization and the collectivization of agriculture, and the bloody purges of the mid-1930s) further diminished Soviet interest in the colonial world. Even after 1945, when the Cold War chilled the relations of the former allies, Stalin's priorities—the reconstruction of a nation devastated by war, the consolidation of Soviet rule over Eastern Europe, the rivalry with the United States over Germany, the challenge of the Titoist heresy, the adaptation required by the triumph of the Communists on the Chinese mainland, and the Korean War—still kept the Soviet purview localized. The Leninist legacy of exploiting the Third World to advance Soviet security and strategic interests found a kindred heir in the ideological revisions of Khrushchev. Starting from the fundamental Leninist assumptions concerning the vulnerability of the Western capitalist countries to pressure from colonial and developing areas, the universal urge of national liberation movements toward independence from their colonial rulers, the irresistible attraction of capitalists to the markets and resources of the Third World, and the inevitability of competition among capitalist countries and groups, Khrushchev modernized Marxist-Leninist thought on Third World developments and gave it an optimism characteristic of his own nature. He substantially modified Stalin's two-camp thesis and, at the twentieth congress of the CPSU in February 1956, proclaimed the existence and growing role of a "zone of peace," which gave ideological recognition to the independent role in world affairs of the former African and Asian colonies that Moscow had already begun to appreciate.[3] Khrushchev also revised Lenin's thesis that the contradictions arising out of the rivalry for the spoils of colonial expansion would drive the capitalist nations to war, maintaining instead that decolonization and the disintegration of Western overseas empires had gone too far to be reversed and that the "camp of socialism" acted as a restraint on old-fashioned imperialism. Therefore, he said, in order to preserve their foothold in the Third World, the Western powers now cooperate through multinational corporations and various associations whose intent is to disguise neo-colonialism, that is, the preservation of Western influence through economic lever-age. On February 26, 1960, during a visit to Indonesia, Khrushchev coined the phrase "collective colonialism" to describe the process.

Khrushchev also devised an ideological justification for differentiating among developing countries and for offering assistance to some noncommunist develop-ing countries but not to others. The concept of the national democratic state was originally advanced at the November 1960 Moscow Conference of Communist and Workers' Parties and later modified in the party program adopted at the twen-ty-second congress of the CPSU in late 1961. It referred to radically oriented non-communist developing countries that adhere to nonalignment in world affairs, adopt anti-Western foreign policies, and pursue domestic programs aimed at building socialism through a "noncapitalist path of development." These national democracies were considered promising candidates for eventual transition to the status of people's democracies. The "national democratic state" was seen as a stage in the consolidation of the anti-imperialist, antifeudal, democratic revolution, as a temporary, transitional form for developing countries desiring to move toward socialism. In 1963, a refinement, ("the revolutionary democratic state") was added—apparently to distinguish the radical Third World regimes that imple-mented many of the programmatic demands of the local Communist Party and tol-erated its active functioning from the ones that persecuted Communists.

But not even Khrushchev relied on ideology as a guide for determining politi-cal alignments. His ideological revisions bore little relationship to the levels of mil-itary and economic assistance that he extended, nor did they have any bearing on the risks he was prepared to run in defense of a particular regime. In practice, Soviet policies were shaped by pragmatic considerations:

- programs of assistance were initiated in response to a less-developed coun-try's (LDC's) request;
- assistance was rendered, irrespective of a regime's political outlook, even if it was anticommunist or repressed local Communists;
- programs or defense commitments were never terminated out of ideologi-cal antipathy, but would be continued as long as a regime followed an anti-American orientation in foreign policy.

Strategically, Soviet leaders sought to eliminate, neutralize, or at least weaken the U.S. military presence in the countries lying south of the USSR, to deprive the U.S. Strategic Air Command of potential refueling facilities, and to end U.S. intel-ligence flights over the Soviet heartland. Accordingly, starting in 1954 with Afghanistan, they gave varying degrees of encouragement to the policies of Third World elites who found military alliance with Western countries difficult to sustain domestically and who therefore opted for foreign policies ranging from coolness to outright hostility toward the West.

Politically, Moscow sought diplomatic normalization, not communization. Its overtures and aid were intended to dispel the suspicion of the Kremlin that was inherent in the attitudes of many of the ruling elites in less developed countries. Some of this anticommunist sentiment derived from the Western European education of the elites, but a deep animus against communism also existed in Muslim countries, and Southern Asia clearly remembered Communist attempts at armed revolution in the late 1940s.

In UN forums and through bilateral relationships, Moscow encouraged the nationalization of key industries and resources, heavy public-sector investment, and central economic planning, stressing the relevance for developing countries of its own experience with modernization and economic development. All of this had a favorable impact upon socialistically inclined elites, at least during the early years of courtship by the "new" Soviet Union.

Ideologically, the Kremlin's "forward policy" in the Third World reflected the optimism of Khrushchev and his associates. Having survived the terror of Stalin's last years, they emerged now for the first time as leaders in their own right. They saw the forces of history as favoring the advance of socialism and the final destruction of capitalism and colonialism. To them, a powerful and economically expanding Soviet Union was a natural ally of the new nations, which basically shared Moscow's anti-imperialist, anticolonialist, anticapitalist outlook. It was a time, too, when Soviet leaders believed that their model of development and internal transformation held great interest for new nations.

Two broad purposes initially underlay the emerging Soviet courtship of key Third World countries: undermining the Western system of alliances and international economic order, and establishing a political and economic presence in areas that had previously been outside the realm of Soviet capabilities. In the 1960s two other broad objectives crystallized: offsetting the Chinese challenge for leadership in the communist world, and acquiring naval and air facilities that would provision the USSR's blue-water fleet, keep close tabs on and counteract U.S. forces operating in strategically important areas, protect clients threatened by their pro-Western rivals, and enable Moscow to project military power more expeditiously into politically promising situations.

GORBACHEV'S NEW DIRECTION

The most significant difference between Gorbachev's Third World policy and that of his predecessors was the shift away from heavy reliance on the military instrument as a means of promoting political objectives. It was reflected in his repeated calls for the "demilitarization of international relations" and an end to the threat or use of force as an instrument of foreign policy. Gorbachev realized that the USSR's role in the militarization of regional politics in the Third World had not brought achievements commensurate with the costs.

A second policy change was the acknowledgment that a contradiction existed between the USSR's projection of military power in the Third World, whether directly or through arms transfers, and its attempts to improve relations with the

United States. This linkage had been explicitly rejected by earlier Soviet leaders and had helped to fuel the Western disenchantment with détente. Gorbachev acknowledged that the invasion of Afghanistan in December 1979 had been an error because, among other things, it had weakened the Soviet Union's ability to pursue better relations with the West.

Third, under Gorbachev the Soviet Union encouraged negotiated solutions to regional conflicts. Instead of exploiting disputes to further the interests of the socialist community as it had done in the past, Moscow actively participated in the search for political solutions and a diminution of regional tensions.

Finally, Gorbachev's approach differed from that of his predecessors in trying to curb unproductive military-economic subsidies to prime clients such as Cuba and Vietnam. He insisted on reducing wasteful expenditures and redirecting resources to the modernization of Soviet society. Long-established client-states like Cuba and Vietnam were told that they must accommodate to an interdependent world in which conflict was to be downgraded as a way of effecting change.

Despite significant revisions, however, many aspects of the old Soviet Third World policy persisted under Gorbachev. The Soviet Union did not abandon the Third World but, rather, by reducing its subsidies, sought to refashion the relationship in a manner that would strengthen socialism.

Like his predecessors, Gorbachev promoted comprehensive relations with all Third World regimes prepared to deal with the USSR, irrespective of ideological or political differences. He nimbly sought opportunities for diplomatic normalization provided by regional actors whose interests and outlooks had changed in response to altered circumstances—as when Iraq's invasion of Kuwait in August 1990 and threat to other Arab states in the Persian Gulf prompted Saudi Arabia to restore diplomatic relations with the Soviet Union in September 1990. Gorbachev continued to use arms transfers to strengthen Soviet ties to key regional actors, and looked to arms sales as a major source of hard currency earnings. Indeed, Gorbachev's policy did not signify an end to competition with the United States in the Third World. Cooperation in containing regional conflicts was deemed compatible with continued competition.

Ultimately, Gorbachev sought a new role for the Soviet Union in the Third World. He courted moderate states so that Moscow could work within a widened network while limiting Washington's policy options.

Having "lost" Eastern Europe and Afghanistan, however, Gorbachev could ill afford to be seen as squandering a generation of investment in forward positions in the Third World. Retrenchment, not disengagement, was thus the key to his policy, and despite the USSR's economic difficulties Soviet resources continue to flow to prime clients. Nowhere in the Third World did Moscow go so far as to tell prime clients that they must be prepared to go on without any Soviet assistance at all.

YELSTIN AND THE THIRD WORLD

With the collapse of the Soviet empire, the ideological rationale for any further Russian involvement in the Third World ended. The precipitous decline in Russian interest in the region illustrates graphically that for the Soviet Union the Third

World held little, if any, intrinsic interest. The only reason it was ever a foreign policy priority was because it was the primary arena of competition between the USSR and the United States. Since 1991, Russian foreign policy has been trying to find a new basis on which to base relations in the region.

One of the first to make specific mention of the potential significance of the Third World for Russia was then Presidential advisor Sergei Stankevich. In a much discussed article in *Nezavisimaya gazeta* entitled "A Power in Search of Itself," Stankevich argued that an alliance with the West was not as desirable for Russia as forging closer ties with the rapidly industrializing countries of the Third World:

> Stability is one of the priorities, one of the most important values, that should be present in Russia's foreign policy. I would add another value to this one—balance, . . . both along the East-West line, which I have already talked about, and along the North-South line. There are gigantic possibilities here that so far have not been used. A quick entry into the markets and full integration into the system of economic relations of such states as the U.S., Japan and the economically developed European states is highly problematic. In this area, we have been deliberately and for many years to come assigned, in the best of circumstances, the role of junior partner, which is not worth accepting.
>
> At the same time, there are much broader and qualitatively better opportunities involving other states, countries that are usually termed second-echelon countries, which are at a historical breakthrough. These are countries that lie to the south of our traditional partners: in Latin America, there are Mexico, Brazil, Chile and Argentina; in Africa, there is the Republic of South Africa; closer to Europe, there is Greece, then Turkey; and in Asia, there are India, China and the countries of Southeast Asia.[4] [translated from the original by Nicolai Petro]

Stankevich's arguments, however, ultimately failed to persuade either Yeltsin or Russia's foreign policy establishment. For them, the underdeveloped countries of Southwest Asia, Africa, and Latin America all share several common traits that make them a low priority for postcommunist Russia. First, with end of superpower concerns and the ideologically driven competition U.S.-Soviet competition, these regions have lost their strategic significance. Since Russia no longer views the United States as a potential adversary, there is no value in maintaining a costly military presence abroad.

Second, these countries are of limited value to Russia as trading partners. Their commodities cannot compete with Western goods on the Russian market, nor are Russian products (with the possible exception of military hardware) especially valued. As a result, much of the trade with the Third World that the Soviet Union subsidized in order to gain political favors, has declined precipitously. Russian analysts estimate that trade with Latin America, for example, declined by more than 35% in 1991 alone.[5] Indeed, in the world market, Russia and the Third World now compete in the sale of raw materials to more developed countries.

Most Russian analysts therefore candidly acknowledge that relations with the Third World are now considered peripheral to Russian interests. Certain regional experts, however, continue to make a case that Russia should pay more attention to the region. They make two points. First, that for the foreseeable future Russia will be at a disadvantage in its relations with the West. (This will not be true in the

Third World, however, where Russian commodities and technology are still found desirable.) Second, by abandoning the region, Russia is needlessly sacrificing the ties forged by the Soviet Union over many years in the region. Although these arguments make good sense in theory, in practice there is still a great aversion to dealing with most Third World countries. Given the economically unprofitable relationships that characterized the Soviet period, it will be a long time before the Third World region becomes a desirable trading partner in Russian's eyes.

Still, Russian leaders are continually faced with a need to balance past interests with future ones. If the opportunity to expand into Western markets is delayed or denied, Third World markets may become increasingly attractive.

THE SUBCONTINENT: INDIA AND PAKISTAN

The shift in Soviet policy toward India may be dated from September 1953, when the Kremlin appointed a personable ambassador who immediately initiated discussions aimed at closer economic relations. The first success was a dramatic agreement, signed on February 2, 1955, under which the Soviet government undertook to finance and construct a million-ton steel plant in the public sector in the Bhilai region of central India. By the time of the visit of Party Secretary Khrushchev and Premier Nikolai Bulganin in December 1955, Soviet-Indian friendship had become important for both countries. For the Soviet Union, it meant a link with the region's leading power and nonaligned country and a safeguard against India's membership in any anti-Soviet military alliance; it offered a showcase for Soviet assistance—a demonstration to the new nations of the tangible benefits to be derived from improved relations with the USSR; it brought the USSR respectability right at the takeoff stage of its courtship of African and Asian nations; and it served as a marked contrast to the military-minded, Cold War-oriented policy of the United States. Moscow's penetration of the "zone of peace" was off to an impressive start. Similar agreements with other nonaligned countries were concluded in the decades that followed.

Under Khrushchev, the USSR sided with India in its dispute with Pakistan. It upheld India's policy of nonalignment and opposition to U.S. military alliances in the area, to Western colonialism in Africa, and to U.S. involvement in Vietnam.

During the undeclared war that erupted between India and Pakistan in September 1965, Moscow was instrumental in persuading the two disputants to cease hostilities and sign the Tashkent declaration of January 1966. This was the first time that the USSR had played the role of peacemaker in a Third World conflict. Its aims were to prevent China's involvement in the region and to improve relations with Pakistan as well as with India.

Soviet prestige in India soared on August 9, 1971, with the signing of a twenty-year Soviet-Indian treaty of friendship and cooperation, which India wanted as a deterrent to possible Chinese intervention on behalf of Pakistan. India's need for the treaty had arisen five months earlier out of the Pakistani government's suppression of the separatist movement in East Pakistan. As millions of refugees fled to India, tensions built up, exploding into war in December 1971. The treaty proved its worth: China stayed out, limiting itself to diplomatic support of Pakistan, while India, well supplied with Soviet weapons, crushed Pakistani forces. In the UN Security Council, the Soviet Union vetoed all resolutions calling for an immediate cease-fire, thus enabling India to complete its military campaign in East Pakistan and help create the independent nation of Bangladesh in its stead.

The Soviet Union did everything to foster intimate ties. For example, in 1973 it signed a fifteen-year economic accord on terms advantageous to India. In late 1976, when oil was difficult to obtain at prices India could afford, Moscow proposed a barter deal on favorable conditions, and it offered a $450 million credit in September 1976 to enable India to expand steel-making capacity in the public sector. Soviet-Indian relations remained close under Prime Minister Indira Gandhi (1966 to March 1977) but Moscow did not receive what it really wanted: naval facilities for its Indian Ocean flotilla; support for Brezhnev's plan, floated in June 1969, for an Asian collective security system; and a special relationship that would keep India at a distance from China. Brezhnev had to settle for Mrs. Gandhi's understanding attitude toward the Soviet invasion of Czechoslovakia, criticism of U.S. policy in Vietnam and the Middle East, and general support on issues that were of little direct interest to India, such as SALT, Berlin, and CSCE. The USSR did not obtain the privileged strategic foothold it coveted.

Under the Janata coalition government, which took office after defeating Mrs. Gandhi in March 1977, India looked increasingly to the West for economic assistance. New Delhi normalized its relations with Beijing in 1977 and was unwilling to condemn China's attack against Vietnam in February 1979. In January 1980, Mrs. Gandhi returned to power in a stunning electoral triumph. Gromyko came in February to strengthen Soviet-Indian ties and obtain its support for the USSR's military intervention in Afghanistan the previous December. India did not endorse its action and urged a withdrawal for "foreign" troops, but neither did it criticize Moscow publicly, which suited Soviet purposes.

Under Gorbachev the USSR continued to accord pride of place to India. Gorbachev's visit in November 1986, his first to a Third World country, was intended to convey a sense of India's importance both internationally and to the Soviet Union; he met often with Prime Minister Rajiv Gandhi (who succeeded his mother, Indira Gandhi, when she was assassinated by Sikh extremists in November 1984) and made a second trip to India in November 1988, at which time he announced plans to build a 2000-megawatt nuclear power station and tried to reassure New Delhi that the USSR's reconciliation with China did not signify a downgrading of ties with India. Although Moscow supplied India with the most advanced conventional weaponry from the Soviet arsenal (for example, starting January 1987, the MiG-29 fighter aircraft) and sold it oil and scarce nonferrous metals at bargain prices, the USSR had no tangible dividends to show for its lengthy and expensive courtship: no naval facilities, no privileged access, and no particular popularity in the country at large.

Relations between Russia and India have been strained by the fall of communism. Unlike many other underdeveloped countries, Indian intellectuals felt a strong affinity for socialism, and were deeply dismayed by Gorbachev's attempts to revise the country's history. This dismay turned to outright hostility when Gorbachev began to improve relations with China and to support American initiatives in the Gulf War. India has long looked to the Soviet Union to support its non-aligned foreign policy stance, and saw the position it had carved out for itself in this regard being undermined by Gorbachev's embrace of the West. Ideological and political differences with the Yeltsin regime have led the Indian government to cut subsidies for Indian exports to Russia, while Moscow decreased the export of oil and raw materials and stopped the financing for the construction of enterprises. India, which had previously been dependent on Soviet weaponry, has begun to approach Western suppliers.

To avoid a further deterioration of relations, in March 1992 the two sides did update the 1985 Soviet-Indian trade protocol. This new protocol allows for a transitional period of two to three years before trade is to be based exclusively on convertible currency.

The main impediment to expanding commercial ties, however, is India's debt to the USSR, currently estimated at over $6 billion. This issue was resolved satisfactorily in late 1992, leading to a cordial state visit by Yeltsin to India in January 1993. Since then relations and trade between the two countries have warmed considerably. After falling to an all-time low in 1992, Russian trade with India increased by 44% in 1994 and is expected to double again in 1995.[6] The lion's share of Russian exports are military equipment—advanced interceptor aircraft like the MiG 29, and fighter bombers like the Sukhoi 30BK—but plans are also going ahead on construction of a Russian nuclear power plant.

At the same time, the Russian Defense Ministry is also arranging the sale of forty military helicopters to Pakistan, India's erstwhile rival, and encouraging the Pakistanis to consider replacing the embargoed U.S. F-16 fighters with Russian SU-2 jet fighters. Russia's utilitarian approach to arms sales in the region illustrates that it is not really concerned with the stability of the Indian subcontinent, as it is with instability in Central Asia, just to the north (see the section in Chapter Six on "Russia and the Near Abroad"). Its relations with India's Islamic neighbors (including Pakistan) and with China, are likely to have greater priority than relations with India because, through their contiguity with the CIS, they are able to have a direct impact on Russia. Until the prospect of instability spilling over the border of these countries into Russian border regions diminishes, Russian-Indian relations are likely to be remain a secondary priority.

AFRICA IN THE SOVIET ERA

Although most African governments of the times were innately conservative and suspicious of communism and kept the USSR at a distance, Moscow persisted and eventually did establish diplomatic ties with most of black Africa.

These ties were partly made effective through an economic program applied with erratic success; its incremental nature suffered because of the encumbrance of experts who could communicate only with difficulty, because of faulty equipment and tardy delivery schedules, and because of a Soviet inability to offer adequate assistance where it was needed most—in agriculture and in light industry.

The principal recipients of economic assistance were Guinea, Ghana, Ethiopia, Mali, Somalia, Nigeria, and Sierra Leone; commitments were made mostly during the Soviet-African honeymoon of the late 1950s when, expecting to acquire prestige, Moscow complied willingly with sometimes vainglorious requests from indigenous elites for showpiece projects and instead wasted resources and reaped disenchantment. Still, Soviet impact on the economies of courted African countries was marginal, mainly because of an unwillingness to transfer substantial economic resources to the continent. In fact, until the Angolan episode, the Soviet Union had been almost niggardly: From 1957 to 1974, it provided more economic credits (approximately $850 million) to Afghanistan than to all of sub-Saharan Africa, which received about $780 million.

In the military sphere, the record was quite different. Arms helped widen and ease Soviet political access to Africa. Realizing that no African proletariat, no well-organized communist parties, and no divisive class antagonisms existed, and that African states were heavily rural, often rent by tribal and ethnic feuds, and as often dissatisfied with colonial territorial divisions, the Soviet Union, by assuming a major role as supplier of weapons and advisers, exploited local rivalries, secessionist impulses, and national liberation movements seeking the end of European colonialism and of white supremacist regimes. Although it spread its stake thinly over a number of actors on the African stage, the USSR usually gravitated toward those elites who were particularly receptive to Soviet ideas and who were anti-Western not because of Cold War preferences, but for reasons relating to inter-African rivalries—for example, to tensions between Somalia and Ethiopia or Congo-Brazzaville and Zaire (formerly the Belgian Congo). As in the economic sphere, these efforts to influence the outcome of internal struggles for power met with mixed fortunes. The Soviet government was stymied in the Congo in 1960, and again in 1964–1965 when it backed an attempt by Algeria and Egypt to maintain a rebel group in Stanleyville (now Kisangani). But its support for the central government in the Biafran civil war vastly improved its relations with Nigeria. Arms supplies were also helpful in establishing closer ties at various times with Guinea, Ghana, Mali, Benin (formerly Dahomey), Burkina Faso (formerly Upper Volta), Burundi, and Uganda (until Idi Amin was toppled in 1979).

In the 1970s and 1980s Soviet strategic planners focused on the Horn of Africa. The reasons were largely strategic and military rather than economic or ideological—an outgrowth of Moscow's Middle East policy and ambitious construction of a blue-water fleet. The prospect of a foothold in Somalia, which dominates the entrance to the Red Sea and the northwest littoral of the Indian Ocean, led in 1969 to a significant flow of military and economic aid and in 1974 to a multifaceted treaty of friendship and cooperation. In a gesture rare for Soviet diplomacy, Moscow canceled Somalia's foreign-aid debt, which amounted to about $45 million (or 16% of Somalia's gross national product for one year). In return, the Somali connection brought Moscow naval and communications facilities at Berbera on the Gulf of Aden (which dominates access to the Red Sea) and at Mogadishu on the Indian Ocean, and privileges at the Soviet-modernized airfields at Berbera and Uanle Uen. Somalia became the most important Soviet client in sub-Saharan Africa.

But privileges and a major presence do not make a satellite. What led to the toppling of the infrastructure that Moscow had built in Somalia was Soviet strategic covetousness and political myopia. Tempted by the revolution that followed the overthrow of Emperor Haile Selassie in 1974 and the anti-Western policies of the self-proclaimed "Marxist-Leninist" military leadership in Addis Ababa, the Soviet Union agreed after two years of hesitation to Ethiopia's requests for arms.

Soviet leaders fully expected Somalia's complete dependence on Soviet weapons to constrain President Mohammed Siad Barre's independence of action. Instead, in July 1977, Somalia invaded Ethiopia in an attempt to annex the Somali-populated Ogaden province. In November, Siad Barre chose to foreclose the Soviet option, renouncing the 1974 treaty of friendship, expelling Soviet military personnel, and withdrawing the use of all facilities enjoyed by the USSR in Somalia. This led Moscow to make a major diplomatic realignment. In late 1977 to early 1978, a massive Soviet and Cuban military intervention on behalf of Ethiopia's ruling Dergue, headed by Mengistu Haile Mariam, drove back the Somalis. The new Soviet-Ethiopian relationship was capped, on November 20, 1978, by a twenty-year treaty of friendship. Soviet military assistance enabled Mengistu not only to expel the invading Somalis but also to contain the Eritrean and Tigrean separatist movements in the country. In return, in 1980 Moscow obtained strategic assets—the privileged use of the Daklak Islands and of airfields near Addis Ababa and Asmara for reconnaissance activities. Then in 1984, after years of Soviet cajoling, Mengistu created a Marxist Leninist party, the Workers' Party of Ethiopia. This made Ethiopia the first communist country on the African continent, at least nominally, because power was still held by the military and was not shared with known Communists.

Gorbachev's disenchantment with the cost of Moscow's Ethiopian policy was quickly evident. First, in keeping with his downgrading of the military instrument as a means of promoting political change, he urged a negotiated solution to Ethiopia's ethnic problem: The campaigns to suppress insurgencies in the provinces of Eritrea, Tigre, Welo, and Gonder were draining the country, dislocating the population, and devastating the countryside. Second, in the late 1980s, Gorbachev signaled an intention to decrease arms assistance, which had exceeded $10 billion in the years since 1975. Third, in the face of droughts in 1984, 1986, and 1989, Moscow urged Mengistu to abandon his radical agrarian policies of villagization and resettlement (which are designed to weaken popular support for the insurgents) and introduce much-needed economic reforms. Fourth, Moscow became more openly critical of Mengistu, not wishing to be overly committed to a leader whose continued ability to survive attempted coups seems increasingly problematical. Accordingly, in early 1990, there were reports that the Soviet Union had stopped using its military advisers to assist Mengistu in his fighting against the Eritreans and Tigreans. Finally, Moscow has improved its relations with Somalia. It supports the agreement signed in April 1988 between Ethiopia and Somalia, ending their war and restoring diplomatic relations.

By contrast, until 1974, southern Africa was less important to the Soviet Union than the Horn of Africa. It was dominated by South Africa, Portugal, and Rhodesia (Zimbabwe); the independent black African states were weak, and the prospects of the various liberation movements based in Zambia, Tanzania, and Zaire were unpromising. Moscow kept its economic assistance to a minimum, although from the early 1960s, the Soviet Union and its eastern-bloc associates helped to train guerrillas and to channel a trickle of weapons to favored national liberation groups, often through second parties such as Algeria and Egypt and occasionally through the Liberation Committee of the Organization of African Unity, which was created shortly after the OAU's establishment in 1963.

However, Moscow preferred bilateral contacts. In the Portuguese colonies its materiel went to Marxist-oriented movements—the Popular Movement for the Liberation of Angola (MPLA) and the Front for the Liberation of Mozambique; and in Zimbabwe, after its unilateral declaration of independence from Britain in 1965, assistance went to the politically more congenial Zimbabwe African People's Union. Except for the MPLA, however, whose Communist antecedents and pro-Moscow orientation date back to 1955, most of the liberation movements in southern Africa seemed able to work better with the Chinese, so Moscow did not press its affiliations with them and until 1974 wielded little clout in the region.

The overthrow of the decades-old military dictatorship in Portugal on April 25, 1974, transformed the political situation in the region with dramatic suddenness and led Moscow to intensify arms shipments, especially to the MPLA. Portugal's decision to pull out of Africa after more than five hundred years of colonial rule accelerated the decolonization process. In Guinea-Bissau, the Cape Verde Islands, and Mozambique, power was transferred smoothly. Only in Angola did the absence of an undisputed indigenous leadership result in civil war and a superpower contest of wills. The massive influx of Soviet arms and Cuban troops in mid-1975 and 1976 brought victory to the MPLA and demonstrated the readiness of Moscow to take bolder risks in promoting strategic goals. (The MPLA controlled the capital of Luanda when independence was formally proclaimed on November 11, 1975. In the civil war that followed, the overwhelming Soviet military hardware—armored cars, tanks, jeeps, small arms, and batteries of 122-mm ground-to-ground rockets—manned by approximately 20,000 Cuban troops proved decisive. This same mix of Soviet and Cuban aid was also prove effective in Ethiopia in 1977–1978.)

The success of the MPLA in Angola was a welcome antidote to the Kremlin's setbacks in the Middle East. In exercising its greatest show yet of resoluteness in sub-Saharan Africa, Moscow calculated that there were few risks and many prospective gains, not the least of which was exposure of China's inability to act in critical periods on behalf of liberation movements and its backing of groups that were also the protégés of Western countries. Moreover, Angola was a tempting plum. Abundantly endowed with oil, untapped mineral resources, and fertile land, it is potentially one of the wealthiest countries in Africa, and air and naval facilities there would position the Soviets to interdict the sea route around the Cape of Good Hope.

Angola required Soviet and Cuban military support (by the mid-1980s, an estimated 60,000 troops) to keep it in power against threats from South Africa and the rival UNITA (National Union for the Total Independence of Angola) group, led by Jonas Savimbi, operating in the southern part of the country. In October

1976, Angolan President Agostinho Neto (who died in September 1979) signed a friendship treaty with Moscow, which became increasingly important as the South Africa–backed UNITA insurgency grew in effectiveness. Repeated Soviet- and Cuban-led military campaigns in 1985, 1986, 1987, and 1988 failed to defeat UNITA. The rising military costs and a new approach to regional conflicts prompted Gorbachev to look to diplomacy for a compromise solution.

By 1987–1988, South Africa realized that the Soviet Union and Cuba were prepared to sustain a virtually open-ended commitment to Angola. Militarily, this was demonstrated in the spring of 1988, when South Africa's attempt to capture the strategic hub of Cuito Cuanavale in southern Angola was beaten back. On the diplomatic front, Gorbachev pressured Angola, Cuba, and South West African People's Organization (SWAPO) to adopt a more accommodating approach. Thanks to the patient, imaginative diplomacy of Chester A. Crocker, the U.S. Assistant Secretary of State for African Affairs in the Reagan administration, a final agreement—the Brazzaville Accord—was reached in December 1988. Under its terms, Namibia became independent on April 1, 1989, South Africa relinquished its control, and Cuban forces withdrew from Angola.

Soviet-Angolan relations remained close, in part because the MPLA relied on Soviet arms (which were paid for in hard currency) to cope with UNITA's continuing insurgency. But having helped to broker an end to the Angolan-Namibian-South African conflict, Moscow took tentative steps toward establishing diplomatic relations with South Africa. In late March 1989, Soviet Deputy Foreign Minister Anatoly Adamishin became the most senior Soviet official to visit South Africa since the two countries broke off diplomatic relations in 1956.

Elsewhere in Africa, Moscow courted "bourgeois nationalist" regimes such as Nigeria, Kenya, and the Ivory Coast, and at the same time sought to retain cordial relations with "radical" states of "socialist orientation" such as Zimbabwe, Mozambique, and the Congo-Brazzaville. Toward the latter group of countries, the Soviet Union consistently worked to establish and maintain cordial if not warm ties, and provided most of the armaments required to meet their needs, but it was not able to compete with or match the level of Western economic aid and technical assistance. "Moscow avoided the temptation to meddle in [their domestic affairs]—having come to recognize that the professed commitment to Marxism-Leninism—[of the ruling political parties] essentially stems from domestic political imperatives rather than ideological conviction."[7]

RETRENCHMENT UNDER YELSTIN

The underdeveloped regions of Sub-Saharan Africa are perhaps the lowest priority on postcommunist Russia's foreign policy agenda. Writing in 1994, two Russian diplomats in the region remarked candidly about the problems they face bringing their region to the attention of policymakers:

> A section of Russian public opinion tends to consider that Russia, which is plagued by internal problems, has ceased to be a great power. . . . [T]hey would like Russia to limit

its presence there to the minimum, giving preference in using its resources and energies to areas closer to its own borders. In other words, they would not mind shutting the door with a bang.[8]

As with other Third World regions, the only reason the Soviet Union got involved in these regions to begin with was to compete with the United States. Now that that competition has ended, involvement has declined precipitously.

Although Africa specialists make the argument that Russia needs to retain a certain interest in the region precisely because it cannot isolate itself entirely from the instabilities and conflicts in the region, their voices fall on deaf ears in the Kremlin. Beyond that, there is the problem of recovering the debt that those nations owed to the Soviet Union (estimated at $14 billion for sub-Saharan Africa).[9]

Russia's interest in the region presently lies in enhancing regional stability and opening African markets to Russian goods. As a result, Russia favors the establishment of nuclear free zones and extension of the nonproliferation treaty, the creation of regional security systems, the reinforcement of international mechanisms for conflict resolution, and the establishment of a climate favorable to trade with Russia and the CIS.

Peacekeeping and economic development are especially encouraged, if conducted under the auspices of the UN Economic Commission for Africa (ECA). More frequently, though, these ambitions are viewed from a purely utilitarian perspective. A frequent theme in Russian writings is that the African experience with multilateral peacekeeping efforts and economic development offers insights into what might work in the context of Russia and the CIS.

A major new concern of Russian diplomacy in the region is discouraging the expansion of Islamic fundamentalism. Russia must learn from the experiences of governments in the region, and halt fundamentalism before it reaches the former Soviet republics of Central Asia.[10]

Finally, there is the hope that profitable trade relations can be established in oil with exporters Nigeria, Angola, and Gabon; or with mineral-rich Guinea, Madagascar, Zaire, and Zambia; or in consumer products with Zimbabwe, Senegal, and the Republic of South Africa. Russian companies are seeking to gain access to mineral rights and fishing rights in a number of regions, and might be able to obtain some advantages in exchange for debt forgiveness.

The end of the apartheid regime in South Africa has brought Russia some unanticipated bonuses. In July 1995, South African Defense Minister Joe Modise and Russian Defense Minister Pavel Grachev signed an agreement on military cooperation that includes joint exercises and training, and collaboration in the development of Russian engines to replace the French engines in South Africa's Mirage fighters. Modise, a former African National Congress (ANC) commander, underwent military training in the former Soviet Union.[11]

For now, however, such agreements tend to be the exception rather than the rule. It is unlikely, however, that either the Russian government or private companies will devote many resources to the region in the near future. As the head of the Africa Department at the Russian Foreign Ministry candidly admits, real opportunities for deepening relations will have to await the next generation, and will be the fruit of long-term investments in the future of relations. He recommends continuing the relatively inexpensive practice of training future African specialists at Russian universities in the hope that this investment will pay off sometime in the future.

MOSCOW'S APPROACH TO CUBA AND LATIN AMERICA

Of all the regions of the Third World, none seemed to the post-Stalin Soviet leadership a less promising target for penetration and influence-building than Latin America. Prior to 1959 Soviet writings accepted U.S. dominance of the region as an established fact. However, the success of Fidel Castro's guerrilla-generated revolution in 1959 and his early self-proclaimed "conversion" to communism opened up new vistas to Soviet leaders. In particular, Castro's successful defiance of the United States alerted Moscow to the general revolutionary potential of the entire region.

Moscow became Castro's arms supplier soon after the formal establishment of diplomatic relations between the Soviet Union and Cuba in May 1960, with shipments expanding greatly after the abortive American-sponsored attempt to overthrow him in April 1961. In the summer of 1962, the Soviet leadership made a bold bid to deploy offensive missiles on the island and thereby to effect a major change in the U.S.-Soviet balance of power. Although Moscow failed in this, the aftermath of the Cuban missile crisis of October 1962 brought it two important chips in the ongoing superpower game: a U.S. pledge not to invade Cuba and an enormously closer relationship with Cuba.

The Cuban connection was expensive. Economically, the Soviet Union made up the large Cuban trade deficit by buying Cuban sugar and nickel at above world market prices and by selling oil at concessionary prices. Throughout the 1980s, the overall subsidy was estimated to exceed $4 billion annually. In addition, Soviet arms, amounting to more than another $1 billion a year, were provided lavishly and virtually free of charge. From this investment, Moscow reaped a rich strategic harvest, which included the largest intelligence collection of its kind in the world, a twenty-eight-square-mile facility that was manned by fifteen hundred Soviet technicians in Lourdes in western Cuba, an airfield that it can freely use for its own reconnaissance and antisubmarine-warfare missions, and the use of Cuban ports by Soviet ships, thus increasing their time on-station off the U.S. coast in the Caribbean. Politically, Cuba served as a constant irritant to the United States, a base for anti-American propaganda throughout the Western Hemisphere, and a conduit for supplies and advisers to revolutionary movements and regimes that are opposed to U.S. "imperialism." Moreover, it proved to be useful surrogate for projecting power in the Horn of Africa and Southern Africa.

Under Gorbachev, Soviet-Cuban relations became increasingly strained. Gorbachev's agenda was difficult for Castro to accept: cooperation with the United States to find political solutions to regional conflicts; deemphasis on Comecon and acceleration of the USSR into the Western-dominated international economic order; and domestic reform and democratization, epitomized by glasnost and perestroika.

Gorbachev was more patient and understanding with Castro than with any other prime Third World client (Vietnam, Syria, or Ethiopia). In April 1989 he visited Havana and signed a friendship treaty, whose provisions more nearly reflected his "new thinking" than Castro's traditional militancy. Unlike the friendship treaties signed in the 1970s with India, Egypt, and Iraq, the Soviet-Cuban treaty does not contain any reference to defense cooperation or even consultation in the event of a threat to one of them from a third party. Ironically, although Moscow had precipitated a nuclear crisis with the United States in October 1962 over Cuba, it avoided a formal commitment to Castro's defense all through the 1970s and 1980s or a friendship treaty of the kind signed in 1989, lest the United States read into it an unintended hostile meaning and overreact. Presumably, in April Gorbachev felt that détente with the United States was firmly on track and could withstand such political reverberations as might result from the treaty.

The treaty was Gorbachev's assurance to Castro that he would not be abandoned: retrenchment, yes, but not rejection. Soviet weapons, including advanced MiG-29s, continued to flow into Cuba, a reassurance to Castro that at a time when their economic ties were in for a major overhaul, the USSR remained committed to the special relationship entertained by both countries since the early 1960s.

Cuba was heavily in debt to the Soviet Union. Estimates of the total debt range from $6 billion to more than $20 billion. During his visit to Havana in April 1989, Gorbachev did not offer to write any of it off, despite his call in the UN General Assembly the previous December asking creditor nations to adopt a more generous approach to major debtor nations. In April 1990, Leonid Abalkin, a deputy prime minister and leading economist in Gorbachev's entourage, told Castro that Cuba's debt repayments would have to be in dollars, starting in 1995.[12] Delays in shipments of grain, oil, and industrial materials were exposing Cuba's vulnerability to economic pressure from the Soviet Union. The insistence of Soviet critics that subsidies for Cuba be drastically reduced heightened the impression that Moscow was looking for a way to cut Cuba's dependence sooner rather than later.

On July 19, 1979, the Nicaraguan dictator Anastasio Somoza was overthrown by a coalition of revolutionaries, which came to be dominated by the Sandinista National Liberation Front (FSLN). From 1980 on, Moscow supplied the Sandinistas with the weapons they needed to consolidate power and defeat the counterrevolutionary insurgents (the "Contras") arrayed against them at the start of the Reagan Administration. Moscow (and the Eastern European bloc) also helped keep Nicaragua's economy operating, by contributing oil, industrial machinery, and food. In addition, the Sandinistas arranged for Cuban and Soviet (the exact extent of Soviet involvement and foreknowledge was a matter of dispute among Western analysts) arms and supplies to be infiltrated into El Salvador to the Marxist-Leninist rebel group, the Faribundo Marti Front for National Liberation (FMLN). Total Soviet aid to Nicaragua in the 1980s exceeded $3 billion; the East Europeans and Cuba contributed upwards of $1 billion. By the mid-1980s more than 80% of Nicaragua's trade was with the Soviet bloc.

Amidst growing U.S.-Soviet tensions over Central America and U.S. military involvement, direct and covert, against the Sandinista government, a group of Latin American countries mounted a diplomatic initiative aimed at finding a way out of the increasingly volatile regional conflict. Costa Rica's President Oscar Arias Sanchez submitted a peace plan in February 15, 1987. Opposed to the Sandinistas but fearful of the spreading violence in the region, he proposed the restoration of "political pluralism," the holding of "free, democratic elections in Nicaragua," and the termination of "any means of support for guerrilla groups in neighboring countries." The U.S. government rejected the Arias Plan, but Gorbachev urged the Sandinista leadership to accept the plan, which held out the possibility of a political solution to the Contra problem. He also favored an end to arms shipments to the FMLN, lest the United States use them as a pretext for invading Nicaragua, in which event the Soviet Union would not be able to help: Gorbachev stressed that the Soviet Union was not in a position to do for Nicaragua what it had done for Cuba. Soviet coffers were too near depletion. Surprisingly, the Sandinistas accepted the modified version of August 1987 and made repeated concessions to conform to the requirements it stipulated.

Then, in a stunning development, the Sandinistas were defeated in free elections on February 25, 1990, and voluntarily relinquished power two months later. Taking his cue from the kind of political pluralism that Gorbachev had promoted in Eastern Europe in 1989, Sandinista President Daniel Ortega agreed to the first orderly transfer of power in Nicaraguan history. The United States ended its support for the Contras, who have disbanded, many returning to Nicaragua. Soviet obligations to Nicaragua (contracted when the Sandinistas were in power) expired at the end of 1990.

In Latin America, as elsewhere in the Third World, Moscow has relied on a combination of subregional rivalries, anti-American sentiments, and the ambitions of local dictators to help it establish a presence, touch off arms races, and exploit consequent polarizations. For example, in the mid-1970s, the USSR extended $650 million to the radical military regime in Peru, which harbored irredentist resentment toward Ecuador and Chile, enabling it to purchase advanced MiG aircraft, tanks, and other weapons; in the early 1980s, Moscow wooed the brutal right-wing military junta in Argentina, purchasing large quantities of beef and more than 60% of Argentina's grain exports in order to offset the partial embargo imposed by the Carter Administration after the invasion of Afghanistan. In appreciation for the junta's business-as-usual policy, Moscow sold Argentina five tons of heavy water and twelve tons of enriched uranium for nuclear reactors, upheld Argentina's position against Britain in the war over the Falklands/Malvinas in April–May 1982, and even blocked discussions in UN bodies of the junta's human rights violations. In both cases, however, the restoration of democracy (1980 in Peru, 1983 in Argentina) limited Soviet prospects for diplomatic gain.

Despite the support for Cuba and, more briefly, Sandinista Nicaragua, the dominant theme in Soviet relations with Latin America was its reluctance to challenge the United States in its own backyard. Even during the heyday of the Sandinista regime, however, many leading Soviet specialists on Latin America and the

Third World like Karen Brutents, Sergo Mikoyan, and Yuri Novopashin were argu-ing that the defense of socialist regimes in the region was economically prohibitive for the Soviet Union.[13] The U.S.-led ouster of the Marxist government in Grenada in 1983 gave added impetus to their arguments that the region was too distant to defend militarily and too costly to prop up economically. Instead, they argued, the Soviet Union should improve relations with capitalist economies of the region and eschew revolutionary upheaval. In what was to become the cornerstone of Gor-bachev's "new political thinking" toward the region, even relations with socialist-oriented governments like Cuba would be based on "mutually profitable econom-ic relations."[14] Moscow breathed a sigh of relief when the Sandinistas were voted out of power, since it eased the economic burden they had to bear.

By contrast, Yeltsin showed his sympathies for the Cuban opposition early on, when it helped to organize his first U.S. visit in 1990. Since 1991, the Russian press has taken a dim view of Castro's "siege mentality" and human rights violations, ominously chastising him for becoming a "Red Saddam Hussein."[15]

Following the pattern established with the repressive communist dictatorships in Korea and Vietnam of withdrawing support, by mid-1993 all Russian forces were withdrawn from Cuba, and Russia refused to provide military equipment to Castro except for cash. The Russian government did agree to finish the nearly completed Juragua nuclear reactor at Cienfuegos, but insisted on immediate repayment of the loan. Although the project was suspended when Cuba failed to pay, it was resumed after Cuba and Russia signed a series of long-term economic agreements in Octo-ber 1995. The new trade protocol for 1996 through 1998 envisages a traditional barter exchange of 4.7 million tons of Cuban raw sugar for 9.5 million tons of Russ-ian oil.[16]

Moscow has also sought to expand commercial and military-technical contacts with other countries, signing bilateral agreements with both Paraguay and Argenti-na in 1992, and selling over $3 million worth of anti-aircraft equipment to Brazil.[17] Russia is also negotiating an extension of important fishing and fish processing agreements with Peru.

What interests does Russia now have in a region as distant as Latin America? The vice-director of the Institute of Latin America, Anatoly Bekarevich, has argued that their similar levels of economic development make Russia and Latin America natural economic partners. In exchange for technology and raw materials, Latin America could provide Russia with a market for its advanced machinery and commercial products at competitive prices. In addition, Russia might learn from the experience of these countries in privatizing their economies and reducing bureaucratic waste.

These relations, however, are only slowly being built up from scratch. There has been some discussion in the Russian Foreign Ministry of encouraging eco-nomic ties between Russia's regions, particularly in the Far East, and Latin Amer-ica, but several obstacles remain. These include the absence of direct flights between Russia and South America, which effectively doubles the travel time. In addition, of the more than one hundred foreign banks in Moscow, only two are from Latin America, and only one Russian bank has offices in the region (in Buenos Aires). As in other regions of low priority, it is likely to be decades before any significant level of relations, diplomatic or commercial, is established.

OBSERVATIONS

What did the Soviet Union achieve for its decades-long commitment of scarce resources in the Third World? Relatively little, say most Russian analysts today, which explains the current government's reluctance to expand contacts with the region.

First, there were never true Soviet satellites in Africa. Moscow has never had the kind of relationship with any African state that it once had with the East European members of the Warsaw Pact. Some countries may have been beholden for military and economic favors, as in the cases of Angola and Ethiopia, and some even granted Moscow air and naval privileges, as did Somalia and Guinea; but as was evident in Ghana, Mali, Somalia, and Congo-Brazzaville the evanescence of privileges made reliance on these countries for the conduct of an imperial policy difficult. Despite these vicissitudes, friendly relations with African countries were a welcome asset that Moscow could rely on in multilateral diplomacy and international forums.

Second, a politically congenial set of circumstances was a prerequisite for the projection of military power in the Third World. For this reason alone, Moscow had to tread gingerly in its behavior toward African states. Despite the varied Soviet military privileges in Guinea, Angola, Ethiopia, and Mozambique, Moscow did not possess the fully controlled land based support facilities so vital for a politically significant projection of military power. Therefore, its naval forces relied on local goodwill, which is an ephemeral phenomenon in Third World politics.

Third, Moscow responded too eagerly to local initiatives in its pursuit of limited objectives. Whatever the strategic rationale and objective for its far-ranging policy may be, each particular move was a result of an African need and an invitation to cooperate, and not of Soviet pressure.

Ultimately, resentment of the West was Moscow's greatest asset in the Third World. Residual regional and ethnic rivalries, economic dislocation, and dissatisfaction were the bases for Soviet involvement in the region, and could provide no lasting foundation for political or economic engagement.

At present, Russia's agenda in the Third World is circumscribed by domestic instability and economic weakness. Even so, three priorities have emerged that are likely to guide its policies in the region in the near future.

First, the pursuit of lucrative trade arrangements, including arms sales. Arms sales have the added benefit of improving relations while maintaining a certain amount of control over access to technology. Russia will continue to reorient its arms sales away from its former ideological and toward its cash-paying customers. While the competition with Western suppliers over arms sales continues, it has shifted from a political-military competition to an economic one.

The difficulty here is that most Third World countries no longer look to Moscow for arms because it can no longer afford to give them away on long-term credit or for free. In addition, many of these countries have difficulty paying for arms with hard currency. The important exception here is the Middle East, which merits closer attention for this very reason.

Second, the pursuit of regional security. With the end of superpower rivalry, Russia is most concerned with the Third World as a source of threats to Russia through terrorism and instability on its borders. Hence, it seeks to incorporate regions of the Third World into international security regimes that would control the spread of nuclear weapons, and limit the spread of armed conflicts. The creation of such security regimes is especially sought in the Middle East. Hence, Yeltsin is likely to focus on a few countries where Moscow continues to have some appeal, such as India, Iraq, and Syria.

Aside from the Middle East, however, the Third World and its concerns now lie outside postcommunist Russia's immediate security concerns and, given its relative weakness, they are likely to remain so for quite some time to come.

SELECTED BIBLIOGRAPHY

Blasier, Cole. *The Giant's Rival: The USSR and Latin America.* rev. ed. Pittsburgh: University of Pittsburgh Press, 1987.

Blight, James G. et al. *Cuba on the Brink: Castro, The Missile Crisis, and the Soviet Collapse.* New York: Pantheon Books, 1993.

Campbell, Kurt M. *Soviet Policy Towards South Africa.* New York: St. Martin's Press, 1986.

Dannehl, Charles R. *Politics, Trade, and Development: Soviet Economic Aid to the Noncommunist Third World, 1955–89.* Brookfield, VT: Dartmouth 1995.

Dinerstein, Herbert S. *The Making of a Missile Crisis: October 1962.* Baltimore: Johns Hopkins University Press, 1976.

Duncan, W. Raymond, and Carolyn McGiffert Ekedahl. *Moscow and the Third World Under Gorbachev.* Boulder, CO: Westview Press, 1990.

Kolodziej, Edward A., and Roger E. Kanet (eds.). *The Limits of Soviet Power in the Developing World.* London: Macmillan, 1989.

Lenin, V.I. *Imperialism, the Highest Stage of Capitalism: A Popular Outline.* New York: International Publishers, 1939.

Lenin on the National and Colonial Questions: Three Articles. Peking: Foreign Language Press, 1967.

Malik, Hafeez. *Soviet-Pakistan Relations and Post-Soviet Dynamics, 1947–92.* Houndmills, Basingstoke, Hampshire: Macmillan, 1994.

Menon, Rajan. *Soviet Power and the Third World.* New Haven, CT: Yale University Press, 1986.

Meshabi, Mohiaddin (ed.). *Russia and the Third World in the Post-Soviet era.* Gainesville: University Press of Florida, 1994.

Miller, Nicola. *Soviet Relations with Latin America, 1959–1987.* New York: Cambridge University Press, 1989.

Mujal-Leon, Eusebio (ed.). *The USSR and Latin America: A Developing Relationship.* Boston: Unwin Hyman, 1989.

Newsom, David D. *The Soviet Brigade in Cuba: A Study in Political Diplomacy.* Bloomington: Indiana University Press, 1987.

Odom, William E. *On Internal War: American and Soviet Approaches to Third World Clients and Insurgents.* Durham, NC: Duke University Press, 1992.

Patman, Robert. *The Soviet Union in the Horn of Africa.* New York: Cambridge University Press, 1990.

Pavlov, Yuri I. *Soviet-Cuban Alliance (1959–1991).* New Brunswick, NJ: Transaction Publishers, 1994.

Prizel, Ilya. *Latin America Through Soviet Eyes.* New York: Cambridge University Press, 1990.

Racioppi, Linda. *Soviet Policy towards South Asia since 1970.* Cambridge, England: Cambridge University Press, 1994.

Rubinstein, Alvin Z. *Moscow's Third World Strategy*, rev. ed. Princeton, NJ: Princeton University Press, 1990.

Sand, G.W. *Soviet Aims in Central America: the Case of Nicaragua.* New York: Praeger, 1989.

Smith, Wayne S. (ed.). *The Russians Aren't Coming: New Soviet Policy in Latin America.* Boulder, CO: L. Rienner Publishers, 1992.

Somerville, Keith. *Southern Africa and the Soviet Union: from Communist International to Commonwealth of Independent States.* London: Macmillan, 1993.

Thakur, Ramesh Chandra, and Thayer, Carlyle A. *Soviet Relations with India and Vietnam.* New York: St. Martin's Press, 1992.

Valenta, Jiri, and Cibulka, Frank (eds.). *Gorbachev's New Thinking and Third World Conflicts.* New Brunswick, NJ: Transaction Books, 1990.

Valkenier, Elizabeth Kridl. *The Soviet Union and the Third World: An Economic Bind.* New York: Praeger, 1983.

Varas, Agusto (ed.). *Soviet-Latin American Relations in the 1980s.* Boulder, CO: Westview Press, 1987.

NOTES

1. Quoted in Jan M. Meijer (ed.). *The Trotsky Paper 1917–1922*, vol. 1 (The Hague: Mouton, 1964), p. 625.
2. Joseph Stalin, *Works*, vol. 6 (Moscow: Foreign Languages Publishing House, 1953), pp. 144–146.
3. N.S. Khrushchev, *Report of the Central Committee of the CPSU to the Twentieth Party Congress* (Moscow: Foreign Languages Publishing House, 1956), excerpts.
4. Sergei Stankevich, "Derzhava v poiskakh sebya" *Nezavisimaya gazeta* (March 28, 1992), p. 4.
5. "Latinskaya Amerika," *International Affairs,* January 1992, p. 116.

6. Scott Parrish, "Russian and Indian Officials Optimistic About Trade," *OMRI Daily Digest,* October 13, 1995.

7. Mark V. Kauppi, "Moscow and the Congo," *Problems of Communism,* vol. 39, no. 2 (March–April 1990), pp. 43–44.

8. Pavel Petrovsky and Vladimir Shestak, "Russia and West Africa," *International Affairs,* January 1994, p. 19.

9. Leonid Safonov, "Russian Priorities in Africa," *International Affairs,* March 1993, p. 45.

10. Petrovsky and Shestak, "Russia and West Africa," p. 23.

11. Doug Clarke, "Closer Military Ties with South Africa" *OMRI Daily Digest,* July 17, 1995.

12. The essentials of the Ablakin-Castro meeting were reported by a Cuban defector who was involved in Soviet-Cuban economic affairs in the *New York Times,* September 13, 1990.

13. See the literature cited in Sharyl Cross, "Gorbachev's Policy in Latin America" *Communist and Post-Communist Studies,* vol. 26, no. 3 (September 1993), pp. 320–321.

14. Cited in Cross, "Gorbachev's Policy," p. 324.

15. *Ibid.,* p. 332.

16. "First Balance Sheet on Cuba Visit," *Monitor: A Daily Briefing on the Post Soviet States,* October 17, 1995.

17. "Expanded Military-Technical Cooperation with Latin America," *Monitor: A Daily Briefing on the Post Soviet States,* October 3, 1995.

Chapter
11

Russian Interests in the Middle East

*I*In the Third World, the Middle East has received the lion's share of Moscow's attention. Geographically, the Middle East is the land bridge linking Europe to Africa and Asia; strategically, it commands key air routes and maritime communications; economically, it possesses vast amounts of oil, the critical energy resource of the next generation; politically, as a region experiencing simultaneous political, social, religious, and economic turmoil and rivalry, it suffers from the systematic instability that attracts great power involvement; and during the Soviet period, it could be used by the United States to threaten the underbelly of the USSR.

Soviet strategy in the Middle East was directed toward three areas: (1) the non-Arab Muslim tier of states situated along the USSR's southern border, namely, Turkey, Iran, and Afghanistan; (2) the Arab-Israeli sector of the Arab world and the eastern littoral of the Mediterranean; and (3) the Persian Gulf–Arabian Peninsula region. Soviet interest in each subregion developed independently in response to a changing combination of security concerns, military capabilities, local opportunities, and U.S. policy. From the mid-1950s, when the post-Stalin leadership first tried to improve its position in parts of the Middle East, to the 1990s, when it became deeply enmeshed in all sectors of the Middle East, Moscow has extended its political horizons from contiguous regions to those lying well beyond its essential security belt.

Since the fall of communism, the strategic importance of Moscow's former allies in the Middle East has fallen dramatically, while sensitivity to the threat posed to Russia's "soft underbelly" by Islamic fundamentalism has grown proportionately. Moscow now finds itself trying to forge alliances with moderate the Arab states and Turkey, and encouraging them to use their influence in Central Asia to promote stability in the region. At the same time though, Moscow would like to keep alive its own role in Central Asia, painstakingly forged over the past century, as a major conduit between the Muslim world and Europe.

MOSCOW'S SOUTHERN TIER: TURKEY AND IRAN

Acentral component of the USSR's policy in southwest Asia has been the relationship with Turkey and Iran. Successive tsars had expanded the USSR's borders in the eighteenth and nineteenth centuries at the expense of the enfeebled Ottoman and Persian Empires; absorbed the feudal Central Asian Turkish-speaking Muslim khanates of Bokhara, Khiva, and Samarkand; and reached the border of Afghanistan by the 1880s. Acquiring real estate always loomed large in Russian military thinking. Temporary Russian military weakness after the Bolshevik Revolution and World War I led the new Communist regime to emphasize "peaceful coexistence." From 1919 to 1945, Moscow lacked the strength or opportunity to do anything but maintain the status quo with its southern neighbors. Victory in World War II, however, revived the imperial impetus. Encouraged by his successes in Europe, Stalin tried in 1945–1946 to wrest territorial concessions from Turkey and Iran and to acquire a UN trusteeship over Tripolitania (Libya), but failed, largely as a consequence of determined U.S. opposition. He did indirectly affect developments in the Arab East, however, by supporting the United Nations' partition of Palestine in November 1947 and by recognizing Israel in 1948 in order to weaken the British position in the area. Indeed, even though 1948–1949 was a period of mounting anti-Semitism in the Soviet Union, Stalin's sanction for the sale of Czech arms to Israel at that critical time was a crucial factor in the survival of the infant Israeli nation. But aside from this, during the Stalin period, Moscow was a sideline observer of the political controversies plaguing the Middle East.

In 1953 the change of leadership in the Kremlin brought with it a readiness to chart new approaches to improve the USSR's security and strategic position in the Middle East. Geographical contiguity mandated special attention to improving relations with Turkey and Iran. This courtship started slowly but was pursued consistently. The note to the Turkish government from Soviet Foreign Minister V.M. Molotov on May 30, 1953, heralded the start of a campaign to repair the damage done by Stalin and to reestablish the accommodation that had prevailed in the 1920s. The note was significant for its unequivocal apology and renunciation of territorial ambitions. By the early 1960s, Ankara was slowly responding to the proffered Soviet olive branch as Washington sought détente with Moscow and as alignments changed in the Arab world. Moscow was prudent and generous. It avoided military provocation, extended economic assistance, and exploited Ankara's disillusionment with Washington, triggered by the U.S. removal of Jupiter missiles from Turkey several months after the Cuban missile crisis (arousing Turkish suspicions of a Soviet-American deal at their expense), and reinforced by the Cyprus crises of 1964 and 1974. Extensive Soviet economic commitments have resulted in the construction of important industrial projects, including an iron and steel complex, an oil refinery, and an aluminum plant. And Soviet loans to Turkey for economic projects have been larger than those extended to any less-developed country in recent years. In 1975 Kosygin's suggestions of a nonaggression pact was politely rejected, but during Turkish Premier Bulent Ecevit's visit to Moscow in June 1978, the two governments signed a political document on the principles of good-neighborly and friendly cooperation, similar to a 1972 communiqué issued from Ankara during a visit by Soviet President Nikolai Podgorny.

All of this helps explain the ease with which Moscow was able to carry out its military deployments and overflights of Turkish (and Greek) airspace during the 1973 October War and the 1977–1978 Somali-Ethiopian war. Turkey looked the other way. In July 1976, at the height of Turkey's anger at the U.S. arms embargo over Cyprus, the Turks interpreted the 1936 Montreux Convention flexibly and, by designating the USSR's Kiev-class carrier an antisubmarine cruiser, permitted it to be the first carrier ever to transit the Turkish straights.

Although the Turks remained wary of Moscow's perennial ambition to control the Turkish straits, this frontier remained relatively quiet during the 1980s. No threatening Soviet military buildups and no serious incidents took place. Indeed, Soviet-Turkish relations epitomized the progress Moscow had made toward undermining containment, encouraging the de facto nonalignment of the entire rimland region from Greece to Afghanistan, and ensuring an easy access to the eastern Mediterranean and the Arab East.

Since the fall of communism, Russian-Turkish relations have increasingly come to resemble a late-twentieth-century version of the "great Game" for influence in Central Asia.[1] Ankara initially reacted cautiously to the declarations of independence of the former Soviet republics. After mid-1992, however, Turkey has been increasingly open about its desire to promote pan-Turkish ties and to serve as a counterweight to Russian influence in the region.

Evoking a common cultural heritage, Turkey has invested more than $1.5 billion in Turkmenistan, more than $2 billion in Kazakhstan, and several hundred million dollars in Uzbekistan and Azerbaijan. Most of this money is being spent in construction projects, but a sizable amount (several tens of millions) is going to restore the sites of important Turkish cultural figures. Building on this ancient bond, in Bishkek (Kyrgyzia) in June 1995 the heads of state of Azerbaijan, Kazakhstan, Kyrgyzstan, Turkey, Turkmenistan, and Uzbekistan declared their intention to forge what Kyrgyz Foreign Minister Roza Otunbayeva terms a "Turkic Alliance." This alliance will include new initiatives on regional security and cooperation, confidence-building measures, and further economic integration among this "community of cultures, languages, and traditions."[2]

This new Turkish assertiveness has spawned concern in Moscow and heightened Russian concerns over its own loss of influence in the region. Tensions have focused on the Russian request for an exemption to the CFE Treaty in order to permit Russia to base more troops in the northern Caucasus (General Gures, chief of the Turkish General Staff has bluntly accused Russia of pursuing an imperial policy in the region and posing a threat to Turkey); and over Russia's support of "Armenian aggression" in Nagorno-Karabakh.[3] In April 1995 Turkish Prim Minister Tansu Ciller and Azerbaijan's president Heidar Aliyev met in Baku to "intensify military cooperation in light of closer military ties between Russia and Armenia." At that meeting, Turkey purchased 5% of Azerbaijan's stake in a deal to develop the oil fields in the Caspian Sea. According to Ciller, this purchase is designed to guarantee "the future of Azerbaijan, which he referred to as "my second homeland."[4]

Turkish organizations, parties, and private individuals have also been openly supportive of the Chechen separatists. Although the Turkish government has denied direct involvement in the conflict (as was alleged by the Russian Counterintelligence Service, the FSB), its "unofficial" reception of Chechen separatist President Dzhokhar Dudayev in 1994 (killed by Russian pinpoint bombing on April 21, 1996) indicated high-level sympathy for the rebels.[5] In retaliation, Moscow allowed the Kurdish Labor Party (PKK) to hold a public conference in Moscow, to let the Turks know that support of regional insurgencies could cut both ways.

Surprisingly, relations in the commercial and diplomatic arena impeded by these conflicts seem to not be seriously affected by these ongoing disputes. After Germany cut off its supply of helicopters and armored combat vehicles (ACVs) in October 1992 in response to domestic pressure against these forces being used against the rebel Kurds, Turkey turned to Moscow for replacements.[6] In the United Nations, Moscow and Turkey share a common interest in lifting sanctions from Iraq: Ankara because it has lost its lucrative oil transit fees from the pipeline through Turkey from northern Iraq; Moscow because lifting the embargo would provide Baghdad with the hard currency to repay its extensive debt for Soviet military equipment. And while Turkish investments in Central Asia have mushroomed, the exchange of goods and services with Russia is equally impressive. Officially, bilateral trade between Turkey and Russia is put at $2 billion for 1994, but the Russian trade paper *Birzhevye vedomosti* estimates that in reality construction work in Russia is worth $6 billion annually and "shuttle" trade between individuals amounts to an additional $5 billion.[7]

For the coming decade, therefore, Russian-Turkish relations are likely to be characterized by a combination of expanding commercial and economic ties, and jockeying for greater geopolitical leverage in Central Asia. It should not be forgotten, however, that while these two regional powers are seeking to attract the newly independent states of Central Asia to their side, the states in the region will also be playing the two of them against each other.

Soviet-Iranian relations, poor between 1945 and 1961, improved gradually after 1962, when the shah announced that no U.S. military bases or missile sites would be permitted on Iranian territory. Although Iran was a member of the pro-Western Central Treaty Organization (CENTO) military pact, it did not keep a large military force along the Soviet-Iranian border, a fact that made its participation in CENTO tolerable to Moscow and played an important role in the Soviet-Iranian rapprochement. Economic ties expanded significantly. The USSR built a major steel plant and various industrial projects; in return, it received natural gas and oil. Increasingly the government-to-government relationship improved to the point that the shah even returned Soviet defectors.

Iran experienced serious social unrest and political protests: the frustrated responses of different groups to rampant inflation, urban blight, agrarian dislocation, extensive corruption, and modernization on the one hand; and dictatorial rule, repressive policies, and rising expectations on the other. For complex reasons, the disparate groups in opposition to the shah found a unifying symbol in the late spring of 1978: Ayatollah Ruhollah Khomeini, the octogenarian religious leader who had been exiled by the shah in 1962. Events moved with tumultuous rapidity, so that by mid-January 1979, the shah was forced into exile; within a month, Khomeini had returned and established an Islamic republic.

The Soviet role in these momentous and unexpected developments remains a subject of speculation. In the early stages of the anti-shah protests—from late spring to early fall 1978—Soviet commentators generally restricted themselves to reporting what was happening in the cities and oil fields. They did not turn against the shah or proclaim his imminent demise. Moscow, like Washington, was surprised by the shah's ineptness. Only gradually did Soviet broadcasts begin to criticize the shah's government, attack U.S. involvement in Iran, and demand that U.S. imperialists be kicked out of the country.

A turning point in the Kremlin's attitude came on November 19, 1978, when Brezhnev issued a statement noting Moscow's opposition to any outside interference in Iran. In effect, he warned the United States that if it attempted to act directly to keep the shah in power, the Soviet Union might undertake an intervention of its own in accordance with a 1921 Soviet-Iranian treaty concerning threats to the territorial integrity of the country. By January 1979 Moscow's role had assumed an incendiary dimension, and communist agents played an important role in aggravating labor unrest in the oil fields (where the Communists were influential among the minority Arab and Kurdish workers), thereby contributing to the general economic paralysis that finally undermined the shah's position.

The fall of the shah was in general a boon to Moscow and, of course, a grievous blow to the United States. Soviet benefits were considerable and primarily strategic. The American-manned intelligence-gathering stations situated along the Soviet border were shut down, Iranian arms purchases from the United States ended, and Iran withdrew from the role of policeman for the West in the Persian Gulf. Moscow watched with understandable satisfaction Khomeini's intense anti-Americanism, Iran's withdrawal from CENTO (which collapsed shortly thereafter), and the legalization of the Tudeh (Communist) Party. Despite different political systems and antithetical ideologies, Soviet leaders expected basic continuation of extensive economic relations, quiet borders, and a prudent, pragmatic handling of divergent regional interests.

Relations with Khomeini's Iran, however, proved pricklier than Moscow had expected. The issues that loomed large in Soviet-Iranian relations during the Khomeini period (the Ayatollah died in June 1989) related to Iraq's invasion of Iran in September 1980 and the USSR's occupation of Afghanistan from December 1979 to February 15, 1989; the inability to agree on a price for Iranian natural gas and Soviet interference in Iran's internal affairs also complicated the relationship. A few comments about each should indicate the strained and self-limiting character of Soviet-Iranian ties and the difficulties the Soviets faced in their courtship of Iran under Khomeini.

The Soviet Union's quest for normalization and continuation of the good state-to-state relationship that it had had with the shah was hampered by Khomeini's suspicion of communism, by the traditional Iranian fear of the covetous colossus to the north, by the communist coup in Afghanistan in April 1978, and by Moscow's insistence on reaffirming, despite Tehran's repeated repudiations, the application of Articles 5 and 6 of the 1921 Soviet-Iranian treaty. These articles stipulate that

Soviet forces may intervene in Iranian affairs if a third country threatens to attack the USSR from Iranian territory or if Moscow considers its border threatened. The latter has been a particularly sore point, a reminder that for more than 150 years successive generations of Russian leaders have looked on Iran as their natural sphere of influence and that Moscow's support for the principles of equality between nations and noninterference in the internal affairs of other countries bears little resemblance to its practice, in dealing with weaker powers.

Soon after coming to power, the Khomeini regime criticized the USSR's interference in the internal affairs of Afghanistan, and Ayatollah Khomeini exhorted the Afghans to resist their communist puppet rulers. Moscow failed to ingratiate itself by adopting a pro-Iranian position in the hostage crisis that erupted on November 4, 1979, when Iranian militants seized the U.S. Embassy in Tehran and held 52 Americans hostage for 444 days. But it was the Soviet military intervention in Afghanistan in December 1979 that became the running sore in their relations. Not even the Iraqi attack on September 22, 1980, and Iran's obvious desire that the Soviet Union be a disinterested observer instead of a partisan patron of Iraq, as could be expected from the 1972 Soviet-Iraqi friendship treaty, mitigated Tehran's hostility on the Afghan issue.

The effort to avoid alienating either side in the Iran-Iraq War created dilemmas for Moscow. Essentially, the Soviet position, as set forth in *Izvestiya* the day after the war began, was that the conflict was a vestige of the two countries' colonial past, that the United States would try to exploit the situation in order to control the region's oil, that Washington hoped the conflict would lessen Iran's ability "to resist the imperialist pressures that are being brought on it," and that the United States viewed the conflict as an opportunity to reorient Iraq's foreign policy toward the West.[8] In this entangled situation, the Soviet government sold arms to both sides and played for time on the assumption that when the fighting ceased, Moscow could continue its courtship of both Tehran and Baghdad.

At first Moscow inclined toward Iran, it being clearly the weaker side, but Khomeini's enmity and Moscow's refusal to condemn Iraq made this tilt difficult. By the summer of 1982, when Iran assumed the offensive and crossed into Iraqi territory, Moscow favored Iraq, who was willing to accept a ceasefire and withdraw its forces to internationally recognized frontiers, in contrast with Tehran, who insisted on reparations, an official apology, and condemnation of Iraq. During this period, the Soviet Union joined the other members of the UN Security Council in calling for an end to the fighting. A major irritation to the Kremlin was Khomeini's crackdown on the Tudeh Party. In February 1983, many members were arrested. At the end of April, Nureddin Kianuri, the Tudeh leader, publicly confessed that the party had been trying to subvert the Islamic Republic and had been spying on the Soviet Union. On May 4, Tehran outlawed the Tudeh and expelled a number of Soviet diplomats. Iran's help to the anti-Soviet resistance movement in Afghanistan and hostility to the Soviet Union's stepped-up arms sales to Iraq were additional factors contributing to the worsening relationship between the two countries.

Despite frictions with the Khomeini regime, Moscow constantly reassured the Arab regimes in the Persian Gulf of its peaceful intentions, hoping to persuade

Saudi Arabia to normalize diplomatic relations. Other than Iraq, Kuwait was the only Arab country in the Gulf with which Moscow had relations, until 1985, when Oman and the United Arab Emirates established diplomatic ties with the USSR. Gorbachev's quest for greater participation in regional affairs led to the introduction of a Soviet naval presence in the Gulf in October 1986: Moscow emulated a practice the U.S. Navy had started earlier in the year and provided a small naval escort for its ships. Gorbachev also agreed (as did the United States) to reflag and protect some of Kuwait's oil tankers. Contributing to Gorbachev's activism was concern over the revelations in November that the United States had covertly sold arms to Iran in an abortive attempt to open a political dialogue with the Khomeini regime and to ransom some American hostages, whose Lebanon-based Shiite kidnappers had links with Tehran.

After months of negotiating with the United States, Moscow joined in adopting UN Security Council Resolution 598 of July 20, 1987, which called for an immediate cease-fire and stipulated that otherwise "further steps" (the imposition of sanctions) would be taken to ensure compliance. However, the war between Iran and Iraq raged on for another year, finally ending with a cease-fire on August 20, 1988.

As often happened in its approach to regional politics, the Soviet leadership reacted to events rather than initiating them. Thus, although it was Iraq's principal arms supplier, Moscow was receptive to the signal for better relations that came from Iran. By 1984 the Iranian government realized that increased tension with Moscow redounded to Iraq's benefit, and it set out to improve the atmosphere, first, with the symbolic whitewashing of the anti-Soviet slogans blazoned on the walls of the Soviet embassy, and second, by an exchange of economic delegations. In February 1986, amidst fierce fighting on the Iran-Iraq front, First Deputy Foreign Minister Georgii Korniyenko became the highest-ranking Soviet official to visit Tehran since Khomeini's 1979 revolution; in December, the Iranian-Soviet Standing Commission for Economic Cooperation met in Tehran for the first time in six years. In August 1987 the two countries agreed to large-scale economic cooperation, including projections for expansion of natural gas deliveries by the early 1990s; construction in the areas of power generation, steel, and oil refining; and the return of Soviet technicians, removed in 1985 because of Iraqi air attacks.

The sudden emergence of fifteen sovereign states in 1991 from the chrysalis of the Soviet Union raised completely new security considerations between Russia and Iran. The most significant has been the end of a shared twelve-hundred-mile border and the creation in its place of a buffer zone of eight new countries. Russia is keenly interested in preserving its influence in the region, while for Iran the key to security lies in fostering nation-building and stability in the new republics of the region.

Ethnically, this buffer zone still contains sizable Russian and non-Russian ethnic minorities, which both sides seek to sway. In the meantime, the political elites of these new republics have grown attached to ruling their own nation-states, and this attachment to sovereignty may transcend irredentist claims, thus giving less excuse for any manipulative Russian intrusiveness. The appeal of nationhood may well serve to keep both Russia and Iran at bay, and in that way coincidentally foster pragmatic policies toward one another in Moscow and Tehran.

A looming challenge in the region is Islam, particularly, the aggressive, Shii'a variety practiced in Iran. The Islamic factor affects Russian foreign policy in three ways: the political demands and the aspirations of millions of Muslims living inside the Russian Federation, some of whom seek virtual independence (Chechnya and Tatarstan, among others); the fate of Russians living in the Central Asia "Near Abroad"; and the efforts of states like Turkey and Iran (but also Pakistan and Saudi Arabia) to influence developments in Central Asia and the Caucasus. Finally, Russia's need for profitable economic relations is a key priority. It needs markets and reliable sources of hard currency earnings. In this respect, no country looms larger for Russia than Iran, which has the hard currency resources to buy Russian arms, industrial equipment, and advanced technology and is an important source for natural gas.

Moscow strongly supports Iran's attempts to foster regional economic cooperation—quite possibly because Tehran is not in a position to challenge Russia's special bilateral connections with the Central Asian republics. For example, the Organization for Cooperation of Caspian Sea Littoral States, Iran's Caspian Sea initiative advanced in October 1992, called for collaboration by the littoral states—Russia, Kazakhstan, Turkmenistan, Azerbaijan, and Iran—in stimulating oil and gas extraction, environmental protection, and the modernization of key ports. But the institutions and infrastructure essential for regional cooperation are still weak. Judging by the successes and failures of other attempts at regionalism, the Iranian variant lacks the necessary preconditions for success—a community of market-oriented economies, decreasing control by the central government, a free trade zone to attract investors, low tariffs, efficient customs operations, and so on.[9] Still, there is serious interest in closer economic ties, and this presumes a commitment to political stability in the region.

This increasing convergence of Russian and Iranian interest can be seen in the policy each has followed toward the Azerbaijani-Armenian war over Nagorno-Karabakh in the Caucasus and toward the civil war in Tajikistan. While Moscow has, through enticements and threats, sought to push Azerbaijan, Armenia, and Georgia back into the Russian fold, Iran has played a very limited role in the Caucasus. The interest is there, but the leverage is not. Although Iran has sought to be active in arranging a cease-fire, the Iranian foreign ministry conceded that Russia is affected by "the situation in Nagorno-Karabakh . . . more than anyone else."[10]

Iran's circumspection may be motivated by the destabilizing consequences of continued fighting. It worries that its own minority population of 15 million Azeris in northern Iran (twice the population of Azerbaijan) could become politicized and polarized along ethnic lines. The longer the war goes on, the more dangerous and unpredictable the political fallout. In such a volatile environment, Tehran is intent on avoiding any confrontation.

Geostrategically, Russia and Iran are both rethinking their strategic objectives, not just toward each other, but also toward Transcaucasia and Central Asia, where they are rivals once again, as they were in the eighteenth and early nineteenth centuries. Russia is better informed on these regions, having ruled them for so long, but Iran may be better able to exploit certain linguistic, religious, and cultural affinities. Their competition will remain political and economic, not military, absent any Russian recourse to force to reincorporate former Muslim republics into its security sphere.

THE AFGHAN CRISIS

In neighboring Afghanistan, Moscow's problems were of a different character. The roots of Soviet interest can be traced to Russian imperial expansion into Central Asia in the nineteenth century and to the "great game" of power politics between Russia and Britain. Russia's expansion to the Oxus River, the northern border of Afghanistan, heightened Britain's fear for the security of its Indian Empire. In 1907, faced with threats to their security in Europe and the Far East, Russia and Britain agreed to respect a buffer role for Afghanistan and the status quo along the entire Central Asian periphery. This accommodation ended with the Bolshevik Revolution.

In 1919, Afghanistan proclaimed its full independence—and neutrality. It maintained correct relations with Soviet Russia and the British raj. However, with the end of British rule in 1947 and the establishment of India and Pakistan as new nation-states, Afghanistan started to press claims to the Pashto-speaking tribal areas of Pakistan, and this policy intensified its desire for modernization, especially for modern weapons. Ironically, this covetous course was to end in subjugation to the power that did the most to feed Afghan ambitions, namely, the Soviet Union.

The Soviet courtship of Afghanistan began in 1954 as part of Khrushchev's overall policy of improving relations with Turkey, Iran, and Afghanistan and undermining the U.S. policy of containment. Sensitive to the xenophobia of its weak, semifeudal neighbor, the Soviet government proceeded slowly. Agreements were signed calling for Soviet construction of two large grain elevators, a flour mill, and road-building equipment. Other economic and social projects followed in rapid succession.

Soviet policy had several objectives: to prevent the possibility of Afghanistan's joining any U.S.-sponsored alliance; to create in Afghanistan a showcase of Soviet aid projects as a way of demonstrating to other Third World countries the benefits of closer ties with the USSR; to offset Chinese inroads; and to draw Afghanistan more intimately into the Soviet sphere of influence, into what Soviet leader Leonid Brezhnev was to term in 1969 a "collective security system for Asia."

Modernization proceeded fitfully—enough to stimulate elite demands for a greater role in policymaking but inadequate to satisfy the social groups that it spawned. Meanwhile, Afghan dependence on Soviet economic aid grew. In July 1973, a group of army officers staged a coup, brought Daoud back to power, and established a republic. Daoud tried, but too late, to veer toward an approximation of the policy that had traditionally been used to preserve independence—*bi-tarafi*, the balancing of external influences. His attempt to become less dependent on the Soviet Union prompted the restive Communists to seize power in a bloody coup on April 27, 1978.

The new communist government was headed by Nur Mohammad Taraki, one of the founders of the People's Democratic Party of Afghanistan (PDPA) in 1965. The party split in 1968, with Taraki leading a majority faction known as the *Khalq* (the "masses") and Babrak Karmal heading the smaller, more pro-Soviet, group known as the *Parcham* (the "flag"). For a time the two communist groups cooperated, but three months after the coup, Taraki purged the Parchamis, and Babrak Karmal took refuge in East Europe.

Taraki's policies triggered open rebellion. By early 1979, attacks on the regime were so widespread that in April Moscow dispatched a high-ranking military mission to Kabul to evaluate the situation. In September, Taraki fell afoul of intraparty factionalism and was killed in a showdown with his Deputy Prime Minister, Hafizullah Amin. For the next three and a half months, Amin pursued an even more aggressive policy, trying to destroy the *mujahideen* (freedom fighters, or "holy warriors"). Like Taraki, he took Soviet support for granted and welcomed the increasing flow of Soviet soldiers and supplies. The Kremlin, however, had other plans. On December 27, 1979, it intervened in force, killing Amin and installing Babrak Karmal as its man in Kabul. Whatever independence of action the communist regime had retained in the twenty months after the April 1978 coup came to an end.

Moscow justified its military invasion on the grounds that it had acceded to the "urgent request" of the Afghan government under Article 4 of the 1978 treaty for help in repelling "outside armed intervention." But it was clear from the very beginning that Moscow used the treaty as a pretext for its invasion: Its aim was to install a compliant communist who would heed Soviet advice on how best to pacify the country and prevent the communist regime from being overthrown by a coalition of "counterrevolutionary" forces.

For more than eight years, the Soviet Union waged a brutal war, aptly termed "selective genocide," to crush the Afghan mujahideen: It bombed and strafed villages suspected of harboring members of the resistance, burned crops in an attempt to starve the population into submission, mounted repeated offensives to depopulate strategic valleys, and conducted a scorched-earth policy. Out of a population of approximately 16 million, more than 4 million Afghans have fled—over 3 million to Pakistan, and the rest to Iran. Despite overwhelming superiority in firepower, the 110,000 Soviet troops were slowly thwarted, and the costs to Moscow rose steeply. Officially, over 16,000 Soviet soldiers died in the conflict. The mujahideen received better weapons—for example, from late 1986 on, shoulder-held surface-to—air missiles such as the U.S. Stinger, which virtually neutralized Soviet control of the air—and their perfected hit-and-run strikes and ambushes exacted a heavy price.

Soon after coming to power, Gorbachev recognized that the war in Afghanistan was his most urgent and difficult problem in the Third World. In his report to the twenty-seventh congress of the CPSU on February 26, 1986, he called it "a bleeding wound." His dissatisfaction prompted changes on a number of fronts. First, in May 1986, he replaced Babrak Karmal as general secretary of the PDPA with Najibullah, a tough, dedicated Communist with a record of complete loyalty to Moscow going back to his student days in the mid-1960s. Second, Gorbachev moved to give credence to his stated aim of bringing Soviet troops home by withdrawing 8000 at the end of October. Third, he accelerated diplomatic efforts, both bilaterally and through the UN-sponsored talks that had started in 1982 between Pakistan and the communist regime in Kabul. Finally, military attacks on the mujadideen were intensified, as was propaganda aimed at dividing and coopting them with offers of status and rewards, as in Najibullah's call for "national reconciliation" in January 1987.

By the end of 1987 Gorbachev had run out of carrots and sticks. His hopes for inducing the mujahideen to support the Najibullah regime were misplaced; and his military escalation—intended to show the impossibility of defeating the Red Army on the battlefield—underestimated the staying power of the resistance. On February 8, 1988, he announced a readiness to withdraw Soviet troops from Afghanistan and went on to say that he would be only too happy to have "as a neighbor an independent, nonaligned, and neutral" Afghanistan. In Geneva, under the guidance of UN Under-Secretary for Political Affairs Diego Cordovez, a carefully crafted package of four separate but interrelated agreements was signed, entering into force on May 15, 1988. On schedule, the last Soviet combat troops left Afghanistan on February 15, 1989. (In the late 1980s, when glasnost opened the way for an assessment of the Soviet intervention, the following essentials emerged: The Soviet General Staff had opposed the invasion, but was overruled by then-Defense Minister Ustinov; the matter was decided without any serious discussion; and the decision was made by a few members of the Politburo—Leonid Brezhnev, Mikhail Suslov, Andrei Gromyko, and Dimitrii F. Ustinov.)[11]

The final withdrawal of Soviet forces from Afghanistan in February 1989 did not end the fighting in that war-torn country. Indeed, the conflict between Islamic fundamentalists and Soviet-supported communist elites in Afghanistan is now mirrored in neighboring Tajikistan, whose population is linguistically and ethnically close to the Afghans. The result has been a bloody civil war in which an estimated 150,000 people have disappeared and half a million have been made homeless.[12]

In the course of the war, the Tajik opposition has fled to Afghanistan and used it as a base of operations. In a political environment dominated by a corrupt Soviet party-state and a rising Islamic movement, Moscow has supported the former, providing border guards and the bulk of troops for CIS peacekeeping operations set up to enforce a fragile cease-fire negotiated in early 1995.

Dependent on Russia's good will for his regime's survival, and eager to retain as many Russians in Tajikistan as possible, Tajik President Emomali Rakhmonov has agreed to institute dual citizenship, and called for an accelerated integration with both Russia and the CIS. Although Russia benefits little from its involvement in this conflict, it fears that precipitous withdrawal would grant Islamic fundamentalists (who in the November 1991 elections garnered 34% of the vote) their first foothold within the CIS. Having made opposition to Islamic fundamentalism a cornerstone of their policy in the southern tier, Moscow now fears that abandoning its allies in Tajikistan might have repercussions throughout the region, and lead other, moderate Islamic leaders in neighboring states, to worry about Moscow's commitment to secular political development in the region. The legacy of the bloody conflict in Afghanistan is thus likely to haunt Russia for many years to come.

THE ARAB-ISRAELI CONFLICT

By concluding an arms deal with Egypt's Gamal Abdel Nasser in August 1955, the USSR discovered that arms were the key to access to the Arab world and erased the diplomatic debits of the Stalin era. The initial targets were Egypt and Syria, both of whom opposed Western military pacts in the area and sought alternative sources of weapons with which to counter their Western-armed regional rivals. Moscow seemed fully in tune with the anticolonialist and anti-imperialist sentiment cresting in the Arab world. Soon afterward, the Arab-Israeli conflict provided Moscow with a convenient issue for exploiting Arab ties with the United States and enhancing its status with radical Arab states. In time, Moscow's goals expanded to include the quest for military privileges.

Moscow sold Egypt arms with several purposes in mind, primarily to establish firm ties with a key Arab country and to encourage its opposition to the Baghdad pact (established in the spring of 1955 and reorganized as CENTO in 1959, following the revolution in Iraq that brought in an anti-Western regime). When Washington's precipitate withdrawal of its offer to assist Egypt in building the Aswan High Dam provoked Nasser to nationalize the Suez Canal Company in July 1956, the Soviet government upheld the Egyptian action. Moscow also championed Nasser's cause during the Israeli-Anglo-French invasion of Egypt in October 1956, and though it was American rather than Soviet pressure on the invaders that forced their withdrawal and saved Nasser, the Soviet Union's prestige nonetheless rose spectacularly in the Arab world as it replaced Egyptian arms lost to the Israelis in Sinai, lent Egypt and Syria several hundred million dollars for economic development, and supported Arab positions in the UN. However, Moscow was careful to avoid any military actions that might occasion a strong response from the United States, still the preeminent military power in the area.

Arab nationalism posed dilemmas for the Soviet Union in the years immediately after the merger of Egypt and Syria created the United Arab Republic (UAR) and the military made an anti-Western coup in Iraq, in March and July 1958, respectively. Although unhappy over the establishment of the UAR because this "nullified some of the gains made in Syria by both the USSR and the indigenous Communist Party" and also served to strengthen Nasser's bargaining position, "making him less amenable to Moscow's wishes and more immune to Soviet pressure," Moscow reconciled itself to the newest manifestation of Arab nationalism and "chose to continue to protect Soviet interests in the Middle East through cooperation with, not opposition to, Cairo."[13] Pleasantly surprised by the overthrow of the pro-Western Iraqi regime on July 14, 1958, the USSR saw in the emergence of the Qasim government a sharp blow to the Western position in the Middle East (Nasser also considered it a move toward Arab unity). An early and unexpected falling-out between Cairo and Baghdad, however, confronted Moscow with difficult choices. How was it to differentiate between two "progressive" Arab regimes without alienating either? How was it to nourish anti-imperialism without rousing Arab suspicions of communism by pressing for better conditions for indigenous Arab Communists? How was it to strengthen the progressive component of Arab nationalism and at the same time minimize its bourgeois component?

For a time, Moscow backed Abd al-Karim Qasim against Nasser because in contrast to Nasser, who repeatedly expressed interest in improving relations with the Western countries, Qasim was militantly critical. Also in contrast to Nasser, who cracked down on local Communists and asserted that communism was imcompatible with Arab nationalism and unity, Quasim brought Communists into the government and relied on their support against his Nasserite opponents; and where Nasser had ambitions to unify the Arab world under his leadership, Qasim represented a force for retaining the existing nation-state system in the Arab world, thus affording Moscow more room for diplomatic maneuvering and lessening the likelihood that Arab nationalism would take on a bourgeois complexion that might impede the move toward socialism. Furthermore, Moscow could not fail to regard with utmost concern the possibility, however remote, of a unitary Arab nationalist state, which might exert a strong attraction for Soviet Muslims.

Shrewdly, Khrushchev kept this mini–Cold War with Cairo over strategy, outlook, and issues from interfering with the expansion of economic ties, as exemplified by the USSR's commitment in October 1958 and January 1959 to help build the Aswan High Dam. Aware of Nasser's enormously enhanced position as the standard-bearer of Arab nationalism, Moscow tolerated his anticommunist outbursts and sporadic moves toward improved relations with the West. Moreover, by 1961–1962, disenchantment with Qasim had set in because of his suppression of Iraqi Communists.

Military considerations were even more important motivations for Moscow's careful courtship of Nasser. In May 1961, Albania evicted the Soviet Union from the naval base it had enjoyed at Vlone on the Adriatic Sea since 1945, and U.S. deployment of Polaris submarines in the Mediterranean was impending. These events prompted friendlier relations with Nasser and serious Soviet efforts to obtain naval facilities in Egyptian ports.[14] This quest for tangible military privileges increasingly absorbed Moscow and muted political differences with Egypt. The collapse of the Egyptian-Syrian federation in September 1961 also helped, and, buttressed by the growing interest of Soviet strategic planners in Aden, the USSR subsidized Egyptian intervention in the Yemeni civil war after 1962.

Egypt's disastrous showing in the Arab-Israeli war of June 1967 proved a boon for Moscow, paving the way for the extensive privileges that the Soviet military had sought. The political and strategic consequences of the June War concern us here only insofar as they relate to Soviet policy. Briefly, the background was this: In the spring of 1967, Moscow feared for the future of the pro-Soviet government in Syria. To rally support behind its Syrian client, it spread false reports of an impending Israeli attack against Syria. (To prove that there was no military buildup, the Israeli prime minister even offered to tour the Israeli-Syrian border with the Soviet intelligence reporters.) He mobilized his army in Sinai and ousted the UN Emergency Force (UNEF), which had kept the Egyptians and Israelis apart since

1957. At this point, Nasser went beyond Soviet expectations. Instead of settling for the tactical political triumph of liquidating UNEF—the last vestige of Israel's advantage from the 1956 war—and thus diverting the supposed threat away from Syria, he announced the closing of the Straights of Tiran, blocking Israel's outlet to the Red Sea and Indian Ocean, and moved the mass of his army into position to invade Israel. However, the combination of Israeli air superiority and surprise was decisive, and in a lightning campaign from June 5 to 10, the Israelis defeated the Egyptians in Gaza and Sinai, the Jordanians in Jerusalem and on the West Bank, and the Syrians on the Golan Heights.

Soviet leaders, unwilling to abandon their ambitions in the Arab world, poured new weapons and Soviet advisers into Egypt and Syria. Cairo's dependence was total; the army and air force had to be re-equipped and retrained to handle advanced weaponry, and the economy required imports of food, industrial materials, and machinery, much of which Moscow bankrolled. Between 1967 and 1969 alone, the Soviet investment into Egypt was in the range of $3 to $4 billion. Nevertheless, against Soviet wishes, Nasser started a "war of attrition" against Israel along the length of the Suez Canal in March 1969, but this effort backfired. In early 1970, Moscow was forced to up its ante to the point of committing 20,000 combat troops to manned missile sites and the air defense of Egypt's heartland. In its complete dependence on the Soviet Union, Egypt granted significant concessions: naval facilities at Alexandria and Port Said, the assignment of airfields for the almost exclusive use of Soviet forces, and approval for the transformation of Mersa Matruh into a naval "facility" (the term Third World countries prefer to "base," since it does not imply surrender of sovereignty or smack of colonial rule) to be used by the Soviet Mediterranean fleet. These privileges marked the high point of Soviet presence in any Arab country. In saving Nasser, Moscow demonstrated that it was prepared to go beyond the supply of arms and advisers to support prized clients and pursue imperial objectives in the Third World, even if these jeopardized the USSR's quest for détente with the United States.

When Nasser died in late September 1970, Moscow expected continuity in leadership but instead watched a struggle for power that resulted in the virtual elimination in May 1971 of Nasser's entire entourage, on which it had predicated its aim of consolidating and preserving the privileged Soviet position in Egypt. Seeking to stabilize relations with Anwar Sadat, the victor in the succession struggle, and to institutionalize its political and military presence, Moscow pressed for the Soviet-Egyptian treaty of friendship and cooperation of May 27, 1971. Article 7 of the treaty held that "in the event of development of situations creating, in the opinion of both sides, a danger to peace or violation of peace, they will contact each other without delay in order to concert their positions with a view to removing the threat that has arisen or reestablishing peace." For the first time, the USSR bound itself to a military commitment in the Third World—a measure of Egypt's importance to Moscow and of the USSR's growing military confidence. Moscow hoped that the treaty would ensure its position in Egypt and serve as a model for cementing ties with other Third World countries. (And indeed, similar treaties were signed with India in August 1971, Iraq in April 1972, Somalia in 1974, Angola in October 1980, to mention some of the most important ones for the Soviet Union.)

Despite the treaty, the Soviet leadership found Sadat difficult. Cairo wanted more weaponry than Moscow, influenced by its developing détente with the United States, was prepared to deliver; the Egyptian military was restive over the patronizing attitude of Soviet advisers; and the completion of the Aswan Dam in January 1971 brought new requests for major economic commitments. Also, Sadat helped to suppress a communist-inspired coup in the Sudan in July 1971, subsequently cracked down on Egyptian Communists, and made independent efforts to deal with the United States and diminish its support of Israel. On July 18, 1972, he publicly announced the expulsion from Egypt of Soviet military personnel (between 15,000 and 20,000), including all Soviet pilots. Of the once extensive Soviet military presence in Egypt, only the naval facilities were permitted to remain more or less as before. This stunning turn of events demonstrated that neither a major presence nor heavy dependency would necessarily bring influence to the patron, and that a superpower unable or unwilling to project its military power directly into the domestic politics of a client state was vulnerable to the vagaries of a client's change of attitude or policy.

By January 1973, Moscow and Cairo had effected a reconciliation, Sadat unilaterally extending Soviet naval facilities beyond the April 1973 expiration date and Brezhnev again turning on the arms tap, in part for strategic reasons and in part for Arab oil money.

When Sadat and Syrian President Hafez Assad launched the fifth Arab-Israeli war on October 6, 1973, they started a conflict that Moscow did not want but did nothing to stop. The Soviet leadership risked the budding détente with the United States in order to back its Arab clients, going nearer to the brink of a confrontation with the United States than ever before, even during the 1962 Cuban missile crisis. By 1973, the Soviet Union had achieved strategic equivalence with the United States and both sides had sizable conventional forces deployed in proximity, so that a small incident might easily have triggered a chain reaction. Moscow acted very much the generous and protective patron, saving Egypt and Syria from another military disaster and enabling both to emerge from the war with significant strategic and political gains.

But Sadat, far from being grateful, repaid Soviet help with contumely and a political rebuff. For a combination of personal, strategic, political, and economic reasons, Sadat turned sharply to Washington, openly alienating the Soviet Union. Acrimony and increasing friction characterized Soviet-Egyptian relations for the next two and a half years, as Sadat looked to Washington for economic assistance and for political solutions to the Arab-Israeli conflict. On March 15, 1976, Sadat unilaterally abrogated the 1971 treaty; a month later, he announced the cancellation of facilities for the Soviet navy. In less than five years, the formerly impressive Soviet military presence in Egypt had turned to sand.

The end of the Egyptian connection forced Moscow to search anew for a secure foothold in that part of the Arab world directly involved in the Arab-Israeli conflict. Thus, while the United States was fashioning two disengagement agreements on the Egyptian-Israeli front and a first-stage pullback in the Syrian-Israeli sector, the Soviet Union was looking elsewhere for an active role and a constituency for itself. It built up Syria's military capability, reluctantly supporting Assad's intervention in Lebanon in 1976; it sold massive amounts of arms to Iraq and Libya; and it followed the lead of the Arab rejectionist front in espousing the maximalist demands of the Palestine Liberation Organization.

President Jimmy Carter took office in January 1977 determined to press for a comprehensive Middle East settlement. Deteriorating relations with the Soviet Union prompted by the President's abrasive emphasis on the human rights issue and introduction of sudden changes in the SALT negotiations led Secretary of State Cyrus Vance to seek Soviet cooperation on the Arab-Israeli problem, in the hope that progress in a Middle East settlement would have a salutary effect on negotiations in other sectors. On October 1, 1977, the Soviet Union and the United States issued a joint statement that would have moved the Middle East negotiations to a Geneva venue and included all the parties. However, Israeli objections and congressional opposition rendered the statement ineffective within a week. This led Sadat to take matters into his own hands. The result was his historic trip to Jerusalem on November 19, 1977, and the pursuit of a separate Egyptian-Israeli accord. Once again the Soviet Union was left outside the bargaining process.

Moscow denounced Sadat's initiative as "an act of capitulation" and strongly supported the position of the hard line Arab states—Syria, Iraq, Libya, and Algeria—who sought to prevent any Egyptian-Israeli agreement. It also bitterly criticized the United States for reneging on the joint statement and encouraging a separate accord. By the end of July 1978, the Soviet Union had reason to expect an American failure—then came the August 8 announcement in Washington of a meeting to be convened on September 5, 1978, at Camp David, Maryland. President Carter's personal commitment and involvement made the difference. The Egyptian-Israeli-American negotiations bore fruit in the signing of a formal treaty between Egypt and Israel on March 26, 1979.

In the aftermath of the Egyptian-Israeli reconciliation and peace treaty of March 26, 1979, Moscow strengthened ties with members of the radical, anti–American, anti-Camp David component of the Arab world, notably Syria, the People's Democratic Republic of Yemen (PDRY), and the Palestine Liberation Organization (PLO). Syria has long been important in the USSR's political-ideological effort to establish sound relations with a key Arab country. The first to receive Soviet arms (in the fall of 1954, admittedly on a small scale), it was attractive because of its radical secular anti-Western political outlook, its toleration of Communist Party activity, and its bitter opposition to any compromise with Israel. In the early 1970s arms flowed to President Hafez Assad, to whose defense Moscow rallied during the October War and whose obduracy toward U.S. efforts to promote a Syrian-Israeli agreement was rewarded with massive quantities of arms. Moscow was unhappy with Syria's military intervention in Lebanon in June 1976, but did nothing to pressure Assad to withdraw—on the contrary, it continually upgraded its commitments and transfers of weapons.

The situation in Lebanon and growing Syrian domestic opposition stemming from ethnic and religious sectarianism forced Assad into a closer political relationship with Moscow. Assad's tightly knit, tough, secretive leadership is primarily Alawite, members of a Shiite Muslim sect representing only about 10% of the Syrian population, which is predominately Sunni, the orthodox mainstream of the

Islamic religion. On October 8, 1980, in Moscow, Assad gave the Kremlin the treaty it had sought for almost a decade and signed a twenty-year treaty of friendship and cooperation. Moscow obtained some immediate advantages: access to Syrian port facilities, prestige in the Arab world as a consequence of having finally concluded a friendship treaty with Syria, and the support of a key Arab country on the issue of Afghanistan.

The treaty's utility to Syria became evident in June 1982, soon after Israeli forces invaded Lebanon. A series of Israeli-Syrian confrontations in the sky over the Bekaa Valley resulted in the downing of more than eighty Syrian Soviet-built MiG aircraft. In addition, the Israelis, using pinpoint bombing, knocked out all of Syria's Soviet-provided mobile surface-to-air missile sites (SAMs) in Lebanon. Furious over foreign reports depreciating the value of Soviet weaponry and intent both on reassuring Syria of its commitment to the 1980 treaty and on signaling Israel not to carry the war to Syria, Moscow quickly replenished Syria's losses of aircraft, tanks, armored personnel carriers, and SAMs. In political terms, its military resupply and buildup of Syria was a response to Camp David and President Reagan's Middle East initiative of September 1, 1982, and a warning to Washington not to underestimate the USSR's determination to play an active role in the Arab-Israeli sector of the Middle East.

Under Gorbachev, Soviet diplomacy made special efforts to improve relations with moderate Arab states such as Egypt, Jordan, and Saudi Arabia and to drum up interest in an international conference that would work toward a comprehensive settlement of the Arab-Israeli conflict. Thus, Soviet relations with Egypt, poor for most of the decade after Sadat's abrogation of the friendship treaty in 1976, were normalized in 1985, when President Hosni Mubarak permitted Moscow's ambassador to return to Cairo after a four-year hiatus. Since Moscow stopped its condemnation of Egypt's peace treaty with Israel and agreed in April 1987 to reschedule Egypt's military debts (estimated at upwards of $4 billion) on favorable terms, there has been a noticeable warming of their relationship. In February 1989, Edward Shevardnadze became the first senior Soviet official to visit Egypt in fifteen years, and in May, Moscow agreed to extend long-term credits for a major power project in the Sinai and modernization of the Soviet Union in talks to promote Israeli-Palestinian negotiations.

Intrinsic to Moscow's efforts to become part of the Arab-Israeli peace process have been the changes in its approach to Israel. The first sign that the Soviet government was rethinking its policy towards Israel was *Izvestiya's* publishing on May 12, 1985, of a telegram from Israeli President Chaim Herzog on the occasion of the fortieth anniversary of the Allied victory in Europe. In printing the Israeli message in the commemorative celebration, Moscow gave rare diplomatic affirmation of Israel's right to exist. By the time that Prime Minister Shimon Peres met Soviet Foreign Minister Shevardnadze and the United Nations in New York in late October, the Soviet-Israeli dialogue had become front-page news.

But matters proceeded slowly, Gorbachev having more pressing issues to attend to than the restoration of relations with Israel. Then, in early August 1986, the Soviets proposed a meeting in Helsinki to discuss "consular affairs." Although nothing came of the one-day session, continued periodic discussions resulted in a low-level breakthrough: In July 1987, a Soviet consular delegation arrived in Israel on a ninety-day visa, the first visit by Soviet diplomats in more than twenty years. Its ostensible purposes were to survey the property of the Russian Orthodox Church and check on the situation of the few dozen Soviet citizens living in Israel; the real purposes were more political and far-reaching.

After repeated delays, in late July 1988, Moscow admitted an unofficial Israeli consular delegation, permitting it to occupy Israel's embassy building but not to issue visas or conduct formal diplomatic activities. Two events hastened a more forthcoming attitude by Moscow: In early December 1988, five Georgians who had hijacked a civilian airliner to Tel Aviv airport were promptly returned to Soviet authorities, and several days later, a major earthquake in Armenia brought an outpouring of international assistance that included Israeli officials, and in early October consular missions were opened in Moscow and Tel Aviv, the penultimate stage in restoration of full diplomatic relations.

On the major bilateral issues—emigration, cultural freedom, and economic interaction—Moscow has made major policy changes. Soviet Jews are being permitted to emigrate in unprecedented numbers, with the prospect that this will continue for the foreseeable future: in 1986, 914 were allowed to leave; in 1987, 8155; in 1988, almost 19,000; in 1989, more than 70,000, surpassing the previous high of 51,000 set in 1979 under Brezhnev; and in 1990, the total exceeded 200,000. Despite pressure from Arab governments, Gorbachev has continued to permit the increase.

The cultural milieu of the Soviet Jewish community has improved. For those who wish to cultivate their religious or cultural heritage, there is an emerging cultural pluralism. In the economic sphere, trade with Israel is increasing, Soviet enterprises are exploring coproduction agreements with Israeli high-tech companies, tourism is expanding, and business contacts were placed on a legal basis, after a protocol was signed in Moscow in January 1990 between the Soviet and Israeli Chambers of Commerce.

A few words may be appropriate at this juncture about the PLO, as it impinges on Soviet-Middle East relations. Under Brezhnev, Moscow supported efforts to strengthen the PLO's international standing and the case of Palestinian statehood. Its attitude toward the PLO evolved as a function of its perceived need to align itself with the mainstream of the anti-American coalition in the Arab world. Thus, as the PLO was accorded a more central position by Arab leaderships, Moscow increased its support. In the summer of 1982, there was an unwarranted rush to assert that Moscow had suffered a severe blow to its credibility as a patron-protector through its failure to intervene in Lebanon and defend the PLO from a crushing military defeat at the hands of Israel. True, for years Moscow had helped arm, train, and encourage the PLO, but this was part of its being a camp follower of the hard-line, radical anti-American Arab regimes it courted. To use the extent of the Soviet Union's readiness to fight on behalf of the PLO as a litmus test of its credibility with those Arab regimes with whom it has treaty relationships or close ties is to misread Soviet policy egregiously. Moscow never agreed to act as the PLO's protector. It was under no obligation—moral, legal, or military—to lift a hand in Lebanon on behalf of the PLO, to whom no single Arab government had provided help.

Gorbachev introduced important changes in the way Moscow related to the PLO and handled the Arab-Israeli conflict in the United Nations. When, on November 15, 1988, the Palestine National Council (the legislative arm of the PLO) proclaimed a state in Algiers, Moscow extended a limited recognition that did not call for the exchange of diplomatic missions, the establishment of a PLO embassy in Moscow, or membership in the United Nations. The PLO, inflated by the diplomatic recognition extended by almost one hundred governments, was disappointed by Soviet equivocation. Thinking it had the votes to succeed, in April 1989 it applied for membership in the World Health Organization (WHO). After heated debate, the WHO General Conference voted to defer consideration of the application, with the USSR joining the majority, to the consternation of the Arab states. Moscow also opposed the PLO's efforts to upgrade its status in the United Nations Educational, Scientific, and Cultural Organization (UNESCO) and the Food and Agricultural Organization. Since committing himself to the strengthening of the United Nations (see Chapter Twelve), Gorbachev has reversed the previous Soviet policy of encouraging the isolation and delegitimation of Israel (as when Moscow supported the challenge to Israel's right to be seated in the General Assembly). At the same time, not wishing to alienate the PLO, in January 1990 Gorbachev permitted it to raise its representation in Moscow to embassy level.

After the failed August 1991 coup attempt, the Russian Foreign Ministry acted quickly to restore diplomatic relations with Israel. Interestingly, it did so despite the opposition of the then-still-active Soviet Foreign Ministry. Diplomatic relations were formalized on October 24, 1991, twenty-four years after they were broken off in the aftermath of the Six-Day war. Since then, direct flights from Russia to Israel have been reinstituted, and efforts have been made to facilitate contacts between the large émigré community from the former Soviet Union living in Israel.

Russia's weakness and self-absorption, however, have dramatically reduced its role in the Arab-Israeli conflict. Although invited to cosponsor the Madrid Peace Talks in 1991, Russia had no role in the subsequent negotiations that led to the accord on Palestinian autonomy signed in Washington in September 1995. Despite the large expatriate community in Israel with Soviet training and contacts, trade contacts have also been surprisingly modest. One reason for this has been Russia's concentration on consolidating its position among the Islamic states of the CIS, and on keeping up good relations with Iran. Israel has vociferously opposed Russia's plans to sell low-grade nuclear reactors to Iran, and relations between the two countries have suffered as a result. A recent accord between Canadian, Russian, and Turkish companies to build a pipeline to carry Russian natural gas to Israel is one of the few large scale projects linking the two countries.[15]

THE GULF AND THE ARABIAN PENINSULA

The differentiated policy Moscow has pursued in the Third World—the adaptability, persistence, and pragmatism as well as the opportunistic and low-risk character of that policy—is very apparent in the USSR's drive to penetrate the Arabian peninsula. In the years since the oil and energy crises roared onto the international scene in the wake of the 1973 October War, the area has assumed greatly increased importance in Soviet calculations. A geographically strategic land mass lying to the south of the USSR's Muslim, non-Slavic union-republics and flanked by busy sea routes whose choke points at the Strait of Hormuz and the Strait of Bab al-Mandab expose Western economic vulnerability to any cutoff of oil, the peninsula is an obvious target for U.S.-Soviet rivalry in the Middle East.

The Soviet Union's interest in the Arabian Peninsula started in the late 1920s and early 1930s, when Moscow established relations with Yemen and Saudi Arabia. However, the essentially marginal commercial ties of that time never took hold. Moscow's attempts to establish firm footholds on the peninsula lagged far behind its efforts in other regions, in part for want of opportunity but also because the less explosive political tensions offered few quick rewards. Post-Stalin Soviet diploma-cy made its first inroad on the peninsula with the treaty of friendship signed with Yemen in Cairo on October 31, 1955, though not until 1968 did the USSR become directly and intimately involved in the Yemeni sector.

Moscow's readiness to assume extensive economic and military commitments in pursuit of strategic interest in the Arabian Peninsula was first demonstrated in Iraq. The military coup that overthrew the pro-Western Hashemite monarchy in Baghdad on July 14, 1958, brought the Soviet Union into an important tributary of Middle East developments quite independent of its growing involvement with Egypt and the Arab-Israeli conflict. After an initial halcyon period, Soviet-Iraqi relations went through a trying ten-year phase, primarily as a result of the chang-ing fortunes of the Iraqi Communist Party. But this did not prevent the steady expansion of government-to-government ties, because regardless of the group in power, Baghdad pursued an anti-Western policy, which Moscow found congenial.

By the late 1960s, with the Baath party in power in Iraq, Soviet-Iraqi relations improved. Moscow looked favorably on the Baath's anti-Western and radical ori-entation, its determination to settle the Kurdish issue, its greater tolerance of local Communists, and its growing reliance on Soviet assistance and arms. Not only did Moscow's concern over its southern tier ease as a consequence of Iraq's nonalign-ment and the shah's decision in 1962 to bar U.S. military bases and missiles from Iranian territory, but its intrusive activities in the Gulf and Arabian Peninsula region were aided by changes in the strategic environment: the end of the British imperial presence in the Gulf; the creation of independent mini-states along the eastern littoral of the Arabian Peninsula, which fueled residual Iraqi-Iranian, Iraqi-Kuwait, and Iraqi-Saudi rivalry; and the growth of Soviet military capability.

Symptomatic of improving Soviet-Iraqi accord was the fifteen-year treaty of friendship and cooperation signed on April 9, 1972 (and subsequently renewed in 1987 for a five-year period, in keeping with the provisions contained in Article 12). The treaty helped convince Baghdad of Moscow's readiness to back the Baath's decision to settle its Kurdish problem, nationalize Western oil holdings, and oppose the threat from the shah of Iran. When the Kurds rejected the Baath's offer of limited autonomy in March 1974 and the civil war was gradually resumed, Moscow sided with Baghdad. The Soviet leadership's desertion of the Kurds and its support for the Baath further dissuaded the shah from interference.

Moscow's aim was to consolidate its ties with Iraq, but also to prevent an Iraqi-Iranian conflict that could have scuttled the Soviet-Iranian rapprochement. The effort succeeded well, and the Soviets used a limited display of military force (overt shipments of sophisticated weapons and occasional strafing runs by Soviet-piloted MiG-25s along the Iraqi-Iranian border) without alienating either party.

Soviet-Iraqi relations were adversely affected by the Iran-Iraq War. After fighting broke out in September 1980, Moscow's calls for a peaceful settlement went unheeded, and it saw again, as it had in Egypt in the 1970s, that in the Middle East, nothing fails like success. It had hoped to maintain its good standing with both sides, but, as with Khomeini's hostility in Iran, again it was frustrated, this time because of Saddam Hussein's conviction that Moscow preferred Iran to Iraq, his dissatisfaction with the level and reliability of Soviet arms deliveries, and his repression of local Communists and expulsion of Soviet diplomats on charges of spying. Although the Soviet Union was Iraq's principal arms supplier during the Iran-Iraq War from 1983 on, its diplomacy was not especially successful. In November 1984, it was unable to restrain Hussein from restoring the diplomatic relations with Washington that Iraq had broken off after the 1967 June War. Despite the Soviet sales (for hard currency) of advanced fighter aircraft, T-72 tanks, and air-to-surface missiles that upgraded Iraq's capacity for precision strikes against merchant ships and Iranian targets; despite the sympathetic Soviet commentaries on Iraq's desire for a just solution to the war; and despite the presence of thousands of Soviet technicians and military advisers, Moscow's relations with Iraq were not close. When the war ended in August 1988, both countries continued their intensive but businesslike relationship.

Since August 2, 1990, however, alignments in the Gulf region are once again in flux. On that date Iraq's invasion and occupation of Kuwait triggered a profound crisis in the Gulf and strained Moscow's ties to Baghdad. The Soviet government issued a statement declaring "that no contentious issues, no matter how complicated, justify the use of force. Such events totally contradict the interests of the Arab states, create new, additional obstacles to the settlement of conflicts in the Middle East and run counter to the positive tendencies of improvement in international life." The statement called for "the immediate and unconditional withdrawal of Iraqi troops from Kuwaiti territory. The sovereignty, national independence and territorial integrity of Kuwait must be fully restored and defended."

In this crisis, the first of the post–Cold War era, the Soviet Union found itself aligned with the United States and the overwhelming majority of the international community against Iraq, a key client of long standing. It voted for UN Security Council resolutions calling for withdrawal of Iraqi troops, the freeing of hostages, imposition of an economic and military embargo, and condemnation and invalidation of Iraq's annexation of Kuwait. On November 29, 1990, it joined with the United States in passing a revolution that sanctioned the use of "all necessary means to uphold and implement" all relevant resolutions to restore international peace and stability to the region. Though not an active participant, Moscow upheld President Bush's decision to lead the international coalition into war against Iraq on January 17, 1991, to liberate Kuwait. After five months of air attacks, it tried to broker a cease-fire to save Saddam Hussein from a ground assault, but Hussein would not agree to the coalition's insistence on compliance with all UN resolutions. The result was Iraq's total defeat on February 27, 1991.

The Soviet Union has championed Kuwait's independence ever since that tiny sheikdom established diplomatic ties with it in March 1963, after Iraqi President al-Karim Qasim was disposed and Moscow showed itself unwilling to support Iraq's territorial claims to the oil-rich 17,800-kilometer land area (slightly smaller than New Jersey) located at the head of the Persian Gulf. Kuwait was the first of the Arab sheikdoms of the Gulf to develop close ties with the USSR. Its motives were to signal the Saudis not to take Kuwait for granted, to buy some Soviet goodwill as a form of protection against Iran or a renewal of Iraqi pressure, and to put Washington on notice that the oil-rich Arabs might turn to Moscow for weapons if the United States did not force Israel to relinquish Arab land seized in the 1967 June War. During the Iran-Iraq War, Kuwait aligned itself with Iraq, a fellow Sunni Arab state, but also maneuvered skillfully to attract support from both the USSR and the United States. After being invaded by Iraq on August 2, 1990, Kuwait was liberated on February 27, 1991, by a U.S.-led international coalition whose actions were supported politically by the Soviet Union.

Gorbachev's inroads in the Gulf have been impressive. Oman and the United Arab Emirates (UAE) in the fall of 1985 and Qatar in 1988 joined Iraq and Kuwait as Arab Gulf countries having diplomatic ties with the USSR. In late September 1990, in recognition of Moscow's opposition to Iraq's seizure of Kuwait and its strong support in the UN Security Council for measures intended to compel an Iraqi withdrawal and safeguard Saudi security, Saudi Arabia reactivated diplomatic ties with the Soviet Union. These relations, which Saudi Arabia had permitted to lapse in 1983, marked Moscow's coming of age as a full-fledged diplomatic actor in the Gulf. Bahrain followed suit two weeks after the Saudis, giving Moscow formal ties to all the regional states.

Although it sided with the West over the Iraqi invasion of Kuwait, Russia, along with Turkey, would now like to see the punitive UN sanctions on Iraq lifted. The basic reason is economic: in order to repay its debt for Soviet weaponry to Moscow, Baghdad needs access to oil revenues. This desire puts Russia in conflict with the United States, which opposes anything that would strengthen Iraq as a regional actor. For the time being this has been a relatively low priority for Moscow; Iraq is unimportant to political developments within the CIS. If relations with the West continue to deteriorate, however, Russia might well feel that it has little to lose and much to gain by abandoning UN sanctions entirely.

On the other side of the Arabian Peninsula, the Soviet Union's inroads had taken hold much earlier. The Yemeni sector of the Arabian Peninsula, stretching in a northerly direction along the Red Sea and eastward along the Gulf of Aden, received attention second only to Iraq in Moscow's quest for footholds on the peninsula. Moscow's quest for a foothold in the region encouraged its opposition to British rule in the Aden-South Yemen region. For a short time after Yemen's accession to the union formed by Egypt and Syria in February 1958, Nasser was uneasy over the influx of Soviet technicians and advisers into Yemen, fearing that the country might come under Soviet domination and that Imam Ahmad might provoke a war with the British in Aden. A military coup in September 1962 and the proclamation of the Yemen Arab Republic (YAR) led Nasser to commit Egyptian forces in order to prop up the pro-Egyptian putschist Brigadier Abdullah al-Sallal, whose forces were no match for the Zaidi tribes supporting Imam al-Badr (who had succeeded to office on the death of his father a week before Sallal's coup). Thus began Nasser's Soviet-subsidized Vietnam: the 60,000 to 80,000 troops were Egyptian; the weapons and supplies were Soviet. Moscow funneled most of its aid through Cairo, avoiding direct involvement in the civil war that pitted the Egyptian-backed republicans and Shafeite tribes against the Saudi-backed royalists and long-dominant Zaidis.

In contrast to its behavior in Iraq, Moscow tried in Yemen to upset the status quo and exploit regional instability. Soviet objectives included deepening Nasser's dependence, with the hope of obtaining naval facilities that would replace the lost Soviet base in Albania, intensifying pressure on the British in Aden and on Saudi Arabia, and establishing close ties with a new progressive force and preventing its overthrow by reactionary, Western-supported forces. Without the Soviet wherewithal, Nasser could not have sustained his overseas adventure. Indeed, it is difficult to imagine that he would have gotten so enmeshed in the first instance but for Soviet assurances and encouragement. Certainly he would not have been able to sustain five years of demanding, inconclusive conflict.

Nasser's defeat in the June War forced him to withdraw and leave the field to the Saudis. Consequently, Soviet prospects in Yemen declined. At the same time, the British crown colony of Aden and the associated surrounding mini-protectorates were emerging to independence under the name of the South Arabian Federation. Instead of fostering the nationalist coalition of the pro-Egyptian Front for the Liberation of Occupied Southern Yemen (FLOSY), the British shortsightedly allowed power to gravitate toward the National Liberation Front (NLF), an umbrella organization for a motley mixture of Marxist-Leninists and Maoists, out of hostility toward Nasser after their humiliation in 1956. When the British left in November 1967, the NLF seized power in Aden and soon extended its control over the entire country, whose population is about one third that of the neighboring YAR. In June 1969, the more radical faction of the NLF gained control; it changed the country's name in November 1970 to the People's Democratic Republic of Yemen (PDRY).

From the start, the PDRY cultivated close relations with the Soviet Union. Military assistance, economic aid, and Soviet, Cuban, and East German advisers and technicians poured in, the first shipment of Soviet arms arriving in August 1968. Moscow's assistance was essential not only for the internal retention of power, but also for waging an ongoing fight with the YAR and sustaining the Dhofari rebellion that started in western Oman in 1965 (the Dhofaris used PDRY territory as training and staging areas and sought with PDRY assistance to overthrow the pro-Western regime in Oman). By the mid-1970s, the Dhofaris were defeated militarily by a combination of Iranian troops and British advisers, and they were stripped politically of leverage when the financially sorely pressed PDRY leadership decided to accept Saudi financial assistance in return for normalization of relations in March 1976. This meant an end to support for the Dhofari insurgency.

With the signing of a friendship treaty in October 1979, Moscow consolidated its presence in the PDRY. Throughout a series of struggles between rival party and tribal factions of the ruling Marxist and pro-Soviet Yemeni Socialist Party (YSP) during 1978–1986, it managed to keep on good terms with the winning coalition. Gorbachev poured generous amounts of economic and military assistance into the country, and the USSR has been able to retain its military presence, flying intelligence missions from PDRY airfields, using Aden and the island of Socotra for its naval ships, and helping to train assorted anti-Western radical groups.

Two developments that occurred in 1990 changed Soviet policy: the unification, on May 22, of the two Yemens, and the resumption of Saudi relations with the Soviet Union in late September.

Moscow has long courted both Yemens (in addition to the 1979 friendship treaty with the PDRY, it signed one with the YAR on October 9, 1984). But unification signaled the beginning of closer ties to the West, greater attention to economic development and modernization, and, quite possibly, a lessened reliance on the Soviet Union. Moscow was no longer willing to subsidize anti-Saudi forces or policies, lest these jeopardize its diplomatic breakthrough with Riyadh.

A few generalizations about Moscow's policy toward the labile politics of the Arabian Peninsula are in order. The Soviet approach has been pragmatic and low-key. Moscow adapted to regional upheavals with flexibility and shrewdness, in the main tempering its activism to political circumstances. Opportunism impelled its policy. Quick to establish diplomatic ties and a presence, it assisted prospective client states and proved its reliability as a provider and protector. The inhibitions on greater activism came primarily from the preferences and domestic pressure of the clients themselves and not from considerations of its prospects for a Soviet-U.S. relationship or the power of the United States, whose capacity for affecting developments was limited.

The level and character of Soviet involvement was determined (except in Afghanistan) by each regional client. Although reluctant to accede to all requests for arms, Moscow nonetheless gave what support was necessary to ensure a client's security, without (it must be noted) always being able to obtain comparably significant returns—witness the limited nature of Soviet naval privileges in Umm Qasr in the 1970s, a period of excellent relations with Iraq. In rendering military assistance, the USSR tried to keep the regional balance of power in mind and to avoid encouraging recourse to war by its clients. Thus, initially it benefited from the feuds between Iraq and Iran, Iraq and Kuwait, the Yemen Arab Republic and the People's Democratic Republic of Yemen, the PDRY and Oman, and Iraq and Saudi Arabia by developing a close working relationship with one party to the dispute; but having once forged a connection, it preferred to dampen regional conflicts and, as in the Iraqi-Iranian and Iraqi-Kuwaiti cases, to try to mediate the disputes and improve its relations with both parties.

Moscow accepted the dilemmas that result from courting opposing sides in regional disputes and the periodic frustration with unmanageable clients as the lot of a superpower pursuing a multiplicity of goals in an age of complexity and change. Moscow was fully aware that its 1972 treaty with Iraq aroused suspicions among Arabs of the lower Gulf and adversely affected its efforts to normalize diplomatic relations, and that its lavish supply of arms to the bitterly antagonistic Syrian and Iraqi regimes would strain its relations with each of them. In case after case, Moscow's efforts to exercise influence aroused nationalist resentment and resistance, and to the extent that it tried to mediate local disputes, divergent tugs set limits to the influence it could wield over either party.

Only in the PDRY did Moscow reap tangible benefits on the Arabian Peninsula. There its position provided privileged access to Aden, the best port in that part of the world. Aden has ample supplies of fresh water, more important than fuel oil, and excellent docking, storage, and repair facilities. Even more valuable to the Soviet military were the air privileges accorded it.

Moscow's interest in the Arabian Peninsula was never a military one. Basically, Moscow seeks influence, not instability, and it is no longer willing to invest the resources needed to exploit and aggravate the latter in its quest for the former. Its policy is essentially one of supporting the status quo, while seeking to enhance its position as an attractive and necessary partner in regional affairs.

OBSERVATIONS

Due to its strategic importance and proximity to Russia, the Middle East is likely to remain a priority for Russian foreign policy. The end of ideological confrontation opens up new possibilities for cooperation in the region, particularly with Israel, though it will do little to ease emerging geopolitical tensions, as the current protracted negotiations over Caspian oil resources illustrate.

The Gulf War effort proved to be a crucial turning point because it illustrated Moscow's willingness to follow the United States' lead in the region. Despite concurring with overall American objectives, Gorbachev still saw the Soviet Union as playing a key role in promoting regional peace and stability. A number of times Gorbachev suggested that military operations in the region might have exceeded the UN mandate, and in the weeks before the commencement of hostilities he sent his advisor Yevgeni Primakov on a separate Soviet peace initiative. Russian Foreign Minister Andrei Kozyrev's statement in January 1991 that the Soviet Union bore a good part of the blame for Saddam Hussein's being in power—"In essence [Hussein] is a child of our totalitarianism who was nurtured under the care of our ideology and with the help of huge arms shipments."[16]—therefore marks a significant departure.

Since the fall of the communist regime, Russian policy in the Middle East has become linked to the broader domestic debate over Russian foreign policy concessions to the West. To critics, the Middle East is a good example of where Russia has sacrificed its own interests in order to cozy up to the West. Despite polls showing that only 5% of the populace feels that the Middle East should be a major area of concern for Russian foreign policy, many observers argue that for strategic as well as economic reasons, the Middle East should have a priority similar to Europe. What makes the Middle East different, they say, is its geographical proximity to Russia, the ties of Russian citizens of Islamic faith to the Arab world, and, most importantly, the fact that unlike other LDCs the Arab states are willing to pay cash for technology.

The resurgence of Islam in post-Soviet Central Asia is of particular concern. To be sure, Islam is not unknown to Moscow. There have been centuries of interaction—first, across porous borderlands, then, through imperial expansion, conflict, and diverse attempts at absorption and coexistence, and finally, the emergence in the late Soviet period of an Islamic renaissance "connected with the growth of nationalism and a slowly growing awareness among the intelligentsia that was reflected in the rebirth of Islamic traditions."[17] What form Islam takes in the republics of the former Soviet Union will depend primarily on internal developments there that are largely beyond Russia's control. These, in turn, will be affected by the way Islam's multidimensionality coheres in different republics. Islam is at one and the same time a religious faith, a political identity, a code of ethics, and a cultural system, but this multidimensionality is rife with fault lines that produce quite different kinds of political systems and foreign policies. The challenge for Russian policymakers will be to deal with the Islamic nations and movements in their vicinity in ways that foster Russia's national interests.

The domestic political infighting between the Ministry of Foreign Economic Relations (MFER) and Ministry of Defense on the one side, and the Ministry of Foreign Affairs on the other over Russian participation in the embargoes against Iraq and Libya has been fierce. During parliamentary hearings on foreign policy in December 1992, the MFER argued that as a result of joining sanctions against Iraq, Libya, and Yugoslavia, Russian had lost nearly $16 billion.[18] When the U.S. Senate threatened to make a $500 million credit contingent on stopping an arms delivery to Iran, an MFER official commented publicly that revenue from the sale would be three to four time as large as the credit blocked.[19]

From the perspective of Russian domestic politics, the issue is not so much improving relations with the Arab world as it is not being seen as constantly bowing to American whims. Under pressure from his domestic critics, Foreign Minister Kozyrev has frequently pointed to what he calls America's "double standard" on arms exports: while calling for unilateral Russian reductions in arms sales, the United States remains by far the largest arms exporter to the region. The debate over the sale of low-grade nuclear reactor technology to Iran in 1995 is but the latest manifestation of this debate.

As Russia abandons its initial infatuation with the West, however, it is also increasingly willing to stake out distinctive policies in the Middle East. The new Russian policy is aimed at trying to steer a path between two competing priorities: first, commercial interest in arms exports; second, arms control and the enhancement of regional stability. Russia hopes to harmonize these two objectives by encouraging military and technological cooperation with moderate Arab regimes in the region, specifically with the monarchies of the Persian Gulf who are committed to enhancing regional stability and have pledged to use their weapons for defensive purposes only. To this end, official Russian delegations to the monarchies of the Gulf have formed half of all official Middle Eastern visits between 1992 and April 1994.[20]

Despite the loss of its superpower status, Russian diplomacy has gained freedom to maneuver in the region since it has abandoned its ideologically driven foreign policy. No longer bound to support the most radical Arab regimes because they were "the enemy of my enemy," Russia is now free to pursue more advantageous economic ties with the moderate states and, at the same time, enhance its security and influence in the region. No longer bound to oppose Israel, Russia has been able to reestablish diplomatic relations and remove a major source of domes-

tic and international tension over Jewish emigration. The Middle East will continue to be an issue of contention, but more as a metaphor in the domestic debate
over priorities, than because of any serious international conflict.

SELECTED BIBLIOGRAPHY

Altstadt, Audrey L. *The Azerbaijani Turks: Power and Identity under Russian Rule.* Stanford, CA: Hoover Institution Press, 1992.

Arnold, Anthony. *The Fateful Pebble: Afghanistan's Role in the Fall of the Soviet Empire.*
Novato, CA: Presidio, 1993.

Behbehani, Hashim S.H. *The Soviet Union and Arab Nationalism, 1917–1966.* New York:
KPI, 1986. (Distributed by Methuen, New York.)

Borovik, Artem. *The Hidden War: a Russian Journalist's Account of the Soviet War in
Afghanistan.* New York: Atlantic Monthly Press, 1990.

Cordovez, Diego. *Out of Afghanistan: The Inside Story of the Soviet Withdrawal.* New
York: Oxford University Press, 1995.

Eickelman, Dale F. (ed.). *Russia's Muslim Frontiers.* Bloomington: Indiana University
Press, 1993.

El Hussini, Mohrez Mahmoud. *Soviet-Egyptian Relations, 1945–85.* New York: St. Martin's
Press, 1987.

Freedman, Robert O. *Moscow and the Middle East: Soviet Policy Since the Invasion of
Afghanistan.* New York: Cambridge University Press, 1991.

Freedman, Robert Owen. *Soviet policy toward Israel under Gorbachev.* New York:
Praeger, 1991.

Golan, Galia. *The Soviet Union and the Middle East.* New York: Cambridge University
Press, 1990.

Hammond, Thomas T. *Red Flag over Afghanistan: The Communist Coup, the Soviet Invasion, and the Consequences.* Boulder, CO: Westview Press, 1984.

Kakar, M. Hasan. *Afghanistan: The Soviet Invasion and the Afghan Response, 1979–1982.*
Berkeley: University of California Press, 1995.

Karsh, Efraim. *Soviet Policy towards Syria since 1970.* New York: St. Martin's Press, 1991.

Katz, Mark N. *Russia & Arabia : Soviet Foreign Policy Toward the Arabian Peninsula.* Baltimore: Johns Hopkins University Press, 1986.

Keddie, Nikki R., and Gasiorowski, Mark J. (eds.). *Neither East nor West: Iran, the Soviet
Union, and the United States.* New Haven, CT: Yale University Press, 1990.

Nissman, David B. *The Soviet Union and Iranian Azerbaijan: The Use of Nationalism for
Political Penetration.* Boulder, CO: Westview Press, 1987.

Page, Stephen. *The Soviet Union and the Yemens: Influence on Asymmetrical Relationships.*
New York: Praeger, 1985.

Ramet, Sabrina P. *The Soviet-Syrian Relationship since 1955: A Troubled Alliance.* Boulder,
CO: Westview Press, 1990.

Rezun, Miron. *The Soviet Union and Iran: Soviet Policy in Iran from the Beginnings of the
Pahlavi Dynasty until the Soviet Invasion in 1941.* Boulder, CO: Westview Press, 1988.

Rubinstein, Alvin Z. *Red Star on the Nile: The Soviet-Egyptian Influence Relationship since the June War.* Princeton, NJ: Princeton University, 1977.

Shemesh, Haim. *Soviet-Iraqi relations, 1968–1988: In the Shadow of the Iraq-Iran Conflict.* Boulder, CO: Lynne Rienner Publishers, 1992.

Shemesh, Haim. *Soviet-Iraqi relations, 1968–1988: In the Shadow of the Iraq-Iran Conflict.* Boulder, CO: Lynne Rienner Publishers, 1992.

Sicker, Martin. *The Bear and the Lion: Soviet Imperialism and Iran.* New York: Praeger, 1988.

Smolansky, Oles M., and Bettie M. *The USSR and Iraq: the Soviet Quest for Influence.* Durham, NC: Duke University Press, 1991.

NOTES

1. Vladimir Socor, "Turkey Asserts Role in Ex-Soviet Orbit," *Prism,* part 2, August 4, 1995.
2. Lowell Bezanis, "Third Turkic Summit," *OMRI Daily Digest,* August 29, 1995.
3. *Izvestiya,* May 23, 1992, in *FBIS/SOV/92-103,* May 28, 1992, p. 5.
4. Lowell Bezanis, "Ciller in Baku," *OMRI Daily Digest I,* April 13, 1995.
5. Ernest Andrews "FSB Tries to Link Turkey to Chechnya Problem" *Prism,* Part 2, September 22, 1995.
6. *Turkish Daily News* (May 25, 1993), p. 11; Doug Clarke, "Iran-Russia's Largest Arms Customer," *RFE/RL Daily Report,* October 17, 1994.
7. Lowell Bezanis, "Russian-Turkish Trade," *OMRI Daily Digest,* August 31, 1995.
8. Lee Suck-Ho, "Evolution and Prospects of Soviet-North Korean Relations in the 1980s," *Journal of Northeast Asian Affairs,* vol. 5, no. 3 (Fall 1986), pp. 23–27.
9. Robert D. Hormats, "Making Regionalism Safe," *Foreign Affairs,* vol. 73, no. 2 (March–April 1994), p. 102.
10. *FBIS/SOV/RUSSIA,* March 31, 1992, p. 14.
11. For example, *Sovetskaya Rossiya,* March 14, 1989; and the symposium with contributions by leading analysts such as Vladimir Lukin, Viktor Kremenyuk, and Aleksandr Bovin, in *S. Sh. A.,* no. 7 (July 1989); and *Krasnaya Zvezda,* November 18, 1989.
12. Richard Sakwa, *Russian Politics and Society* (New York: Routledge, 1993), p. 376
13. Oles Smolansky, *The Soviet Union and the Arab East Under Khrushchev* (Lewisburg, PA: Bucknell University Press, 1974), p. 80.
14. George S. Dragnich, "The Soviet Union's Quest for Access to Naval Facilities in Egypt Prior to the June War of 1967," in Michael MccGwire, Ken Booth, and John McDonnel (eds.). *Soviet Naval Policy: Objectives and Constraints* (New York: Praeger, 1975), pp. 252–269.
15. "Russia Branching into the World," *Monitor: A Daily Chronicle of the Post-Soviet States,* vol. 1, no. 74 (August 15, 1995).
16. Cited in Fred Wehling, "Three Scenarios for Russia's Middle East Policy," *Communist and Post-Communist Studies,* vol. 26, no. 2 (June 1993), p. 186.
17. Alexei V. Malashenko, "Islam Versus Communism: The Experience of Coexistence," in Dale F. Eickelman (ed.). *Russia's Muslim Frontiers* (Bloomington: Indiana University Press, 1993), p. 67.
18. Cited in Andrei Kasatkin, "Will the Middle East Become a Russian Priority?" *International Affairs,* no. 7 (July 1993), p. 61.
19. Fred Wehling, "Three Scenarios," p. 191.
20. Kasatkin, "Will the Middle East Become a Russian Priority?" p. 60.

Chapter
12

Russia and International Organizations

*T*he antecedents of the Soviet attitude toward the United Nations are to be found in the Kremlin's ideological perceptions and diplomatic experience with the League of Nations. The League was created after World War I to preserve an international system based on capitalism and colonialism, and epitomized the antithesis of the world revolution and anticolonialism propagated by Soviet and Comintern leaders. Dominated by Britain and France and their visceral fear of communism, it barred the USSR from membership. During 1920–1934, therefore, Moscow saw it as an instrument of "imperialism" designed to promote the encirclement and eventual destruction of the Soviet state. Lenin called it "a League of bandits." Maxim Litvinov, then deputy foreign minister, termed it "a masked league" engaged in anti-Soviet intrigues. He said the Soviet Union had no desire to be a member, knowing that

> it would then be confronted, in the form of partners, or even judges, with states, many
> of which have not even recognized it, and [which] consequently do not conceal their
> enmity toward it, and with others, even among those which have recognized it, which
> even now behaved toward it with ill-concealed hostility."[1]

Expediency, however, dictated accommodation. Global realignments of power prompted the Soviet Union and the Western powers to draw closer together in the face of the common threat from Hitler. When Hitler discarded Rapallo, Stalin could no longer rely on the special relationship with Germany. He turned to France, which was interested in reviving a variation of the pre-1914 Franco-Russian alliance against the threat of a strong and expansionist Germany. To ease the way for the Franco-Soviet rapprochement, which the French believed would be facilitated by Soviet membership, Stalin—who was increasingly concerned also over Japan's military threat in Manchuria—joined the League of Nations.

For the next few years, Moscow championed the concept of collective security and tried to fashion an effective security arrangement with Britain and France.

However, the Western sellout at Munich and Hitler's subsequent readiness (in contrast to Britain and France) to meet Stalin's stiff terms for friendship set in motion the chain of events that resulted in the Nazi-Soviet pact and the outbreak of World War II. The denouement of the Soviet Union's experience in the League came after its invasion of Finland; the League, already an anachronism in a dying era, denounced the USSR's aggression and expelled it from the organization on December 14, 1939.

As World War II drew to a close, the enthusiasm of the Western powers for a new international organization was not shared in Moscow, but Stalin obliged Roosevelt and Churchill once he had secure guarantees for safeguarding Soviet interests. The Soviet Union joined the United Nations as an act of accommodation, not out of conviction. Its aim was to ensure that the League's successor would not become an anti-Soviet alliance; and its participation was predicated on the assumption that the United Nations would function primarily to handle political and security problems, and that the ultimate responsibility for the maintenance of international peace and security would devolve on the permanent members of the Security Council, the five great powers: the USSR, the United States, Britain, France, and China. In essence, Stalin envisaged an extension in peacetime of the wartime condominium of the United States, Britain, and the Soviet Union, which would preserve the peace, determine and respect spheres of influence, and settle disputes among themselves at clubby summit meetings. The USSR approved the UN Charter, but only after the inclusion of the veto power in the Security Council and the provision that amendments to the charter would be subject to the approval of the five permanent members.

By contrast with influential private circles in the United States, Soviet leaders never had any illusions about what the UN was and what it was not. They considered the UN "an inter-state organization, an organization of sovereign independent states":

> As an inter-state organization, the United Nations does not, and cannot, stand above states: it is not and cannot be a self-sufficient body, independent of states. . . . It is for this reason that no United Nations body, except the Security Council, can take any decisions, binding on all member states of the Organization, on any question except administrative matters and procedural questions.[2]

There was no visionary interest in integration or supranational institutions. Soviet writers denounced all proposals to transform the United Nations into a world parliament, emphasizing that this would undermine national sovereignty.

Postcommunist Russia actively sought the USSR's seat on the Security Council, and continues to see the United Nations as an important forum for achieving its goals. It has used this forum to try to speed up Russia's acceptance into important international financial institutions like the International Monetary Fund (IMF) and the GATT. Through the United Nations it seeks to play a role in defining the scope of peacekeeping efforts, an issue of particular concern in Bosnia and Tajikistan. Finally, it hopes to establish a permanent presence for the CIS at the United Nations, thus validating the commonwealth as a fullfledged international actor. Although the Soviet Union then and Russia now share a similarity in their eagerness to advance the national interest through international forums, since the fall of communism Russia has sided with the West in a number of areas in which it previously sided with the lesser-developed countries.

THE EARLY YEARS AT THE LEAGUE AND THE UNITED NATIONS

The Cold War and the polarization of political alignments dominated the period from 1945 to 1953. From the very first session of the Security Council in January 1946, when the USSR was severely criticized for its failure to withdraw Soviet troops from Iran in accordance with the 1942 treaty among Iran, Britain, and the USSR, Moscow felt its isolated minority position in the UN. Its attention was riveted on issues directly affecting Soviet interests. To offset Western "mechanistic voting" majorities, the Soviet government used the veto, which Molotov strongly justified in a speech at the United Nations on September 14, 1946. He noted that the veto prevents one group of powers from organizing themselves to act against one or another of the five permanent members and that its very existence encourages frank discussions on disputed issues and provides an incentive for concessions and eventual agreement; and he pointed out that unlike the League, which in theory was built on the principle of equality of large and small states, the United Nations institutionalizes a process of ensuring that the interests of the great powers in matters of international peace and security are not ignored.

During the first postwar decade, the USSR exercised the veto eighty times, usually to keep out new members pending a deal with the United States on quid pro quos. It also used the veto to prevent attempts to interfere in any way with its hegemonic position in Eastern Europe and to assist client states. For example, in December 1971, during the Indo-Pakistani war, the USSR vetoed a resolution calling for a cease-fire and troop withdrawals, because the Indian government, which was favored by Moscow, was not yet interested in halting military operations; and in July 1979, the mere threat of a veto was sufficient to terminate the UNEF operation in Sinai, a move favored by the anti-Sadat Arab states that Moscow was courting. In 1960 Khrushchev himself warned the General Assembly (which at the time was discussing possible revisions of the charter) that "if there is no veto, there will be no international organization; it will fall to pieces."

Stalin's only interest in the United Nations was to ensure that it would not serve an anti-Soviet function or interfere with the realization of Soviet objectives in Eastern Europe. Moscow thwarted all UN efforts to function in that region; it denounced UN reports implicating the communist governments of Albania, Bulgaria, and Yugoslavia for their role in fueling the Greek civil war, and it refused entry to economic survey missions and investigators of human rights violations. The USSR also tried to keep the UN's authority as circumscribed as possible. It interpreted the concept of national sovereignty to mean the exclusion of any out-side interference in the domestic affairs of Soviet-bloc countries.

But consistency is not a strong card in the ongoing international game of weakening the enemy. When the target of interference was noncommunist countries, especially Western-dominated colonial areas, adherence to a narrow interpretation of the charter's provisions on sovereignty and nonintervention in the domestic affairs of member states was supplanted by espousal of the principles of national self-determination and the need to act against "threats to international peace." The principles were given a very broad interpretation by Soviet officials, who wished to align themselves with Third World countries and undermine the overseas empires of the Western powers.

During the Stalin period, the USSR was slow to perceive the advantages of active participation in the United Nations. Wedded to the two-camp conception of international alignments, Moscow made tactical errors on colonial questions, alienating Indonesia, India, and the Philippines, among others; and its support for the creation of Israel in 1948 alienated the Arabs. A miscalculation with far-reaching consequences occurred in January 1950 when the USSR abruptly walked out of the Security Council, the General Assembly, and the other UN bodies over the question of Chinese representation; Moscow argued that the People's Republic of China (PRC), proclaimed on October 1, 1949, and not the Kuomintang regime of Chiang Kai-shek, was the legitimate government of China and should be seated in the Security Council. The USSR announced a boycott of all UN organizations and activities until the PRC's admission was procured. The resultant absence of the Soviet Union at the time of the North Korean aggression on June 25, 1950, enabled the Security Council to pass resolutions calling for the cessation of hostilities, the withdrawal of North Korean forces from South Korea, and the rendering of all possible assistance to South Korea by UN members. No doubt Moscow assumed that the United Nations, like the League, would take no effective action to repel the aggression; hence its absence from the council. It returned on August 1, 1950, but too late to block the UN's authorization of a police action to "restore international security in the area."

It was during the Korean War that the Soviet leadership came to the realization that participation in the United Nations was important, not just to prevent the United Nations being used by the United States as an anti-Soviet instrument, but to establish closer relations with the emerging Afro-Asian group of nonaligned countries, which were neither Western puppets nor necessarily opposed to policies advantageous to Moscow. Moscow perceived that it could actively exploit, not merely thwart, the United Nations to keep the West on the defensive and strengthen the international position of the Soviet Union. Stalin's death brought a new flexibility and activism to Soviet policy in the United Nations.

Soviet interest in the United Nations is an outgrowth of the changed environment within the United Nations in the 1960s, when the membership more than doubled, America's reliable voting majority came to an end, the LDCs developed a heightened radicalism and anti-Western attitudes on a growing number of political and economic issues, and the Soviet bloc's isolation within the organization drew to a close.

THE COMINTERN: MOSCOW'S INTERNATIONAL COMMUNIST INSTRUMENT

As Moscow saw it, the country's security and strategic objectives could be pursued simultaneously both through the League of Nations (in the 1930s) and the United Nations, after 1945, on the one hand, and through a distinct, Moscow-dominated system of "socialist" (that is, communist) states, on the other. Moscow never trusted the former, and it felt comfortable with the latter only as long as it could manipulate foreign communist parties.

The world communist movement was an important instrument of Soviet diplomacy during Moscow's period of greatest military weakness, vulnerability, and relative international isolation. This period extended from 1919 until the late 1950s—at which time its own strength, global foreign policy interests, and confidence drew it to increasingly active engagement in the United Nations.

Paradoxically, Moscow's manipulation of foreign communist parties to defend Soviet state interests was never managed with more telling effect than in the period of the USSR's maximum weakness. At the time of Soviet diplomatic isolation and military vulnerability in the 1920s and 1930s, the foreign parties were truly the handmaiden of Soviet policy. There was no questioning of Stalin's injunction that internationalism required proletarians of all countries to support the Soviet Union, since an internationalist is one who "unhesitatingly, unconditionally, without vacillation is ready to defend the USSR because the USSR is the basis of the world revolutionary movement, and it is impossible to defend and to advance [this movement] unless the USSR is defended."[3]

From 1919 to 1945, the world communist movement was characterized by two fundamental considerations: the existence of the Soviet Union as the only communist state, and the complete subservience, especially under Stalin, of foreign communist parties to the will of Moscow. Those who disagreed either quit or were expelled from the movement. During this period, authority devolved on Moscow because of the esteem in which it was held by the membership despite periodic disagreements, and not because Moscow was in a position physically to compel obedience. The early adherents to Soviet authority willingly followed Lenin, who uniquely combined "the individual prestige of a charismatic personality with the authority of the idea of world revolution."[4] Stalin's authority came from manipulation of symbols, personalities, and bureaucracy and the use of force.

Foreign communists accepted Moscow's policies, often at the sacrifice of their own interests and prospects for power. They did so because the Soviet Union, as the only communist state, embodied the ideal of world revolution; because the realization of world revolution was feasible only as long as the Soviet state survived and thrived; because of the exalted feeling that comes from membership in a universalistic movement; because Moscow's approbation meant that an otherwise political nonentity would be "taken seriously not merely by his party but also by his fellow countrymen, for whom he personifies Moscow's power locally"[5]; and because of the power over an organization, however small, that flowed to a leadership willing to do Moscow's bidding. Their blind obedience brought disaster to many parties in the 1920s and 1930s, including the German, Chinese (before Mao), Indonesian, and Spanish. During the honeymoon period of the Nazi-Soviet pact, West European Communists did nothing to help their countries resist German aggression; not until Hitler's attack on the Soviet Union in June 1941 did they take up arms against nazism. In all of this, Soviet state interests transcended those of world revolution, though Moscow rationalized the former in terms of the latter, and the party faithful voluntarily did as Moscow asked.

The big change came in 1945, when the Soviet Union extended its authority over Eastern Europe through the Red Army. With this coercive instrument, it created new communist states, although at the time they were merely compliant, exploited Soviet imperial possessions. Intent on subordinating Yugoslavia to Soviet wishes, Stalin tested his authority, trying by dint of his prestige to have Tito removed, but he failed and, unwilling to use the Red Army to compel obedience, resorted to excommunication. But the heretic survived and in the process retained his credentials as a communist and a revolutionary.

However, Tito's rejection of Soviet authority was a minor matter compared with the situation that was inherent in Mao's conquest of mainland China. At first Mao acknowledged Moscow's ideological preeminence and leadership in foreign affairs. The charisma of Stalin and the convergence of national interests ensured unity, and the nature of Soviet authority did not become an issue as long as Stalin lived. Stalin died in 1953, and the turning point in the relationship of authority between Moscow and Beijing came in February 1956. Khrushchev's denunciation of Stalin at the CPSU's twentieth congress compromised his own standing in Beijing and led Mao to stake his claim to leadership of the world communist movement. The November 1957 attempt to paper over the policy differences between Moscow and Beijing failed, and the rift widened. It became public knowledge after 1960, and forced foreign communist parties to take sides. The quarrel ended Moscow's pretension to speak for all parties on matters of doctrine and policy. Its authority was being challenged by a major center of power fully qualified to carry on the mission of the proletariat to bring about world revolution and communism.

By Khrushchev's time the rival claimants of authority in Beijing and Belgrade were forcing Moscow to confront the challenge of reconciling unity with diversity. But Moscow lacked the instruments necessary for restoring bloc unity: It had neither the charismatic leader nor the monopoly of force. A series of irreversible developments inevitably weakened Soviet authority in the Socialist camp and in the world communist movement: the USSR's de-Stalinization that spread to Eastern Europe and nurtured nationalistic demands for greater independence; the Sino-Soviet dispute that enabled the mice in the socialist camp to play, while the two cats fought; the Soviet leadership's surrender, implicit in its acceptance of the notion of "many roads to socialism," of the prerogative of proclaiming the universality of the Soviet model, in return for support of the Soviet position in the dispute with China and on major foreign-policy issues; Moscow's readiness to discard the former exploitative economic relationship with Eastern Europe and seek bloc cooperation; and its realization that greater independence from the center was essential to preserve the communist character of the countries in Eastern Europe.

After the monolithism that existed until the end of 1948, the Kremlin had to cope with three different types of communist parties in order to exercise what little remained of its once preeminent authority. The first type was the ruling communist parties that were part of the Soviet bloc (that is, the Warsaw Pact and Comecon) and could be forced into line by the Red Army. In 1989–1990 Gorbachev rejected this course and accepted the fall from power of pro-Muscovite communist oligarchs. Second, there were the ruling parties lying outside of Moscow's ability to impose its authority forcibly. These were China, Albania, North Korea, Vietnam, Cambodia, and Laos. The third type were the nonruling communist parties, which may for convenience be subdivided into two groups: those that are permitted to operate openly and have some electoral support (ranging from minimal in the United States and much of Latin America to substantial in Italy), or that attained parliamentary status (as in Western Europe, India, and Japan); and those proscribed parties whose political possibilities, at least through legitimate channels, were severely curtailed.

In its efforts to reimpose a measure of authority, Moscow used two types of forums: (1) the worldwide meeting, epitomized by the conferences of world communist and workers' parties held in Moscow in 1957, 1960, and 1969 (and supplemented by frequent annual gatherings of the dozen or so leading communist-front organizations in the fields of labor, education, science, and culture); and (2) the regional forum, intended primarily for European communist parties, exemplified by the meetings in 1967 in Karlovy Vary, Czechoslovakia, in 1976 in East Berlin, and in 1980 in Paris. Even more important were bilateral meetings between the CPSU and one other communist party.

An indication of how far the Soviet Union's authority had slipped can be seen in the difficulty Moscow experienced in trying to convene an international communist conference to condemn or excommunicate Beijing. Khrushchev determined in late 1963 to hold such an ecumenical kangaroo court but encountered stiff opposition from the Yugoslav, Romanian, Polish, and the Italian party leaders. The Italian Communist Party's (PCI's) secretary-general, Palmiro Togliatti, told his Central Committee in April 1964: "When talk arose of a new international meeting of all communist parties to examine and assess the attitude of the Chinese comrades this was likely to end in another excommunication; and it appeared to us unnecessary and dangerous." Togliatti, a highly respected veteran communist—a survivor of the Stalin period—carried his criticism of Khrushchev's course and his insistence on the independence and equality of all parties to the Kremlin itself and to the movement as a whole.

By the time of Krushchev's deposal in October 1964, Moscow could count on attendance by only some forty-six parties, not the seventy Khrushchev had originally claimed. Brezhnev postponed the December conference, convening instead a "preparatory meeting" in Moscow in March 1965, which was attended by only eighteen of the twenty-six parties invited. Faced with widespread resistance to the excommunication of the Chinese and to any return to the monolithism of the Stalinist period, Soviet leaders groped through subsequent meetings in 1967 and 1968 for a way to accommodate both the diversity demanded by foreign parties and the minimal unity the Kremlin could accept and still retain the authority necessary for promotion of foreign policy priorities.

Far from forging the movement's unity, the world conference finally held in Moscow from June 5 to 17, 1969, demonstrated conclusively that the Balkanization of world communism had taken place. The very holding of the conference was a minor feat of sorts for Moscow. Seventy-five parties attended (five did not sign the final document)—the remaining twenty-five followed China and stayed away (absentees who had been present in 1960 included the communist parties of Vietnam, North Korea, Japan, Burma, and Indonesia). The final document, which did not mention China or the Soviet invasion of Czechoslovakia, was a bland mélange of generalities.

In the years after the 1969 international conference, Moscow made no headway in regaining any of its former authority. Indeed, the statements of individual leaders became even more forceful in the assertion of their independence.

By the time of the pan-European communist Conference on Peace and Disarmament convened in Paris at the end of April 1980, the Eurocommunist swell had crested. The conference attracted twenty-two delegations, but was boycotted by the Italian, Spanish, British, Swedish, Yugoslav, and Romanian parties, whose reasons varied from their opposition to the USSR's invasion of Afghanistan to dissatisfaction with the lack of preconference consultations to interest in exploring closer cooperation with the noncommunist socialist Left.

Frustrated with the fragmentation and unruliness of the world communist movement that it had established—a movement comprised of literally hundreds of communist and workers parties, international and national institutions, and front organizations—after 1960 Moscow turned increasingly toward the UN General Assembly for international support.

DECOLONIZATION

Moscow's claim to being a noncolonial power, and the legacy of Western antagonism made it seem like a natural ally for many newly decolonized nations. From the beginning Moscow staked out a position in the UN debates that placed it in the vanguard of anticolonialism. The USSR did not face any agonizing dilemmas; its imperial system did not include Asian or African territories agitating for independence. Moscow generally applauded the mushrooming national liberation movements, including peoples' wars waged against colonial regimes. But though aware that such struggles weakened its Western rivals, Moscow could offer only moral support and rhetorical encouragement during the first postwar decade. Such ambitions as the USSR had in 1945 to become the administering authority for one of the trusteeships that were to be established for former Italian colonies—that is, Libya and Somalia—were blocked by the United States. But the Soviet Union did join the call in the United Nations for the dismantling of the British, French, Dutch, and Portuguese overseas empires.

After the early 1960s, however, Moscow could increasingly rely on large voting majorities in the General Assembly, thanks to the good will garnered when Soviet Premier Nikita Khrushchev introduced a draft Declaration on the Granting of Independence to Colonial Countries and Peoples at the fifteenth session of the UN General Assembly. Khrushchev shrewdly seized the moment to propose a declaration, subsequently adopted in modified form as General Assembly Resolution 1514 (XV), embodying the most radical denunciation of colonialism in all of its aspects and calling for the independence of all colonial countries and peoples. This resolution advanced the notion that all forms of struggle, including armed struggle, were legitimate to achieve this goal. The abstention by the Western powers enhanced the political impact of the Soviet proposal among the African and Asian leaders.

The following year the Soviet Union again laid claim to a bold initiative, proposing the establishment of the Special Committee on the Situation with Regard to the Implementation of the Declaration on the Granting of Independence to Colonial Countries and Peoples (known informally as the Special Committee of Twenty-four) to ensure that Resolution 1514 (XV) was implemented and decolonization brought to a successful completion. Under the weight of its African membership, the committee militantly pressed for independence of the Portuguese colonies (Angola, Mozambique, and Guinea-Bissau) and of Zimbabwe (Rhodesia), and starting in the late 1950s, it zeroed in on South Africa and urged independence for Namibia, the former German colony of Southwest Africa that was taken over by South Africa after World War I and administered as a possession until December 1988, when Pretoria agreed to Namibia's independence as part of an overall settlement that led to the withdrawal of Cuban and Soviet troops from Angola.

For Moscow, the colonial issue went a long way politically. Because it had no direct links with Afro-Asian colonial areas and could not bring influence to bear on Britain, France, or Portugal outside the framework of the United Nations, the USSR used the United Nations as the forum in which it could directly address itself to the decolonization issue and hope to exert some leverage, if only by exhortation and escalatory, declaratory initiatives. In later years, with Soviet support, the United Nations recognized militant independence movement like the PLO, ANC, SWAPO, MPLA, and Frelimo (Mozambican Liberation Front). Many were granted observer status, allowing them to participate in UN discussions. The General Assembly even set aside funds to aid national liberation movements that had achieved observer status.

Between 1945 and 1992 more than ninety-three non-self-governing territories achieved political independence and joined the United Nations, swelling the ranks of the nonaligned movement, but in practice often supporting the Soviet position against the industrialized democracies of the West. By 1990, however, the decolonization process had largely run its course.

GLOBAL DEVELOPMENT

As part of a further reconceptualization of Soviet security policy, Gorbachev assigned global development a prominent place on the Soviet foreign policy agenda. In a reversal of policy, he embraced the view, then popular among influential Soviet analysts of Third World, that the problems of Third World countries were not useful levers "for tilting the balance of power in favor of the Soviet Union," but were threats to international stability and peace. Conceding that the Soviet bloc countries did not have all the answers, he urged "the broad, constructive cooperation of all the advanced countries in solving the problems that create unrest in the LDCs—overpopulation, food shortages, and backwardness."[6] Soviet writers had, in the early 1980s, developed an interdisciplinary branch of knowledge—globalistics (*globalistika*), which dealt with environmental concerns, growth, global warming, and so on; but they were restricted to a rigid party-imposed ideological framework that "assailed the idea of 'convergence' between socialism and capitalism and any forecast or prescription of movement in that direction" and that blamed global problems on capitalism.[7]

By the latter part of 1988, however, Gorbachev succeeded in altering the ideology so that "universal interests" were held to transcend "class interests." This transformed the term *global problems* from an ideologically divisive concept to a positive one holding that such problems superseded class and economic rivalries, and could be solved by a cooperative, nonclass approach. Andrei V. Kozyrev, a high-ranking official in the Soviet foreign ministry (and later Russian Foreign Minister), put the matter forcefully:

> The restoration of reasonable principles in our foreign policy makes it possible to identify a platform for searching *a balance of interests* of the USSR and other states with a view to shaping a comprehensive system of confidence and security. . . . [T]here is a need to readjust stereotyped perceptions concerning the desire of the imperialist centers for all-out plundering of newly free nations. Lenin stressed that, unlike its undeveloped forms, advanced capitalism is not interested in deception but in "honest" profits from trade and economic transactions. . . .
>
> It appears to be only natural that Soviet literature raises the question of a crisis of civilization and a need for new forms of international cooperation in overcoming it. The watershed here lies not so much between the systems and ideologies as between common sense and the sense of self-preservation of the human species, on the one hand, and lack of responsibility, national egoism and prejudices, on the other." [italics added][8]

The changing Soviet approach under Gorbachev was best exemplified in the issues of economic development, the law of the sea and environmental protection, and human rights and affiliation with international organizations.

Economic Development   During the Stalinist period, the Soviet Union did not contribute "one Red ruble" to UN programs designed to promote the development of the new nations. Soviet delegates criticized the West's emphasis on agriculture and light industry and, oblivious of the resource base and immediate needs of developing countries, insisted that only heavy industry could make the countries truly independent. They opposed any kind of direct investment, saying that it led inevitably to political interference, but refused to assist in the creation of a fund that would instead disburse loans and credits, allegedly because the amounts contemplated were inadequate to the task. Nonparticipation in any of the UN economic and technical assistance programs was the policy.

When Stalin died, this damaging legacy was ended, and the USSR began to contribute to UN technical assistance programs. It sought thereby to make its bilateral assistance, which it was then dangling before developing countries, respectable and desirable. The Soviet courtship of the LDCs in turn induced Soviet participation in UN activities, though Moscow was more interested in image-building than nation-building. It opposed the view that aid should be given primarily in the form of grants and insisted that the problem "could not be solved by the creation of a charitable society." Neither the establishment of the Special Fund in 1959 nor the UN Capital Development Fund in 1966 brought forth any generous Soviet response. Moscow's niggardliness reinforced the impression that its small contribution to UN programs was the price it paid to play power politics in the United Nations.

Soviet delegates argued to often-sympathetic delegates from Third World countries that they were underdeveloped because of past imperialist exploitation, and that "the principal sources of means for the economic development of underdeveloped countries should be their own exploitation of their natural resources and natural wealth." The elites of these countries found the Soviet diagnosis of their economic backwardness plausible, sufficiently familiar in essentials to be readily accepted, and comforting to believe, as it relieved them of any responsibility for their present malaise and instead blamed foreign rule, exploitation of national wealth by foreign monopolies, forced dependence on a single crop, and lack of industry.

In the 1970s, especially after the dazzling success of the OPEC nations in revolutionizing their economic situation and the adoption by the nonaligned movement at its 1973 summit meeting in Algiers of a charter for a New International Economic Order, the LDCs deluged the General Assembly with resolutions for redistributing the world's wealth. Particularly at the UN Conference on Trade and Development (UNCTAD), first convened in 1964, and then at approximately four-year intervals, they pressed for higher commodity prices, lower tariffs, concessionary loans, more favorable terms of trade, and debt rescheduling.

Moscow's reaction to all of this was to play up the anti-Western, anti-imperialist, and anticolonial animus underlying LDC demands and to repudiate Western efforts to link the industrialized capitalist and Soviet-bloc socialist states together or to equate "the socialist community countries with the imperialist countries." Despite its oft-proclaimed sympathy for the plight of needy Third World countries, the Soviet Union offered little and played an insignificant part in UN deliberations.

Nor did Moscow modify its commercial practices. Soviet foreign trade organizations drove hard bargains, exacting high prices for their products, unless political considerations were controlling, as when dealing with Cuba; they bought primary products at the lowest possible prices and would not increase their purchases—for example, of cocoa beans, coffee, or fresh produce—to assist the producing countries in disposing of surpluses (and, incidentally, to give Soviet consumers a better choice of food); and Soviet terms of trade were rarely more favorable than those offered by the Western countries. Indeed, as a practitioner of the double standard, the USSR was notorious. For example, in the mid-1970s, it began requiring Western firms to purchase some of the finished goods produced in the factories built by them in the Soviet Union; however, when Moscow helped LDCs (India was a case in point), it resisted such "industry-branch" or cooperative arrangements and refused to link its production needs to the supplies from Soviet-built factories in Third World countries.

A complete reversal of attitude occurred under Gorbachev. In his December 1988 UN speech, Gorbachev made several proposals of market debt relief mechanisms for LDCs, saying the Soviet Union was "ready to establish a long-term (up to one hundred years) moratorium on the repayment of the debt by the least developed countries, and to write if off completely in a whole number of cases." Given its own difficult economic situation, however, Moscow was in no position to help LDCs.

The Law of the Sea   Examination of another global issue shows that the emergence of the Soviet Union as a major naval and maritime power had the curious effect of aligning it with the United States against the LDCs on many issues affecting the regulation of the high seas. The necessity of clarifying and modifying traditional practices on such issues as the establishment of the limits of the territorial seas, innocent right of passage, fishing rights, and exploitation of the mineral resources to be found on the seabed prompted the 1958 convening of the United Nations Conference on the Law of the Sea (UNCLOS I); a second conference was held in 1960, and a third was started in 1973 and ended in April 1982. However, not until November 1994 did the Law of the Sea Treaty (LOST) receive the votes of sixty governments needed to bring it into force. But neither Russia nor any other leading maritime power, such as the United States, Great Britain, or Japan, has yet ratified it. The net effect of the widespread objections to key sections of the treaty relating of seabed mining, environmental regulations, and the conservation of fisheries has been to intensify the conflicting positions of domestic pressure groups. Eventual ratification by all the leading maritime and naval powers seems likely because of the treaty's strong defense of traditional rights of navigation and control by coastal states to fishing in their territorial waters out to two hundred miles.

The Soviet Union was a vigorous advocate of retaining the traditional freedom of the seas. Although claiming twelve miles for its territorial sea since 1927, in opposition to the previously Western-preferred norm of three miles (on December 28, 1988, President Reagan extended the territorial waters of the United States to twelve miles, making the United States the one hundred-fifth nation to do so since UNCLOS adopted the provision in 1982), the USSR favored the traditional limiting of national jurisdiction over fishing zones. However, as many countries unilaterally extended their territorial waters and claims to exclusive fishing rights in these waters, the USSR followed suit. Thus, on December 10, 1976, the Supreme Soviet extended to two hundred miles the coastal waters limit over which the USSR was prepared to exercise control on all fishing, most likely in response to similar actions by other states, including the United States, which were unwilling to await the final results of UNCLOS III. The move was taken reluctantly, because the Soviet fishing fleet was the world's largest and ranged from the English Channel to the waters off the Arabian Peninsula to Antarctica. Like the United States, the Soviet Union adapted to the restraints imposed by increasingly nationalistic governments on previously unfettered fishing rights. On March 1, 1984, it officially established sovereignty over all mineral and maritime resources within the two-hundred-mile zone.

An issue of particular strategic significance on which the superpowers found themselves aligned against radical Third World countries was the right of innocent passage through international straits where the extension of sovereignty to twelve miles offshore (from the present generally practiced three-mile limit) would restrict the free movement of naval ships. However, whereas the USSR advocated a twelve-mile limit for territorial waters, it disputed the extension of the present right of innocent passage through international straits to straits that are situated wholly within the territorial waters of one country—for example in Soviet territorial waters. (The United States favors this extension.) Thus, when "in 1967, the United States sent two Coast Guard ice-breakers, the *Edisto* and the *Eastwind,* along the Northern Sea Route, outside a line 12 nautical miles from the Soviet Arctic coast, intending them to pass through the Vilkitskii Straits,"[9] they were turned back at the straits by the Soviets, who contended that these waters are "Historic Bays and Straits" for which no right of innocent passage is held to exist under Soviet law. Although "Soviet law in fact refrains from defining Soviet historic or internal waters—either theoretically or geographically"—Soviet jurists include all the Arctic Seas "in the category of what are called 'historic internal waters'"[10] The effect is to deny other countries access to the vast Arctic areas north of Russia and innocent passage through straits located in its waters. On a related issue, the Soviet Union allowed merchant ships the right of innocent passage through its territorial waters (that is, twelve miles off shore), but insists that naval vessels must obtain prior permission, a position the United States rejects.

Human Rights   Gorbachev repeatedly called for greater attention to human rights issues, and for a global system to safeguard them based on international law. In his December 1988 UN speech, he reaffirmed the USSR's commitment to the Universal Declaration of Human rights, adopted on December 10, 1948:

> We intend to expand the Soviet Union's participation in the human rights controlling mechanisms under the UN aegis, and within the framework of the European process. We think that the jurisdiction of the International Court in the Hague with regard to interpretation and application of agreements on human rights must be binding on all states.

And three months later, underscoring its new commitment to an expanded role for the International Court of Justice, the Soviet government announced that it would accept the Court's jurisdiction "over interpretation and application" of

> the 1948 convention condemning genocide, the 1949 convention banning trafficking in prostitutes and similar forms of slavery, a 1952 convention guaranteeing the political

rights of women, a 1965 convention banning racism and a 1984 convention outlawing torture.[11]

For many, the ultimate proof of Soviet intentions lay in how Gorbachev would treat organizational and personnel policy in the United Nations. Moscow's use of its nationals as intelligence agents in international organizations was confirmed by Arkady N. Shevchenko, the Soviet citizen who was under-secretary-general for political and security affairs, when he defected to the West in April 1978.

The Soviet Union usually tailored its position on organizational issues such as membership and accreditation of nongovernmental groups, including national liberation movements such as the PLO, to the sentiments prevailing among its Third World constituents. But exceptions clearly occurred, for example, differences between the USSR and Third World nations over restructuring the composition of international secretariats; Soviet reluctance to expand the membership of the Security Council (from eleven to fifteen) and the Economic and Social Council (from eighteen to twenty-seven) during the decade from 1955 to 1965; and Soviet opposition to increasing the UN budget or expanding the UN's authority in the economic, social, and humanitarian realms.

Under Gorbachev there were changes in organizational issues. In 1988 the government agreed "to phase out its policy of sending staff members to the Secretariat only on a temporary basis" and to permit more of them to take career appointments, though by the end of the Soviet era, still only six of the three hundred and sixty-four Soviet citizens employed by the United Nations had accepted permanent positions.[12] On other issues, however, policy shifts are being implemented more successfully. The USSR showed itself committed to universality of membership: after autumn 1989, it opposed Arab efforts to expel Israel from the General Assembly and UN specialized agencies; and, on many political issues, it signified its preference for consensus-building instead of confrontation or even competitive rivalry with the United States.

UN PEACEKEEPING AND INTERDEPENDENCE

Under Gorbachev the Soviet attitude toward UN peacekeeping operations underwent major changes—from tactical exploitation on behalf of Third World clients under Khrushchev and Brezhnev, to support for UN involvement in fashioning regional settlements in Afghanistan, Namibia, and the Gulf, among others, under Gorbachev. Previously, Moscow's policy was quintessentially Leninist, judging each operation in terms of Soviet interests and its effect on U.S.-Soviet rivalry in the region involved; it did not try to establish precedents or principles to guide future UN efforts, but acted only to take whatever advantage a particular crisis offered.

The first UN peacekeeping operation was organized after the combined British, French, and Israeli attack on Egypt at the end of October 1956 and the paralysis of the Security council because of the British and French veto. The creation of the UNEF suited Soviet aims: to bring about a withdrawal of British, French, and Israeli forces; to preserve Nasser in power; to weaken the position of Britain and France in the Middle East; and to sow discord in NATO.

At the same time, however, Moscow bitterly opposed the General Assembly's attempted intercession in the Hungarian crisis of November 1956, arguing that the "unrest" was purely an internal matter and came under the domestic jurisdiction of the Hungarian government—despite the presence of 5000 Soviet tanks and 250,000 Soviet troops. In this instance, it invoked Article 2, paragraph 7 of the UN Charter, which says that the United Nations shall not "intervene in matters which are essentially within the domestic jurisdiction of any state" nor shall it "require members to submit such matters to settlement." Eastern Europe was off limits to the United Nations.

In the Congo crisis of 1960, the USSR approved the United Nations Peacekeeping Operation in the Congo (ONUC) in order "to ensure the immediate and unconditional withdrawal of the Belgian troops," but soon reversed itself when the possibility of acquiring a foothold in the Congo disappeared. It has not opposed the United Nations Force in Cyprus (UNFICYP), created in March 1964 to keep Greek and Turkish Cypriots separated, in part because the operation has been financed by voluntary contributions and in part because the nonaligned government of Cyprus favored the peacekeeping operation.

In 1964–1965, the Soviet Union's unwillingness to help finance the peacekeeping operations that it supported politically precipitated a major crisis in the United Nations. At issue was the Soviet conception of what should be the outer limits to political and economic commitments by a UN organization. The USSR (as well as France) refused to pay its assessed share of the UNEF and ONUC operations on the grounds that they were not legal, having been authorized by the General Assembly and not the Security Council. As mentioned, it maintained that the charter invests the Security Council with the sole responsibility for defining the terms, including the financial terms, under which armed forces may be employed by the United Nations to maintain international peace and security. To substitute the General Assembly or the UN Secretariat for the Security Council (and its Military Staff Committee) is to undermine the principle of great-power unanimity that is embodied in the charter and that must be controlling in situations involving the use of armed forces under UN auspices. The July 1962 advisory opinion of the International Court of Justice, which ruled that the UNEF and ONUC operations were legitimate expenses of the United Nations and thus subject to the budgetary authority of the General Assembly, was dismissed by Moscow as devoid of legal value, since advisory opinions are not binding on the parties. Also, in company with other countries such as France and the Arab nations, the USSR insisted that full responsibility for these operations must be borne by the countries most directly responsible for their having been undertaken by the United Nations.

The financial crisis erupted in late 1964, at the nineteenth session of the General Assembly, when the U.S. delegation contended that Article 19 of the charter should be invoked against delinquent countries. Under this article, a nation that falls two years behind in paying its assessments "shall have no vote in the General Assembly." With Moscow threatening to withdraw from the United Nations—having refused to pay its assessment in the regular UN budget for activities it considered illegal—the General Assembly adjourned in February 1965 without debating the issue. The crisis passed soon thereafter, only because the United States, sensing the reluctance of the membership to implement Article 19, decided not to press the issue. From time to time, Moscow indicated that it would make a "voluntary contribution" to help ease the UN deficit caused by peacekeeping expenditures, but not until September 1987 did it do so.

The USSR's policy on peacekeeping was largely determined by political considerations, as developments in the Middle East have shown. In the aftermath of the Suez War of October 1956, UNEF contingents were stationed in Gaza and Sinai and for a decade helped create a situation that allowed the uneasy truce between the Egyptians and the Israelis; but Nasser's summary termination of the UNEF presence on May 18, 1967, set in motion the chain of events that triggered the Arab-Israeli war of June 5 to 10, 1967. In the wake of the Egyptian defeat and with the approval of the Security Council, the secretary-general assigned UN observers to the Suez Canal zone, but they played a minor role.

After the 1973 October War, the Security Council, with Soviet approval, established two peacekeeping forces to preserve the peace and uphold the interim agreements reached between Israel and Egypt, and Israel and Syria: a second UNEF in Sinai, and a United Nations Disengagement Observer Force (UNDOF) on the Golan Heights. During 1974–1978, the USSR went along with a series of six-month extensions because the Arab states wanted them. However, Egyptian President Anwar Sadat's decision to sign a separate peace treaty with Israel on March 26, 1979, polarized the Arab world and precipitated Soviet opposition to a renewal of UNEF, that is, the UN units supervising the gradual Israeli withdrawal from Sinai and safeguarding the peace in that sector. Rather than incur a Soviet veto, Washington accepted the withdrawal of the four-thousand-man armed force on July 24, 1979, and the substitution of the unarmed United Nations Truce Supervisory Organization (UNTSO), which has operated in different parts of the world since 1949, is directly responsible to the Security Council, unlike UNEF, and is a part of a non-UN policing force.

Just as the USSR's opposition to UNEF's continuation was in deference to the wishes of the Arab states opposed to Sadat's treaty with Israel, so its support for UNDOF's renewals has been conditioned by the desires of Syria, Moscow's prime client in the Arab world. Since May 1974, UNDOF's thirteen-hundred-man force has supervised the cease-fire and disengagement between Syria and Israel on the Golan Heights, which has remained quiet even during the worst period of Israeli-Syrian fighting in Lebanon's Bekaa Valley in the summer of 1982 and the Palestinian uprising (*intifada*), which erupted in December 1987 in territories occupied by Israel since the 1967 June War.

The first sign of a change in Soviet policy came on April 18, 1986, when the USSR voted with the fourteen other members of the UN Security Council to renew UNIFIL's (the United Nations Force in Lebanon, established in March 1978) mandate for another three months, whereas on previous votes it had abstained. Even more unexpected was the Soviet delegate's statement that Moscow intended to pay its assessed share of the UN operation.

On September 17, 1987, in a major article in *Pravda,* Gorbachev proposed the wider use of "UN military observers and UN peacekeeping forces in disengaging the troops of warring sides, and observing cease-fire and armistice agreements." The plan called for greater use of the permanent members of the UN Security

Council, who could act as guarantors of regional security; cooperation in "uprooting international terrorism"; and more frequent use of the International Court of Justice "for consultative conclusions on international law disputes."

On October 15, Gorbachev's sweeping proposals for revitalization of UN functions—not just in the area of peacekeeping—gained credibility when the Soviet government announced that it was paying its $225 million debt to the United Nations, of which $197 million was for peacekeeping operations and $28 million for the regular budget. With this sharp policy reversal, Gorbachev enhanced Soviet prestige and highlighted U.S. indebtedness, which is larger than any other country's. His address to the UN General Assembly on December 7, 1988, elaborated the Soviet Union's commitment to a stronger United Nations and a restructuring of international relations. By calling for invigoration of the United Nations, he was able to (1) dispel some lingering Cold War suspicion and reaffirm Moscow's interest in an improvement in the international climate, (2) enhance Soviet prestige and status as a coequal of the United States, (3) find a welcome reception among the less developed countries and the members of the nonaligned movement, and (4) constrain U.S. unilateralism.

Two weeks later, the USSR joined with other members of the UN Security council in dispatching the UN Angola Verification Mission to oversee the withdrawal of Cuban troops and the transition of Namibia to full independence. In 1989 and early 1990 Moscow also gave its approval for peacekeeping operations in Afghanistan and Central America (where ONUCA—the UN Observer Group in Central America—helped bring the Nicaraguan conflict to a peaceful political conclusion).

Gorbachev's commitment to a strengthened United Nations was demonstrated in the Gulf. On August 2, 1990, Iraq invaded and annexed Kuwait, prompting condemnation by a series of UN Security Council resolutions and the formation of a powerful multinational military force in Saudi Arabia under the leadership of the United States. Soviet leaders agreed that aggression could not be permitted to go unchallenged, and they supported all the Council's resolutions.

Under Yeltsin, Russia has been active in UN efforts to contain and mediate regional conflicts in Cambodia, Haiti, and Bosnia. Its special interest in Transcaucasia and Central Asia caused some tension with the United Nations and the United States, which have been reluctant to give Russia a green light to intervene as unilateral guarantor of stability in CIS disputes. Nonetheless, Moscow has pursued its own course in Moldova and Tajikistan. However, in Georgia, it received a mandate from the UN Security Council in July 1994 to preserve the shaky cease-fire between the government of Georgia and the secessionist rebels in the western region of Abkhazia.

Bosnia has proved to be the most contentious issue between Russia and the United Nations. Although supportive of Security Council resolutions seeking to end the conflicts that broke out in Croatia, Bosnia, and Macedonia in the wake of the collapse of Yugoslavia in 1991, Russia has tilted toward Serbia and tried to insulate it from strong UN sanctions. The two countries share a common Slavic heritage, Orthodox Christian faith, and historical memories as allies in both world wars. Moscow is also sympathetic to the desire of the Serbs in the Krajina region of Croatia and of the Serbs of Bosnia to merge eventually with Serbia.

For a time after the West backed his successful showdown with the Russian parliament in October 1993, Yeltsin did not veto Security Council resolutions that increased pressure on Serbian President Slobodan Milosevic, whose covert aid made possible the continued resistance of the Krajina and Bosnian Serbs to UN efforts to impose a settlement. But domestic pressure from his ultranationalist opponents has nudged Yeltsin toward more open support. The dismissal of a Russian general in April 1995 from the UN peacekeeping forces in Croatia on grounds of corruption and connivance with the Krajina Serbs in permitting a "thriving trade in United Nations gasoline with the Serbs" and smuggling artillery and antitank weapons into the area, increased tensions between Moscow and the United Nations.[13] Russia is clearly not prepared, judging from its veto of a resolution sponsored by Muslim countries that back the Bosnian government, to permit the United Nations to impose a peace plan that is unacceptable to the Serbs.[14]

Russian confidence in the whole UN peacekeeping process was deeply shaken by the two-week NATO bombing campaign over Bosnia in early September 1995. The decision by the UN Secretariat to approve a secret memo abdicating authority over the use of air power over Bosnia, without consulting all the permanent members of the Security Council (of which Russia is a member) was tantamount, according to the chairman of the Duma's International Affairs Committee, Vladimir Lukin, of dividing the Security into first- and second-class members. Although the bombings ended shortly after the memo was released, and Russian troops were offered a key role in acting as a buffer for withdrawing Bosnian Serb forces, the entire experience heightened anti-Western and anti-NATO sentiment among the Russian political elite.

INTERNATIONAL ORGANIZATIONS AND THE NEW RUSSIA

Constrained by economic necessity, the new Russia has had to curtail its ambitions to be a major actor in the world arena. This has led to an even greater than customary emphasis on strengthening its position in international organizations.

Russia's first objective was to retain and enhance its political status in international organizations by obtaining recognition for itself as the legal successor to the USSR. Russia's adoption of the rights (and obligations) of the USSR in these international forums has, by and large, been successfully completed.

Russia's second objective is to enhance Russian security interests by inviting multilateral international organizations to play a greater role in regional peacekeeping. Given its prominent political status, Russia expects to play a major role in all peacekeeping efforts. At the same time, given its financial constraints, it expects the international community to help with the costs of any such efforts in which Russia participated.

These expectations are modeled after the support given to the efforts of the United States in regions like the Persian Gulf, Somalia, and Haiti, where the United States volunteered to act with the support—financial and diplomatic—of the international community. The Russian foreign ministry has made this analogy with regard to Russian peacekeeping efforts within the CIS, which it sees as an international issue on its own borders that no other nation will send troops to contain.

This desire to establish a quid pro quo helps to explain Russia's involvement in conflict resolution in Bosnia-Herzegovina, as well as persistent attempts by the Russian Foreign Ministry to drum up international support for an expansion of peacekeeping inside the CIS.

Russia under Yeltsin is also attempting a more systematic balance between two competing objectives in this arena. It seeks to utilize international forums to enhance Russian security; it seeks to enhance Russia's role in world affairs and integration into the world community. The former objective sometimes has given rise to Western suspicion that Russia seeks an increased role for international organizations in conflict resolution merely to manipulate the international community into supporting Russian interests.

It would be wrong, however, to dismiss the current Russian policy of enhancing the authority of international organizations as mere window-dressing. It is clear that Foreign Minister Andrei Kozyrev is an ardent supporter of internationalism. His own background lies in this area, and he has consistently argued that an enhanced role for international organizations coincides with the Russian national interest. Russia's current military and economic weakness also necessitates significantly more accommodation to the international community than in the past. This will not always be the case, as is becoming evident in Bosnia, and there appears to be a window of opportunity for the West during these early years in the formulation of post-Soviet foreign policy to shape the outlook of Russian leaders.

Currently, Russian interests fall into two broad categories: regional security issues, and economic and trade issues.

Regional Security Issues Russia is especially interested in ending internecine conflicts at its frontiers before they expand or lead to a massive population exodus that would further burden the Russian economy. Hence, Russia has sought both international support for its peacekeeping efforts and the expansion of international mechanisms that will enhance domestic stability and safeguard human rights (most notably those of the Russian minority) in the region.

As it did in the past, Russia's ultimate definition of regional security involves the dismantling of military blocs and their replacement with collective security arrangements that involve Russia and its neighbors. This involves creating what Yeltsin has called "a new mechanism of international power" under the aegis of the United Nations. Ideally, for the Russians, this new structure ought to replace the bipolar structures established during the Cold War with a "Euro-Atlantic" collective security system.[16] At the very least, however, Russia seeks to prevent any enlargement of NATO.

The collective security structure Russia has proposed would not dismantle existing institutions such as NATO, North Atlantic Cooperative Council (NACC), the Western European Union, the Council of Europe, and the CIS, but would enhance the coordinating function of the OSCE, by setting up a UN-style Security Council for European states, in which senior members would have a veto right.[17] By advocating participation in such a broad regional framework, Russia hopes to achieve several objectives: (1) to end the division of Europe into East and West that serves to isolate Russia; (2) to create conditions that make NATO's existence as a military alliance superfluous; (3) to obtain political, economic and military support from the West for its peacekeeping efforts in the CIS; and (4) to publicize and combat violations of human and civil rights in the region due to "aggressive nationalism."

This is a risky strategy for Russia, since it involves obtaining international recognition for the CIS as an international organization on a par with the EC and NATO. By subordinating the CIS to the OSCE, however, Russia risks limiting its own ability to intervene in those states unilaterally. By broadening the forum through which grievances are to be adjudicated, Russia's relative weight in internal CIS matters might well diminish. So far this appears to be a risk the Russian government is willing to take in return for a commitment to expedite Russia's integration into European-wide economic, political, and military institutions.

Economic and Trade Issues   In contrast to the Soviet Union which, even under Gorbachev retained a substantial degree of economic autarky, Russia is pursuing a strategy of seeking full participation in international financial and economic institutions so that it may obtain loans to assist in rebuilding its economy and integrate fully into the global economy. On this score, Russia's success has been mixed, partly because of Russia's lack of organized market structures, and partly because of the reluctance of international financial institutions (IFIs) to integrate such an unstable economic and political entity too quickly. While the Russian government tends to argue that more rapid integration would help stabilize the Russian economy, IFIs like the World Bank have generally taken the position that stabilization must precede participation.

Oddly enough, the Soviet Union was an active participant in the Bretton Woods Conference, which established the IMF and the World Bank. In fact it was Vice-President of the conference and signed the agreement, but failed to ratify it. For more than two decades after that the Soviet Union attempted to create an alternative, socialist world trade system, constructed around the Comecon, while maintaining its state monopoly on international trade. This policy of economic autarky, dictated far more by ideological than commercial considerations, was gradually abandoned by Gorbachev. As a step toward encouraging it to participate more actively in the global economy, the Soviet Union on May 16, 1990 was granted observer status in the General Agreement on Tariffs and Trade (GATT), an organization established in 1948 to liberalize world trade. Shortly thereafter, it also joined the European Bank for Reconstruction and Development (EBRD). It was not until after the collapse of the USSR, however, that the United States and other major Western powers agreed to expedite Soviet membership to the IMF and World Bank. These changes mark a dramatic shift in policy, but given the secrecy that has traditionally enshrouded Moscow's trade and economic policy, Russia's progress toward integration into the world economy has been slow.

Under Yeltsin this process faces not ideological obstacles, but obstacles of a more technical and domestic political nature, such as a lack of reliable economic data, burgeoning unemployment and falling productivity. The austerity measures imposed by the IMF are no more popular than in other underdeveloped countries, and are frequently criticized by politicians as an intrusion on national sovereignty, making them painful for Russian legislators to swallow.

Still, despite these difficulties, since 1991 the Russian economy has made considerable progress toward integrating into the world economy. For the first half of 1995, Russia's foreign trade turnover equaled nearly $60 billion, an increase of 19% over the previous year.[18] During this same period, goods exported to the former Soviet republics rose 9%, while goods exported to other countries of the world rose by more than 23%. Already more than three quarters of Russia's trade is with countries outside the former Soviet Union, a trend that is likely to accelerate despite efforts to forge greater integration among the CIS economies.[19] Direct foreign investment in Russia is still low by world standards, but is expected to increase as the political situation stabilizes. Russia's new dependence on foreign markets and financial institutions may be troubling to many in the older generation, but there is a general recognition among the young that the Russian economy must learn to become globally competitive if the country is to prosper.

SELECTED BIBLIOGRAPHY

Assetto, Valerie J. *The Soviet Bloc in the IMF and the IBRD.* Boulder, CO: Westview Press, 1988.

Boardman, Robert. *Post-Socialist World Orders: Russia, China and the UN System.* New York: St. Martin's Press, 1994.

Clemens, Walter C. *Can Russia Change?: The USSR Confronts Global Interdependence.* London: Unwin Hyman, 1990.

Frieheim, Robert L. *Negotiating the New Ocean Regime.* Columbia, South Caorlina: University of South Carolina Press, 1993.

Geron, Leonard. *Soviet Foreign Economic Policy Under Perestroika.* New York: Council on Foreign Relations Press, 1991.

Haigh, R.H., et al. *Soviet Foreign Policy, the League of Nations and Europe, 1917–1939.* Totowa, NJ: Barnes & Noble Books, 1986.

Hallas, Duncan. *The Comintern.* London: Bookmarks, 1985.

Haus, Leah A. *Globalizing the GATT: The Soviet Union's Successor States, Eastern Europe, and the International Trading System.* Washington, DC: Brookings Institution, 1992.

Hewett, Edward A. *Open for Business: Russia's Return to the Global Economy.* Washington, DC: Brookings Institution, 1992.

Hohmann, Hans-Hermann, et al. (eds.) *Economics and Politics in the USSR: Problems of Interdependence.* Boulder, CO: Westview Press, 1986.

James, Alan. *The Politics of Peacekeeping.* New York: Praeger, 1969.

Lall, Arthur. *The UN and the Middle East Crisis, 1967.* New York: Columbia University Press, 1968.

Nogee, Joseph L. *Soviet Policy Towards International Control of Atomic Energy.* Notre Dame: University of Notre Dame Press, 1961.

Palmieri, Deborah A. (ed.). *Russia and the NIS in the World Economy: East-West Investment, Financing, and Trade*. Westport, CT: Praeger, 1994.

———. *The USSR and the World Economy: Challenges for the Global Integration of Soviet Markets under Perestroika*. Westport, CT: Praeger, 1992.

Raevsky, Andrei, and Vorob'ev, Igor. *Russian Approaches to Peacekeeping Operations*. Research paper (United Nations Institute for Disarmament Research) no. 28. New York: United Nations, 1994.

Rubinstein, Alvin Z. *The Soviets in International Organizations: Changing Policy Toward Developing Countries, 1953–1963*. Princeton, NJ: Princeton University Press, 1964.

Shevchenko, Arkady N. *Breaking with Moscow*. New York: Knopf, 1985.

Smith, Alan. *Russia and the World Economy: Problems of Integration*. New York: Routledge, 1993.

Sorokin, Konstantin E. *Russia's Security in a Rapidly Changing World*. Stanford, CA: Center for International Security and Arms Control, Stanford University, 1994.

Taracouzio, T.A. *The Soviet Union and International Law*. New York: Macmillan, 1935.

NOTES

1. A statement made to the press, as quoted in Jane Degras, *Soviet Documents on Foreign Policy,* vol. 2 (New York: Oxford University Press, 1952), p. 66.
2. M. Lvov, "United Nations: Results and Prospects," *International Affairs,* no. 9 (September 1965), p. 4.
3. Jane Degras, *Soviet Documents on Foreign Policy,* vol. 2, p. 243.
4. Bernard S. Morris, *Communism, Revolution, and American Policy* (Durham, NC: Duke University Press, 1987), p. 10.
5. *Ibid.,* p. 13.
6. Elizabeth Kridl Valkenier, *The Soviet Union and the Third World: An Economic Bind* (New York: Praeger, 1983), p. 149.
7. Walter C. Clemens, Jr., *Can Russia Change? The USSR Confronts Global Interdependence* (Boston: Unwin Hyman, 1990), p. 127; see chap. 5.
8. Andrei Kozyrev, "Confidence and Balance of Interests," *International Affairs,* no. 11 (November 1988), pp. 11–12.
9. Elizabeth Young and Viktor Sebek, "Red Seas and Blue Seas: Soviet Uses of Ocean Law," *Survival,* vol. 20, no. 6 (November–December 1978), p. 256.
10. *Ibid.*
11. *New York Times,* March 9, 1989.
12. *New York Times,* July 26, 1990.
13. Roger Cohen, *New York Times,* April 12, 1995.
14. Alessandra Stanley, *New York Times,* December 4, 1994.
15. Scott Parrish, "Russia Criticizes UN and NATO," *OMRI Daily Digest I,* September 14, 1995.
16. Victor Yasmann, *RFE/RL Daily Report* December 2, 1994.
17. Doug Clarke and Vladimir Socor, *RFE/RL Daily Report,* October 11, 1994.
18. Thomas Sigel, "Foreign Trade Turnover Up," *OMRI Daily Digest* July 14, 1995.
19. Thomas Sigel, "Export-Import Balance up 23%," *OMRI Daily Digest* August 17, 1995.

Chapter
13

Russian-American Relations

At the end of World War II, the USSR's expansion in Europe and the Far East placed it astride areas that were vital to the United States. An imperial-minded and tyrannical Stalin pursued policies that increased Western insecurity and residual ideological antipathies and that polarized East-West relations. His obsession with security—an understandable reaction to a war that had brought the USSR to the brink of disaster—became more acute as the United States gained obvious superiority in strategic weapons and developed its policy of containment. Tension was endemic.

By the mid-1950s, however, relations between the two blocs had stabilized, and the fear of war in Europe had receded. Soviet development of nuclear weapons ushered in an era of deterrence predicated on mutual assured destruction, and the Khrushchev leadership inched toward a limited accommodation with the West, based on the preservation of the territorial-political status quo of a Europe divided along bloc lines. But the essentially conflictual character of Soviet-American relations did not significantly diminish; indeed, it grew with Moscow's power projection capability and assertiveness in the Third World. In the consequent globalization of the rivalry, the Soviet-American relationship assumed an adversarial nature in which competition overshadowed cooperation; the latter was served by a mutual desire to avoid nuclear war and direct confrontation of Soviet and American forces, but the former lasted for decades in a wide number of areas.

Before moving on to discuss the post-Soviet period, it is worth summarizing the dynamics of the relationship during the Cold War. Even during this period of intense rivalry, both countries shared certain characteristics that kept their rivalry within acceptable limits even during the worst of the Cold War.

First, despite tense crises and regional conflicts, the Soviet Union and the United States never fought a war against one another, not over Berlin in 1948–1949, Korea in 1950–1953, Hungary in 1956, Cuba in 1962, Czechoslovakia in 1968, Vietnam in the late 1960s to early 1970s, or the Middle East in 1970 or 1973. Both refrained from taking steps that might have precipitated a direct confrontation between them.

Second, neither coveted the territory of the other. There are no outstanding irredentist claims. Real estate was not at the heart of their difficulties. A rivalry that was imperial rather than nationalist in character did not generate volatile emotional passions and thus was far easier for the elites in power to manage domestically and was less likely to get out of hand. Each side could more easily accept limited gains by the other.

Third, as peoples, the Russians and Americans have many positive images of one another. Russians and Americans appreciate each others' literature, music, theater, and sports, as is evident in the general popularity of the visiting artists and cultural troupes of both countries.

Fourth, Soviet and American societies shared the admirable but quixotic belief of the eighteenth-century Enlightenment that through science, education, and humans' reason, society can be transformed. If, as many scholars have suggested, Marxism is a quintessentially Western ideology, then its durability in the USSR was at least partly attributable to the fact that Russia in the early twentieth century was already an integral part of the West. This fundamental outlook predominates despite mushrooming ecological, social, and economic problems. For both, gleaming technology still stands at the center of the societies that their elites seek to build; for both, technological "fixes" are seen as the cure for man's ills.

Fifth, both the United States and the Soviet Union were often disliked and mistrusted by their immediate neighbors. Both had alliance problems. Concerns over maintaining intra-alliance cohesion helped to limit the temptation to interfere directly in the other's primary sphere of influence.

This complex legacy of superpower rivalry has lingered on even after the end of the Cold War. Despite declarations of partnership and amity, practical disagreements and mutual mistrust have led some analysts (both in Russia and the United States) to speculate about the emergence of a new Cold War. Still, it is noteworthy that in a very short time relations between these two nations have taken on a decidedly friendlier tone than would ever have been thought possible with the former communist regime.

RELATIONS WITH THE WEST: THE RISE AND FALL OF DÉTENTE

After the death of Stalin in March 1953, the Soviet leadership consciously sought to improve relations with the United States and other Western countries. The origin of this policy can be pinpointed to 1954–1955 and Khrushchev's withdrawal of Soviet military power from Austria and Finland. Whatever the other considerations, Moscow's pullback from forward positions in Europe signified its readiness to pare its territorial ambitions somewhat and to seek an accommodation with the West, even at the expense of Soviet relations with China.

The process of negotiating with the West, however, was erratic and periodically disrupted by intra-Soviet bloc crises, such as the 1956 upheavals in Eastern Europe, and by tensions with the West, such as the Berlin crisis between 1958 and 1961 (when the wall surrounding West Berlin was erected), the U-2 affair of May

1960 (when the shooting down of a U.S. spy plane over the USSR reminded the Soviet military of their vulnerability to a U.S. nuclear attack), and the Cuban missile crisis of October 1962. The Cuban missile crisis was the most dangerous Soviet challenge to the United States during the Khrushchev period. It had a profound effect on Soviet-U.S. relations and on the acceleration of the USSR's buildup of strategic forces in the 1960s and 1970s.

After Fidel Castro came to power in January 1959, his commitment to revolution elsewhere in Latin America prevented a normalization of Cuba's relations with the United States. Moscow was slow to court Castro, but it upheld Cuba's increasingly anti-American policy and revolutionary outlook. In July 1960, Khrushchev said the Monroe Doctrine "has outlived its time, has outlived itself, has died, so to say, a natural death. Now the remains of this doctrine should best be buried as every dead body is so that it should not poison the air by its decay."[1] After the abortive CIA-engineered effort to overthrow Castro at the Bay of Pigs in April 1961, Moscow undertook a program of economic and military assistance to Cuba. In the spring of 1962, the Kremlin decided to install intermediate range missiles in Cuba, ostensibly to protect Castro (who had proclaimed himself a Marxist-Leninist) from another U.S.-organized invasion, but it is difficult to accept this explanation as the single reason for the deployment. Khrushchev already had, as Washington knew, upwards of 30,000 troops on the island—a more than adequate deterrence against a possible U.S. attack. More likely, the missiles were intended for some far more ambitious strategic objective—to effect a sweeping shift in the balance of power or to obtain U.S. concessions on Berlin or in the arms control negotiations.

According to Khrushchev, it was during his visit to Bulgaria in mid-May 1962 that he conceived the idea of installing nuclear-tipped missiles in Cuba without allowing Washington to find out about them until it was too late for anything to be done.[2] In late July, after obtaining Castro's permission, Moscow began pouring in men and materiel. On September 2, it announced an expanded program of arms deliveries and the sending of unspecified "technical specialists" to help Cuba meet the "threats" from "aggressive imperialist quarters." On September 11, in a major policy statement, the Soviet government gave assurances of peaceful intent, asserting that "the armaments and military equipment sent to Cuba are designed exclusively for defensive purposes" but warning that "if war is unleashed," the Soviet Union will render assistance to Cuba "just as it was ready in 1956 to render military assistance to Egypt at the time of the Anglo-French-Israeli aggression in the Suez Canal region." During the next few weeks, the Kremlin carried on an intensive program of disinformation and deception, issuing placatory statements and sending diplomats to assure officials in the Kennedy Administration, including the President, of the defensive nature of the weapons being introduced into Cuba.

The dramatic account of the "eyeball-to-eyeball" Soviet-American confrontation in the Caribbean is well known. On October 22, President John F. Kennedy told the American people that the United States had "unmistakable evidence" that the USSR was constructing a series of offensive missile sites in Cuba and that the United States aimed "to prevent the use of these missiles against this or any other country and to secure their withdrawal or elimination from the western hemisphere." By the end of October the crisis was over. The denouement was determined by the preponderant U.S. superiority in conventional forces in the Caribbean and not by its advantage in nuclear weapons—six thousand to about three hundred. In this situation, Moscow calculated that Washington would not, despite its edge in nuclear weapons, resort to a nuclear strike because it could not be certain of destroying all the USSR's missiles and thereby avoid the destruction of some American cities (as was revealed almost thirty years later). Khrushchev was forced to back down. He removed the missiles and, as was revealed years later, forty-eight nuclear warheads that were inside vans near the missiles and that had been undetected by U.S. intelligence. Though disappointed at his failure to redress the strategic imbalance between the Soviet Union and the United States, which would have enabled him to impose a sharp decrease in military spending on his defense establishment, he did ensure the security of his Cuban protégé, having extracted a U.S. pledge not to invade Cuba in return for the removal of the missiles and the undetected nuclear warheads. But at home he had to accede to the Soviet military. As a result, a massive and accelerated buildup of Soviet strategic and conventional forces was undertaken, reflecting the determination of the conservatives in the Kremlin never again to have to back down to the United States because of military inferiority.

In the realm of foreign policy, the crisis led to renewed efforts to reach an accommodation through negotiation, "but within a mutually acceptable balance of strategic power." It gave new impetus to the quest for an improvement in Soviet-American relations, leading to the conclusion of the limited nuclear test ban treaty in the summer of 1963 and the establishment "of the so-called hot-line of instant communications between Washington and Moscow. In general, these ameliorating measures were intended to lower the level of tension, facilitate the management of future crises, and clear the way for greater accommodation."[3]

After Khrushchev's deposal in October 1964, the Brezhnev-Kosygin team continued to improve relations with the United States, but headway was slow. Complicating the process were Moscow's decisions to help North Vietnam, to rearm the Arabs after the June War, to invade Czechoslovakia, and to strengthen Soviet forces in Europe. But West German Chancellor Willy Brandt's *Ostpolitik* and readiness to accept the division of Germany, and the momentum of Moscow's buildup of strategic weapons made the United States more receptive to an improvement of Soviet-American relations.

By the early 1970s, the Soviet Union's interest in détente derived from a series of compelling policy objectives. First was the desire for Western, especially American, technology and credits to increase industrial and managerial efficiency and modernization in the nonmilitary sectors of the economy. In March 1971, at the twenty-fourth congress of the CPSU, the Politburo made the decision—which had been deferred in late 1969 and frequently discussed in 1970—to seek better relations with the United States in order to ensure the importation from that country of large amounts of advanced technology and equipment. It did so after five years of futile efforts to overcome lagging productivity and technological weakness in the nonmilitary sectors of the Soviet economy. In September 1965, the Brezhnev-

Kosygin leadership had introduced a series of major economic reforms to overcome the shortcomings that had allegedly resulted from Khrushchev's "harebrained" policies; but like the fabled monkey who tried to organize the barnyard animals into a symphony orchestra by continually reassigning instruments, they realized that domestic realignments were not sufficient to stimulate innovation and efficiency. For this they would have to turn to the West.

Some argue that the USSR's need for advanced technology was the only reason for its interest in détente in the 1970s. By importing on an enormous scale, the leadership sought to offset the deleterious combination of party and bureaucratic interference in the operation of industry and the imbalances between the military and nonmilitary branches of the economy that accounted for shortages and shoddy goods and that plagued planners and decimated production targets. Western technology had been in vogue before, both under Lenin and Stalin and under the tsars, but the scale of Brezhnev's need was enormous, and meeting it was crucial for overcoming the critical bottlenecks in important sectors.

A second factor in Brezhnev's interest in détente was Moscow's problems with China. Despite their preponderance of military power, Soviet fear of a Chinese threat was aggravated by periodic outbreaks along the thousands of miles of exposed border; by Beijing's vestigial territorial grievances, its growing nuclear capability, and its formal termination of the 1950 treaty of alliance.

A third important consideration for Brezhnev—and a constant in Soviet thinking after 1945—was the desire to obtain formal Western recognition of the territorial status quo in Europe and acceptance of the Soviet imperial system in Eastern Europe. That gained momentum with Chancellor Willy Brandt's policy of accommodation with the Soviet Union in 1969 was completed at the Conference on Security and Cooperation in Europe in Helsinki in July 1975.

Fourth, Brezhnev was interested in furthering détente in order to stabilize the strategic arms race and limit the escalation of defense expenditures. Moscow's keen interest was evident in the SALT I agreement in 1972 and the Ford-Brezhnev accord at Vladivostok in November 1974, when "essential equivalence" or parity was determined (though at a much higher threshold than had been expected by Western proponents of arms control). Nevertheless, the Carter Administration's attempt in March 1977 to lower the quantitative ceilings that had been agreed to at Vladivostok occasioned bitter Soviet opposition, and led to the formal lapsing of SALT I. Moscow's agreement to the on-site inspection mandated by the INF treaty, its campaign for deep cuts in strategic delivery systems in the SALT/START talks, and its efforts to contain the competition in the expensive, high-tech realm of SDI-type research and deployment all reflect the Soviet desire to stabilize the arms race, in order to keep its own swollen arms budget within tolerable economic limits and to avoid an open, all-out weapons competition with the United States. Finally, like his predecessors, Brezhnev viewed détente as a form of political struggle that was compatible with avoidance of conventional and nuclear war. He saw no essential contradiction between the USSR's seeking much-needed economic and technological supplements to its industrial network and simultaneously maneuvering for strategic and political advantages to improve its overall global position vis-à-vis the United States. For Moscow, this was the competitive aspect of peaceful coexistence.By the second half of the 1970s, Moscow's ambitions in the Third World had seriously compromised its efforts to improve relations with the United States. The optimistic expectations for détente raised by the signing of SALT I and the subsequent round robin of summit visits had begun to wane by the convening of the Conference on Security and Cooperation in Europe in July 1975. A number of developments adversely affected the Soviet-American relationship: the near-confrontation during the Arab-Israeli war in October 1973; the resignation of Richard Nixon in August 1974; the uncertainty that followed the military coup in Portugal in April 1974, which led to the Portuguese Communist Party's coming close to gaining effective control of the country; the passage in 1974 of the Jackson-Vanik amendment restricting U.S. credits to the USSR and denying most-favored-nation treatment in tariffs until Moscow eased restrictions on the emigration of Soviet Jews; and the USSR's consequent abrogation of the economic agreement reached with Nixon for the repayment of World War II lend-lease debts. The Soviet-Cuban intervention in Angola in late 1975, which successfully brought to power a pro-Soviet regime, and the USSR's intervention in Ethiopia in 1976–1977 also contributed to the growing difficulties.

In the late 1970s and early 1980s, the USSR and the United States stood essentially in an adversarial relationship. From the start of the Carter Administration in January 1977, Soviet leaders went from uncertainty to disappointment, and then to uneasiness over their relations with the United States. In their view, the principal responsibility for the steady deterioration in Soviet-American relations rested with Washington. They were annoyed by Carter's stress on human rights, which was viewed as a move toward intensification of ideological struggle. His letter, written soon after taking office, to the dissident nuclear physicist Andrei Sakharov, and his support for Anatoly Shcharansky, the Jewish refusenik (that is, one who sought to emigrate from the USSR), when the latter was arrested by Soviet authorities in 1977 and accused of working for U.S. intelligence, were especially irritating to the Soviets. More important, after a visit to Moscow by Secretary of State Cyrus Vance, Kremlin officials sharply criticized the Carter Administration in March 1977 for seeking to undermine the essentials of the SALT II agreement that Moscow had regarded as all but sealed by negotiations with the Ford Administration.

In Geneva in May 1977, Vance suggested cooperation on the Arab-Israeli problem as an indication of Washington's desire to put relations back on track. After some very secret discussions (only Carter, Vance, and National Security Council Adviser Zbigniew Brzezinski were involved on the American side), a U.S.-Soviet statement on the Middle East was issued on October 1, 1977, calling for a return to the Geneva venue and agreement on bringing the PLO into the negotiation process. However, within a week the Carter Administration was forced by Israeli and congressional objections to renege on the agreement, to the ire of Moscow. Sadat's dramatic initiative and trip to Jerusalem in November and Carter's subsequent efforts on behalf of a separate Egyptian-Israeli agreement reinforced Moscow's view that divergence rather than convergence characterized Soviet-U.S. aims in the Middle East. Moscow questioned Washington's seriousness about détente.

During the following year the relationship continued to be troubled. Moscow resented the Camp David process that brought an Egyptian-Israeli treaty on March 26, 1979, without Soviet participation; the encumbrances that Washington placed in the way of greater trade and technological imports from the United States; U.S. attention to the normalization of Sino-American relations, at the expense, Moscow thought, of Soviet-American relations; and the fracas in August–September 1979 over the Soviet "combat brigade" in Cuba. Developments in Afghanistan and Iran further aggravated the Soviet-American relationship: A Soviet-backed communist coup in Kabul in April 1978 triggered an anticommunist nationalist guerrilla war that brought increasingly blatant Soviet involvement, culminating in December 1979 in a formal Soviet military invasion to prop up its Afghan puppets; and the toppling of the pro-Western regime of the shah in February 1979 ushered in a time of turmoil in Iran, highlighted by the seizure of U.S. embassy personnel in Tehran in early November 1979 and Moscow's unhelpful attitude throughout.

Symptomatic of the soured state of Soviet relations with the United States was the imbroglio over Cuba—it was hardly a crisis—that erupted in July 1979. Soon after President Carter returned from his Vienna meeting with Brezhnev, reports surfaced in Washington of a Soviet military buildup in Cuba. The Administration's mishandling of the issue led to an escalation of tensions with Moscow out of all proportion to any substantive threat. Terming the Soviet combat brigade of twenty-six hundred men, forty tanks, sixty armored personnel carriers, and other equipment an "unacceptable" military presence, Carter apparently expected the Kremlin to make some token concessions or conciliatory statements assuring the United States of the nonthreatening character of these troops, if only in the interest of strengthening his hand against the opponents of SALT II in the U.S. Senate. But Moscow obdurately denied that any buildup had taken place, insisting that the Soviet military presence in Cuba had not significantly changed since the 1962 Khrushchev-Kennedy understanding that settled the Cuban missile crisis.

Moscow refused to budge and successfully faced down Washington's efforts to pressure a change in the size and character of the Soviet military presence in Cuba. The advent of the Iranian hostage crisis in November 1979 and the Soviet invasion of Afghanistan the following month finished off efforts to improve Soviet-American relations during the Carter Administration.

During the 1970s, however, all was not tension and disagreement. After Nixon's 1972 visit to Moscow and the signing of the SALT I agreement, the two countries concluded a series of agreements covering such diverse fields as science, public health, culture, space, housing, agriculture, oceanography, and nuclear energy, whose underlying rationale—at least for Washington—was the creation of a network of interdependence that would help stabilize and strengthen détente in the political-military fields.

Nonetheless, in the early 1980s, largely as a result of the Soviet arms buildup in Europe and its involvement in Afghanistan, Soviet-American relations were at an all-time low. When Ronald Reagan entered the White House in January 1981, he brought with him a profoundly hostile attitude toward the Soviet Union, which he characterized as an "evil empire." Within days of taking office, he said that the only morality Soviet leaders recognize "is what will further their cause, meaning they reserve unto themselves the right to commit any crime, to lie, to cheat in order to obtain that."[4]

The Soviet press quickly responded in kind, but the Kremlin, though blaming the United States for poisoning the atmosphere of relations between the two countries, sounded a few conciliatory notes. After all, it had negotiated agreements with the conservative, anticommunist Nixon Administration, so it approached Ronald Reagan in much the same way. At the twenty-sixth CPSU congress in late February 1981, Brezhnev said there was a need for "an active dialogue at all levels" and "we are prepared to have this dialogue," and he suggested the possibility of a summit conference.[5] But none of his proposals—for example, the suggestions that a special session of the UN Security Council be convened to discuss ways of "improving the international situation and preventing war," or that the two sides agree to

a moratorium on the development in Europe of new medium-range nuclear missile weapons of the NATO countries and the Soviet Union, that is, to freeze the existing quantitative and qualitative level of these weapons, naturally including the U.S. forward-based nuclear weapons in this region,

was attractive to the Reagan Administration, whose agenda gave top priority to a massive and rapid defense buildup and force modernization to counter the growing threat that it perceived from the Soviet Union. Whether on missiles, Afghanistan, Poland, Persian Gulf security, Central America, the Far East, southern Africa, or conventional force levels in Central Europe, Soviet and American leadership perceptions were virtually diametrically different.

In early May, the Soviet media accused Secretary of State Alexander M. Haig, Jr., of "rabid anti-Sovietism and anti-Communism." Condemnations of the Reagan Administration's military buildup intensified, as Moscow mounted a major "peace offensive" hoping to forestall the Pershing-II/cruise missile deployment and to split the Western allies by playing on West European fears of Reagan's inexperience, strident anti-Soviet rhetoric, and opposition to the Soviet-European natural-gas pipeline project.

U.S.-SOVIET RELATIONS ON THE EVE OF PERESTROIKA

Throughout 1982 and 1983 Soviet-American relations went from bad to worse, leaving little of détente intact. In Europe, Moscow alleged U.S. interference in Poland's internal affairs, when the Reagan Administration imposed sanctions against the Jaruzelski regime in the wake of the crackdown on Solidarity; decried U.S. opposition to East-West trade and the natural gas pipeline accord (Reagan grudgingly lifted sanctions against participating American and West European firms in November 1982); and bitterly opposed the deployment of Pershing-II missiles, using propaganda, pressure, and infiltration of antiwar groups in an attempt to forestall the deployment that began in November 1983. In the Third World, Moscow expanded its military commitments to Syria, opposed U.S. involvement in Lebanon, and continued to wage its war in Afghanistan; in Central America, it used Cuba to funnel arms to rebels in El Salvador and build up the Sandinista government in Nicaragua; in Africa, it denounced U.S. backing of South Africa, involvement in the nonaggression treaty that South Africa and Mozambique signed in March 1984, and hostility toward "progressive" regimes; and in Southeast Asia, it upheld Vietnam's policy in Kampuchea and Laos. Moscow's mistrust was heightened by fears that Washington intended to provide China with advanced weaponry and technology. The USSR's downing of a civilian Korean airliner on the night of August 31–September 1, 1983, which Reagan called a "crime against humanity," occasioned a Soviet charge that the United States was "mounting a worldwide rabid anti-Soviet campaign."

Beyond the specifics of Soviet-American disagreements and differing perceptions of security and international problems, and even beyond the stridency and anger that characterized so many of their public exchanges, there was a dangerous impasse over how and what to negotiate. Perhaps more than ever before in the postwar period, Soviet leaders discerned in the attitudes and actions of the United States "ruling circles" confirmation of their worst fears of a sorely wounded but still powerful capitalist America trying to stem its decline by recourse to military power and ideological warfare. They saw in Reagan's policies a "crusade against communism," a basic unwillingness to negotiate, and a propensity toward high-risk, unpredictable behavior. On the eve of the Pershing-II deployment, a Soviet diplomat averred that "détente has been deliberately murdered by the United States."[6] Aleksandr N. Yakovlev, director of a leading Soviet think tank, told a Japanese audience that "our relations with the United States are indeed at a very low level, whatever yardstick we use. A lot of bitterness, unpleasantness, and danger—I would say much danger—have accumulated in these relations."[7] Yet despite some early attempts to improve the Soviet Union's foreign policy position, by the early 1980s the Kremlin leadership had essentially failed to compete successfully with the United States, and faced a most ominous set of choices. With domestic productivity declining, and the relative burden of defense expenditures on the economy increasing, there seemed to be no way for the Soviet Union to prevent a decline in the standard of living without sacrificing its military might and its foreign policy influence abroad.

Perhaps realizing the perilous situation into which they were rapidly drifting, the superpowers agreed in January 1985 to resume formal talks on the whole range of nuclear issues. Fortuitously, and perhaps even providentially, Konstantin Chernenko's death two months later brought to power a new generation of leaders with a political agenda that aimed at transforming the Soviet-American relationship.

A NEW MAN IN THE KREMLIN

The CPSU's new general secretary, elected in March 1985, was born in 1931 in Stavropol, an agricultural area between the Black and Caspian seas. Before graduating from Moscow University in 1955 with a degree in law, he worked on a machine-tractor station and gained recognition as a leader in the Komsomol (the Young Communist League). After joining the party in 1952 he rose rapidly, attracting the attention of Brezhnev and Andropov for his work in the Stavropol region. There he remained throughout his professional career, until called to Moscow in November 1978 to become a member of the CPSU Secretariat, responsible for agriculture. Two years later, he was appointed a voting member of the Politburo as well. He impressed foreign leaders, who describe him as intelligent, extremely self-assured, energetic, well informed, possessed of a solid grasp of difficult issues, unshakable in his views, argumentative, skilled in debate, and shrewd at negotiating. In brief, Gorbachev was a formidable national leader.

During the process of consolidating his power and reordering the country's foreign policy agenda, Gorbachev carried out sweeping personnel changes. Perhaps most important was the elevation of Andrei Gromyko to the ceremonial position of chairman of the Presidium of the Council of Ministers (the titular post of president of the USSR) and his replacement as foreign minister by Eduard Shevardnadze, the head of the Georgian SSR, who had shown himself to be efficient and reform-oriented. In his many appointments in the foreign affairs field, Gorbachev's choices demonstrated the importance that he attached to relations with the United States and with the West in general. Also important was Aleksandr Yakovlev, who came to the United States in the late 1950s as part of the Soviet-American cultural exchange, served many years as ambassador in Canada, contributed much to the intellectual case for glasnost, and had been Gorbachev's closest confidant. All of the many bureaucratic changes were essential for infusing the ministry of foreign affairs with "new thinking," which superseded the "old thinking" associated with Andrei Gromyko's domination of the Ministry of Foreign Affairs for three decades.

By mid-1985 Gorbachev assumed the diplomatic offensive, presenting the United States with a range of arms control proposals for an early summit. The first of the four summits that Gorbachev and Reagan held was convened in Geneva in November 1985 and succeeded in taking the frost out of Soviet-American relations. The second, in Reykjavik, Iceland, in October 1986, foundered on Gorbachev's heavy-handed attempt to kill the SDI. At the third, held in Washington, DC, in December 1987, there was a precedent-setting agreement abolishing an entire category of weapons—intermediate range missiles—and instituting an elaborate procedure for on-site inspection to verify the consequent INF treaty. The fourth was held in Moscow from May 29 to June 2, 1988; while it did not break important new ground, it strengthened the case for regular summits, even in the absence of concrete achievements.

Improved relations with the United States were the centerpiece of Gorbachev's approach to foreign affairs, and arms control dominated his American agenda.

A quantum improvement in U.S.-Soviet relations was partly the result of significant progress toward solutions of regional conflicts, lessening of human rights abuses, and transformation of the Soviet political system (contested elections, political pluralism, the strengthening of the Supreme Soviet, and the striving to establish a legal system that will act as a constraint on the arbitrary exercise of executive power, and so on). There were hopeful signs of change: In Gorky (now Nizhnyi Novgorod) in December 1986, exile came to an end for Andrei D. Sakharov, the Nobel Peace prize winner, father of the Soviet hydrogen bomb, and prominent critic of the regime; many dissidents were released from prison in early 1987, including Yurii Orlov (one of the founders in 1976 of the Moscow Helsinki Group to monitor human rights violations in the USSR), Anatoly Koryagin (a psychiatrist who spoke out against the KGB's misuses of psychiatry to discourage dissent), and Sergei Grigoryants (a literary critic and activist on human rights issues); Soviet Jewish emigration increased from less than 900 in 1986 to more than 70,000 in 1989; glasnost flowered in a wide range of critical commentaries on communist rule and misdeeds and in the publication of previously suppressed works by writers such as George Orwell, Arthur Koestler, Alexander Solzhenitsyn, and Boris Pasternak; and in January 1988 legislation was passed making it illegal to incarcerate individuals in psychiatric hospitals controlled by the secret police on the basis of hearsay and without judicial approval.

The Bush Administration was slow to react to panoply of Gorbachev's changes. For months after coming to office in January 1989, it delayed taking any stand on key issues, pleading the need to familiarize itself with the situation. A key report submitted to the president in April argued that the process of change introduced by Gorbachev was likely to continue even if he were deposed. The debate within the administration was basically between skeptics and cautious optimists— between those who argued that Gorbachev wanted a respite (*peredyshka*) to gain time to modernize the Soviet economy and better prepare the USSR for continued military-political rivalry with the United States in the twenty-first century, and those who saw his reforms as aiming at a fundamental restructuring (*perestroika*) of Soviet foreign policy and society.

Gorbachev's acquiescence in the disintegration of the Soviet imperial system in Eastern and Central Europe convinced Bush that the era of the Cold War was ending. In mid-October 1989, a month after meeting with Shevardnadze in Wyoming, Secretary of State James Baker declared, "We want perestroika to succeed." Reservations about arms control, Afghanistan, and sundry issues remained, but a month later, with the opening of the Berlin Wall, the success of peaceful revolutions against communism in East Germany and Czechoslovakia, and Gorbachev's visit to Rome to meet with the Pope, there could be no denying the transformation of East-West relations.

Gorbachev's signal historical importance lies in his public recognition that the USSR was suffering from systemic dysfunctions. The only solution to these dysfunctions was to embark on a systemwide reform that, he hoped, would revitalize the Soviet system and restore the popularity of socialism. In the tradition of previous Soviet leaders, Gorbachev recognized that domestic constraints required a shifting of foreign policy priorities. Unlike previous leaders, however, he viewed these constraints as endemic to the Soviet system. If the system was to survive, he argued, it must learn to deal with these constraints realistically, rather than simply tolerate them.

Gorbachev thus laid a groundwork for long-term improvements in Soviet relations with the West. His approach was essentially conciliatory, as he made major concessions on key issues affecting arms control, reduction of Soviet forces, self-determination in Eastern Europe, human rights, settlement of regional conflicts, and participation in the tackling of key global problems. Under his leadership, the hoary bugbear of ideological conflict all but disappeared from Soviet policy considerations.

Yet, for all his attempts to break the mold of his predecessors, in many ways he remained bound by it. To the end he opposed any movement toward federalism, even sending troops to squash the movements toward political autonomy in Georgia and Lithuania. He opposed any meaningful economic reforms, including the "500 Days" program of gradual transition toward privatization proposed by his own leading economists, and subsequently embraced by Boris Yeltsin. He remained ambivalent about true freedom of the press and meaningful political choice, insisting always that the Communist Party retain its tutelage over society and guide it toward a reacceptance of socialist values. By stubbornly refusing to break decisively with the regime's autocratic past, despite the populace's obvious disdain for Marxist-Leninist ideology, he sealed the demise of the USSR and made the transition to democracy more painful. Whether this was due to his own unwillingness to recognize that society had outgrown any further attempts to sanitize and salvage Marxism-Leninism, or to the stubborn recalcitrance of the party bureaucracy, in either case, it quickly became apparent to Russians after the August 1991 that only with the demise of the USSR could the search for a new foundation for Russian foreign policy begin.

THE ABANDONMENT OF IDEOLOGY

Gorbachev's domestic policies and structural changes undermined the foundations of the centralized, hierarchical system that Lenin founded and that Stalin totalitarianized. In the process of implementing glasnost, Gorbachev permitted a torrent of criticism, including exposés of systemic and endemic criminality and brutality, and ended the Communist Party's monopoly on power. The anger and despair over the tyranny that characterized Soviet rule for so long were captured in the slogan, seen often in Soviet rallies and protests: "Communism—Seven Decades on the Road to Nowhere."

Even more than the average person, the elite knew how irrelevant Marxism-Leninism had been in guiding foreign policy. Whether Gorbachev was a strategist with a coherent vision, or a politician increasingly driven to ever more desperate tactical moves in order to hold power is still the subject of debate. It is clear, though, that he ended the penchant for "creative" reinterpretations of the tenets of Marxism-Leninism, which was so prominent a part of the Soviet foreign policy establishment in the past. "New Political Thinking" meant that Soviet scholars no longer sought typologies and explanations that fit into doctrinally devised makeshift boxes. Ideology lost its legitimating function within the Soviet communist hierarchy and its usefulness as a medium for communication within a severely splintered world communist movement.

Deideologization, what may even be called "the end of ideology," can be illustrated by the changes in the meaning of the term *peaceful coexistence*. Prior to

1945, an isolated Soviet Union resorted to the idea of peaceful coexistence to buttress its essentially defensive strategy; peaceful coexistence was a policy dictated by weakness. But by the end of the Stalin period and particularly under Khrushchev and Brezhnev, it was refashioned for a strong, internationally vigorous, imperial Soviet Union. It then applied to a strategy of conflict, short of nuclear war, in which the Soviet camp was strengthened and extended to encompass new members. As an authoritative Soviet publication explained:

> Peaceful coexistence is a specific form of class struggle between socialism and capitalism. In peaceful competition with capitalism, the socialist system will win, that is, the socialist method of production has decisive advantages over the capitalist system. Peaceful coexistence concerns relations between states. It does not touch upon relations within states; it does not touch upon the revolutionary struggle for the transformation of society.
>
> Peaceful coexistence among the states of two [different] systems does not mean compromise in ideological questions. The bourgeois and communist world outlooks cannot be reconciled; moreover, this is not necessary for peaceful coexistence among states. Each can maintain its own position on ideological questions without having this serve as a roadblock preventing cooperation in economic questions and in questions concerning international peace and security.
>
> Naturally, the concept of peaceful coexistence as a condition of relations among states is inapplicable to the internal relations of a state. Therefore, the attempts of the revisionists to extend the concept of peaceful coexistence to class relations within a state are absurd. The recognition of the necessity and possibility of peaceful coexistence does not signify rejection of the class struggle, of the idea of the idea of the inevitability of the victory of communism over capitalism.[8] [translated from the original by Nicolai Petro]

What often confused Westerners was the way the term was variously used, at some times to convey a spirit of conciliation and at others, conflict.

Perhaps nothing illustrated the ambiguity of the term better than Khrushchev's attempt to explain away the implied threat in the ominous words "We will bury you." For example, on one occasion, at a reception at the Polish Embassy in Moscow on September 4, 1959, he went out of his way to reaffirm the USSR's belief in the peaceful competition implied in peaceful coexistence and to calm Western uneasiness:

> Some representatives of the capitalist countries reproach me for having allegedly said that we shall bury capitalism. I have already said that I want only one thing—that they should understand me correctly. The imperialists are digging their own grave. Such is their nature. Karl Marx long ago explained how this is being done, but they still do not understand it.
>
> I want to say only one thing: You must know that physically we shall not dig a grave for you. If you like the capitalist system so much, live under capitalism to your heart's content as long as you can, but how long you will be able to do so I cannot tell.[9]

In general, to the Soviets, peaceful coexistence meant competition and incessant struggle in all spheres short of total war. "Imperialist" wars would be resisted, just as all national liberation movements would be aided, irrespective of the effect on Soviet-U.S. relations. Khrushchev and Brezhnev shared the belief that the balance of world power was shifting inexorably toward the Soviet camp and that capitalism was no more capable of preventing the triumph of communism than feudalism was of forestalling the advent of capitalism. Implicit in peaceful coexistence was continued rivalry, endemic suspicion, and unrelenting effort to weaken the adversary in order to alter the correlation of world forces through a combination of political, economic, cultural, and ideological means. As Brezhnev told the 1976 CPSU congress:

> Some bourgeois leaders affect surprise and raise a howl over the solidarity of Soviet Communists with the struggle of other peoples for freedom and progress. This is either outright naiveté or more likely a deliberate befuddling of minds. It could not be clearer, after all, that détente and peaceful coexistence have to do with interstate relations. This means above all that disputes and conflicts between countries are not to be settled by war, by the use or threat of force. Détente does not in the slightest abolish, nor can it abolish or alter, the laws of class struggle.
>
> We make no secret of the fact that we see détente as the way to create more favorable conditions for peaceful socialist and communist construction.[10]

When relations between the Soviet Union and the West began to improve in the early 1970s, the word *détente*—the French world for a relaxation of international tension—was widely used in the West. But in the English language, unlike the French, it connotes not only easing tensions but also developing extensive, friendly relations in all areas of national interaction. During the heady days after the signing of SALT I in May 1972, the Soviets too began to use the word *détente* in conjunction with calls for peaceful coexistence. But the crucial term for the Soviets was *peaceful coexistence,* not *détente.*

Soviet ideology was highly malleable. Policy shifts occasioned by changes in the correlation of forces were incorporated in refurbished ideological formulations. Thus, Khrushchev, recognizing in 1956 that nuclear weapons had made war between great powers unthinkable as a means of acquiring tactical political and strategic advantages, announced in a sweeping doctrinal change that war between capitalism (that is, the United States) and communism (the Soviet Union) was no longer "fatalistically inevitable." But though Khrushchev dropped the inevitability-of-war thesis from Moscow's doctrinal baggage, he did not say that war was impossible, nor did he cease in his efforts to undermine his adversaries and extend Soviet influence, he also did not suggest that peaceful coexistence meant cooperation with other powers to alleviate global ills.

Gorbachev not only used less contentious formulations but drastically revised content as well. In its fourth programmatic document published in October 1985 and adopted at the twenty-seventh congress in February 1986 (the previous party program had been adopted in 1961, the second in 1919, the first—Karl Marx's Communist Manifesto—in 1848), the CPSU declared that

> the peaceful coexistence of states with different social systems is not simply the absence of war. It is an international order under which good-neighborliness and cooperation, not military power, would dominate, and broad exchanges of scientific and technical achievements and cultural values to benefit all peoples would take place.

This roseate formulation was, however, tempered by the assertion that the present era is one "of the transition from capitalism to socialism and communism and of the historic competition of the two world social and political systems[—]an era of the struggle against imperialism [that is, the United States] and its policy of aggression and oppression." At the congress, Gorbachev emphasized the cooperative dimensions of peaceful coexistence:

> We are realists and are perfectly well aware that the two worlds are divided by very many things, and deeply divided, too. But we also see clearly that the need to resolve most vital problems affecting all humanity must prompt them to interaction.
>
> Such interaction is essential in order to prevent nuclear catastrophe, in order that civilization could survive. The realistic dialectics of present-day development consists in a combination of competition and confrontation between the two systems and in a growing tendency towards interdependence of the countries of the world community. This is precisely the way, through the struggle of opposites, through arduous effort, groping in the dark to some extent, as it were, that the contradictory but interdependent and in many ways integral world is taking shape.
>
> That means recognizing that in the present situation there is no alternative to cooperation and interaction between all states. Thus, objective conditions—and I stress objective—have arisen in which the confrontation between capitalism and socialism can take place only, and exclusively, in the form of peaceful competition and peaceful rivalry. For us, peaceful coexistence is a political course which the Soviet Union intends to rigorously keep to in the future.[11]

The transformation of *peaceful coexistence* into a phrase meaning cooperation with capitalist societies was basically completed by the fall of 1988. Gorbachev's political opponents, notably Yegor Ligachev, unsuccessfully used the newly defined concept as a symbol in his attack on Gorbachev's entire reform program.

Under Gorbachev, peaceful coexistence was described not as a surreptitious form of class struggle, but as a "universal principle of interstate relations."[12] This turnabout is explained not only as the result of changes in the world scene since détente, but also as the correction of previous errors of judgment. Peaceful coexistence, according to the new political thinking, entailed not only the absence of armed conflict, but the active cooperation of all states in all spheres.

Class interests were thus subordinated to the notion of "common human interests"—i.e., those interests that threaten the existence of mankind and cannot be resolved by the efforts of single nations or small groups of nations. These interests, according to Aleksandr Bovin, "set an objective limit to class confrontation in the international arena—the threat of self-annihilation."[13]

If ideology is seen as an important signpost in the evolution of Soviet foreign policy, then changes wrought by Gorbachev were truly remarkable. In a nutshell, foreign minister Eduard Shevardnadze has described them as the "de-ideologicization of international relations."[14] Yet, although class struggle and the ideological approach had been rejected as the source of many of the current problems of Soviet foreign policy, Gorbachev had only the vaguest answer as to what should take their place. His inability to see that society at large had rejected the values of Marxism-Leninism meant that the task of defining a new national interest would fall to his successor, Boris Yeltsin.

YELTSIN AND STRATEGIC PARTNERSHIP WITH AMERICA

In many ways, Yelstin's biography is that of a typical Soviet bureaucrat. Born in 1931 into a peasant family in Sverdlovsk oblast (now Yekaterinburg), he began his career as a construction engineer in a large factory. He proved to be an effective organizer and soon came to the attention of the regional Party committee, which appointed him party secretary (chief local executive) for Sverdlovsk in 1976. When Mikhail Gorbachev became General Secretary in March 1985, he invited Yeltsin to join the CPSU Secretariat, and in December 1985 he appointed Yeltsin to lead the Moscow city party organization, by tradition one of the most influential in the country. Gorbachev asked Yeltsin to root out opposition to perestroika, which he did with considerable zeal, gaining many enemies in the process.

Yeltsin won popular acclaim by calling for an end to the special privileges enjoyed by the nomenklatura, and by appearing often in public, even riding public transportation with his fellow citizens.

Increasingly disillusioned with the slow pace of change, at a Central Committee meeting in October 1987 Yeltsin attacked not only his politburo colleague Yegor Ligachev for opposing reform, but also Gorbachev for failing to make tough choices and surrounding himself with sycophants. Removed from office and publicly humiliated, popular support saved him from a minor posting in the Urals. Instead, he remained in Moscow, nominally as deputy minister for construction, and began to rebuild his political career in alliance with more radical reformers. Standing for election in Moscow in the 1989 elections to the new Congress of People's Deputies, Yeltsin won over 90% of the popular vote despite official harassment and the opposition of Gorbachev.

In July 1990 he dramatically resigned his Communist Party membership, and called on the CPSU to end control over the army, police, and economy. Less than a year later, he won election as the first popularly elected president of Russia. His opposition to the attempted coup of August 19–21, 1991, consolidated his image as the most stalwart opponent of the old regime. Immediately after the coup, he signed a series of decrees outlawing the activities of the CPSU on Russian territory and nationalizing its assets. By December 1991, all real power had passed from the center to the republics; Gorbachev resigned his figurehead position as head of the USSR, the union was dissolved and a new Commonwealth of Independent States was instituted by common agreement of Russia, Belarus, and the Ukraine.

Even before the formal demise of the USSR, however, Yeltsin and his young foreign minister Andrei Kozyrev had set out to establish a distinct Russian foreign policy agenda toward the United States. Its guiding principles were already in place when he was elected Russian president, allowing Kozyrev to reiterate them immediately following the August coup attempt: the United States and the other Western democracies are now to be deemed as much friends and even perspective allies of democratic Russia, as they were enemies of the totalitarian USSR.

The fear that the tenor of Russian-American relations could be quickly reversed from hostility to amity underlies Russian attempts to promote a "mature strategic partnership" with the United States. According the Russian Foreign Ministry, such a partnership was now possible because Russia now shared the same basic values of the Western democracies, including the view propounded by the Reagan Administration that the national interests of democratic states do not conflict, but rather complement each other in the international arena.[15] According to the Russian Foreign Ministry, the major long range task of the West should be the creation of a democratic Russian state open to the rest of the world, and the transformation of the volatile CIS states into a region of stability and democracy.

Since these tasks are vital to the security of both Russia and the United States, the two countries should work jointly to achieve them. Russia recognizes the United States' unique historical opportunity to assist democratic developments. At the same time, however, Russia insists on playing a key role, particularly in the CIS, in encouraging regional stability and democratization.

PROBLEMS IN RUSSIAN-AMERICAN RELATIONS

As much as the United States and the Soviet Union once confronted each other, and sought to undermine each other's influence, Kozyrev argued that it is now in the mutual interest of both countries to support each other in a special partnership that will play a dominant role in guaranteeing a democratic and peaceful international system after the fall of communism. Given its financial resources and diplomatic status, the United States is in a unique position to assist the stabilization of the CIS by financial support and encouraging Western investment in the former Soviet states. The quid pro quo, as the Russians see it, is that given the West's unwillingness to commit troops to quell ethnic and civil conflicts in the region, Russia would assume the responsibilities of regional peacekeeping and the immediate financial support of collapsing regional economies.

The strategic partnership is to be coordinated action in five major arenas. (1) In obtaining guarantees of a global security regime. Key initiatives here are the ratification of START I, which was formally implemented in December 1994, the ratification of START II, and the strengthening of the nuclear nonproliferation regime. (2) In peacekeeping. The end of the cold war has taken the lid off a number of regional conflicts. Just as the United States has taken a role in preserving the peace in Somalia and Haiti, so Russia must take a role in preserving domestic tranquillity in the regions on its border. As Foreign Minister Kozyrev remarked,

> The principle difference, between Somalia and Abkhazia or Tadjikistan is that we cannot 'leave' the conflict points of the former Soviet Union as the Americans left Somalia. I think that even the United States, if similar conflicts were to occur next to them, close to wide open borders, could not permit themselves [this luxury].[16]

(3) There should be an explicit recognition of the "special role and responsibility of Russia" for stability within the states of the former Soviet Union. Logically, this entails special support of Russian efforts to promote economic ties and prosperity in the entire region, which necessarily means closer economic ties with Russia.

(4) The West and the United States in particular, should support Russia's concern for the equal treatment and concern for human rights violations within the

former Soviet republics. Kozyrev has remarked that the problem of human rights for Russians in the Near Abroad is so important for Russia because nearly every Russian citizen has a relative or someone they know who has experienced some form of discrimination or been forced to become a refugee. Besides, in light of America's emphasis on human rights issues, refusal to acknowledge the violation of such rights in the Near Abroad would smack of hypocrisy.

(5) There should be Western assistance for Russian integration into the world economy. As the Russian foreign ministry sees it, political partnership between Russia and the United States should not only provide important support for the reform process inside Russia, but should also encourage Western investment in the region. Russia's key priorities here are a speedy acceptance into regional and international financial arrangements (particularly the GATT and the World Trade Organization) that would allow for the reduction and eventual elimination of tariff barriers against Russian goods. At the same time, support for Russia as "the locomotive of economic reforms in the CIS" would help to stabilize the entire region.

Kozyrev has been severely criticized in Russia for uncritically adopting positions advocated by the United States, and for sacrificing Russia's long-term interests for the dubious privilege of becoming America's junior partner. Since 1994, although the rhetoric of partnership still ostensibly guides the relationship, a number of issues have arisen that indicate that the strategic objectives of the two states do not always coincide. The most significant areas of disagreement have been the expansion of NATO, the export of Russian nuclear technology to Iran, and arms control issues.

NATOs plans to expand eastward have been the greatest sore point between Russia and the United States. There is near universal agreement in the Russian government that the enlargement of NATO, absent a solid foundation of cooperation between Russia and the West, would undermine Russian security and make the reintegration of the CIS more difficult. If NATO is indeed meant eventually to include all the former Eastern bloc countries, Russian officials ask rhetorically, then why expand it in a divisive, piecemeal fashion? If NATO is meant to be an alliance that includes Russia, then whom is it meant to defend against? In September 1995 both Yeltsin and Defense Minister Grachev reiterated that if the Baltic States are encouraged to join NATO, then Russia would feel forced to support the creation of a new military-political bloc of CIS states. Russia will seek to do all that it can to prevent NATO expansion, fearing that the real purpose of such an expansion is to draw a new curtain between it and the rest of Europe.

The issue of the sale of Russian nuclear technology for peaceful purposes loomed large in mid-1995, when the United States urged Russia not to sell two low-grade nuclear reactors to Iran, threatening Russia with unspecified aid cut-offs if it did.

While from Americas perspective the issue was one of nuclear nonproliferation and preventing Iran from becoming a dominant player in the Middle East, in Russian domestic politics the issue quickly became one of the double standard America was applying to protect its own commercial interests. In this view, why should Russia give up a lucrative contract with Iran, a member in good standing of the International Atomic Energy Agency (IAEA) which inspects nuclear development programs around the world, when at the same time the United States is helping the North Koreans to build the same type of reactors in a country notorious for flaunting international inspection. If a state in good standing with the IAEA can be denied access to civilian nuclear technology because of the suspicions of another state, the Russian government argued, then there is little incentive for any state not to go it alone. Despite vociferous protests, the Russian deal did go ahead.

In the arena of arms control, disagreements have loomed over the ratification of START II Treaty. Although President Yeltsin submitted the treaty to the Duma in June 1995, ratification is far from ensured. Russian legislators have criticized the treaty for placing an excessive financial burden on the budget. Russia will have to commit scarce funds to destroy its heavy ICBMs, and additional resources to replace them with single-warhead missiles at a time when funds for housing and military pay are already depleted. Some Duma leaders have advocated extending the START II time frame beyond 2003 so that weapons need not be withdrawn before the end of their usefulness. Also, unilateral U.S. changes in the interpretation of the Anti-Ballistic Missile (ABM) Treaty to permit the deployment of Theater Missile Defense (TMD) systems have led to calls in the Russian Parliament for strict implementation of the ABM treaty as a precondition for ratification of SALT II.

Still, there have been tangible signs of cooperation as well as disagreement. In response to Russian complaints that the restrictive "flank" limitations of the CFE Treaty are unfair and outdated in the post–Cold War environment, NATO has proposed moving some oblasts from one military district to another as a way of allowing Russia greater flexibility in the allocation of its forces.

Also, the Cooperative Threat Reduction (CTR) Program that provides U.S. assistance in dismantling the nuclear and chemical arsenals in the CIS has been quite successful. In addition to dismantling ICBMs, SLBMs, bombers, and chemical weapons, this program provides assistance in accounting, control, protection, transportation and storage of weapons components. Unfortunately, there is increasing pressure in Congress to reduce funding to this program, with the result that the dismantling of weaponry could be delayed.

For its part, the United States has responded with a mixture of early euphoria followed by an equally deep disillusionment. Early on, President Clinton endorsed many of the principles of a strategic partnership in its Charter on US-Russian Partnership and Friendship, signed on June 17, 1992. These principles, reaffirmed at subsequent presidential summits in Vancouver in April 1993 and Moscow in January 1994, declare the relationship to be one of "mature, strategic partnership, based on equality, mutual advantage and recognition of each other's national interests." After the December 1993 elections gave a large share of the votes to extremist Vladimir Zhirinovsky, however, the attitude among U.S. policymakers seems to have shifted to deep pessimism about the prospects for Russian democracy. In a key speech in March 1994, Defense Secretary William J. Perry warned that Russian democracy had a good chance of failing and that "it is possible that Russia will emerge from the turbulence as an authoritarian, militaristic, imperialistic nation hostile to the West."[17]

With the election of a Republican majority in the Congress in 1992, the "new Cold War" as some pundits have already dubbed it, gained support. While former democratic policy advisers like Zbigniew Brzezinksi called for the United States to support "geopolitical pluralism" in the CIS, Republican leaders criticized the President for "turning our foreign policy over to the Russians."[18] One staff member on the Senate Foreign Relations Committee even remarked in a speech that the United States should promote the "encirclement" of Russia with democracies and free market economies, bolstered by NATO protection. It was time, according to this staffer to "start acting like victors in the Cold War, not apologists."[19]

As of this writing, though the future of Russian-American relations looks decidedly less rosy than it did immediately in late 1991, there is still a clear desire on both sides not to allow relations to deteriorate beyond friendly competition. There is evidence of this in the attempts to include Russia in the settlement of the Bosnian conflict, and in the slow pace established for NATO expansion. For its part, Russia has had to show clear signs of progress toward democracy in its efforts to join the Council of Europe, and has worked hard to satisfy the OSCE observers in Chechnya of its good faith in ending the war in Chechnya. Finally, in early 1995 U.S. Chamber of Commerce reported that U.S. companies had become Russia's largest foreign investors. Clearly, even if governments disagree, the expansion of trade relations continues, and this makes a return to the animosity of the past highly unlikely.

PROSPECTS FOR THE FUTURE

Although the pendulum of public sentiment in both nations may well continue to swing between euphoria to hostility, the fundamental quality of Russian-American relations will be based on the mutual recognition of common interests. In order to understand what these are, we must look at both the similarities and dissimilarities between current Russian and past Soviet foreign policy objectives. Like the Soviet Union, Russia seeks to play a key role in international organizations, even though this has burdened it with obligations as well as privileges in the international arena.

Also, Russia includes the former Soviet republics in its sphere of vital security interests. Although it has lost direct control over these regions, it will seek to do everything in its power to ensure compliant regimes on its borders that will take Russia's lead in foreign policy and defense matters.

These, however, should not mask some very significant changes in Russia's foreign policy toward the United States. For one thing, the current Russian definition of partnership is quite different from the limited partnership envisioned by détente. The Soviet leadership envisioned détente as reducing the risk of warfare between states, while permitting the continuation of geopolitical rivalry between the capitalist and communist systems. The current "strategic partnership," by contrast, is based on the assumption of an ideological consensus between Russia and the United States. The removal of ideological hostility, at least theoretically, removes any intellectual impediment to a close partnership.

There is also the opportunity to continue and deepen substantive cooperation between the world's two largest nuclear powers on the reduction of nuclear weapons. By 1990 Soviet-American efforts had brought one hundred and forty countries to sign the Nuclear Nonproliferation Treaty. As bilateral arms negotiations become less important, however, the importance of multilateral cooperation of nuclear weaponry among other states will be enhanced. Prominent Russian analysts have suggested a plan to internationalize nuclear weaponry ("an updated edition of the old Baruch Plan").[20]

Finally, there is today virtually no danger of serious conflict between Russia and the United States in the Third World. Beyond its immediate sphere of security concerns, Russia has chosen not to commit its resources to any distant region of the world. The only real possibility of conflict, therefore would arise from a substantive American involvement in the affairs of the CIS states, which, despite efforts to promote "geostrategic pluralism" is unlikely to gather long-term support either in the United States or among its NATO allies.

Still, in looking ahead it is important that we temper our expectations for Soviet-American relations with an awareness of some persisting sources of the two sides' rivalry. There are geopolitical and societal differences that destine the two countries for some form of competition. Differing values, perceptions, interests, and ambitions cannot be wished away. These need not result in violence or produce hostility like that of the period from 1945 to 1985, but they act as constraints on long-term friendship. It is useful to recall that it took the United States and Great Britain more than one hundred years to realize they were not really implacable enemies.

Similarly, in evaluating future sources of Russian-American tensions, Western leaders must pay serious attention to the views given by the Russian national security elites as explanation for the erratic evolution of Russian foreign policy. First, Russian leaders contend that the United States is unwilling to recognize and deal with Russia as an equal superpower, having legitimate global interests and views that must be considered in the management of the international system.

What George F. Kennan observed regarding the far-reaching changes in Gorbachev's foreign policy may be appropriate for the Russia of Yeltsin and his successors as well:

> That country should now be regarded essentially as another great power, like other great powers—one, that is, whose aspirations and policies are conditioned outstandingly by its own geographic situation, history and tradition, and are therefore not identical with our own but are also not so seriously in conflict with ours as to justify any assumption that the outstanding differences could not be adjusted by the normal means of compromise and accommodation.[21]

Russian-American relations are entering a critical period. But in this we are not unique. Each generation has tended to regard its own challenges as particularly difficult and has wistfully envied previous generations their comparative security and tranquillity. Yesterday's dilemmas seem uncomplicated and manageable when viewed from today's perspective. Time passes and the seemingly insurmountable ills of humans somehow find solutions, however imperfect, that in turn give rise to new problems.

Despite the best efforts of foreign policy leaders, it often seems that both countries are not yet ready to move from hostility to cordiality. Too many psychological, cultural, and historical impediments persist that lead each side to be suspicious of the other. Indeed, historically, except for Russia's brief support of the

North against the South in the American Civil War, it would be difficult to characterize Russian-American relations as friendly. The typical attitude could best be described as cordial indifference. A return to this tradition of cordial indifference is not only possible, but quite likely so long as the vital concerns of one nation do not intrude directly on the vital concerns of the other.

SELECTED BIBLIOGRAPHY

Beschloss, Michael R., and Talbott, Strobe. *At the Highest Levels: The Inside Story of the End of the Cold War.* Boston: Little, Brown and Company, 1993.

Bialer, Seweryn, and Mandelbaum, Michael (eds.). *Gorbachev's Russia and American Foreign Policy.* Boulder, CO: Westview Press, 1988.

Bochkarev, Andrei G., and Mansfield, Don L. (eds.). *The United States and the USSR in a Changing World: Soviet and American Perspectives.* Boulder, CO: Westview Press, 1992.

Boyle, Peter G. *American-Soviet Relations: From the Russian Revolution to the Fall of Communism.* New York: Routledge, 1993.

Clark, Susan L. (ed.). *Gorbachev's Agenda: Changes in Soviet Domestic and Foreign Policy.* Boulder, CO: Westview Press, 1989.

Felshman, Neil. *Gorbachev, Yeltsin, and the Last Days of the Soviet Empire.* New York: St. Martin's Press, 1992.

Gardner, Hall. *Surviving the Millennium: American Global Strategy, the Collapse of the Soviet Empire, and the Question of Peace.* Westport, CT: Praeger, 1994.

Garthoff, Raymond L. *Détente and Confrontation: American-Soviet Relations from Nixon to Reagan.* rev. ed. Washington, DC: Brookings Institution, 1994.

———. *The Great Transition: American-Soviet Relations and the End of the Cold War.* Washington, DC: Brookings Institution, 1994.

Ginsburgs, George, Rubinstein, Alvin Z., and Smolansky, Oles M. (eds.). *Russia and America: From Rivalry to Reconciliation.* Armonk, NY: M.E. Sharpe, 1993.

Hyland, William G. *The Cold War is Over.* New York: Times Books, 1990.

Jervis, Robert, and Bialer, Seweryn (eds.). *Soviet-American Relations After the Cold War.* Durham, NC: Duke University Press, 1991.

Lockwood, Jonathan S. *The Russian View of U.S. Strategy: Its Past, Its Future.* New Brunswick, NJ: Transaction, 1993.

Mandelbaum, Michael, and Talbott, Strobe. *Reagan and Gorbachev.* New York: Vintage Books, 1987.

Mills, Richard. *As Moscow Sees Us: American Politics and Society in the Soviet Mindset.* New York: Oxford University Press, 1991.

Nelson, Keith L. *The Making of Détente: Soviet-American Relations in the Shadow of Vietnam.* Baltimore: Johns Hopkins University Press, 1995.

Oberdorfer, Don. *The Turn: From the Cold War to a New Era: The United States and the Soviet Union, 1983–1990.* New York: Poseidon Press, 1991.

Schweizer, Peter. *Victory.* New York: Atlantic Monthly Press, 1994.

Taubman, William. *Stalin's American Policy.* New York: W.W. Norton, 1982.

Ulam, Adam B. *The Rivals: America and Russia Since World War II.* New York: Viking, 1971.

Yeltsin, Boris. *The Struggle for Russia.* New York: Random House, 1995.

Zacek, Jane Shapiro (ed.). *The Gorbachev Generation: Issues in Soviet Foreign Policy.* New York: Paragon House, 1988.

Zimmerman, William (ed.). *Beyond the Soviet Threat: Rethinking American Security Policy in a New Era.* Ann Arbor: University of Michigan Press, 1992.

NOTES

1. *Pravda,* July 13, 1960.
2. *Khrushchev Remembers* (Boston: Little, Brown, 1970), pp. 546–547.
3. Joseph G. Whelan, *Soviet Diplomacy and Negotiating Behavior: Emerging New Context for U.S. Diplomacy* (Washington, DC: Committee on Foreign Affairs, 1979), pp. 360–361.
4. *New York Times,* January 30, 1981
5. *Pravda,* February 24, 1981
6. *New York Times,* November 26, 1983.
7. *FBIS/USSR International Affairs,* March 9, 1984, p. AA5
8. "Mirnoe sosushchestvovanie" [Peaceful Coexistence], *Diplomaticheskii slovar'* [Diplomatic dictionary], vol. 2 (Moscow: Politizdat, 1961), p. 299.
9. *Soviet News,* No. 4107 (September 8, 1959), p. 142.
10. L.I. Brezhnev, "Report of the CPSU Central Committee and the Immediate Tasks of the Party in Home and Foreign Policy," *Socialism: Theory and Practice,* no. 3 (March 1976), p. 39.
11. *FBIS/SOV/Party Congresses* (February 26, 1986), 0 = 9, 0 = 30.
12. Eduard Shevardnadze, "Dobivat'sia vseob"emliushchei bezopasnosti" *Pravda,* September 28, 1988, p. 4
13. Aleksandr Bovin, "Novoe myshlenie—novaia politika" *Kommunist,* June 1988, p. 121.
14. Shevarnadze, "Dobivat'sia," p. 4.
15. Andrei Kozyrev, "Strategiya partnerstva" *Mezhdunarodnaya zhizn'* no. 5 (1994), pp. 5–6.
16. *Ibid.,* p. 13.
17. Steven Greenhouse, "US to Russia: A Tougher Tone and a Shifting Glance" *New York Times* (March 21, 1994), p. A9
18. "Europe" *The Washington Post,* December 26, 1994, p. A34.
19. *Ibid.*
20. Andrei Kortunov, "Russia and the United States," in Robert D. Backwill and Sergei A. Karaganov, *Damage Limitation of Crisis?* (Washington, DC: Brassey's, 1994), p. 296.
21. George F. Kennan, "Just Another Great Power," *New York Times,* April 9, 1989.

Chapter
14

Russian Foreign Policy: Looking Ahead

*A*re we headed back toward a period of imperial confrontation with an expansionist Russia, or forward toward a "new world order" in which Russia will be a full fledged member of the international community? This question haunts foreign policy analysts and conditions the public's perception of Russian foreign policy initiatives from Iran to Bosnia. Although the answer will be several decades in the making, it is not too early to begin a preliminary assessment of how well the international community and Russia are responding to the opportunities offered by the end of the Cold War.

The precipitous declaration that a "strategic partnership" had been forged between the United States and Russia raised false hopes that Russia would be content with a distinctly subordinate role within the Western alliance. To many in the United States this seemed entirely appropriate because of Russia's economic weakness and its "loss" of the Cold War.

Herein lies one source of misunderstanding between the two nations. Russian policymakers, regardless of political outlook, do not describe themselves as "losers" vis-à-vis the West. Rather, they see themselves as partners in the victory over a common enemy—communist totalitarianism. As Dimitri Simes has noted from his extensive discussions with members of the new Russian political elite:

> Most Russian perceive their country not as a defeated villain, but rather as both the victim of and victor over the Soviet empire. As such, they feel that Russia should be embraced and supported by the community of democratic nations. No special restrictions on Moscow's freedom on international action—beyond say, what the United States would be prepared to accept for itself—are considered justified.[1]

Russia emerged from this struggle terribly weakened and in need of Western assistance. Hence Russian leaders feel that the West should help Russian, which peacefully withdrew from Europe and the CIS and which has continued to shore up the economies of its neighbors through economic credits and subsidized sales of raw materials, to become a full partner in the international system; while recognizing, as Foreign Minister Kozyrev put it, that "a partnership based on common values and even sympathies does not at all imply renouncing a firm, occasionally even aggressive policy of defending one's national interests.[2]

This divergence of views between the Russian and Western elites is exacerbated by the failure to consider the first five to ten years after the demise of the USSR as a transitional period, during which new Russian foreign perceptions are being formed. Years of regarding Soviet foreign policy as a natural extension of the "Russian" national interest has led Western analysts to underestimate the trauma involved in creating a new foreign policy for a new country—Russia.

In many respects, therefore, postcommunist Russia is a fundamentally different state from the USSR. Its borders have been pushed several hundred miles eastward. It has lost most previous ports of access to the Baltic and Black Seas. Although still tremendously rich in natural resources, it is now far more dependent on its neighbors for transportation and processing. More than ever, Russia is on Europe's periphery; and it faces new security problems in the south, in Central Asia, and in East Asia. The impact of this fundamental geopolitical realignment is only just beginning to be understood by the Russian elite—and by their counterparts in the West. Finally, regionalism, the new multiheaded monster of the CIS, has also raised its head in Russia, threatening to undermine the national unity, as in Chechnya.

On the plus side, although its population is smaller, Russia is now more ethnically compact and has proved to be more politically stable than many observers had anticipated. Democracy has always been a messy way of conducting political affairs, and Russian democracy has been messier than most because it lacks the benefit of established patterns and avenues through which to exercise political choices.

In this political transition Russia did not have any preexisting alternatives to fall back on. The communist regime had done a most thorough job of eradicating those national political and cultural traditions that could have formed the basis for popular rule. Having suffered under communist rule the longest, Russia is having a more difficult time reconnecting the threads of its national political tradition than the countries that fell under communist rule as a consequence of the Second World War. Moreover, it has had to undertake the arduous task of constructing a new social and economic order, at the same time that it is forging a new basis for foreign policy and redefining the Russian national interest.

Adding to the confusion is the fact that Russian foreign policy, while different in many of its basic assumptions, is still carried out by personnel trained in the Soviet period. The result is a schizophrenic foreign policy, whose contradictions are exacerbated by the fact that foreign policy issues are often used as targets in the domestic political debate over Russia's future, or in squabbles among competing personalities in the government.

With time these growing pains of the transitional period should ease and give way to a new and distinctively Russian foreign policy agenda. Some of the differences between that agenda and its Soviet predecessor are already becoming apparent. Thus, unlike the Soviet Union, Russia does not want to change the international system, but only to adapt itself to it. Although the Soviets participated in international institutions, it was always with the understanding that this reflected temporary accommodation, not acceptance of the prevailing market-oriented international system. This two-track policy of negotiating while simultaneously preparing for the inevitable demise of capitalism led to feelings in the West of Soviet duplicity that ultimately scuttled détente. We now know that it also fed the frustrations of Soviet career diplomats, some of whom felt they were forced to take positions contrary to the national interests of their country. Before leaving office, former Soviet foreign minister Eduard Shevardnadze spoke of the "dogmatism" and "missionary zeal" that "drastically limited the possibilities for rational and controlled action," while the former Soviet Ambassador to the United Nations, Aleksandr Belonogov, remarked that "the super-ideologicization [*sverkhideologizatsiia*] of foreign policy in the past often strongly prevented us from seeing where our interests lay in the international arena. . . ."[3]

For the first time in generations Russian interests are defined in regional rather than global terms. Contemporary Russian analysts look at the world through the prism of *realpolitik,* assessing which nations can threaten the domestic tranquillity of Russia proper. The result is a concentric view of Russian national security interests that places highest priority on the CIS states; next on relations with the United States, the West European powers, China and Japan; next on the East European, Middle Eastern and middle level Asian states (including India); and with the lowest priority assigned to states most distant from Russia. By contrast, in its latter decades the Soviet Union was impelled to project power and influence in all parts of the world. Regarding the Third World, by contrast with the Soviet Union, Russia sees little need for anything but trade relations. This concentric vision of national priorities seems to be widely accepted across the breadth of the Russian political spectrum, and it offers important insights into the long-term patterns that may emerge in Russian diplomacy.

Clearly, the region of greatest importance to Russia is the Commonwealth of Independent States. In this region Russia seeks to establish a collective security arrangement and close cooperation for a variety of reasons: to prevent isolation; to enhance economic prosperity; to improve commerce and living conditions since this has a direct impact on regional stability; to protect Russians in the Near Abroad so that they will have an internal source for redress of human rights grievances and not be forced to emigrate; and, possibly, to assert neo-imperial ambitions in ways that would enhance self-esteem at home and acceptance as a great power abroad.

The second most important region to Russia seems to be Europe. Russia strives to anchor herself to Europe economically, politically, and militarily and to become a key component in any further European integration. Russia seeks a collective security arrangement that would link Russia militarily and politically to other European states, and make the preservation of territorial integrity and threat of nationalism issues of common concern and responsibility. It has legitimate security concerns along its western border from the Baltic to the Black Sea. Much hinges on what kind of relationship it fashions with NATO and the leading powers of Western Europe, as well as the United States.

While the West argues that such a collective security arrangement already exists in the form of NATO, Russia is promoting the OSCE (Organization for Security and Cooperation in Europe) as an alternative structure because the latter is less dominated by Western Europe and the United States, and because it originated as a pan-European and transatlantic forum that included Eastern Europe and the Soviet Union. Despite notable differences, there is common agreement on the need for some new collective security structure that will embrace all of Europe, from the Atlantic to the Urals, and it is quite possible that some sort of compromise in this area will be reached. There are cautious grounds for optimism in NATO's agreement to permit a modification of the 1990 Conventional Forces in Europe (CFE) agreement that will sanction larger Russian troop deployments in the Caucasus region in recognition of the unrest that faces Russia there. The loss of the westernmost CIS states has made Russia's identification with Europe an issue of even greater importance than ever before, and all attempts to separate Russia from European-wide trends will be strongly opposed.

Asia, not traditionally a region of prominence for Russian foreign policy, will become much more critical as Siberia and the Far East, driven by regionalism and economic necessity, pursue their own course. If Russia ever becomes an economic powerhouse, it will be through the development of this region's fabulous natural resources. No one has a greater vested interested in this area than local elites. In Asia, therefore, Russia's primary interest lies in reducing instability along the Chinese border and in the northern Pacific region generally. Maintaining good relations with China, for both trade and security, is of paramount importance and also serves to put added pressure on Japan to come to terms on the Kurile Islands dispute.

The most significant threat to regional stability, after the coming struggle to succeed Deng Xiaoping in China, is the collapse of the communist regime in North Korea. Having come to the conclusion that the South will eventually absorb the North, Russia has abandoned Soviet support of North Korea and embraced the South, in the hope that this will position it well to profit from the future reunification of the Korean peninsula. As for the rest of Asia, Russian commercial interests have a long way to go before they will become important to foreign policy considerations.

Least significant from the current vantage point of Russian foreign policy is the Third World. With the exception of the Islamic Middle East, which because of its proximity and potential for exporting religious fundamentalism remains a key concern, Russia has all but abandoned this region to its fate. While it may be true that both Russia and less-developed countries (LDCs) face similar problems in their economic transition, Russia's present self-absorption make attention to matters far beyond its periphery highly unlikely.

Finally, relations with the United States, in Soviet times of paramount importance to the leadership, are likely to remain important, if only because of nuclear-related issues. The threat of nuclear confrontation and global ideological rivalry have passed, leading to unwarranted optimism that other issues would quickly be resolved in their wake. Indeed, many Russian and American diplomatic historians like to point out that there are no abiding reasons for enmity between the two nations since their interests rarely intersected before World War II.

A return to the indifference that characterized Russian-American relations before the October Revolution is not likely because of the very different global positions that these two nations came to occupy after World War II and that they still hold today thanks to their nuclear status. In addition, while Russia has been forced to rethink its forward global position, the United States continues to play a very active role in influencing political developments in regions throughout the world, including regions like the CIS deemed to be of vital interest to Russia. Paradoxically, this one-sided withdrawal from the world arena has heightened Russian sensitivity to American involvement overseas, especially on its flanks. Having lost the ability it once had as a global superpower to force the United States to be more circumspect, many in the Russian political elite resent America's prominence on the world stage.

However, looking ahead, there is reason to believe that Russian-American relations will remain important, not just to Russia but also to the United States. For many years to come, the centerpiece of Russian-American relations will remain the common interest in nuclear arms control. Both countries are committed to sharp reductions in strategic nuclear forces. Even if the START I and II treaties are fully implemented, the countries will remain major nuclear powers. Follow-up agreements in the realms of inspection and verification, and in the chemical and biological fields, all are high on their defense agendas. Even as the danger of nuclear confrontation between the two countries recedes, the difficulties in implementing the existing agreements will, by their very nature, become more time-consuming and attention-riveting. Benign neglect is just not a feasible option for either country. As has frequently been noted, the devil is in the details. According to General Colin L. Powell, then-chairman of the U.S. Joint Chiefs of Staff, in carrying out the START agreements, "there are over 80 different kinds of notifications which cover each system and facility from cradle to grave," and more than "a dozen different kinds of inspections." These include on-site inspections that monitor missile plants, share data, ensure a ban on encrypting radio signals, and oversee the dismantling of warheads and missiles.[4]

Other points of convergence mentioned earlier in this book include a shared interest in stability in Europe and the Middle East, Russia's engagement in the world economy and reorientation along market-based lines, and cooperation in the United Nations. Two other issues may be noted briefly: energy and the environment. Russia possesses enormous untapped resources of oil and natural gas. Tapping into this wealth is a major attraction for U.S. and Western multinational corporations, who see Russia and some of the oil-rich CIS states like Kazakhstan, Azerbaijan and Turkmenistan as a counterweight to reliance on Iran and the Arab states of the Persian Gulf.

In addition, Russia's environmental situation has a direct impact on Europe. The decades of communist despotism and centrally controlled economic planning will be remembered for generations as a time of unparalleled despoliation and destruction of natural and human resources. There is no more polluted part of the world than the former Soviet Union. Another Chernobyl-style nuclear accident, which spread radioactive waste over thousands of square miles, could easily recur. There are still some forty Chernobyl-type reactors operating in Russia, the

Ukraine, and Eastern Europe under unsafe conditions. Nuclear dumping in the high seas by Russia is raising further international protests. All of this mandates closer collaboration between American and Russian leaders.

THE STRATEGIC OBJECTIVES OF RUSSIAN FOREIGN POLICY

Russia is today weaker and more disoriented than at any time since the end of the Russian Civil War. While some attribute this disorientation to the debate between Eurasianists and Atlanticists over the "soul" of Russian foreign policy (described in Chapter Five). In fact, the differences between these two groups are more tactical than substantive. Neither group denies that Russia is a country whose cultural roots firmly link it to Europe and to the West. With 80% of the country's natural resources located east of the Urals, Eurasianists argue that Russia's major sources of political opportunity (as well as the major sources of potential instability) lie in Asia. In an increasingly multipolar world Russia can ill afford to focus attention exclusively on Europe and the United States. Some supporters of the shift from "Atlanticism," to "Eurasianism" see it as merely a synonym for "pragmatism;" the opposite of the "inverse moralism" that led foreign ministry officials to idealize the West in 1992.[5]

Foreign policy analysts seek to discern the future even in uncertain circumstances. It is not too early to ask which of the many competing visions currently being discussed will survive to become part of the permanent concerns of Russian foreign policy after the current transition period has ended.

It is already clear that Russia will seek to reestablish its role as a great power— an essential actor balancing competing interests in a multipolar world. At his very first press conference after being appointed Foreign Minister, Yevgeni Primakov reasserted Russia's intention to be treated as a great power. What this is likely to mean in practice is that Russia will utilize its position in the Eurasian heartland to act as a power-broker and to prevent the emergence of opposing coalitions in Europe, Central Asia, or the Far East. As a territorially satisfied power, Russia's objectives in these outlying regions will not be territorial aggrandizement, but trade advantages and stability on its borders.

It is likewise easy to predict that the CIS will continue to be Russia's main foreign policy priority. Though it has neither the capability nor the inclination to reabsorb any of these regions by force, Russia will likely use everything short of force to make sure that the domestic and foreign policies of these states coincide with Russian priorities. The ultimate objective, foreshadowed by the June 1995 accord on economic and political integration signed with Belarus, is to establish an European Union–like transparency in political, economic, and security arrangements in the region. It may take several generations before the trust needed to establish such arrangements is in place, but reintegration of the former Soviet republics remains a driving force in Russian politics, and hence an important objective for Russian foreign policy.

In Europe, Russia will strive to become a permanent partner in the process of European integration. At the same time that it is strengthening ties with Europe, however, it is safe to predict that Russia will also be devoting more resources to becoming an Asian power. This predictable consequence of Moscow's historical neglect of Siberia is made all the more likely by the rapid growth of federalist sentiments and independent commercial activities in the region.

RUSSIAN FOREIGN POLICY AFTER YELTSIN

How certain, however, can we be that Russia's currently relatively benign course in world affairs will continue? Many analysts have speculated openly that the resources of Russian civil society may be too shallow to sustain democracy. The collapse of the economy, they say, along with the weakness of democratic traditions, and the resentment against the loss of empire and superpower status could all easily combine to make Russia's current democratic experiment a brief interlude preceding a chauvinistic and aggressively militaristic regime—a "Weimar Russia" to use the phrase popularized by former National Security Council staffer Steven Sestanovich—destined by analogy to be a prelude to a Hitlerite Russia.

Émigré writer Alexander Yanov has written that Russia has historically dealt with the threat of systemic crisis "by the establishment of a garrison-state based on a fortress mentality." He speculates that a form of reactionary, xenophobic, "Orthodox patriotic" constellation of alienated Great Russians could serve as the cement for a new Russian elite. Under such circumstances, a beefed-up military establishment, again commanding a disproportionate percentage of the national wealth and restored to privileged status, could be relied on to defend the empire from threats, both external and domestic. The December 1995 communist victory in the Duma elections, and the prospect of a communist victory in the June 1996 presidential elections have heightened concerned about Russia reverting to confrontation with the West.

Russia's current foreign policy priorities could certainly change dramatically if domestic political priorities shift. A more nationalistic government in Moscow could easily conceive of some distinctively Russian concept of a "new world order" that is both anti-Western and anticapitalist. Domestically, such a shift would find favor among the lingering remnants of the old bureaucracy, still solidly entrenched in the security forces, local government and, to a lesser extent, the military. Abroad, such a policy would no doubt find support among Third World regimes unhappy with the one-sided influence that America now exerts in the world.

Yet, given Russia's economic and military weakness, there are limits to how much even a militantly chauvinistic regime could undertake. Attempts to assert Russian military might, even just to preserve the territorial integrity of the Russian Federation in Chechnya, have proved so unpopular that anything more ambitious would quickly unravel any political coalition that militant nationalists might attempt to forge. It is telling that the most nationalistic-sounding groups in Russia today are advocating a retreat into xenophobic isolationism and economic autarky, not military expansionism.

On the other hand, should a more pro-Western government emerge in Russia (like the one briefly led by Yegor Gaidar in 1992), it too would be constrained by Russia's economic morass. As much as it might want Russia to become an active member of the G7, the GATT, and other Western alliance structures, Russia's role in such institutions would be minimal. For any pro-Western government this discrepancy would be a painful reminder of the need to emphasize domestic political and economic priorities.

What then will Russia's foreign policy look like over the coming decade? Although specific actions are impossible to foretell, the most plausible scenarios recognize the very real constraints on Russian ambitions that economic weakness impose. These will almost certainly force a centrist political orientation on national politics, and a foreign policy that is modest in its ambitions and focused on reconnecting the severed ties of the former Soviet republics. Much, of course, will depend on the future course of Russian domestic politics. While it is quite possible that a more autocratic, communist led regime will come to power in 1996, the objective constraints of contemporary Russian politics and economics would force such a government to pursue much the same foreign policy as its predecessor. The consensus achieved between Yeltsin and his opponents in the Duma on key foreign policy priorities leads one to suspect that there is little support among the political elite for a policy of direct confrontation with the West.

What, then should the United States anticipate in the event of a communist victory in the June 1996 presidential elections in Russia? Most likely, a heightened sense of suspicion about the West, offset by a begrudging recognition of Russia's new political and economic realities. In Gennady Zyuganov, the Communist Party's candidate for the Russian presidency, the party seeks a nostalgia that will appeal to the older generation, with a lukewarm tolerance for private economic activity and an avid appeal for greater Western investment in Russia that will appeal to young entrepreneurs. At the World Economic Forum in Davos, Switzerland, in February, 1996, Zyuganov argued that under the communists, foreign investors in Russia would be better off than they are now because could rely on clearer rules of the game.[6] But whether this suspicion turns to hostility may well depend on the West's response to a communist electoral victory. If the West begins to shut Russia out of financial institutions, reversing the progress already made, it will only serve to confirm the communist's argument that the West did not really want economic integration with Russia.

On the other hand, an approach that continues to support democratic forces and independent Russian entrepreneurs—a "constructive engagement" in support of Russian democracy of the kind that former Assistant Secretary of State Chester Crocker once advocated for South Africa—would strengthen pluralism while undermining the arguments of those inside Russia who argue that the West's policies are motivated by fear of a strong and prosperous Russia. This seems to be the tack taken by the Council of Europe, which despite reservations concerning Russia's ability to comply with the terms of membership, voted overwhelmingly in January 1996 to approve Russian admission. Supporters argued that it would be easier to influence Russian policies as a member of the organization than as a pariah.

In the past, efforts by Russian rulers to reform their system has often led to serious domestic instability that threatened the security of the state. The state may then seek to guarantee its security by relying on its own military potential, by combining the latter with the potential of allies, or by seeking to reduce the threats facing it. During past Russian efforts at domestic reform and economic renewal (e.g., the 1860s, 1880–1890s, and 1920s) its leaders have chosen to place heavy emphasis on the third alternative: that is on the diplomacy of threat reduction.[7] Today, this threat requires dealing forthrightly with the reality of newly independent states in the CIS, and with the aspirations of Eastern Europe to join NATO, recognizing the limits of what Russia can accomplish.

In sum, there is no predictable correlation between the character of a political system and the foreign policy that it follows. Too much depends on the international environment, the nature of the external threat, and the ambitions of the ruling elite. Developments in the United States and on the European continent-in Western Europe's step toward integration in 1992 and in Eastern Europe's progression toward market economies and open societies—will all affect Moscow's choice of foreign policy.

It is also possible that the resilience of Russia's new democratic institutions has been underestimated. Writing in 1994, Stephen Sestanovich commented quite positively on the transformations that had occurred in Russian politics since he had warned of a Weimar Russia. "Russia," he said, "had turned the corner" on the road to political and economic pluralism and would not be able to turn back.[8] By the end of 1995, a number of sources noted the stabilization of the Russian economy, and a study prepared by the Organization for Economic Cooperation and Development (OECD) projected that if present trends continue, Russia's gross domestic product (GDP) could be growing at the astonishing rate of 10% annually in a few years.[9] Moreover, just as an autocratic Russia may pose less of a threat than we suspect, a democratic and prosperous Russia may be less to our liking than we think. Our former adversaries Japan and Germany now challenge American industry; similarly, a resurrected Russian economy would be a formidable economic force in the world.

The most likely scenario for Russia's relations with the West, therefore, is neither confrontation nor cooperation, but competition in some areas and collaboration in others. Unlike the Soviet period, however, the competition will move increasingly away from the military arena, and into the economic-political arena, and will not preclude friendly relations on a variety of issues.

We may not be moving into the best of times, but we are assuredly not entering the worst. The challenges facing Russia are far different from any it has ever known: a security that depends more on political accommodation and cooperation than on a huge military machine; the strengthening of democratic institutions and processes, even as the society undergoes severe economic and sociological upheavals; the shedding of past grandiose imperial and global ambitions and a tailoring of national objectives to the means at Russia's disposal; an opening to the outside world that is consonant with participation in the global information revolution and that will require psychological changes in the Russian political mentality; and finally, a reordering of foreign policy priorities with far greater attention to the limits of power and available resources.

Although currently experiencing a "time of troubles" whose end is not yet in sight, Russia is at the same time trying to shift from an age-old reliance on subsidized, secretive, enormously influential military-industrial institutions and elites to civilian production and to foreign investment in key industries, like the energy sector. In Yeltsin's general foreign policy orientation and strong attachment to partnership with the West, and in the erosion of the military establishment under the pressure of domestic alienation, economic privation, and budgetary constraints, there are signs for guarded optimism.

With so much still in flux, it is premature to be either overly optimistic or unduly pessimistic about the future of Russian-American relations. But it would not be amiss to emphasize that the conditions that gave rise of the Cold War at the end of the Second World War are gone and are not apt to reappear in a way they would again pit Russia and the United States against each other as global rivals. This alone recommends a modicum of optimism. If, in the past, Russia and America had little to link them in friendship, in the future there are also few objective reasons for hostility. A state of modest amity and friendly competition should be achievable. It all depends on the choices leaders will make. Machiavelli put very it well: "There is nothing more difficult to take in hand, more perilous to conduct, or more uncertain in its success, than to take the lead in the introduction of a new order of things."

SELECTED BIBLIOGRAPHY

Blackwill, Robert D., and Karaganov, Sergei, eds. *Damage Limitation or Crisis? Russia and the Outside World*. Washington, DC: Brassey's, 1994.

Dunlop, John B. *The Rise and Fall of the Soviet Empire*. Princeton, NJ: Princeton University Press, 1993.

Hirsch, Steve (ed.). MEMO 2: Soviets Examine Foreign Policy for a New Decade. Washington, DC: Bureau of National Affairs, 1991.

Odom, William, and Dujarric, Robert. *Commonwealth or Empire?* Indianapolis: Hudson Institute, 1995.

Petro, Nicolai N. *The Rebirth of Russian Democracy: An Interpretation of Political Culture*. Cambridge, MA: Harvard University Press, 1995.

Sherman, Peter (ed.). *Russian Foreign Policy Since 1990*. Boulder, CO: Westview Press, 1995.

Yergin, Daniel, and Gustafson, Thane. *Russia 2010—And What It Means for the World: The CERA Report*. New York: Random House, 1993.

NOTES

1. Dimitri Simes, "The Return of Russian History," *Foreign Affairs*, vol. 73, no. 1 (January–February 1994), pp. 77–78.
2. Cited in A. Akulov, "Strenuous Transfiguration," *International Affairs*, no. 5, (1995), p. 94.

3. Cited in Nicolai N. Petro, "New Political Thinking and Russian Patriotism," *Comparative Strategy*, vol. 9, no. 4 (1990), p. 353.

4. "Cheney Urges Swift OK of Nuclear Pacts," *Air Force Times*, August 10, 1992, p. 22.

5. Andrei Kortunov and Sergei Kortunov, "From 'Moralism' to 'Pragmatics': New Dimensions of Russian Foreign Policy," *Comparative Strategy*, vol. 13, no. 3, pp. 261–276.

6. "Communist Party Leader to Attend World Economic Forum," *Monitor: A Daily Briefing on the Post-Soviet States*, January 31, 1996.

7. David R. Jones, "Domestic and Economic Aspects of Gorbachev's Foreign Policy," in Carl G. Jacobsen (ed.). *Soviet Foreign Policy: New Dynamics, New Themes* (New York: St. Martin's, 1989), p. 40.

8. Steven Sestanovich, "Russia Turns the Corner," *Foreign Affairs* vol. 73, no. 1, (January–February, 1994), pp. 83–99.

9. Marshall Ingwerson, "Russia's Bear Economy Goes Bullish as Reforms Kick In," *The Christian Science Monitor*, October 10, 1995, p. 6.

1996 Post-Election Epilogue

The first round of the June 1996 presidential elections went pretty much as pollsters had predicted: the incumbent president, Boris Yeltsin, and his communist rival Gennady Zyuganov emerged as clear leaders, with a scant 3% difference between them. Observers were caught by surprise, however, by the strong third place showing of retired general Aleksandr Lebed. By gaining 15% of the vote, he made himself an indispensable ally for the run-off, prompting Yeltsin to offer him the powerful positions of national security advisor to the president and secretary of the Security Council. In addition to giving Lebed a broad mandate to combat crime and corruption, Yeltsin apparently intends to rely on Lebed to advance reforms in the military.

Lebed's appointments (which Yeltsin called "the union of two politicians and two programs") set the stage for a series of dramatic personnel changes.[1] Yeltsin immediately dismissed Defense Minister Pavel Grachev, national security adviser Yuri Baturin, and Oleg Lobov, who had headed the Security Council since September 1993. Two days later, he fired his first deputy Prime Minister Oleg Soskovets, the head of the Federal Security Services Mikhail Barsukov, and the head of presidential security apparatus, Aleksandr Korzhakov. All had been seen as hard-liners supporting a military resolution to the conflict in Chechnya. Less than a week later seven senior generals (including three deputy chiefs of the General Staff) were also ousted.

Who is Aleksandr Lebed, and how will he affect the course of Russian foreign policy? A 45-year-old professional military man, Lebed has served as a battalion commander in Afghanistan and seen action in internal "hot spots" such as Azerbaijan, the Caucuses, and Georgia in 1988 and 1989. He rose to national prominence as commander of the 14th Army in Moldova, where his cautious intervention in support of the local Russian minority helped end ethnic fighting there.

A first inkling of Lebed national security concerns can be gleaned from a memo leaked to the press just days after he assumed office. The document, entitled "A New Approach to National Security Issues," places particular emphasis on economic security. It calls for stricter government control over export earnings, reducing the size of Russia's foreign indebtedness, greater efforts to stem the "brain drain" of scientists, stricter controls over foreign banks and firms, and an amnesty for tax evaders now abroad in order to encourage them to invest in the Russian economy.[2]

Arguing that "it is difficult to find strategic partners in Europe," the document also advocates drawing closer to the countries of the Pacific rim, "especially China," in order to create a more balanced, multipolar world.[3]

All in all, this document fits neatly into the foreign policy outlined by President Yeltsin and foreign minister Yevgeni Primakov during the presidential campaign. The general's rise, therefore, seems to reinforce the consensus that has emerged about what constitute Russia's vital interests. As articulated by Yeltsin in his re-election platform, these interests are as follows.

First, Russia will strive to be "a leading power without whose participation no key [international] problem can be solved". In this context, priority will be given to relations with the CIS, with the aim of both hastening peaceful reintegration and defending the rights and interests of Russians living in the Near Abroad.

Second, Russia will seek equal partnership with the West, the creation of a European-wide collective security system, and the removal of trade blocs to Russian exports.

Third, although certain interests with the United States differ, there are also many areas of mutual interests where Russia and the United States can cooperate. These include combating terrorism and drug trafficking, limiting the proliferation of weapons of mass destruction, and ratification of START-2 (which Russia sees as dependent on continued US adherence to the 1971 ABM treaty).[4]

Rejecting the arguments of isolationists, Primakov argues that Russia must remain active in world politics to ensure peace and tranquillity at home. The key tasks facing Russia, such as restructuring the Russian economy and military, securing peaceful borders with Russia's neighbors, and establishing relations with the Near Abroad that are conducive to future integration, cannot be accomplished without an active Russian diplomacy. Leaving the field to others during Russia's current time of weakness, Primakov argues, would be a costly abdication of responsibility to future generations.

With Yeltsin's decisive victory in the July run-off election (or, more accurately, communism's decisive defeat), the transition period in Russian foreign policy seems to be coming to a close. Russia is defining its role in the world as other great powers have in the past i.e., as a counterbalance to the hegemony of the dominant power (currently the United States). Russia thus seeks to reprise the role that it once played in counterbalancing the British Empire in the late 19th century. The West, in turn, should expect a protracted period of both competition and cooperation, with traditional diplomatic maneuvering gradually supplanting ideology as Russia pursues its transition from empire to nation-state.

NOTES

[1] Robert Orttung, "Yeltsin Makes Lebed Top Security Aide," *OMRI Daily Digest I*, No. 118 (June 18, 1996).

[2] Peter Rutland, "Economic Security a Top Priority for Lebed," *OMRI Daily Digest I*, No. 125 (June 27, 1996).

[3] *The Straits Times* (Singapore) June 28, 1996.

[4] "Defending Russia and Russians," *The Jamestown Foundation Prism*, vol II, #12, part I (June 14, 1996).

Index